IN SPIES W

IN SPIES WE TRUST

TRUST

THE STORY OF WESTERN INTELLIGENCE

RHODRI JEFFREYS-JONES

OXFORD
UNIVERSITY PRESS

OXFORD

UNIVERSITY PRESS

Great Clarendon Street, Oxford, OX2 6DP,
United Kingdom

Oxford University Press is a department of the University of Oxford.
It furthers the University's objective of excellence in research, scholarship,
and education by publishing worldwide. Oxford is a registered trade mark of
Oxford University Press in the UK and in certain other countries

First Edition published in 2013

Impression: 1

British Library Cataloguing in Publication Data

Data available

ISBN 978-0-19-958097-2

Printed in Great Britain by
Clays Ltd, St Ives plc

for Josephine

Preface and Acknowledgements

Some might say that secret 'intelligence' is a euphemism for espionage and is not intelligent at all. True or false, in the twentieth century it became a prominent feature in nations' pursuit of security. Rightly or wrongly, it came to be seen not merely as a means of winning wars, but also of avoiding them.

The First World War taught the lesson that having a trusty ally was a means of improving national intelligence and security. International liaison remained a vital element in intelligence. The Dutch intelligence specialist Cees Wiebes estimated that during the Cold War the CIA acquired 60 per cent of its information from Allied foreign intelligence agencies.

Few would dispute that the century's leading example of an intelligence alliance was the Anglo-American 'special' relationship. It was a relationship that dominated western intelligence and contributed to the US–British shaping of world politics. The first nine chapters of this book are an account of the rise, decline, and obsolescence of that special intelligence relationship.

The relationship did not command undeviating support. To give an example, just after Britain's declaration of war against Germany in 1939, the US State Department's Adolf Berle warned how British intelligence had tricked his country into entering the last war by means of 'half truths, broken faith, intrigue'.

Berle was being unreasonable. Nevertheless, there were real problems. For example, the British would not let Americans into their codebreaking secrets until the US superiority in computing gave America a lead in the field. At that point, it became America's turn to threaten intelligence blackouts. Nevertheless, the intelligence alliance held fast until the advent of terminal factors: British decline made the partnership too unequal, the end of the Cold War melted the icy grip of friendship, and America became unBritish in composition and outlook.

Britain and America studied each other's intelligence experiences, and this book explores the mutual learning process and some of the controversies surrounding it. Ultimately, the British were too poor and too reluctant to emulate America's informational wizardry. However, the book argues that America was an effective teacher in one regard. Its lesson on how to reconcile intelligence and democracy found listeners in Britain and throughout the West.

Now that the picture has changed, which way should Britain look for intelligence partners? Chapters 9 to 11 examine the United Nations (UN) and the European Union (EU) as alternatives or supplements to America. From the American point of view, Washington has already made two decisions. The first is to opt for hegemony where cooperation is not forthcoming. The second is to change the terms of cooperation. Here, the UK remains a valued intelligence partner, but it is in the demoted position of being one of several. These decisions still leave questions for Washington to ponder—about the merits of the UN and EU as intelligent intelligence options.

The Leverhulme Trust's award of an emeritus fellowship facilitated the research for this book. The Carnegie Trust for the Universities of Scotland and the School of History, Classics, and Archaeology at the University of Edinburgh granted funds for supplementary travel. I am most grateful for this support.

I would like to thank also all those individuals who generously helped with their time and advice. Some have for good reason asked for their names to be withheld from the following alphabetical list. Unless otherwise stated in the notes, no single fact or opinion can be attributed to any one person: Paul Addison, Rosita Agnew, Richard Aldrich, Martin Alexander, Malcolm Anderson, Christopher Andrew, Rod Bailey, Gill Bennett, Merete Bilde, Gustaaf Borchardt, Niels Bracke, Duncan Campbell, Mark Castillo, Doug Charles, Malcolm Craig, Jeremy Crang, Graeme Davies, Philip Davies, Richard Dearlove, Walter Dorn, Simon Duke, Thérèse Duriez, Huw Dylan, Mauro Falesiedi, Jonathan Faull, Peter Filardo, Burton Gerber, Michael Goodman, Nick Hacking, Patrick Hagopian, Margaret Harman, Philippe Hayez, John E. Haynes, Michael Herman, Nick Hiley, Fabian Hilfrich, Claudia Hillebrand, Fred Hitz, Gerald Hughes, Peter Jackson, Keith Jeffery, Matthew Jones, Tim Jones, Daniel Keohane, David Langbart, Scott Lucas, Paul McGarr, Paul Maddrell, Buffy and Ian Manners, Kaeten Mistry, Angelika Molnar, Robin Monro-Davies, Christopher Moran, Elizabeth Brennan Moynihan, Björn Müller-Wille, Paul Murphy, Bill Newton Dunn, Yukiko Ochiai, Eunan O'Halpin, Kathryn Olmsted,

David Omand, José-Miguel Palacios, Søren Kragh Pederson, Natalie Pensaert, John Peterson, John Prados, Charles Raab, David Robarge, Priscilla Roberts, Len Scott, William Shapcott, Jennifer Sims, David Stafford, Kristan Stoddart, Adam Svendsen, Gerry Thomas, Larry Valero, Rob Wainwright, Tom Wales, Wesley Wark, Michael Warner, Cees Wiebes, Hugh Wilford, Aled Williams, Charles Williams, Brian Willis-Jones, and Marilyn B. Young.

My agent Sydelle Kramer was as ever helpful in bringing this project to frution. At Oxford Univerity Press, Christopher Wheeler and Matthew Cotton were most supportive, as were the whole OUP team on both sides of the Atlantic, together with Jackie Pritchard my copyeditor. I am grateful to all.

My wife Mary helped by being her constant and loving self. Josephine inspired by being born as I was finishing the book. This is one lucky author.

Contents

List of Illustrations

Prologue: An American in Bruges

The American arrived in Bruges in 1995. It is understandable why she enjoyed the city. Scores of red-roofed medieval buildings testified to Flemish good taste, a soaring clock tower dominated the elegant town square, Renaissance art was there for the taking. Added to this was the stimulating nature of her mission. She spent her year in Bruges studying for the master's degree at the city's College of Europe, an institution that groomed future leaders of the European Union.

The college encouraged students to live in its hall of residence. At 32, the American was a little older than other members of her class who were typically 22–28 years of age. She studied harder than most and held herself slightly apart from the common run of student activities. Plus she was the only student at that time to have a telephone in her room. Still, she lived in the dorm and talked with classmates who would remember with fascination her time with them.

And there would have been plenty to discuss both in the dorm and in class. There was a buzz in the air about further European integration. Amongst the plans under discussion were European police and intelligence coordination. Though Bill Clinton was popular in Europe, there was an anti-American tinge to the debate, with Europe's media indignant over the Echelon revelations—under the satellite-based Echelon scheme, American agencies were eavesdropping on European conversations, invading individual privacy and threatening trade secrets.

She added the Bruges degree to those she had already acquired at Pennsylvania State University and the London School of Economics. But her interest in Bruges had been more than academic. She was an experienced officer of the CIA.

Valerie Plame had already operated under diplomatic cover in Athens. When she arrived in Belgium, she exchanged that relatively comfortable arrangement for more adventurous types of cover—as a student and later as a business executive in Brussels she had fewer restrictions, and got to know a wider variety of useful people with more interesting information to divulge. But should her cover ever be blown, she was also open to retaliation from America's adversaries.

The retaliation, however, would not come from her country's enemies. We now cut to the time when Plame had re-located to Washington. From 2002, she worked there for the CIA's Weapons Intelligence, Non-Proliferation, and Arms Control Center. It was in connection with this work that she found herself at the centre of a shameful Anglo-American intelligence scandal.

Her story became an illustration of a failure in efficacy, and of the wresting of intelligence away from the professionals to the politicians, making the value of intelligence zero.

When the Bush administration opted for military means to achieve regime change in Iraq, it decided that the best way of drumming up support for the policy was to convince the American public that Iraq's dictator, Saddam Hussein, was producing weapons of mass destruction (WMDs). Plame recalls that in early 2002 Vice President Dick Cheney made frequent and unprecedented visits to the CIA to try to persuade the agency to produce persuasive evidence of Saddam's intentions.

By this time, Plame had married a career diplomat, Joseph Wilson, who in common with her had expertise in non-proliferation investigations and had spent some time in the African country, Niger. When rumours came through that Saddam was buying from Niger a supply of uranium 'yellow-cake' that might help him produce nuclear weapons, Plame suggested that Wilson be sent to Niger to find out. Perhaps there is evidence to suggest that she had by this time already shown signs of wobbling, having 'gone native' in Europe and become disillusioned with her CIA career, but there is nothing to suggest that Wilson's evidence was in any way skewed when on the basis of his Niger investigation he reported that the yellowcake story was in all probability an unfounded rumour.

Both British and American intelligence officials concluded by September 2002 that other rumours were also untrue, for example the one that Iraq would be able to assemble WMDs within 45 minutes. Britain's Joint Intelligence Committee chairman John Scarlett specifically rejected the charge that Iraq had purchased aluminium tubes for uranium enrichment purposes. But all this was *sub rosa* and, anxious to please the Americans, the Tony Blair government proceeded to 'sex up' the evidence to suggest that Saddam was plotting WMDs. News of the deception leaked to the BBC, but not in a conclusive manner.

In his State of the Union address in January 2003, President Bush cited British sources for his statement that yellowcake was going to Iraq, and made the WMD allegation the basis of his case for war. Blair issued supportive statements. The Anglo-American attack on Iraq started in March.

In July, Joe Wilson published an op-ed in the *New York Times* saying, 'we went to war on false pretences'. A furious Bush administration immediately exacted revenge on him by outing Valerie Plame as a CIA official via a leak to the *Washington Post*, thus destroying her career and potentially placing her life in danger. A few days after that, the body of Dr David Kelly was found in English woodland. A Ministry of Defence adviser on biological weapons, he had been fingered as the source of the BBC WMD-deception story, and had fallen into a depression.

The intimidation of the truth-tellers did not in the long run succeed. True, both Bush and Blair won further general elections in their respective countries, but the drip, drip of ebbing credibility continued remorselessly. The outing of Valerie Plame had been illegal under the terms of the Intelligence Identities Protection Act of 1982. The US Attorney General John Ashcroft refrained from pursuing the matter, and for this neglect of duty had to resign. In October 2005, Vice President Cheney's chief of staff, I. Lewis 'Scooter' Libby, was indicted on a charge of revealing Plame's CIA affiliation.

Her viability having been destroyed, Plame resigned from the CIA in December 2005. Other events now seemed to confirm that the powerful were crushing the weak. When Libby was convicted of perjury and obstruction of justice, President Bush commuted his prison sentence. When Plame's autobiographical account of the intelligence scandal was ready for publication, the administration attempted to suppress it, and when it finally appeared in October 2007, the CIA had severely 'redacted' (censored) the book.

But Plame was not the loser. How could she be? Her life story was a bonanza for the press. Her narrative spoke to the issues of the day. Gifted and with a firm sense of women's rights, Plame had by an ironic twist owed her rise in the CIA to Bush senior's 'Glass Ceiling' study that led the agency to reform its recruitment policies and hire talented females. Then there was the really human element. When her story appeared in *Vanity Fair* and then in a movie starring Naomi Watts and Sean Penn, women could sympathize with her workplace problems and with her personal life—she suffered from post-natal depression following the birth of her twins in 2000.

Nor were the men disappointed, as Valerie Plame was a gift to media photographers—a curvaceous blonde, yet with comforting hometown looks. *Fair Game*, the title of her book, conveyed the basis of her appeal to both sexes—an all-American beauty hunted down and victimized by vile men. Plame won the publicity war by a mile.

I tell the Valerie Plame story not to criticize the Iraq War—the world was well rid of that latter-day Hitler, Saddam Hussein—but as a parable that illustrates the sad state of modern intelligence process. I say process, because the intelligence analysts themselves did not go far wrong in their estimates.

In the case of the WMDs, the process involved the subordination of the special British–American intelligence relationship to the special British–American diplomatic relationship. Blair politicized intelligence in that way because he cherished the diplomatic link. Meantime, Bush also politicized intelligence. In doing so, he evidenced a trend. Contemporary thinking explicitly rejected the traditional separation of estimative and political process. A leader here was Robert Gates, former CIA chief who would become President Obama's Secretary of Defense.

I would defend the traditional separation of the intelligence and political processes. Less traditionally, I argue that the extra-close UK–USA intelligence relationship has in recent years been both corrosive and obsolescent. I show that it was not always so. Anglo-American intelligence cooperation was the main espionage liaison story of the twentieth century and, in spite of its blemishes, was often successful. My book narrates its history and its lessons; the last of these is that the story should now be told in the past tense.

For the future lies with other types of intelligence liaison, if not through the UN, then through the EU—as Valerie Plame may have begun to realize in those balmy days in Bruges.

I

The Separate Origins of American and British Intelligence

They were the original Ku Klux Klan. They issued warnings to their opponents that were 'written in a disguised and cramped hand'. Their missives displayed 'a methodical ignorance in the orthography and composition, done with the evident intention of concealing their origin'. They were sworn to secrecy. The 'low whites' amongst their numbers might talk, but their leaders were utterly silent, deviously concealing their identities and social rank. They carried out their threats and committed daily outrages against those who voted Republican. Their inflictions of physical abuse sometimes lasted long after their victims had 'ceased to scream'.

So wrote Hiram Whitley, chief of the US Secret Service in 1871. It was at the time of Reconstruction, when America's former slaves had acquired freedom, votes, and other civil rights, and when elements in the defeated South tried to restore white racial dominance.[1]

All this may seem far removed from the twenty-first-century saga of Valerie Plame and Anglo-American connivance over weapons of mass destruction. And it is. The Secret Service's war with the Klan illustrates how the geneses of the modern American and British Secret Services were different and separate.

Separate, one should emphasize on the US side, and not inferior. Far from being laggardly in these matters, as is so often assumed, the Americans injected expertise into their commitment to a moral cause. These very qualities enabled them later to contribute a distinctive building block to the edifice of US–UK intelligence cooperation. That edifice would be a bastion of twentieth-century security, even if it would be a source of controversy by the time of the Plame affair.

Secret intelligence was nothing new in America. In 1793 the 'contingency' or 'secret' fund at President George Washington's disposal had amounted to a million dollars, or 12 per cent of the national budget. But there was no permanent organization at the disposal of the executive until President Abraham Lincoln called for its creation. After the carnage at the Battle of Appomattox, Lincoln had issued his proclamation freeing slaves in lands conquered by the Union armies. It gave his soldiers' sacrifice a new meaning and his cause a greater vigour. Yet, the economic consequences of the war were grim, and Lincoln had to attend to that front, too. In the spring of 1865 inflation and an unstable currency gave cause for concern. Against this background there emerged a threat to the Union cause that was less heroic than the men in grey, but still a source of acute worry. A band of counterfeiters exploited America's crisis to line their own pockets. Just before his assassination on 14 April 1865, President Abraham Lincoln held his last cabinet meeting. It established the United States Secret Service. The agency was located in the Treasury Department, and its remit, far removed from that of the future CIA, was simply to hunt down greenback forgers.

The Secret Service trained America's first force of federal detectives. At the end of the Civil War, they turned their attention to the South and especially to Tennessee and the Carolinas, where they focused on a new threat to federal revenue: moonshiners. These were men who regarded the federal government with its taxes as even more poisonous than the whiskey they illegally distilled. Some of these anti-federalists would join the Klan.

Hiram C. Whitley was one of the Secret Service agents who operated against the moonshiners. He was a towering personality in more senses than one. Two inches short of being seven foot tall, he was man of prodigious physical vigour. In the antebellum years he had worked as a bounty hunter in Missouri, and run down thirteen fugitive slaves. In the war he drilled with the Confederates in New Orleans before changing sides and serving behind enemy lines for the Union Army. In May 1869, Whitley became head of the Secret Service.

The Republican-dominated US Congress would soon give him a new task. Worried by the activities of the Klan, in June 1970 it authorized the creation of the Department of Justice. The intention was to deliver justice to the terrorized black population of the South. Though still part of the Treasury Department, the Secret Service loaned all its detectives to the newly created department. Poacher turned gamekeeper, slavecatcher turned freedmen protector, Whitley directed his men to gather evidence against the Klan with a view to its destruction.

Catching the leaders of the secretive Klan was no easy task. They rode at night, and in disguise. But Whitley and his agents knew the ground. They also received help from local people who were brave enough to resist the lily-white terrorists. In South Carolina, John Good was a black man who shoed horses. By hammering a bent nail into the shoes of Klansmen's mounts, he made it possible for Whitley's trackers to identify the night-riders' movements. The Klan grew suspicious of Good and killed him. But the evidence against their leaders piled up. In September 1871, Whitley anticipated the 'crushing of the Ku Klux'. Just under a year later, he reported a burgeoning success rate, and the figures for arrests and convictions support his finding.[2]

The US Secret Service was a national detective force in a federal land. This made it controversial when the South re-entered the Union and asserted its states-rights principles. From the late 1870s to the late 1890s, states-rights southerners forced the service to assume a low profile. But the service nevertheless had a longlasting influence. It formed the basis for the future Federal Bureau of Investigation, and the FBI would in turn be a much-emulated model for domestic policing and for counterintelligence. The emulation happened in individual nations—and arguably in another federalist enterprise, the European Union.

In the 1880s, when the Secret Service had sunk temporarily into obscurity, America took further steps in the direction of organized secret intelligence. The Office of Naval Intelligence (ONI) came into existence in 1882, and the Military Intelligence Division (MID) three years later. These agencies differed from the Secret Service in clear and significant ways. Though the Secret Service had cooperated with the US Army in the South, the service itself was civilian in character. ONI and MID were in contrast military in both composition and objectives, and, unlike the Secret Service of the 1870s and 1880s, sought intelligence in foreign countries.

Another feature of the ONI was its association with the principle of emulation. Mutual learning would be a feature of the twentieth-century intelligence relationship between Britain and America, and, as the example of Alfred T. Mahan shows, it had nineteenth-century origins. Captain (later Rear Admiral) Mahan was a naval officer who hated going to sea. In 1886 he became president of the Naval War College, where he helped shape both naval intelligence and the rise of the US Navy generally. He became influential by propounding to a receptive audience the views that Britain had achieved imperial power by means of its navy, that America should become an imperial power and challenge Britain, and that the key to American dominance also lay in naval strength. In the very long term, his insistence that history's lessons 'remain constant' hinted at a dangerous rigidity, but for a number of decades important elements in the United States followed his lead by studying the British and trying to emulate them.[3]

In the year of ONI's formation, Lieutenant Commander French Ensor Chadwick arrived in London as US naval attaché. Like other powers, the USA was sending military and naval attachés abroad, where they used secret agents or other means to acquire military secrets. Chadwick warned about British naval tactics for undermining US influence in Asia, but also reported a surprising phenomenon. British Admiralty officials were discreetly turning over to him the technical specifications for the latest UK warships. To put this into an interpretative context, Britain was keen to ensure US friendship. A well-disposed America would ensure the western rim of that great strategic pond, the Atlantic Ocean, against any incursion by a power hostile to Great Britain. For this reason, the Royal Navy acted as a de facto enforcer of the 1823 Monroe Doctrine, the American ban on European colonial-style activities in the western hemisphere. It made sense to facilitate US naval capability so that America itself could share the burden.[4]

At least, that was true up to a point. Britain was beginning to become sensitive to commercial and military challenges to its imperial dominance. Unauthorized disclosure by civil servants became a crime under the Official Secrets Act of 1889. Chadwick's successor William H. Emory reported in 1892 that his official British sources of information had dried up, and that he now had to try to obtain naval technology from manufacturers and ship builders, rather than through official sources. When war broke out between Spain and America in 1898 and Britain proclaimed its neutrality, officials operating under the cover of the American embassy in London obtained UK armour-piercing shells and other equipment to help the US war effort. However, they had to use devious means to circumvent the British authorities.[5]

The MID as well as ONI was active in the War of 1898. In June of that year, the Secretary of War requested a 'secret service' subvention of $100,000 to meet wartime needs. But the war was more significantly a time when the Treasury Department's Secret Service once again became prominent. The old wounds of the Civil War began to be forgotten in the face of a mutual foe, and Americans from all sections of the nation now took pride in the Secret Service. Its activities gave rise to a precedent-forming chapter in the history of British–American intelligence relations.[6]

According to official US rhetoric, the war's aim was to rid the western hemisphere of a significant vestige of European imperialism, Spanish rule in Cuba. Neutral Britain had every reason to desire friendly relations with Spain. But an undercover operation by the US Secret Service put the British in a difficult position. It established that Ramon de Carranza, formerly the Spanish naval attaché in Washington, was running an intelligence operation against the USA. Its centre of operations was in the British Dominion of Canada.

Carranza hated being land-bound just as much as Mahan had loathed the thought of going to sea. From an aristocratic family, he wanted to engage in naval combat in his nation's maritime tradition. He complained that espionage was a dishonourable activity. In more than one western country, the profession of intelligence 'officer' would soon be portrayed as an occupation fit for gentlemen. But aristocratic disdain for espionage of the type that Carranza expressed was not yet quite out of fashion.[7]

Suppressing his disgust, Carranza obeyed orders and, following his expulsion from Washington, set up a credible spy ring in Montreal. Carranza's agents pinpointed East Coast targets—civilian as well a military—for long range bombardment by Cadiz's flotilla of five armoured cruisers. Carranza identified as one of his 'two best spies' George Downing, a former petty officer on the US Navy cruiser the *Brooklyn*. One day, Carranza briefed Downing in what he thought was a secluded hotel suite. The Secret Service had its man in the adjoining room. He listened through the partition door and made notes. Downing was now a marked man. On 7 May 1898, the Secret Service had him arrested after he had travelled to Washington, DC, in possession of a compromising letter. He was found dead in his cell two days later. Carranza remarked that he might have killed himself, 'or else they did it for him'. It was one of a series of episodes that led to the uncovering and exposure of the Montreal spy ring.[8]

Britain was responsible for Canada, and the exposure of Carranza presented London with a dilemma. What should the mother country do? British intelligence had already in the post-Civil War era operated in the USA. It had spied on the Fenians in the 1860s and 1870s, when the Irish nationalists had planned to invade Canada from a US base. Then in the late

1870s Plains wars, when native warriors defeated Colonel Custer's Seventh Cavalry at the Battle of Little Big Horn, British intelligence again favoured Washington. It gave the US Army a secret report on the elusive Sioux leader, Sitting Bull, who was duly shepherded into obscurity across the Canadian border. However, these activities came with little cost. Irish rebels and Sioux warriors were diplomatically weak; the government of Spain was not.

It fell to Colonial Secretary Joseph Chamberlain to deal with the problem. As the historian Alex Campbell noted, although there had been some recent London–Washington friction, cooperation was still 'an axiom of British policy'. Chamberlain's wife was the only daughter of the former US secretary of war, W. C. Endicott. It is not at all surprising that the colonial secretary telegraphed the Canadian governor general, Lord Aberdeen: 'The Law Officers of the Crown advise that Carranza should be requested to leave British territory, if the facts are as stated.' They were, and Carranza had to leave. It was Anglo-American intelligence cooperation. Though not of a service-to-service type, the cooperation was an indication of the shape of things to come.[9]

Towards the end of the first decade of the twentieth century, both America and Britain established intelligence bureaucracies that began to take a recognizably modern shape. The developments were simultaneous, yet separate. In spite of the ties of language and other similarities between the two nations, there appears to have been no mutual learning on this occasion, no correspondence between the officials responsible for the developments, and no hint at Anglo-American cooperation. Perhaps, nevertheless, the two nations were so similar that the outcome reflected parallel stimuli and development? But no, a look at the stories in the two countries suggests this was not the case. It may be a hazardous thing for a historian to say, but we are in this case looking at a coincidence.

The American initiative sprang from a reform initiative of President Theodore Roosevelt (1901–9). A charismatic figure in the Progressive movement, Roosevelt achieved worldwide significance as a political pioneer of the conservation movement. One of that movement's principal objectives was to withhold from sale to commercial developers significant tracts of land, for example the redwood forests on the Pacific slopes. A number of corrupt timber merchants frustrated these goals by manipulating small land owners and bribing politicians. Matters came to a head in the state of Oregon, where Secret Service agents, once again on loan to the

Justice Department, dug up evidence leading to the arrest of a number of individuals. The US Senator John H. Mitchell was convicted on land fraud charges. He escaped going to prison only because he died before he could be sentenced.

To those who saw America as falling into the hands of capitalist robber barons and the Senate as little more than a millionaires' club, Roosevelt was doing a good job. But there was another side to the story. James A. Tawney (R-MN), chairman of the House Appropriations Committee, complained that the Justice Department was increasingly employing Secret Service agents to snoop on private business—and on members of Congress. The Constitution gave Tawney's committee the right to cut off funds, and he duly threatened to do so.

Roosevelt exploded with anger. Complaints about government 'spies', he raged, were 'cheap'. Crippling the investigatory powers of the federal government would let corrupt corporations off the hook. Playing on the fact that the self-proclaimed anarchist Leon Czolgosz had assassinated his predecessor President McKinley, he claimed his opponents were encouraging anarchists seeking to destroy America. The chief reason for Tawney's objection, though, was that 'congressmen themselves did not want to be investigated'.[10]

Roosevelt now decided to create a new agency within the Department of Justice. The president entrusted the reform to its head, Attorney General Charles Bonaparte. A larger than life figure prone to the kind of witticism that gets you into trouble, Bonaparte had once suggested that guards on the ever-permeable Mexican border should be encouraged to develop better marksmanship by being put to shoot at each other.

Bonaparte and his plan were a gift to journalists. Perhaps he wanted to introduce a 'political secret service', Russian-style? But the historically literate focused on the fact that he was the grandson of Napoleon's brother. Inevitably the comparison was with Joseph Fouché, Napleon's ruthless spymaster. So vigorous was the opposition in the press and on Capitol Hill that President Roosevelt waited for a congressional adjournment before creating his new agency by executive decree.[11]

Under the authority of the attorney general's directive of 26 July 1908, the Secret Service transferred nine agents to Justice in an arrangement that it declared to be temporary, but which proved to be permanent. By the start of 1909, people were referring to this new branch of Justice as the 'bureau of investigation'. The bureau would perform a significant role in counterintelligence in the First World War and later. After a number of further name changes, it came to be officially dubbed, in 1935, the Federal Bureau of Investigation, or FBI. For the sake of clarity and following a common custom, this book will use the term FBI as well as the terms MI5 and MI6 for the entire period from 1909 on.[12]

The FBI had come into existence for reasons of high principle. With its roots in the racial progressivism of Reconstruction, it later drew on the nutrients of the conservationist crusade. Arguably, this gave rise to a moralistic flavour in US domestic intelligence, but at least American intelligence had an ethical basis. Not only this, but also there was an open debate in the press and Congress at the time of the FBI's creation. On the subject of transparency, America already had a lesson to offer the world.

The British Secret Service Bureau, ancestor of both MI5 and MI6, came into existence in October 1909. It stemmed from a recommendation, after a few years' discussion, by a subcommittee of the Committee of Imperial Defence. The bureau's operating charter tasked it to conduct foreign espionage and domestic counter-espionage activities, and to be a bridge between the Admiralty, the War Office, and the Home Office. Secrecy was a top priority, and to this end the original charter remained a unique script with no copies.[13]

There was no debate in parliament. It is uncertain how that body might have reacted, as it had a mixed record. In 1711 parliament had authorized the interception and opening of mail. Starting in 1797 it had (like the US Congress in the same decade) voted to supply the government with a fund for 'foreign and other secret services'. Yet, it revoked the mail-opening permission in 1844, and in the 1860s began to lay down stricter conditions about how 'secret vote' money should be spent. There was no way of telling how parliament might have reacted to the idea of a permanent intelligence bureaucracy, and—if any thought was devoted to the matter—the decision appears to have been taken not to risk stirring up trouble by having a debate.[14]

As in other countries, there was ambivalence towards espionage. While today's MI6 values its association with the Foreign Office, British diplomats like some of their American counterparts have had reservations about that link. Responding to new proposals in 1905, the British minister in Copenhagen was horrified by the suggestion that British spies might use embassy cover. Intelligence work 'should be left to specialists. Any connection of a diplomatist with espionage which got to the ears—say of the German

Foreign Office—would militate very significantly against such diplomatists in future times in Germany.'[15]

Powerful forces swept aside such reservations. These forces were not moral in character. They reflected, on the one hand, mounting international tensions and the beefing up of intelligence provisions in Germany. In 1901 the German admiralty staff established an intelligence department, the *Nachrichten Abteilung im Admiralstab*, 'N' for short. Its responsibilities were different from the continental remit of the army. Matching the rise of the German navy, it was to spy on foreign navies including the British Royal Navy, and in addition on Britain itself.

Another amoral force boosting the mood in favour of British intelligence revival was confrontational nationalism. The chauvinism that led Britain and Germany to fight a bloody war contributed also to the formation of the Secret Service Bureau, and that bureau was in turn unable, as well as indisposed, to stem the flood of prejudice—as were its German counterparts.[16]

In the years leading up to the creation of the bureau, anti-German feeling welled up in the British Isles. Journalists, novelists, and politicians fanned fears of invasion, and promulgated the views that a German spy network was putting British defences in peril.

Writers of spy fiction helped to shape those perceptions. Spy novels may not be realistic in cleaving to existing 'reality' however that be defined, but they can shape the mythologies that create future realities. Police detectives, previously despised, had in mid-century found a champion in the journalistic writings of the novelist Charles Dickens, and by 1900 were distinctly in vogue. Through the persona of Sherlock Holmes, Arthur Conan Doyle's stories meantime elevated private detection. There was a sharp contrast with America, where the use of private detectives to break strikes had brought them into political disfavour.

Where the English detective trod, the spy followed. British spy fiction enjoyed a boom, marked in some cases by a quality of writing never matched on the other side of the Atlantic. It must be borne in mind that spy fiction writers do not just create but also reflect the popular mood, and profit from it commercially. But even if they were mere readers of the opinion barometer their articulation of the results was influential, and a factor behind the emergence of modern British espionage.[17]

Here are some examples of British spy novels. The Franco-Prussian War, in which German spies had played a role, alerted George Chesney to the possibilities, and he wrote *After the Battle of Dorking* (1871). Other countries like France and Russia also fed British paranoia, but Germany shaped up increasingly as the main enemy. The prolific novelist E. Phillips Oppenheim singled out the German spy menace in *Mysterious Mr Sabin* (1898), in which he anticipated future trends by depicting American scenes and engaging American readers.

Then, on a higher literary plane, came Erskine Childers's *The Riddle of the Sands: A Story of Secret Service* (1903), a tale of how two Englishmen of maritime disposition spotted furtive Teutonic plans to launch an invasion from the Frisian Islands off Germany's North Sea coast. Already the lines between fiction and present reality were being blurred. Both the army and the navy commissioned intelligence reports to assess the Frisian menace. On this occasion, both reports dismissed the idea as nonsense. The water was too shallow, the coastline lacked transport infrastructure, there was insufficient warehousing. Potentially, the military reports were an example of how intelligence can soothe anxieties, and contribute to the peace.[18]

But the discrediting of *The Riddle* did not put public anxieties to rest. Like Oppenheim (and like their low-literature American equivalent, Robert Chambers), William T. Le Queux produced around a hundred novels. Less sluggish than Oppenheim who could manage only five novels a year, Le Queux at his peak could churn out eight before buying his Christmas presents. His spy novels were low in quality, intellect, and accuracy, but high in impact and popularity, placing him in the same literary earnings bracket as H. G. Wells and Thomas Hardy.

In pursuit of those literary earnings, Le Queux could move effortlessly from one phobia to the next. In 1894 he wrote of a possible French invasion. Then, the Germans took over. His novel of 1906, *The Invasion of 1910*, told how England was infested with German spies preparing for an invasion. Can the echo of an assertion prove its veracity? The novel urged the nation to heed the warnings issued by Britain's pre-eminent military commander, Field Marshal Earl Roberts—and included a facsimile reproduction of a letter by Lord Roberts recommending the book for its forcible illustration of 'our present state of unpreparedness'. The book first appeared in serialized form in the *Daily Mail*, whose proprietor, Lord Northcliffe (future owner of *The Times*), loved a good hate yarn with its stimulus to sales. Indeed, *The Invasion* boosted *Mail* circulation by 80,000. In novel format it appeared in twenty-seven languages and sold a million copies.

Whether because of opportunism or because he suffered from a personality disorder that convinced him he was one of his own protagonists,

Le Queux considered himself to be a patriot helping to save England from Germany. He took an inflated view of his/his protagonists' role. In a later novel, he claimed that his fictional secret agent, Hugh Morrice, had the aptitude to turn the tide of history in Britain's favour. Little wonder that *The Invasion* impressed William Melville. This was an officer who carried out security investigations for the military and who wanted to boost Britain's alertness. He said he was thankful to Le Queux for 'waking up the public'.[19]

An excited public opinion helped to create the new intelligence bureau of 1909. However, that bureau could not hope to calm the chauvinists. There was no chance that a new-model intelligence officer might tell the *Mail* to cool it, explaining that tales of German perfidiousness were exaggerated. This was in part because intelligence officers like so many other people are loath to put themselves out of work, in part because there was, indeed, a job to do in the wake of the Germans' creation of the 'N' department. As international tension increased, there would certainly be spies to round up, and foreign secrets to be obtained.

One definitive reason why the new intelligence organization could not calm the nation was because it chose to be silent. True, there were chinks in the curtain of secrecy. Le Queux wrote to the *Manchester Guardian* in January 1910 pouring scorn on that newspaper's assertion that there was no German spy menace. Demonstrating his credentials as an insider, he told the editor: 'it may be news to you to know . . . that a special Government Department has recently been formed for the purpose of watching their movements.' By and large, though, the new intelligence bureaucrats aimed to keep their very existence out of the public eye. They reported only to politicians and in the eventuality of a manufactured crisis would have been unable to dampen public expectations and save England from the toll of war. At this stage the probability was that they would fight wars, not prevent them.[20]

At the beginning, the Secret Service Bureau had just two officers, Commander Mansfield Cumming of the navy and the army's Vernon Kell. Christopher Andrew, the authorized historian of MI5, speculates that continental European defence leaders would have been surprised at the 'enfeebled' condition of Britain's fabled intelligence service. Their reading of Edwardian spy fiction would have led them to expect something on a grander scale.[21]

The American military historian Thomas Fergusson addressed the issue of reputation from a different angle: 'If British intelligence was as outstanding during the two world wars as we Americans generally believe, and if our military commanders and intelligence organizations received more from the British in the way of timely, reliable intelligence and assistance than they gave in return, as the evidence seems to indicate, the development of British military intelligence before 1914, including its Secret Service branches, is a topic worthy of careful examination.' Fergusson was wrong in his premiss— America was more competent than he assumed. Yet he was right to hint that British intelligence was already potent in its pre-modern incarnation. British aptitude did not develop overnight.[22]

British national intelligence had a longer tradition than its American counterpart, which by definition could not be dated earlier than 1775, when the revolutionary Continental Congress established the Continental Army. Sir Robert Walsingham organized an effective espionage network for Elizabeth I when Spain threatened to overwhelm England in the 1580s. Much earlier than that, William the Conqueror had a counterintelligence service to warn him of plots to strip him of the crown he had won in battle in 1066. In citing these episodes one should beware of 'originalism'—just because the Normans and Queen Bess did it, it does not mean spying was good morally or qualitatively. Nevertheless, there is no denying the tradition and its inspirational value.

In the century prior to 1909, the inhabitants of the British Isles had witnessed a rich variety of counterintelligence activities. Chartists, Irish nationalists, and anarchists all came under state surveillance. At first, a critical factor was missing from the scene, institutional memory. Consciousness of a long tradition was no substitute for the handing down of expertise from one generation to the next within the framework of institutions that guaranteed continuity. To be sure, one could argue that common preconditions might produce similar outcomes, but a certain level of bureaucracy is necessary to the retention of memory about know-how.

In 1887, Britain began to remedy that deficiency with the creation of the posts of Director of Military Intelligence and Director of Naval Intelligence. This was a tardy move, as in the United States ONI and MID had already sprung into existence. In 1902, however, the UK took continuity a step further with the formation, in the premiership of Arthur Balfour, of the Committee of Imperial Defence. Hitherto, it had usually fallen to the Admiralty to respond to invasion threats as they arose. From now on, there would in principle be continuous peacetime planning of national security, whether to counter invasions or threats from within—as we have seen, the committee would set in motion the steps that led to the creation of MI5 and MI6. From now on, there would be coordination and civilian control. It was the beginning of British central intelligence and would in 1936 spawn the present-day Joint Intelligence Committee. Advocates of the US Central Intelligence Agency would in future point to the merit of what they considered to be British centralized practice. But, before the First World War, the Americans had no such facility for across-the-board coordination.

The Second Boer War (1899–1902) had alerted the British military to the need for improved intelligence. A small 'special section' developed in the War Office, coordinating Secret Service efforts on behalf of the navy and Foreign Office as well as the army, and in 1905 the War Office drew up a plan for 'Secret Intelligence Arrangements in the Event of War with Germany'. Spies would be based in German towns, and a system of 'couriers' would bring the information out. The army thought that women, 'gypsies', and commercial travellers could do the latter job as they could move around without arousing suspicion. The plan was not a response to hysteria about German espionage in Britain, but the reverse, a declaration of intent to conduct aggressive intelligence operations against Germany. The establishment of the Secret Service Bureau in 1909 sprang, then, from more than one source.

The British had superior 'tradecraft' in 1909. The US Secret Service was a first-class detective agency, and private detectives like W. J. Burns who became famous in America generally had Secret Service training. But the British had skills more finely tuned to international espionage and counterespionage. In October 1909, Cumming and Kell received a procedural briefing about their new jobs. They were to isolate key personnel, thus observing vertical integration of information flow without horizontal leaks (in later years, Americans saw this as a procedure that had gone too far, giving rise to 'stovepiping' and the hoarding of key data). They were never to write names and addresses on the same sheet of paper, and never use identifiable paper. They were to use false addresses and assumed names. They would never meet an agent on official premises.

It was not entirely a case of briefing ingénues. Vernon Kell, who would develop the counterintelligence capability that led to the creation of MI5, was the son of a well-travelled army officer, and through the Polish count who was his maternal grandfather had connections throughout Europe. He spoke five languages by the time he went to Sandhurst, then learned to speak Chinese. Asthmatic, he concentrated on a deskbound intelligence career. He had already served as assistant secretary of the Committee of Imperial Defence by the time he took up his bureau post at the age of 36.

In the long run, Kell's performance would prove controversial. At the outset of the First World War, he claimed MI5 had arrested twenty-one German spies, the entire network operating in Britain. Parliamentary patriots celebrated the news with cries of 'Shoot them!' At 7 a.m. on 6 November 1914, the first execution took place. Carl Hans Lody, a German naval lieutenant travelling on an American passport and speaking with a credible American accent, had spied on installations in Edinburgh and Liverpool. Just before he was hanged, he wrote to his sister, 'I will die as an officer, not as a spy.' He impressed the British public with his courage and gentlemanly behaviour at the scene of execution. German intelligence 'officers', like their British and American counterparts, were acquiring social cachet.

German intelligence officers no doubt hoped for local support. Kell accordingly denounced the German colony in Britain, depicting what appears to have been an innocent community as a nest of spies, and encouraging nationalistic fervour against the conjectured menace. Parliament passed a law restricting the rights of aliens.

Oft repeated by Kell and others, the twenty-one arrests claim became part of MI5's 'foundation myth'. It was based on shaky premises. As the historian Richard Rowan pointed out in the 1930s, judging counterintelligence efficacy by the number of arrests was 'like judging a business community by its bankrupts'. Not only this, but in later years it emerged that the number of evidentially supported arrests was eight. At the time Kell himself had suspected that other German agents were still at large, as indeed they were—the MI5 arrest rate never mopped up more than 20 per cent of the German spies at large at a given time. To promote wartime morale, the welfare of his agency, and his own ambitions, Kell had overstated MI5's immediate effectiveness. What saved Kell's longer-term reputation was the fact that 'N', the German intelligence service ranged against him, was a chaotic organization enfeebled by poor tasking, inter-service rivalries back in Berlin, and an ethical sense in Germany that forbade the full deployment of chemical weapons against the civilian population of Britain.

At the time, Cumming must have appeared to be more in need of the tradecraft briefing. Though older than Kell—he was 50 in 1909—his experience of life was more mundane and less cosmopolitan. He came from a professional family of moderate wealth, and had served with average competence in the Royal Navy. At the time of his appointment, he was no more capable in intelligence matters than any one of a dozen US naval officers. When the bureau split in 1910 into the two components that would become MI5 and MI6, Cumming would take over the latter responsibility. He acquired a legendary status and the head of MI6 would forever thereafter be known after the initial letter of his surname, 'C'. But to claim that at the time of his appointment he was an illustration of British intelligence superiority would be to stretch a point.[23]

The legend of British intelligence superiority needs to be studied critically. At its inception American intelligence was no copycat operation, but an independent creation with virtues of its own. But in the first half of the twentieth century the reputation of British intelligence would be boosted in a way that made for continuing awe in some circles, and would help to ensure US respect and the survival of the 'special intelligence relationship' for many decades, perhaps even beyond the time when America needed it. The relative potency of British intelligence and its reputation for excellence would soar for a specific reason. This was early British and late American entry into two world wars.

2

Great War Origins of the Anglo–American Intelligence Partnership

A dolf A. Berle awaited his guest. A short but ample middle-aged, middle-class figure, he was a little fidgety and impatient. In turn, he fingered the college ring on his wedding finger and a packet of cigarettes. A Harvard graduate at the age of 18, Berle expected things to happen quickly. Life had for many years obliged him. His 1931 book attacking the concentration of power in the hands of capitalists brought him fame. He became one of a group of three, the 'brains trusters', who helped to shape the New Deal policies of President Franklin D. Roosevelt. Since 1938 he had been assistant secretary of state. His special responsibility was for Latin America, and he had an interest in intelligence affairs.

The guest who had requested to see him was an Englishman. For some years, though, Sir William Wiseman had worked for American banks, notably Kuhn, Loeb, & Co. Perhaps that did not recommend him to Berle. And no doubt the assistant secretary was upset by the outbreak of war in Europe some days earlier, an event that threatened the progressive world order for which he had striven. But there was another reason for his distrust, one that he chose to conceal from his visitor.

Wiseman announced that he was helping London's new ambassador in Washington, Lord Lothian, to explain America to Britain and vice versa. He especially desired to smooth the path, politically, for British purchasing in the United States. Could Berle, 'as an old friend', help him?

Berle gave an affable but non-committal reply. Soon afterwards, he circulated to his colleagues a minute that gave the reason for his reserve. It said he 'felt it unnecessary to recall' that Wiseman 'had played a very considerable part in the exchanges between Sir Philip Kerr (now Lord Lothian), Walter Hines Page, Cecil Spring-Rice, Colonel House, and others, by which the United States was ultimately committed to enter in the [First] World War almost without knowledge of the State Department. Caution is suggested.' Improving this account for his diary, he referred to Wiseman as 'a ghost [who] walked on two legs into my office', and as a contributor to a 'history of half truths, broken faith, intrigue' in Anglo-American relations who now imagined that Berle would be his 'easiest mark'.[1]

Did Sir William Wiseman and his colleagues in British intelligence trick America into entering the First World War? There is an alternative narrative, which suggests that in those years Britain and America laid the foundations of an intelligence partnership that would be of mutual and lasting benefit and would have significance for international security for many decades.

At the start of the war, British intelligence was too feeble for either role. In the spring of 1919, the American diplomat Edward Bell delivered a retrospective assessment of the British set-up designed to inform future US policy. He noted that in 1914 Britain was unprepared for war. Once the war started, there was a sudden, mushroom expansion in intelligence personnel and activities. There was 'overlapping of authority', 'reduplication of labor', and 'waste of time and money'. Americans residing in Britain were sometimes arrested on suspicion of being German spies, and it was a reflection of the prevailing confusion that they did not know where to seek redress: 'it became almost a question of flipping a coin to decide whether application for information should be made to Scotland Yard, the Home Office, or MI5.'[2]

In less critical vein, it can be said that this lack of preparedness was neither unique nor long lasting. The opposing German intelligence services had to undergo similarly rapid adjustment. 'N', the agency charged with spying on Britain, furthermore received orders from the German admiralty that changed with bewildering regularity—at first it had a worldwide remit, then had to concentrate on the North Sea, and finally had to focus on submarine warfare. German intelligence officers were not so utterly incompetent as Anglo-American propaganda later implied. But, whether on account of poor tasking or because of their own shortcomings, neither did they come up to the standards some of them claimed in their memoirs. The German scholar Markus Pöhlmann caustically remarked, 'the autobiographical writings of former intelligence officers...make us wonder how the *Reich* could ever have lost the war'.[3]

The British took three steps that gave them an intelligence edge. First, a new Official Secrets Act—*the* Official Secrets Act—superseded the 1889 law. Much admired later on by those on the right in American politics, this law went down badly with British libertarians. The British press had risen in concert in 1908 to thwart an early attempt to amend the original law. Three years later, Home Secretary Winston S. Churchill managed to sneak it through parliament with virtually no debate. Putting the onus of proof on the arrestee, the law eroded the habeas corpus and free speech rights of British citizens. In future years it was used to prosecute not just spies but also investigative journalists, for example Duncan Campbell in the 1970s and *Guardian* writers in 2011.

The sociologist Ken Robertson argued that the 1911 law was not a reaction to fictional and press hysteria about German spies. Rather, 'it was the culmination of a prolonged campaign to eliminate leaks by civil servants'. Another scholar, David Vincent, suggested the law stemmed from 'the growing requirement to recruit to government offices those whose breeding, education, and pay excluded them from the rank of gentleman'. Government administrative offices were expanding, and a host of new recruits were neither privately educated nor immune to trade union membership. There was a presumption that the lower orders were by nature untrustworthy. It was convenient to forget that at the pinnacle of 'society' King Edward VII had, when Prince of Wales, succumbed to some indiscretions with cardsharps. It was enough that there had been some examples of impecunious clerks leaking information to the press. The prejudice contributed to the rationale for legislation to plug a potential hole in national security.

It could be argued, further, that the Official Secrets Act of 1911 marked a step in the direction of the professionalization of the management of secrecy. This was a step consistent with the emergence of an intelligence establishment based on the premiss that those of 'officer' status could be trusted, but lower-order 'spies' had to be subject to vigilant discipline. Here, there is a parallel with America, where intelligence work could be regarded as a gentleman's escape from democratic politics of the kind that involved getting one's hands dirty and dealing with the teeming immigrant multitudes.

It brings to mind the 'status' thesis about the American political elite of the 'Progressive' period. The historian Richard Hofstadter held that the old upper middle-class introduced reforms at least partly in order to fend off the challenge of the lower orders—as well as the new rich. Both the American and British hypotheses are open to prosopographical objections—were all the proponents of secrecy and espionage and political reform elitist, and none of their opponents?

These insights and debates should not be allowed to obscure the fact that the 1911 law also constituted a step on the road towards a British national security state. For better or for worse, it protected secrets of state. In that way, it improved the prospects for effective counter-espionage.[4]

The second step giving the British an edge was the formalization of the work of the cryptographic unit known as 'Room 40'. This had been the chamber in the Old Admiralty Building where the codebreakers of pre-expansion days had laboured. In the words of its first director Alfred Ewing, Room 40 had 'two amazing pieces of good fortune'. The first arose from the Russian navy's destruction of the German light cruiser the *Magdeburg* at the outset of the war. With the *Magdeburg* in its death throes, one of its crew grasped the onboard copy of the German navy's codebook, and held onto it as he drowned. As Ewing put it, 'To save the book from the enemy was, one may conjecture, the impulse of a gallant man.' But the German sailor's gallantry was in vain, as the Russians retrieved the book, realized its significance, and gave it to their British allies.

The second stroke of luck was the acquisition in December 1914 of 'a secret conversation book of the German Admiralty', which according to Ewing turned up in a parcel of books hauled in along with the rest of his catch by a Lowestoft fisherman. The keying procedure used in the book was of further assistance to the mathematicians and other bright graduates Ewing was now recruiting for the Room 40 team. The team made gradual headway in reading German cable and radio traffic, making it possible, for example, to track the location of German submarines.

Churchill, by now First Lord of the Admiralty, recognized the significance of Room 40. As far back as 1897, when he had reported for the *Daily Telegraph* on British action against an Afghan rising on India's North-West Frontier, Churchill had remarked on the need for good military intelligence. Now, on 8 November 1914, he issued a charter to the Room 40 unit, written in his own hand. He had a clear idea of how things should be run. He emphasized security: with the exception of the original, which should be kept in a safe, all copies of intercepts were to be 'collected and burnt'. Ewing having established Room 40 resigned, to be succeeded by Captain Reginald Hall, known as 'Blinker' after his eye twitch. Room 40 and its signals intelligence (SIGINT) successors would be a key ingredient in the Anglo-American special intelligence relationship.[5]

The third step was of more immediate Anglo-American significance. In December 1915, Captain Mansfield Cumming ('C') sent Sir William Wiseman to America, ostensibly to run the British purchasing committee but actually to take charge of the American section of MI1c, better known to posterity as MI6. Wiseman was a Cambridge University dropout and failed playwright. He had represented a British bank in Mexico until the outbreak of the war, when he volunteered to serve with the duke of Cornwall's light infantry. Gassed at Ypres in 1915 and suffering a partial loss of vision, he was invalided out of active service and became an intelligence officer.

There is another claimant to the unofficial title of chief British intelligence officer in First World War America. The naval attaché at the British embassy, Guy Gaunt, later claimed to have been Wiseman's boss, and in a memoir styled himself 'Chief of the British Intelligence Service in the United States, 1914–1918'. There was no such post. Nor was Wiseman foolish enough to crave the status of being an intelligence supremo. Like 'C', he valued anonymity. At one New York dinner party, his hostess introduced him to Gaunt, triumphantly identifying the latter as the head of British intelligence in the city. Glad of the error and amused by it, Wiseman kept his counsel. Gaunt did perform a significant role, but his retrospective assertion of seniority was just an attempt to defy English privilege. For Gaunt had been (in his own words) 'a harum-scarum boy born and bred in the Australian bush', who had concentrated on shooting possums and flying squirrels before escaping to sea at the age of 14.

Wiseman's personality was a study in contrast. Diminutive in physique yet dapper in appearance with his neatly groomed moustache, he was a Cambridge bantamweight boxing blue, and heir to a baronetcy stretching back to 1628. He appealed to a certain type of influential American partly for that reason, but he was also politically adroit. Wiseman convinced his American friends that he had a channel to British leaders independently of the Washington embassy (untrue at first, but then a self-validating fallacy). Similarly, he won the support of British officialdom by stating that he had the confidence of the American foreign policy-making elite. As the European war dragged on with no decisive outcome, it became clear that the

United States was the one power that could break the impasse. Wiseman would play a measurable role in achieving that outcome.

Wiseman and his British colleagues found themselves dealing with a newly constituted American intelligence elite. In June 1915, unhappy with the belligerency of President Woodrow Wilson's policy towards Germany, William Jennings Bryan resigned as secretary of state. Bryan was a pacifist, and a leading critic of British rule in India. Although the president continued to denounce the secret diplomacy taking place in Europe and to call for a better world, the departure of the idealistic Bryan made possible the creation of a US central intelligence mechanism run from the office of the counsellor of the Department of State. Its personnel oversaw and coordinated both domestic counterintelligence and foreign intelligence. The office of the counsellor changed its name in 1919 to the office of the undersecretary, and the intelligence unit was known, after the first letter of that word, as U-1, from then until its abolition in 1927. Just as we backwards-stretch the terms MI5, MI6, and FBI, we can for the sake of convenience refer to the unit as U-1 from 1915 onwards.

President Wilson was an erudite man who took a personal interest in foreign intelligence, as did his influential adviser. Colonel E. M. House was an individual with whom Wiseman, too, enjoyed a special relationship. In the running of U-1, the new secretary of state, Robert Lansing, took a back seat, leaving day to day responsibility to Frank L. Polk. From one of America's oldest political families, Polk was created counsellor in September 1915. He continued from 1919 as undersecretary and acting secretary of state. This senior intelligence overlord would also head the American commission to negotiate peace.

Reacting against what they considered to be the political depredations of America's capitalist 'robber barons' as well as against challenges to their political authority from the lower orders and an incipient socialist move-ment, a group of the country's older-established middle-class elite felt at this time that they had a duty to take the helm and guide their nation in a more expert and less corrupt manner. Hofstadter may have exaggerated its socio-economic homogeneity and influence, but a group defining itself in that way did exist. Its members were well connected and privately educated, and supplied the new intelligence elite.

Polk attended Groton and Yale. Gordon Auchincloss, appointed assistant counsellor in May 1917, was also at Groton and Yale, and had the further advantage of being Colonel House's son-in-law. Leland B. Harrison, who from 1916 carried the title 'diplomatic secretary' within U-1 and had foreign liaison duties, was educated at the English prestigious public school Eton College, and then at Harvard. Harrison's key overseas intelligence colleague was Edward (Ned) Bell, second secretary at the US embassy in London since 1913 and future author of the abovementioned assessment of British intelligence. Bell came from an 'old New York' family that had kept the arriviste Astors off the Social Register. Educated at the Cutler preparatory school and at Harvard, he belonged, like the rest of our cast, to exclusive social clubs. Bell on at least one occasion wrote an official memorandum on Racquet Club headed stationery, deleting the printed heading and writing in 'Department of State' instead.[6]

The elite background of the pioneering central intelligence group invites consideration. On one level, it spawned a gormless preppiness. When Bell heard that a German military attaché had lost his job for sleeping with a Frenchwoman, he joked that the officer's defence might be that it was 'peaceful penetration in the interests of the Fatherland'. Hearing of a row between the Ministry of Defence and the Admiralty in London, he sagely observed that 'the latter look upon the former in about the same way as Harvard look on Yale'.

On another level, the top U-1 officials were well informed and able, and had direct access to the White House. Furthermore, the recruitment of secret service personnel from such an intimate circle made it easier to keep the secrets. Looking back at the Anglo-American intelligence experience in the First World War, Polk was sufficiently confident in his own team's discretion to complain that British secret operations had been 'carried on with a brass band'.[7]

The U-1 people represented a further contemporary trend, the American elite's Anglophilia. This was a pronounced feature of what later came to be known as the special intelligence relationship. Discernible in the novels of Henry James and in millionaires' daughters' habit of marrying into English titles, the disposition was rooted in assumptions about shared values and in fashionable contemporary notions of 'Anglo Saxon' racial and moral superiority. Institutions attested to its force: the Rhodes Trust (established in 1902) sent American scholars to Oxford University; the US National Security League (1914) was pro-British and advocated 'preparedness'; the English Speaking Union came into existence in 1918. Former president Theodore Roosevelt (private tutors, Harvard) was the prime example of a number of powerful Republicans who strongly favoured Britain in the period of America's neutrality. Henry Cabot Lodge (Harvard) was later vilified for having used his position as chairman of the Senate Foreign Relations Committee to oppose US membership of the League of Nations. However, he represented a powerful group that, unlike President Wilson, thought the League should take second place to an Anglo-American alliance, an alliance that would impose a world order to the advantage and moral satisfaction of both countries.

Especially in the case of U-1, the Anglophilia plugged into a joint elitist mindset. Just as Groton and Yale might propel you into the Department of State, so Eton and Balliol could be a passport into the Foreign Office. The diplomatic/intelligence cousins on each side of the Atlantic found they had things in common.

The phenomenon did not sweep all before it. If around half of the US population was of British or Canadian descent, it was also true that a fifth was of German or Austrian empire extraction. The wartime hysteria whereby *dachshunds* were kicked on sight and renamed sausage dogs for their own good was not a foregone conclusion, and Germans had previously ranked highly in American ethnic hierarchies. There were close German–American personal ties. These were evident in the case of the official with ultimate responsibility for German wartime espionage, Johann Heinrich Count von Bernstorff. German ambassador to the United States between 1908 and 1917, Bernstorff had spent the first ten years of his life in London, and spoke English as fluently as his mother tongue. His wife of more than twenty years, Jeanne, was an American.[8]

Again, it should be remembered that the UK is a monarchy, and that America had fought a revolution largely against that principle. Leland Harrison's ancestor, Thomas Harrison, had been a general in Cromwell's New Model Army and signed Charles I's death warrant. After his father's gruesome execution at the time of the Restoration, the regicide's son emigrated to America, and one of *his* descendants fought against the forces of George III in George Washington's Revolutionary Army. Proud of this ancestry, Harrison was at least cerebrally aware of the problem of royalist Britain's rule-the-world arrogance. In a letter to House in January 1916, he said he feared US public opinion would become pro-German because Britain was using the Royal Navy to blockade Germany in a manner that rode 'roughshod over the small neutrals, Denmark, Holland, Norway, Sweden, and Greece. He hoped America could prevail on the Foreign Office to modify its tone.[9]

Yet it is clear from his letter that, even as early as 1916 with Wilson about to campaign for re-election as the president who kept America out of the war, Harrison, House, and their circle took it for granted that they were on the side of Britain. At the operational level, American and British intelligence officers would behave as if they were virtually indistinguishable. When Ned Bell sailed for England in 1913 to take up his embassy post, his close friend and Harvard classmate Franklin D. Roosevelt cabled him, 'Goodbye and good luck. Don't acquire an accent with the other things British.' And there were other things. Once in London, Bell divorced his American wife and married an Englishwoman. This may have had to do with the inclination that later led the first Mrs Bell to join a group of Parisian literary lesbians. At the same time, there was compensation for Ned Bell, as his new matrimonial partner was well connected in English society. He could be forgiven for having come to the conclusion that he was now an English gentleman. As for Harrison, a student of Anglo-American cryptographic cooperation offered the following verdict on his contribution: 'Those who had known him during World War I would have expected nothing less from this American ex-Etonian.'[10]

When America's entry into the war was imminent, Wiseman and Auchincloss had lunch at a New York club and discussed 'the kind of [secret service] cooperation that we should endeavor to establish between this country and England'. Auchincloss further noted in his diary that Wiseman promised to communicate with the State Department through him. Wiseman would have had no such intention as he liked to keep channels open to more senior officials, but he continued to cultivate his impressionable American counterpart. In November 1917, he dined Auchincloss in the House of Commons, gave him a tour of the war intelligence offices, and took him to an English version of the Folies Bergères. Additionally, Auchincloss made daily visits to Wiseman's tailor. For the American group, London was the centre of everything—Ned Bell went shopping there to take care of the sartorial needs of Leland Harrison, buying everything from shoes to collars. Even the austere President Wilson was not immune to the charms of English social prestige. When he met 'Blinker' Hall to thank him for his war work, the venue was Buckingham Palace.[11]

There was a flip side to the Anglophile coin. Anglophilia meant distrusting people who were not of British descent. More precisely, as Ireland was still a part of Britain it meant being suspicious of those who were not of English, Scottish, Scotch-Irish, or Welsh descent. The anti-Irish attitude is evident in Polk's intelligence files. The counsellor received counterintelligence reports from the US Secret Service—the venerable agency was at this time reporting to President Wilson's son-in-law, Secretary of the Treasury, William McAdoo. In May 1916, Polk received one such report on a Friends of Irish Freedom meeting in Chicago attended by 1,500 supporters, ranging from hod-carriers to priests, who plotted anti-English actions. The words describing the meeting as one of the 'worst exhibitions ever witnessed' were in the report, and not penned by Polk. However, he who tasks, receives reports to his liking. The Anglo-oriented president and his entourage were friends neither of the Irish Americans nor of the Irish cause.[12]

Also evident in Anglo-American intelligence circles was prejudice against the French. It was partly humour, but like a lot of jokes had a cutting edge. Echoing a complaint by Blinker Hall in January 1918, Bell warned Harrison that 'Frenchmen simply cannot keep their mouths shut' and that 'the French Foreign Office leaks like a sieve'. Later in the year, Wiseman told a receptive Colonel House that the French premier Georges Clemenceau was incapable of putting French intelligence on a proper footing. Knocking the French would become a familiar feature of the cosy Anglo-American intelligence arrangement.[13]

Even Sir William Wiseman fell victim to racial slurring. It happened after the war, when Americans were becoming a bit more curious about the nature of his activities. It was a time when suspicions, often paranoid, circulated about communist plots, banking plots, and Jewish orchestration of both of those plots—and Wiseman's firm, Kuhn, Loeb, was New York's premier German-Jewish bank. Tales of British deviousness were in the air. A New York pamphlet of 1919 that addressed British perfidiousness spread throughout the nation. It featured a forged letter from Wiseman to Prime Minister Lloyd George detailing how British intelligence had successfully brainwashed America.[14]

Then in September 1920, Wiseman fell under suspicion in the eyes of U-1. By this time, U-1 had a counterintelligence operation headed by R. C. Bannerman. Bell's successor as second secretary and U-1 operative at the American embassy in London, L. Lanier Winslow, contacted William Hurley, a counterintelligence official at U-1. Winslow's cable was about 'Willie Wiseman'. Though Wiseman was an 'old college chum' he felt he was up to no good, manipulating his passport to obtain diplomatic cover, and embarking on a possibly dubious banking venture to Mexico.

There followed a correspondence based on the Jewish-sounding nature of the surname 'Wiseman'. The American officials speculated that Wiseman might be 'a Yid' (Winslow), insisted that the 'dope' was required on whether he was a Jew (Bannerman), or perhaps had 'Semitic blue blood' (Winslow); it had to be ascertained whether he was a 'follower of the tribes of Israel' (Hurley). Wiseman remained under suspicion in America throughout the 1920s. Though Winslow had an attack of remorse, it fell short of racial tolerance. He produced Wiseman's entry in *Burke's Peerage* to show the Englishman was beyond reproach, pointed to his wartime collaboration with Colonel House, and clinched the argument by reporting that the suspected Jew must be all right because he had an 'antipathy to Jerusalem'.[15]

It is here worth revisiting Adolf Berle's recollection that Wiseman conspired behind the back of the State Department. It may have been a question of appearances. Secretary of State Lansing was less in control of the intelligence brief than his subordinate and successor Frank Polk, and may for that reason have given the impression of having been outwitted. He was not on the same wavelength as President Wilson, and was known to doodle in cabinet meetings rather than paying close attention. Evidently he had no consuming interest in intelligence. Additionally, he may well have been aware of the danger of being too closely associated with espionage, and of the need to have, and to stand back from, a circuit-breaking mechanism like U-1. There is no evidence that he impeded the collaboration of Polk and Wiseman, or resented British manoeuvres.[16]

Still, another charge invites examination. This is that Wiseman, Hall, and their British colleagues led corresponding US officials by the nose, playing on their susceptibility to flattery and Anglo-snobbery. The first period to be examined with this charge in mind is 1914–17. It was a time of professed American neutrality, during which in reality America drifted towards the Allied (British–French–Russian) camp. However, the transgressions against neutrality in these years were not the product of UK subterfuge. Rather, they reflected an American preference for cooperating with the British, and for treating German agents and their allies as the enemy.

That preference was the product of pro-British bias but also, to some extent, a reaction to German actions, vulnerabilities, and mistakes. On the high seas, German submarine warfare offended because it resulted in civilian casualties. The U-boat sinking of the Liverpool-bound *Lusitania* in May 1915 resulted in the deaths of 128 American passengers and outraged US opinion. At the time, rumours were rife that the *Lusitania* was carrying munitions. However, until the year 2008 when divers went down to the wreck off the Irish coast, the British propaganda machine successfully hid the fact that the vessel was carrying four million US-made bullets, making the passengers a human shield. At the time, the allegedly indiscriminate firing of German torpedoes seemed more offensive than the Royal Navy's transgressions; its high-handed interference with neutral shipping. To attack the *Lusitania*, a luxury liner that habitually carried members of the American upper-class elite to and fro across the Atlantic, was politically foolish.

And then there were the German spies in North America. They came to be associated with the German embassy, and with Count Bernstorff himself. It must have been a burden for him to bear. The ambassador was a cultured and reasonable man who eventually died in exile having resisted Hitler's persecution of the Jews. In 1914–17, he tried his best to persuade his superiors in Wilhelmstrasse that the burgeoning economic superpower to which he was accredited mattered in world affairs, and should be treated with respect.

As for the prospects of success, the ambassador was not ideally suited to subterfuge, and a little accident-prone. In 1916 he vacationed in the Adirondacks and was careless. A photograph fell into the hands of Wiseman's assistant, found its way into a New York newspaper office where it was duplicated, then mysteriously reinserted itself (as it were) into the photo album of the unsuspecting ambassador. The image depicted Bernstorff posing between two American women attired in the garb of bathing beauties. It made the rounds of the press on both sides of the Atlantic and was a gift to hawks in Berlin who wanted to undermine his standing with the Kaiser. The episode did not force Bernstorff's recall. But for Britain and France, it was a propaganda coup. The Countess Bernstorff was, after all, an American.[17]

In the first few months of the war, Berlin established an intelligence network in the United States. Some of the US-based spymasters reported directly to the Fatherland and had little to do with Bernstorff. Notably, Frantz Rintelen communicated with the German admiralty. One of his jobs was to sabotage cargoes of war supplies sent to Britain from the Black Tom railway and warehouse facility. This was in New York Harbor at the location that is now Liberty State Park, the tourist gateway to the Statue of Liberty and Ellis Island. With the help of unsuspecting Russian intermediaries, Rintelen arranged for a number of ships to catch fire. Then early one morning, German agents possibly with Irish nationalist assistance destroyed a munitions dump at Black Tom. The massive explosion of 30 July 1916 rocked the skyscrapers of Manhattan and was heard in three states.[18]

Unlike Rintelen, the military attaché Franz von Papen mostly went through Ambassador Bernstorff. The future chancellor of Germany had been assigned to Mexico City before the war and, according to Hall, had there 'been ordered to study Mexican methods of blowing up trains'. Bernstorff, though, did not warm to the idea of being a rogue diplomat. In fact he tried to discourage some of the wilder clandestine plans, and Rintelen thought of him as an appeasing liberal. In a Berlin-authorized effort to save the embassy from being 'compromised' Papen ran most of his operations from a separate office in New York, where Wolf von Igel was in charge. It was a circuit-breaking strategy, but it also meant that if caught, Germany's New York-based spies would lack diplomatic immunity.

This and the sheer scale of operations meant that regardless of intentions the evidential trail was likely to lead back to the Washington embassy. There was documentary evidence to link Bernstorff directly to sabotage, to attempts to recruit ethnic and racial minorities, to efforts to bribe members of Congress to vote down trade with Britain, to schemes to encourage industrial unrest in a way that would disrupt that trade, and to plans to spread influenza to the same end. Bernstorff could not have known it at the time, but Room 40 was reading his communications—all this came out after the war, when victims of sabotage seeking reparations from the defeated Germans hunted for documentary evidence of Wilhelmstrasse–embassy complicity in the destruction of property. With Room 40 in the know, the German ambassador's direct participation in clandestine operations was bound to end in disaster.[19]

The Germans' vulnerability was an open invitation to America's counterspies, and these agents demonstrated an outright pro-British and anti-German bias. Take the case of the unfortunate Dr Heinrich F. Albert. He was a German civil servant who had been sent to New York to work at his country's Central Purchasing Company (*Zentral-Einkaufs-Gesellschaft*)—like the British in both world wars, the Germans rather obviously ran their espionage from an office whose ostensible purpose was to purchase war supplies. Albert had a double mission, buying and spying.

On Saturday 24 July 1915 at 3.30 p.m., Albert boarded a Harlem elevated train. At the end of a working week it is hardly surprising that he was tired and nodded off to sleep. It could happen to any of us, and the same could be said for what happened next. For when he woke up, something important was missing.

Albert reckoned the disappearance took place at the 50th Street station. He inserted an appeal for the item's recovery in the following Tuesday's *New York Evening Telegraph*: 'Lost . . . brown leather bag containing documents . . . $20 reward'.

Perhaps he thought an absent-minded commuter had mistaken his bag for his own and made off with it by accident. Or maybe a quick-witted Harlemite had committed an opportunistic theft and would be tempted by the twenty-dollar reward. From the German viewpoint, however, the truth was more sinister. Frank Burke had seized the bag. Burke was a Secret Service special agent experienced in counter-espionage—he had worked against the Spanish spy ring of 1898. It was a scoop for the Secret Service boss William J. Flynn, who was losing a turf war with the burgeoning FBI.

The stolen papers contained information on German intelligence operations. Washington gave the press some details, and there was a clamour for the expulsion from the USA of Papen, Albert, and other German agents. In an attempt to preserve the appearance of neutrality and to conceal their counterintelligence capability, the Americans put out the story that British intelligence agents had stolen the bag. According to a contemporary British source, Papen now swallowed that line, writing to his wife, 'Unfortunately they stole a fat portfolio from our good friend, Dr Albert, in the elevated. The English Secret Service, of course.' If as seems likely Room 40 alerted U-1 to Albert's activities in the first place, London would not have been too happy about the American cover story.[20]

So why was Frank Burke's action an example of American bias and an illustration of the workings of the special Anglo-American intelligence relationship? Surely, it might be argued, the US authorities could be expected to take action against alien spies operating on its own territory, breaking the law, and endangering life and property? But there is an effective riposte to that argument. British agents operated on American soil, too, and (as we shall see) engaged in illegal activities such as assassination. But they did not have their bags stolen. Instead, American agents cooperated with their British counterparts.

Anything the Secret Service could do, the FBI could do better. Notably, its agents raided Wolf von Igel's New York office. In a secure safe in that location, documents weighing a full seventy pounds detailed the identities, phone numbers, and functions of German secret agents. In charge since

Papen's expulsion, Igel had feared that even the latest model of safe was not good enough to protect such information. He had decided to remove the documents to the Washington embassy, where they would be protected by diplomatic immunity. On 18 April 1916, he began to lay out the documents on a table, methodically readying them for packing. Just as he was finishing, and with perfect timing, four Justice Department agents burst into the room. One of them held Igel's guard at gunpoint. Another pounced on Igel as he desperately tried to shovel the papers back into the safe. The other two appropriated the documents.

The papers on Igel's desk documented the German plot to assist a rebellion in Ireland—the Easter Rising that heralded Irish independence. The episode can be seen in the context of a set of universal promises that masqueraded as war aims in the global conflict. The British and French promised self-determination for the peoples of the German, Austrian, and Ottoman empires (the Central Powers), though not for their own. The Central Powers promised to liberate the peoples of the British and French empires, but not their own. In each case, the motive was to encourage demoralization and rebellion in enemy ranks. As for the Americans, they promised self-determination for all. Though home rule movements did not originate in America and were already part of the post-colonial landscape, they came to be defined eponymously as 'Wilsonian'. But President Wilson and his colleagues even before the give and take of the Paris peace conference were prepared to countenance two damaging exceptions. First, they did not think coloured people could be trusted to rule themselves, Second, they turned out not to be serious about decolonizing the French and British empires, and that included Ireland.

German encouragement of Irish nationalism ran partly through Igel's office with the assistance of Irish Americans and Irish exiles who wanted to free their ancestral land. In a counterpart operation in Berlin, Arthur Zimmermann, an undersecretary of state in the German foreign office, agreed to assist the Irish patriot Sir Roger Casement. Germany sent a shipment of arms to Ireland, but the Royal Navy intercepted it. When a German submarine landed Casement on the west coast of Ireland on 21 April, he was arrested. By 30 April, British troops had crushed the Easter Rising—you can still see the bullet holes on the face of Dublin's General Post Office. In August, Casement was executed for treason.

Analysis of these events remains inconclusive. The historian A. J. Ward argues that the Americans did not process the Igel documents quickly enough to help the British. Bernstorff's biographer Reinhard Doerries hints that the effective tip-offs to the British authorities in Ireland came from Room 40. Perhaps one might add that the remarkable timing of the FBI raid must have been the result of good intelligence, intelligence that could have come from the British side.

What cannot be disputed is the Americans' partisanship. For the Wilson administration, suppressing German operations was more important than upholding the cause of Irish freedom. In the wake of the Easter Rising, Leland Harrison at U-1 received a stream of intelligence reports on Irish American nationalist activities. Some of then came from a prejudiced source. With security awareness heightened, the Secret Service supplied British Ambassador Cecil Spring-Rice with three personal bodyguards. The diplomat would slip them choice documents in the knowledge they would find their way to the State Department.[21]

The burgeoning intelligence relationship between the UK and the USA was assuming a worldwide significance. It was part of the bond that tied two countries given to global vision. Britain had its empire, with a debate taking place between its outright defenders and a younger group of thinkers including Berle's bugbear Philip Kerr who were turning their minds to the issue of how to devolve power within it. America had long-established interests in the western hemisphere and a world vision articulated by President Wilson and lobbying groups like the League to Enforce Peace, together with the economic power to give effect to at least some portions of that vision. All this gave added force and poignancy to intelligence collaboration.

The story of Gadar illustrates how, in the tug of war between conservative and progressive visions, the latter to a significant degree lost out. 'Gadar' (alternative spellings Ghadar or Ghadr) is an Urdu/Punjabi word of Arabic origin meaning 'revolt', and its political use dates back to the Indian Mutiny of 1857. The Gadar Party on the West Coast of the United States and Canada drew on a community of several thousand immigrants of Punjabi and other sub-continental extraction. They were of mixed religious and ethnic adherence—the American press misleadingly called them 'Hindoos' instead of 'Indians' to avoid confusion with native Americans. Lala Har Dayal, a native of Delhi and graduate of Oxford University, supplied leadership in the United States, establishing the San Francisco newspaper *Ghadar* in 1913—at first published in Urdu and then in several languages.

His support for 'free love' and anarchist principles made Dayal a controversial leader of his cause, yet he was an inspirational character. With its commitment to armed struggle against the British Empire, his Gadar attracted support from Irish American nationalists and, more dangerously from London's viewpoint, Berlin. The German emperor took a personal interest in Indian nationalism. On the eve of war, Wilhelm II urged his officials to incite Muslims to a 'wild uprising' against that 'hateful, mendacious, ruthless nation of shopkeepers', England. Cynically anticipating stalemate in the trenches, he proclaimed, 'If we are to bleed to death, then England shall at least lose India.'[22]

At first, Dayal and his followers had reason to expect support from America with its anti-imperialist tradition, especially with William Jennings Bryan as secretary of state. But Gadar was up against the immovable phalanx of Anglo-American solidarity. On the West Coast, they had to contend with William Hopkinson. A member of the Vancouver Immigration Department, Hopkinson had served in the Indian police, spoke Punjabi and other Indian languages, and cooperated with British, Canadian, and American intelligence authorities. In April 1913, he reported he 'had only to give the word and the US immigration authorities would effect Har Dayal's deportation'. The American authorities duly arrested Dayal under anti-anarchist legislation. He skipped bail in April 1914 and fled to Switzerland. From there he moved to Berlin where, with help from the foreign office, the military, and others, he participated in efforts to foment US-based Indian revolutionary activities. Back in the USA, Ram Chandra Bharadwaj took over as leader of Gadar.[23]

With the outbreak of war, Indian nationalist activities and British–Canadian–American opposition to them intensified. In Vancouver, there were assassinations, revenge assassinations, and shootouts involving pro-Hopkinson and anti-Hopkinson Sikhs. The role of assassination as an instrument of Anglo-American intelligence policy would be controversial in future years. In the case of the British, it was an established practice in the First World War. In October 1914, Hopkinson himself reaped the consequences. He was standing outside a courtroom in the quintessentially English town of Victoria, British Columbia, awaiting the verdict in the case of one of his men who had confessed to killing an Indian revolutionary. A nationalist Sikh, Mewa Singh, stepped forward and shot him in the chest at point blank range. Pulling out a second revolver, Singh finished him off with another five bullets.[24]

With Canadian counter-terrorism hotting up on account of the wartime emergency, Gadar moved the focus of its operations south of the 49th parallel. It had substantial German support. Both before and after the abortive Punjab rising of 1915, German secret agents tried to supply revolutionaries in India with weapons via the United States. The details of the story are a bit murky, but British intelligence and the Royal Navy appear to have intercepted most of the shipments. In further pursuit of anti-imperial activities, Dr Chandra H. Chakravarty visited Zimmermann in Germany and secured $60,000 and then a second tranche of $40,000 in funding. British intelligence at first let him run. Then in April 1916 Chakravarty was out walking on a dark and foggy night in Washington, DC, when an automobile appeared from nowhere and almost killed him. This could have been an early example of British intelligence's weakness for modish technology, but one should not jump to conclusions. For by this time the badly shaken Chakravarty had other enemies—he was suspected of being a British double agent.

Both the British and the American authorities wanted to mop up the Gadar 'conspiracy'. But neither side wanted to fuel the charge that America had violated its declared neutrality by spying on and harassing Indian nationalists. Though the involvement of Wiseman's secret service colleagues in the eventual arrest of Chakravarty and in the preparation of a case against Gadar built partly on his confessions was, in the words of one historian, 'an open secret', appearances to the contrary had to be contrived. There was the further complication that British interrogators suspected Chakravarty of deceiving them—for his part, he distrusted the British and insisted on State Department officials being present whenever he was questioned. However, by March 1917, the case was ready. US entry into the war in April removed any element of political risk and meant that professions of fair play went by the board. A show trial took place in San Francisco between November 1917 and July 1918, with over a hundred under indictment. Supporters of Indian independence were now enemies of the United States, and a guilty verdict was a foregone conclusion.[25]

The conspiracy trial was still a delicate matter for MI6 and U-1 because details of pre-war collusion might have been revealed. But they had a stroke of luck. Ram Chandra was the trial's key witness. When he took the stand, a fatal shot rang out. One of the accused, Ram Singh, was the assassin. Had there been a British conspiracy to silence the nationalist leader? How did Ram Singh smuggle the weapon into court? We shall never know, as a deputy sheriff pulled out his automatic and with uncanny aim fired a single shot through the crowded courtroom that killed the assassin.

For helping to crush movements that might have threatened British interests and its war effort, the United States paid a price. Future Indian independence leaders like Jawaharlal Nehru would incline to the Soviet Union. As late as 1976 and the bicentennial commemoration of the American Revolution and even beyond, the memorialization of the Gadar struggle on the West Coast was a vibrant issue for Indian government officials.[26]

Pro-British bias on the part of American officials seems evident, but at the same time there was the question of whether British secret agents had tricked America into complicity with the perpetuation of imperial rule, as a prelude to drawing the United States into the war. As Berle's suspicions confirm, British intelligence officials concerned with drawing America into the Second World War were not unreasonable in their sensitivity to the charge that could be levied against them. Guy Gaunt was at pains to dismiss as 'the wildest of fiction' Rintelen's claim that Britain had saturated the United States with secret agents. Wiseman had always been circumspect about American public opinion. As he warned 'C' in the autumn of 1917, in America there were 'people who are still afraid of George III'.[27]

An ad hominem pursuit of the British conspiracy theme might be better directed at Blinker Hall. While the Room 40 boss managed to retain the confidence of his superiors he was to an appreciable degree, as historian Eunan O'Halpin put it, a 'law unto himself'. Hall's later actions indicate he had a political agenda, and that it was unprogressive. In 1919 he would found the Economic League, a union-busting outfit that engaged in industrial espionage and strikebreaking. Working for the Conservative Party Central Office from 1923, he was associated with the affair of the Zinoviev letter. This letter was a forgery of mysterious provenance purporting to be from Grigori Zinoviev of the Comintern to the British Communist Party. Circulated without authentication by MI6, the Conservatives, and the Tory press, it urged the party to press for pro-Soviet policies by organizing industrial unrest, sympathetic action by the Labour Party left, and even mutiny in the armed forces. The publication of the letter on the eve of the 1924 general election allowing no time for rebuttal heralded the decisive defeat of the sitting and first-ever Labour government. Though it may not have been the decisive cause of the election result, its publication was an undemocratic act that left a stain on the reputation of the intelligence services and the Conservative Party.

Hall was already a ruthless Tory at the time of the Liberal-led wartime administration, and a chauvinist to boot. His intelligence reports indicating that Germans not Irishmen were behind the Easter Rising may well have contributed to the bloodiness of British repression in Dublin and beyond. The von Rintelen of British intelligence, Hall insisted on victory at any price. Neutral America had opposed that principle. With the war in Europe at a stalemate and with the prospect of millions more being slaughtered, President Wilson sent Colonel House to Europe on two mediation missions, in the spring of 1915 and 1916 respectively, to try to mitigate the killing and end the war. At first House concentrated on trying to achieve a maritime compromise—Britain would agree to freedom of the seas in return for a cessation in German submarine warfare. In the second mission, he reached a secret understanding with Britain expressed in the House–Grey memorandum: at an appropriate point, London would trigger an American call for a peace conference. This never happened.

Hall despised peace missions. He used his privileged intelligence position to attack them. Though Room 40 did not at first have the capacity to crack the Wilson–House communication codes, War Office codebreakers were able to do so, and Hall got hold of the messages. It should be noted that whenever they could, and that was much of the time, the British broke American secret codes and read their encrypted messages. The practice continued until 1941, when Hall's successor Alastair Denniston proposed a suspension. The British avowal of discontinuation, and reciprocal American pledges of abstinence, became an additional feature of the special intelligence relationship.

By the standards of the day there was nothing remarkable, then, in Hall's prying approach. What is more significant, though, is the way in which he proactively sought out diplomatic information and used his prior knowledge of House's initiatives in efforts to lobby officials, for example leading figures in the Admiralty who were sympathetic to his cause, in an attempt to defame House and discredit his peace efforts. This is not to say that the Americans would otherwise have succeeded in stopping the war. With casualties mounting there was entrenched bitterness on both sides, and no popular desire for peace. House was an Anglophile who became increasingly hostile to Germany, and by the time of his second peace mission was much less optimistic about the prospects of success than his boss, President Wilson. Hall was machinating to a purpose that was already a foregone conclusion. That the Admiralty spymaster was trying to manipulate the United States is, however, beyond question—and this was just a trial run.[28]

3

Implications of the
Zimmermann Telegram

S ir Alfred Ewing served as principal of the University of Edinburgh from
1917 to 1929. Some of the incumbents of that post had been intellectually distinguished—William Robertson in the eighteenth century wrote
the first secular history of America. Mostly, however, leaders of academic
institutions have to demonstrate more humdrum talents to do with people
management and dexterity on committees. Born in Dundee, a son of the
manse, Ewing had shown mechanical ability that might have made him
famous had he not come from a nation of engineers. He compensated for
any relative deficiencies with abundant self-esteem and with displays
of initiative. Lifting his gaze above his native land, he married a woman of
significant descent. A great-great-niece of President George Washington,
Annie was according to her son attracted by her suitor's 'keen blue eyes' and
'disarmingly quiet Scottish voice'. In further pursuit of his ambitions, Ewing
served as a professor first in Tokyo, then Cambridge.[1]

Today, his name is familiar to Edinburgh students only because it
identifies a 1960s student hall of residence of undistinguished appearance.

But there were other stories behind Ewing. One of them landed him in
trouble with just two years of his principalship to go. On 13 December
1927, the grey-suited university administrator delivered an address to the
Edinburgh Philosophical Institution. His theme was 'Some Special War
Work'. In the lecture, he regaled his audience with an account of his
exploits in Room 40. He credited the 'force, vision, courage' of Winston
Churchill in supporting the unit and mentioned the good luck that attended
its efforts. He listed by name the cryptographers he had recruited. He
described their work. He recalled wistfully the day when 2,000 intercepts
a day had been addressed to 'Ewing, Admiralty', and even gave the

impression that he and not Hall had presided over Room 40's most notable triumphs.

Ewing seemed to realize that he was courting danger. Pre-emptively, he noted that the Germans were on record as being now aware that their messages had been read. The former American ambassador to Britain, Walter Hines Page, had, in the year before his lecture, alluded to Room 40 codebreaking. Former Prime Minister and Foreign Secretary Lord Balfour had said that these disclosures had 'untied his tongue regarding the work which is the subject of this lecture' and had sent a letter endorsing in advance its theme—in fact, the chairman of the meeting had read out the letter before Ewing rose to speak.

However, these precautions were not enough. Ewing had breached the *omerta*-like wall of silence that was supposed to govern the conduct of British secret service. The Admiralty did not want to broadcast the information that it had ever read the correspondence of other nations' diplomats, let alone the fact that it continued to do so in peacetime. Room 40 had given way to the Government Code and Cipher School (GC&CS), which, under the guidance of Alastair Denniston from 1919 to 1942, broke numerous codes. A graduate of the Sorbonne and former Scottish hockey international, Denniston was a countryman of Ewing's but a stickler for discretion. Three days after Ewing's talk, an official circular went out to Room 40 veterans: 'The Lords of the Admiralty view with grave concern this disclosure of information which has at all times been regarded by them as of the utmost secrecy. The publication of such information is prejudicial to the interests of the State, and is in fact contrary to the provisions of the Official Secrets Acts of 1911 and 1920.'[2]

There were reasons for the clampdown. British spymasters did not want their methodologies to be known, believing they might be needed in the future and could only work again if they were kept secret. In the case of human intelligence, they did not want to imperil or neutralize their agents by revealing their identities. And the authorities were thinking not just of future wars. Intelligence as an instrument of national security had come to stay, and was practised in peacetime as well as in war. Of particular sensitivity was the fact that it was deployed against friends not just potential foes.

This security issue was just one of the implications of Room 40 work and especially of its most famous coup, the Zimmermann decrypt. Another was the notion that Room 40 managed to manipulate events so that America entered the First World War, or more plausibly brought in America sooner than might otherwise have been the case—thus winning the war for the French and British Allies and, with far-reaching consequences, humiliating Germany.

Over a longer term, Room 40's signals intelligence (SIGINT) cooperation with the USA was a binding force in the Anglo-American intelligence relationship from 1917 right through to the start of the next war in 1939, and then with even greater force when the USA entered the Second World War in 1941. It is, on the other hand, important to note that there were other dimensions to intelligence cooperation, and that SIGINT could be, was, and remains today an irritant to Anglo-American accord. Equally, there is an Anglo-American tradition of counter-secrecy and a yearning for open government that is evident in embryonic form in the inter-war years. Indeed, it prompted the security campaign that made Ewing nervous, and many others after him on both sides of the Atlantic.

The story of the Zimmermann Telegram and its aftermath merits re-telling with the assistance of new scholarship and documentation, and with the foregoing considerations in mind.

The tale begins at 3.30 a.m. on 4 August 1914 in the murky expanse of the English Channel. Hands aboard the General Post Office specialist ship the *Alert* (not the *Telconia* as in earlier accounts) felt a tug on the rope attached to the grappling hooks they had lowered to the seabed. They had found the first of five cables linking Germany to France, Spain, the Azores, and the United States. The crew now set themselves the task of hauling up and cutting each and every one of the cables. As they were working on the last severance, a dark silhouette loomed out of the dawn. It was a destroyer, and not British. But all was well. It turned out to be French. Its matelots lined up along the warship's rails and cheered as the three-hour cutting operation reached its conclusion. Like those on board the *Alert*, they knew that Germany had just refused to respond to a British ultimatum. France had declared war the previous day, and a state of hostilities now existed between Britain and Germany, too.

The sabotage operation by the civilian cable ship was the first British act of war, and a devastating one. It meant that London, the hub of worldwide communications, would be able to deliver its version of events to the United States much more effectively than Berlin. President Wilson realized the implications, and he made available to Wilhelmstrasse a United States cable linking Berlin and the USA via Britain. The proviso was that the

Germans would use the cable only for peaceful purposes. Berlin surreptitiously ignored the provision, but there was nothing it could do about a further problem. The British could intercept messages passing through their territory, and, if only they could break the codes, read them. This is what happened. One consequence was that Britain could disrupt German commercial communications and blacklist American companies trading with the Central Powers. This helped to skew transatlantic trade in favour of the Allies, giving the USA an economic interest in the defeat of Germany. But there was another consequence, too.[3]

On 16 January 1917, Arthur Zimmermann, by now Germany's secretary of state for foreign affairs, sent his soon-to-be famous secret telegram to the German ambassador in Mexico, Heinrich von Eckhart. It was in high encryption, intended to be difficult to decode. He used the American cable routing the message through Ambassador Bernstorff in Washington. He notified Eckhart of Germany's intention to resume unrestricted submarine warfare. This would reverse earlier pledges given to the still-neutral Americans. With continuing deadlock in the European theatre of war, Berlin calculated it could disrupt transatlantic supplies and starve the British into submission. Though America might declare war, it might not be immediately, perhaps not until the U-boats had killed some more American passengers. And in any case it would take so long to mobilize US troops and get them battle hardened that the risk would be worth taking.

Zimmermann went on to instruct his Mexican envoy on what to do if the United States were in due course to enter the war. Mexico would be invited to enter the conflict on Germany's side. In the case of victory, territories the United States had seized by force in 1846—Texas, New Mexico, and Arizona—would revert to Mexico. Perhaps not realizing that California had also been part of the 1846 seizure from Mexico, Zimmermann also wanted the Mexicans to try to persuade Japan to join the attack on America—in exchange for California should the new allies succeed.

Room 40 had partly decoded the message even before it reached Mexico, and soon had the whole translation in hand. Foreign Secretary Balfour at this point decided to leave the handling of the matter to Hall, giving as his reason his view that Hall knew 'the ropes better than anyone'. Hall and his admirers later treated the decision as a compliment to the Room 40 chief's acuity, and it was. But the decision also gave Balfour an opportunity to disown Hall if things went wrong.

Germany having duly declared unrestricted submarine warfare on 1 February, on the 19th of that month Hall summoned Ned Bell from the US embassy and showed him the letter. By 24 February, the text was in the hands of US officials in Washington. Some of them may have welcomed it as a pretext for war, but a more characteristic reaction was horror and moral affront. President Wilson felt let down by the Germans' use of the American cable not just for unpeaceful goals, but actually for the purpose of plotting against the United States. Though he was not alone in being shocked at the plan to slice off areas of the United States and hand them to Mexico, revisionist historians like Walter Millis and the German scholar Zoachin von zur Gathen have questioned the logic of Wilson's reaction. Millis pointed to double standards: 'Informed Americans understood perfectly well that the Allies had bribed Japan, Italy and Rumenia into the war with the promise of slices from the enemy carcass.' He thought Wilson was naive to think he could go to war with Germany 'without having the Germans fight back'.[4]

On 1 March, the story appeared in the American press, with coverage taking a chauvinistic turn that ignored Zimmerman's conditional language and depicted his message not as a plan to be enacted in the event that war broke out, but as a war plot and stab in the back. Wiseman now deployed his powers of diplomacy. In a display of intimacy with Edward House, he had the colonel at his elbow as he drafted a memorandum, 'Relations between the United States and Great Britain'. It communicated to both governments that if America were to go to war 'which she probably will', it would be for reasons of an American nature. Following its brutal repression of the Easter Rising, Britain was not in good odour. America could not be pressurized or propagandized by London, but should be left to make up its own mind—it was a principle that Britain would try to observe in the Second World War, as well. There was still opposition and suspicion in the US Senate, but the president called for a declaration of war on 2 April, and Congress obliged.[5]

The telegram having been intercepted and decoded in mid-January, why did Hall not show it to Bell and his superiors until mid-February? There has been speculation about the delay. One reason was that the Admiralty wanted to prevent Germany from knowing it had cracked its high-security code. To overcome that problem, British intelligence needed time for a deception to be arranged whereby the telegram was re-procured by means of a bribe in Mexico City—this was the version the British authorities released. The Admiralty wanted to distance itself from that telegram, too. A sham decoding event was arranged in Bell's presence. It took place in America's London embassy partly to reassure the USA that the message was genuine, but also so that it could truthfully be said that the German code was broken on US territory. American newspapers even carried apocryphal stories explaining how US secret agents had pulled off the coup.

The deception was useful because the onward transmission from Germany's Washington embassy to its Mexico City embassy had been in a lower code called 13040. The hope was that Berlin would swallow the Mexican theft story and not, therefore, change its more difficult higher code, meaning that Room 40 could still read vital communications in a manner that would help the war effort.

It is not entirely clear how far the ruse worked. Additional Berlin–Mexico City decodes do show that there was a great deal of German hand wringing and recrimination about who might have been responsible for 'losing' the Zimmermann Telegram. However, Eckhart assured the imperial chancellor, Theobald von Bethman Hollweg, that the original missive had been burnt. He received from the German foreign office a telegram exonerating him and his staff: 'After your telegram it is hardly conceivable that betrayal took place in Mexico.' If that was a candid view, Berlin must have suspected that at least its lower codes had been compromised.

But there was a further reason for the delay and for the concoction of the Mexico City story. It was two-pronged. First, the British wanted to conceal from the United States the fact that they, too, had been abusing the American cable—by intercepting messages flowing along it. Once America was in the war, this did not matter. London dropped any pretence on the subject. Via Bell, Hall supplied the USA with a flood of decoded intercepts showing how German spies and saboteurs had operated in the period of America's neutrality, and a further tranche providing background information on the Zimmermann Telegram. But in the critical weeks between mid-February and early April when America was making up its mind, it was prudent to conceal the tapping exercise. As Hall later put it, London 'was averse from any step which could possibly convey the impression to Washington that there was a chambre noir in the Foreign Office or that the British Government was endeavouring to influence a neutral state in its favour'.[6]

Secondly, Britain wanted to conceal from the Americans the fact that Room 40 was decoding American as well as German messages. This practice might have seemed innocuous in wartime in light of the close cooperation that developed between the two countries. But it was something worth concealing until America's declaration of war, as the news would have played badly with the US administration and with anti-interventionist senators on Capitol Hill. Nor, in the event, was the practice admitted during the war, or in its aftermath. In the naval arms-reduction negotiations of 1921–2, the British were reading American cards before they were played.

While each side was coy about the matter, Bell does appear to have developed suspicions. In October 1917 he suggested to his superior Leland Harrison that he might want to warn the State Department's 'cipher sharps' to have a re-think. One of his embassy colleagues had recently amused himself by attacking the encryption in a secret US diplomatic communication. To his gratification and alarm, he succeeded in short order. 'The moral is, if he did it what could not persons do who are picked for this kind of a job & who spend their lives at it?' Bell did not say which secret service he had in mind.[7]

The British placed a high value on Hall's achievement in the First World War. In the wake of the Zimmermann Affair, he was promoted to the rank of rear admiral and received a knighthood. The American Barbara Tuchman echoed this high esteem. She wrote a history of the Zimmermann Affair in 1958, arguing that without it the American people would not have followed their president's call to go to war. Given the major impact the United States had on the outcome of the war and on the nature of the peace that followed, this was a significant claim. Intelligence devotees took their cue from the Tuchman verdict. A US Army manual of 1973 informed intelligence initiates, 'it was this British success in communications intelligence that brought America into the war. As a matter of fact, if historians had to single out the one individual responsible for bringing the United States into World War I, they would most likely select Admiral Hall.'

In the writing of intelligence history, the Zimmermann Affair has been a useful myth. Hyperbole about its importance became a stick with which to beat those accused of over-reducing US intelligence resources in the 1920s. The genius of British intelligence as manifested in the brilliant work of Hall and exported again to America in 1939–42 has been upheld as a seminal influence on the Office of Strategic Services in the Second World War when US intelligence once again needed to be vitalized, and on the Central Intelligence Agency afterwards.

Yet as Tuchman herself acknowledged, the Zimmermann Telegram was not the only cause of US entry into the war. Other factors played their part, not least German submarines' infliction of US civilian casualties and the inherent Anglophilia of the American political elite. Like the Great Man theory of historical causation, the Great Event hypothesis needs to be treated with caution.[8]

The breaking and handling of the Zimmermann Telegram were, of course, important. The cooperation between Room 40 and U-1 was significant in the First World War and ultimately prefigured the vital Anglo-American SIGINT collaboration in the Second World War. While there is no question about that, at the same time it should be remembered that British intelligence in the inter-war years had a mixed record and was not necessarily a good model. Nor should it be forgotten that misinformation, as evidenced in Hall's deception of his US counterparts, is not a recipe for mutual trust. It should further be noted that U-1's First World War work was by no means confined to SIGINT liaison. It conducted wider liaison work with British intelligence that also contributed to the shaping of the post-war world.

Military liaison was less closely tied to U-1, but still an important part of the picture. It was by no means a straightforward Anglo-American love-in. The point is evident from a reputed proclamation of General John J. Pershing, commander of the American Expeditionary Force (AEF) to France. On 4 July 1917, at the tomb of the French soldier who came to America's assistance in the Revolutionary war, he is said to have intoned, 'Lafayette, we are here.' No matter that in fact it was his subordinate Colonel Charles E. Stanton who uttered the words. The symbolism was that American soldiers were in France to repay their country's debt for help *against the British*. Pershing and his fellow officers were keen to show that they were not just an adjunct to the British Expeditionary Force, and made a political point of being as respectful of their French allies as they were of the British. The Americans studied both the French and the British intelligence models. When they designated their reformed military intelligence 'G-2', the numeral was taken from the French military's *Deuxième Bureau*.[9]

Major Stewart Graham Menzies worked for both MI6 and British Army intelligence. It is an indication of existing stresses that he was given the job of repairing mistrust in order to improve Anglo-American morale in the war zone. Using 'cinematic representations' and other means, he combated what he called 'American ignorance and baseless antipathy' towards the

British. Menzies may or may not have been the illegitimate son of Edward VII as rumour suggested, but he certainly had an upper-class aura—family money made in an Edinburgh distillery, an expensive address in London, Eton-educated. His demeanour went down badly with some American soldiers who remembered the republican roots of American independence. It would not necessarily have offended the Anglophile American elite, but US military distrust of British intelligence did exist at higher levels—General Marlborough Churchill, newly installed chief of the US military intelligence service, in June 1918 ordered an investigation of that entrepôt of intrigue, the British Passport Control Office in New York.[10]

American military personnel nevertheless arrived at the intelligence college in Harrow, England, studying there alongside their British counterparts and a small representation from New Zealand and Australia. As in other areas of intelligence, the British were in a position to instruct because they had been in the war since August 1914 and had thus had the opportunity to reform and fine-tune their system to the requirements of war against the Central Powers. Viewed from the standpoint of a relative novice, British expertise must have seemed impressive. In practice, there were problems with British military intelligence. On the Western front, the British commanding officer Field Marshal Douglas Haig listened uncritically to over-optimistic estimates of German weakness supplied by his intelligence chief Brigadier John Charteris. This was so at the calamitous offensive on the Somme. Delusional intelligence prolonged the war. Yet with their country committed to combat, American officers had little choice but to learn alongside their allies.

General Dennis Nolan, the AEF's chief intelligence officer, studied both the French and British models. He decided the US Army would adopt the latter. In the words of one of his subordinates, 'British Intelligence methods appeared to be better adapted to our army than those of the French.' Against the background of these educational and administrative collaborations, there was Anglo-American intelligence cooperation in the field. It happened in counter-espionage, aerial photography, sound ranging, and frontline radio interception. There was a joint deception operation to try to persuade Germany's generals that American military-industrial strength was even more formidable than it was.[11]

There was also cooperation in the area of decryption. William F. Friedman was a refugee from Russian anti-Semitism whose lifelong service to American cryptography can be traced in part to a youthful fascination with Edgar Allan

Poe's cipher-leads-to-treasure short story, 'The Gold Bug'. In 1917 he worked with the British on German codes in pursuit of the 'Hindu' nationalists, and in so doing developed the frequency technique, an analysis of letter recurrence in messages that could help with the breaking of codes. He then worked with AEF G-2 and collaborated again with his British counterparts. So did his superior officer back in Washington, Ralph Van Deman. A Harvard law and medicine graduate and career army officer, Van Deman was in charge of military intelligence for the US War Department until he gave way to another Harvard graduate, Marlborough Churchill, and departed to serve with Nolan in France.

The circumstances of Van Deman's removal to France were inauspicious and a considerable career setback. His ambitiousness had alienated more senior officers, and he had violated civil liberties by engaging in private initiatives to spy internally on critics of the war and on black radicals. Yet by this time he had made his mark by reconstructing US military intelligence. He modelled G-2 partly on the British example—though in aid of internal liaison, it also reflected the departments of U-1. The intelligence reformer took another leaf out of the British book when he set up a cryptographic unit and to run it imported from the State Department's code room a young cryptographer. Herbert O. Yardley would prove to be second only to Friedman in ability, and successfully promoted the unit known as MI8 and its successors even if he did drink, gamble, womanize, and talk too much. In the meantime, Van Deman relied on British help to decode messages that were potentially significant for the USA, such as one that Berlin sent to the German legation at Bogota in January 1918.

The British regarded Van Deman as the sound man in American military intelligence. During the war, the MI6 officer Claude Dansey lobbied Colonel House, urging him to ensure that Van Deman's reforms met with sympathy in the White House. After the war, MI6 chief Cummings did not realize or could not accept that Van Deman's star was on the wane. He was keen for Anglo-American liaison to continue and saw Van Deman as a key collaborator in the fight against communism. He asked Menzies to cultivate the American. In his study of UK intelligence, Ned Bell emphasized the British determination to do so. Bell noted that MI6's chief, Cumming, 'spoke in the highest terms of Colonel Van Deman, as in fact do all British intelligence officers who came in contact with him'. According to the study, 'C' told Bell he thought Van Deman 'the soundest secret service officer he had ever met or dealt with'.

So military intelligence liaison was an additional component of the Anglo-American secret relationship in the First World War era. While it was distinctive, there was interplay between it and civilian intelligence. This was evident at the elite level, where everyone knew everyone else. For example, in January 1919 'C' gave a dinner party for the civilian Ned Bell, and the civilian-military officer Menzies was in attendance. London's 1b Club teemed with intelligence alumni of both sorts and from both countries. Menzies and Wiseman were members, and the American officers Nolan and Van Deman regularly visited. Thus, while U-1, G2, and MI6 were separate entities and occasionally rivals, they were still intimately bound together.[12]

In the realm of human intelligence, the British conducted a variety of autonomous operations. In the estimate of Keith Jeffery, writer of the authorized history of MI6, *La Dame Blanche* was 'the most successful single British human intelligence operation' of the First World War. 'The White Lady' was one of those women, like Rebecca of the Welsh anti-tollgate movement or Molly Maguire of Irish and American fame, whose mythical identity served as a cover for a dangerously pursued cause, in this case the overthrow of the Kaiser. Belgian patriots, more than 800 of them by war's end and one-third of them women, watched German military trains moving men, horses, and artillery behind the lines. Some spied from fixed posts, others were 'walkers' (*promeneurs*) who went out and about in their German-occupied country. All risked their lives. They smuggled their reports across the combat lines in an assortment of containers, ranging from broom handles to ladies' corsets. Like the captured codebooks that kick-started the efforts of Room 40, it was a gift to British intelligence.

Already by 1916, 'C' had a thousand men and women reporting to him from across the globe. The more senior operatives, reflecting military terminology, were called officers, the rest, mostly non-British nationals, were known as agents (American terminology is similar, with the additional gloss that FBI and Secret Service personnel are called 'special' agents). The MI6 operatives included some startling individuals. In Greece, the challenge was to counter the efforts of Baron von Schenck. This German spymaster had hit on the idea of recruiting seductresses to wheedle information from British agents. It was in answer to this ploy that MI6 sent out a new Athens station chief. American on his mother's side and of Scottish ancestry on his father's, Compton Mackenzie was already a writer of some note.

The roll call of agents sent to Russia, first to try to keep that country in the war and next to combat the Bolsheviks, is legendary. It included writers W. Somerset Maugham and Arthur Ransome and the historian Bernard Pares. It included also Paul Dukes, the only British person knighted for espionage. There was additionally the less fortunate 'ace of spies', Sidney Reilly, who in 1925 met his death as the hands of the OGPU—the Soviet secret service, which, with its successor the KGB, would mount the strongest challenge to Anglo-American intelligence hegemony. In vain did Reilly's two wives sue MI6 for compensation.

British agents concentrated on winning the war, an aim they shared with the United States, and on preserving the Empire, a goal that troubled America. In India, as well as in the Far East and North America, MI6 and local British intelligence services were successful in stalling the effort of their German counterparts. At first, they met with similar success in countering Soviet covert aid to anti-imperialists. In short, it was a world war, and British intelligence operated worldwide.[13]

MI6's extensive reach meant there was little apparent need for human intelligence cooperation with the United States. There was, furthermore, an in-built problem with human intelligence (HUMINT) joint operations. According to the practitioners, this branch of intelligence, as distinct from other branches like SIGINT, lends itself least to mutual trust. Neither partner wants to reveal its HUMINT assets to the other, for the stated reason that enemy penetration of one's partner's intelligence will lead to the betrayal of one's own agents. America's Cold War counterintelligence chief, James Jesus Angleton, observed that 'there are no friendly services'. The NOFORN principle (no foreign eyes to see) has always operated on both sides of the Atlantic on a hierarchical principle—the more vital the information, the more secret it is. Senior British intelligence officials agree that difficulties over HUMINT and penetration have accounted for many of the 'bumps' in Anglo-American intelligence relations.[14]

A little incident in connection with Mexico illustrates the distrust that could exist on the human side of intelligence. Ned Bell wrote to Leland Harrison in January 1918: 'I was shown a telegram at the Admiralty which had been received from Washington (whether by the F.O. from the Embassy or by Hall from Gaunt I couldn't quite make out and didn't like to ask)'. The parenthetical observation shows how Bell still adhered to the etiquette of SIGINT unilaterally imposed by Room 40. He asked no questions about intercepts and decoding, and for security reasons even kept mum about the identities of the sender and addressee. However, when it came to the content of the telegram, it was a different matter.

To sketch in the background to this telegram, there were political and business difficulties over Mexican oil reserves. The British coveted them—Winston Churchill had recognized the strategic importance of oil now that the Royal Navy was converting from coal. The USA, too, saw Mexican oil as important to defence, to business, and to its proclaimed hegemony in its own 'backyard'. The problem was that Venustiano Carranza, elected president of Mexico in 1917, imagined that Mexican oil was an asset for the Mexican people. He was moving towards a policy of nationalization. Influential elements in the US government, including navy secretary Josephus Daniels, wanted the removal of Carranza.

In anticipation of US support, opponents of Carranza in Mexico plotted a coup d'état. According to the telegram Bell saw, one of them then 'got cold feet' and told an official at the British embassy in Mexico City, Thomas Hohler. Through diplomatic intermediaries, Hohler ensured that President Wilson learned about the plot (Wilson eventually decided against both covert action and military intervention). Bell reported to Harrison that the Admiralty was 'frightened' by the possibility of rogue covert action in Mexico and 'up in a balloon' about the prospect. He warned British officials that the coup plot might have a degree of US official backing. But in spite of this evidence of US deviousness masquerading as disarray, Bell reserved his distrust for a *British* official: 'I cannot help having the feeling that somehow Hohler is at the bottom of this. I have never trusted him and I do not think he is really well disposed to us.' This reaction suggests that at least one US intelligence officer, Ned Bell, compartmentalized his trust in Anglo-American liaison—he chose to invest it in the realm of SIGINT, but less so in the fields of human intelligence and intrigue.[15]

Elsewhere, though, there was evidence of HUMINT trust and cooperation. It is evident in the case of Jerusalem. Turkey, which had entered the war on the side of the Central Powers, administered that city as part of the Ottoman empire. But in the autumn of 1917, the sky darkened over the Arab population of the Holy Land. War loomed when Prime Minister David Lloyd George promised Jerusalem to the British people as, in the words of historian John Gray, 'a Christmas present'. To complicate matters further, Britain's foreign secretary issued what came to be known as the Balfour Declaration, giving support to the principle of a Jewish homeland in Palestine.

Sir Edmund Allenby's British Egyptian Expeditionary Force marched north to secure the prime minister's objective. It met with Ottoman resistance. But a bombardment of Gaza, together with an advance disguised as an intelligence probe, ended with British troops on the commanding heights of Ramallah. Confronted with this threat, Jerusalem's commander, Ali-Fuad-Pasha, issued a notice that is in itself revealing of attitudes towards British–American collaboration. It required the expulsion from the city of US citizens between the ages of 17 and 50. Those who refused to go would be treated as spies.

Jerusalem fell to Allenby on 11 December 1917. By February 1918, the British authorities were spying on its inhabitants. They intercepted ordinary civilian correspondence, and passed to the Americans copies of letters they thought might be of propaganda value. There were letters sent to US relatives by Jewish Americans, and a letter from a German saying it 'would be impossible to describe the joy we felt when the English took Jerusalem'. Invasions of privacy and a disposition to self-congratulation bordering on delusion are evident here. But it is also an instance of intelligence cooperation.[16]

The deployment as a secret agent of the English novelist W. Somerset Maugham is another illustration of how human intelligence liaison could run smoothly. Maugham already had some experience of intelligence work, in Switzerland. Like Compton Mackenzie, he found much to deride in the British intelligence establishment. He had found it irritating to work under his MI6 boss John Wallinger. Fictionally, he portrayed Wallinger as 'R', a man who pursued a certain woman in the belief that she would enhance his social standing. Ashenden, Maugham's alter ego in his short stories, took it upon himself to instruct 'R' on the social niceties. One day he admonished his boss who was in the act of pouring a brandy. 'In my youth I was always taught that you should take a woman by the waist and a bottle by the neck.'[17]

Still, the Swiss experience together with the facts that America had entered the war, and that he had an American gay lover, may have made Maugham receptive to a phone call he received one day in East Hampton, Long Island. He was vacationing there with his wife Syrie and 2-year-old daughter Liza (if unenthusiastically, Maugham was bisexual). The man who called out of the blue was Wiseman. He was a distant relative by marriage, and acquainted with the author. Could he interest Maugham in another mission?

Wiseman was worried about post-tsarist Russia. Following the February 1917 revolution, Alexander Kerensky led a provisional government. There was a danger that a debilitated Russia would leave the war, freeing German soldiers fighting on the Eastern front to leave the region and reinforce their comrades fighting the Allies on the Western front. If the Bolsheviks took over, that danger would become a certainty. Wiseman wanted to launch an intelligence probe, and the British and Americans each gave him $75,000 to start the job. Wiseman sent Maugham to St Petersburg as his chief Anglo-American agent, drawing on the joint funds to pay him. Maugham embarked for the Russian capital with $21,000 at his disposal. His subsequent reports went both to MI6 and to U-1, where Gordon Auchincloss gave them his attention.

Maugham later reproached himself because the Bolsheviks did launch a successful coup, and did take Russia out of the war. In his defence, he had been sent not to prevent a revolution from taking place, but on an intelligence mission with the additional remit of making suggestions on how to guide the storm. He was one of the first to predict the demise of the ailing Prince Kerensky. He furthermore devised a strategy of cooperating with nationalist leaders from east central Europe, notably Emanuel Voska, an American secret agent bent on establishing the state of Czechoslovakia.

For in order to stabilize the former territories of the crumbling Austrian empire, it was necessary to create a new order. Lloyd George had his own intelligence network working towards the creation of a new Europe. For example, his private secretary Philip Kerr oversaw the efforts of the Edinburgh scholar James Y. Simpson, who worked to establish the Baltic territories' independence from Russian control. Through Kerr, Simpson also kept the prime minister abreast of the William C. Bullitt mission to Russia, an abortive attempt to establish diplomatic relations between the USA and the new Soviet government. However, in east central Europe the United States applied its own doctrine, self-determination, in pressing for a broader network of nation states that would replace the Austro-German hegemony and act as a buffer against communist expansion. It also had human assets, the many immigrants from Poland, Bohemia, Hungary, Serbia, and so forth, who spoke the languages and had the local expertise to liaise, at first secretly, and, after Austria's defeat, openly, with nationalists in the region. Maugham recognized and cultivated the opportunity, and in that sense was a significant Anglo-American intelligence link man.[18]

In some ways SIGINT liaison went less smoothly than HUMINT. The whole business was frustrating for the Americans. Whereas Room 40 was supplying U-1 with decrypts of German messages, the Americans wanted, in addition, the German codes and ciphers so that they would have the codebreaking capability themselves. Hall and his colleagues stalled on this issue, arguing that because the Germans kept changing their encryption methods, a one-off gift of codes would be of little help, so it was better to leave things to Room 40's experienced personnel. This was disingenuous, as most cryptological breakthroughs come after a flying start such as the acquisition of a codebook. Unimpressed and wanting their own flying start, the Americans kept on demanding the information.

The task fell to Ned Bell. He reported that Hall was 'very shy at giving up any more than he has to' and thought that the 'only way to manage these things is to establish an atmosphere of confidence'. But Hall just strung him along. Leland Harrison now intervened from his position of greater authority, and must have received some kind of assurance. Bell wrote to Harrison in January 1918, 'I am glad you are glad you are going to get your code books.' From the way in which the Americans kept on pressing, though, it can be deduced that Hall did not pass on very much.[19]

The US demands continued after the end of the war. In December 1918, H. O. Yardley turned up in London in pursuit of British code expertise. He reported to Van Deman that he was making headway with breaking German codes, but he needed help. He told Bell that 'Washington is still desirous of a German Naval Code with the form of encipherment used by the Germans'. He understood 'that these codes, as well as the form of encipherment, were changed very often', but still needed a recent sample to work on. He knew 'it was impossible to get this information before the armistice', but now saw no reason for the British to remain uncooperative.

Although Bell helped him at first, Yardley got on indifferently with American colleagues who might have furthered his cause. A brash midwesterner with little education, he had limited appeal to the Ivy League contingent. The feeling was mutual. Yardley characterized his intelligence colleagues at the State Department as 'smartly dressed pygmies, strutting around with affected European mannerisms'. In the event, Hall, too, took against him. Yardley's booster approach was not unusual in America, but Hall thought ill of his exaggerations and indiscretions. He barred Yardley from Room 40, and when he dribbled a few lower-level German codes to the Americans, it was through Bell. When Yardley moved to Paris to work with the US peace delegation, the French cryptanalyst Georges Jean Painvin gave him similar cold shoulder treatment. The more Yardley pressed, the more irritated people became.

Irritation aside, the British had good reason to withhold the crown jewels of secret intelligence. Knowledge is power, and America was a rival as well as a friend. If the American authorities had pressed harder and at a higher level, the outcome might have been different. They had the economic and military clout to make things difficult for Hall and the British government. However, in the hard bargaining across the Atlantic, there were bigger chips on the table. They included territorial realignments in Europe and the incorporation of the League of Nations in the peace settlement. It was the old story. In order to win some, you lose some.

Yet the Americans were not minded to give up in their quest for more effective intelligence. Partly out of admiration for British intelligence and partly out of distrust of it, they turned their attention to peacetime espionage. The president regarded it as a break with tradition. The US Constitution had authorized Congress to conduct some of its business in secret, but generally Americans had favoured openness in diplomatic relations. There was a feeling that the hidden machinations of European leaders had contributed to the outbreak and prolongation of the First World War. In the very first point of his Fourteen Points address setting out Allied war aims in January 1918, President Wilson called for 'open covenants of peace, openly arrived at'. But it turned out to have been a utopian aspiration. The Paris peace conference went immediately into closed session. When the Republican-dominated US Senate plotted against majority opinion in a successful attempt to keep America from joining the League of Nations and thus discredit the Democratic president, Wilson retaliated with this warning. If America did not join, it would have to set up a 'spying system. The more polite call it a system of intelligence.'

In his January letter to Bell, Yardley had already explained that a 'permanent organization of my bureau in Washington has been worked out between Mr Harrington and General [Marlborough] Churchill. The personnel will include several officers, fifty clerks, and thirty cryptographers.' In May 1919, Churchill signed the order. The army would contribute an annual sum of $60,000 and the State Department $40,000 to meet the cost of a cryptographic bureau that would become known as the American Black Chamber.[20]

There were other signs of an American desire to emulate British intelligence practices. Ned Bell's report of 1 May 1919 met with the approval of Leland Harrison, who encouraged Bell to pursue his UK contacts with peacetime liaison in mind.

In his report, Bell outlined the post-war changes that were taking place. Hall and other stalwarts were retiring. MI10, the 'joy-riding section' of military intelligence that had looked after US and French liaison, would disappear along with the British Expeditionary Force. In another threat to liaison, the Admiralty seemed set to lose some of its functions to MI6 (at that point still called MI1[c]). Following the direction of the wind, Bell had had a conversation with MI6's director 'C' about the future of intelligence.

Cumming 'hoped in a general way it might be possible to come to some understanding with our Secret Service in regard to co-operation after the war'. He suggested to Bell how U-1 and MI6 could complement each other. Perhaps with post-war cuts and economies in mind, he suggested a worldwide division of responsibilities. For example, the Americans might take the lead in Mexico, and the British might take a greater interest in Danish fortifications. He ceded there would be areas of overlap—MI6 would want to inform itself directly on the situation in the Mexican oil district of Tampico, and 'if our interests clashed in any one particular country both Governments could maintain complete services there and "cut each other's throats" quite happily'.[21]

In the coming decades, Americans would report on the state of British intelligence on several occasions. Two such investigations followed Bell's at short intervals. Nolan, now director of the army's Military Intelligence Division (MID), presented the first of them in the autumn of 1920. Written by one of the general's officers, it examined MI6 activities within the USA. It set out to describe changes in personnel and organization, and gave details of individual agents some of which were accurate, others being speculative or reflective of the nativist paranoia then sweeping America. The claim that Kathleen Scott, sculptress and widow of the Arctic explorer, was a secret agent flowed rather too easily from the observation that she was 'a very attractive woman'. The fleeting mention that Wiseman received indicated ignorance of his role. Complaints that MI6 was out to give British commercial companies an unfair competitive advantage were a little shrill, if true. Overall, Nolan's report offered the reassuring view that MI6 was spying on rival firms and on Reds and black radicals who might undermine the British Empire, but not on the US military.

A report in 1921 bore the imprint of the FBI's Radical (that is, *anti-radical*) Division though it appears in MID files. It focused on British espionage in New York. Noting that MI6 had identified 600,000 'armed men' who threatened revolt in America—they included mainly radical, labour, and black elements—the unidentified author of the report jealously observed that MI6 had 'better information' on US radicals than the US authorities themselves. Taking fear and awe to unreasonable heights, the author assumed MI6 had achieved top-level penetration everywhere. Amongst the MI6 secret agents it listed were the Jamaican-American radical Marcus Garvey and the American-based Irish socialist James Larkin.[22]

On a more rational plane, those wishing to enhance the efficacy of US intelligence included specialists in the area of secret communications. The communications historian Jonathan Winkler notes that U-1 and the Cipher Bureau anticipated modern US intelligence arrangements and that they began to fight for autonomy in the wake of Zimmermann. There was an American 'dream of wiring the world'. It was partly commercial in intent, but also connected with the goal of an independent intelligence capability. In December 1920, America, Britain, Japan, and others on the winning side in the First World War met in a communications conference where the main bone of contention was, who should control the Pacific cable hub on the island of Yap? The Germans had laid the cables, Japan now had mandate powers over the island, and America wanted control and to exclude Britain and other rivals. Helped by the fact that Yardley's unit was reading Japanese messages and reported that Tokyo would concede if pressed, the US won a favourable outcome.[23]

Such rivalries with other powers including Britain were real enough. It is still possible to say, though, that British and American intelligence had a mutual history in the 1920s and 1930s. The two intelligence communities were more separate than they had been in the war. But at the same time, they had more in common than before the war.

On both sides of the Atlantic, there were reductions in the size of intelligence communities. Once the war was over, government expenditure on national security plunged. What had seemed justified during a national emergency seemed less so in peacetime. Knowing that it would be offensive to their commercial clients, telegraph and cable companies were less keen to cooperate with traffic interception, and on both sides of the Atlantic code-breakers found they had fewer messages to handle.

Incipiently, at least, the chill wind reflected new social attitudes. After complaints that American diplomats in London were walking to work in top hats and speaking with British accents, the Foreign Service Act of 1924 (known as the Rogers Act) sought to broaden the social spectrum from which diplomats were drawn by introducing an entrance examination. This attempt at professionalization potentially had a reverse effect to that intended, as the best educated tended to be the well off. Nevertheless, in 1927, amidst further complaints that a 'Harvard clique' was fixing jobs in the foreign service, U-1 was abolished. More than this, the State Department relinquished its interest in codebreaking. In 1929, the American Black Chamber lost the State Department's financial support and Yardley found himself out of work. The unit continued under military funding, but the dissolution was a psychological as well as a financial blow.

A general revulsion against war took its toll in both America and Britain. In the United States, the revisionist school of history swept aside wartime nationalist assumptions. It argued that America should never have entered the war of 1914–18. The young historian C. Hartley Grattan was one of those who believed that pro-British bias had played a disastrous role. He charged that Walter Hines Page, Anglophile ambassador to London until his death in 1918, had been a 'traitor' to America in the mould of Benedict Arnold. He teamed up with Frederick Bausman, a Washington State judge who conceived of himself as a latter-day Paul Revere, to argue in a book called *Why We Fought* (1929) that British agents had conspired to recruit the USA in defence of the British Empire. Unlike Adolf Berle who thought such agents had gone behind the backs of US diplomats, Grattan and Housman saw them as having operated hand in glove with State Department officials.

There was a post-war wave of Anglophobia and a renewed aversion to spying. In the 1930s, Senator Robert M. LaFollette Jr (R-WI) contributed to the latter sentiment when he conducted an inquiry into industrialists' use of spies against labour unions. However, it should be noted that spyphobia played a minor role in the annals of foreign policy revisionism. The more influential revisionists attributed America's entry into the First World War not to underhand British tactics, but to the lobbying activities of financiers and arms manufacturers, the 'Merchants of Death' who stood to gain. It was these economic arguments that helped to persuade Congress to pass the neutrality legislation in the 1930s banning trade with belligerents. With bankers and arms manufacturers in the firing line, hatred of British intelligence remained relatively low key.

Winston Churchill and other British advocates of higher levels of security expenditure found themselves in the political wilderness for reasons comparable to those that obtained in America. But for them, too, the outlook was not entirely bleak. For although the wartime intelligence establishment was lampooned by writers like W. Somerset Maugham and Compton Mackenzie, in reputational terms it got off relatively lightly, like its US counterpart. In the 1930s, the British journalist William Makin even suggested that 'the spy makes for peace'. The Anglo-American spy was down, but not out.[24]

Another mutual element in the inter-war history of the American and British intelligence communities was their tendency to engage in undemocratic practices, and to ignore civil liberties. It was the modern conundrum—how to make democracy secure, without in the process undermining that democracy. Mistakes were made on both sides of the Atlantic, and sometimes in tandem.

America had its Red Scare of 1919–20, with future FBI director J. Edgar Hoover playing a prominent role and with British intelligence operatives in New York in full support. Both MID and the Office of Naval Intelligence joined in the anti-radical hunt of 1919 and the early 1920s. Their targets included the left, the so-called 'Pink Sisters' who pursued feminist objectives, and African Americans who asserted themselves in the decade of the 'Harlem Renaissance'.

With Admiral Hall mired in strikebreaking activities and MI6 contaminated by the Zinoviev affair, things were little better in the UK. The British authorities were quite capable of matching the inanities on the other side of the Atlantic, as the case of Marcus Garvey shows. Blowing hot and cold on the idea of Anglo-American intelligence cooperation, J. Edgar Hoover pursued his obsession that Garvey was not what he said he was, a Pan-Africanist leader, but a British secret agent. By now director of the FBI and forgetting that his agency traced its origins to the fight against racism, he harassed Garvey and had him indicted on a charge of mail fraud. In 1927, after Garvey had served two years of a five-year sentence, President Calvin Coolidge pardoned him and the US government deported the Jamaican to his native island.

Now it was the British Empire's turn to persecute. Canada deported Garvey when he moved there, and Jamaica sentenced him to prison when he went back home again. Relying on their intelligence sources in the western hemisphere, the British tried to prevent Garvey from visiting various parts of the West Indies, and banned his *Negro World* publication from West Africa. A Foreign Office memorandum explained that the short-term goal was to keep the black nationalist from 'sowing the seeds of discontent and revolt' and from 'deliberately' fomenting 'racial antagonism'. In the longer term, the story of Garvey's persecution did not bode well for the acceptability of the Anglo-American imperium.[25]

A final sphere of synchronicity in intelligence history was censorship. Both the USA and the UK bore down on those who would divulge secrets of state. In the 1920s and 1930s, there developed in both countries oppressive tendencies that came to be associated with the growth of the national security state. At the same time, there was a reaction against excessive secrecy that foreshadowed freedom of information campaigns in future decades.

The proliferation of secret documents increased the opportunities for security leaks. In Britain, Sir Maurice Hankey brought greater order to government business in his capacity as secretary to the Committee on Imperial Defence and cabinet secretary from the First World War to 1938. But his efficiency came at the cost of more paperwork, and the greater the number of secret documents, the greater was the temptation to use—or abuse—them.

The post-war years were a boom time for memoir writers like Winston Churchill and Lloyd George. However, both of them held trenchant views that might not go down well with the guardians of public discretion. Both, for example, initially regarded the First World War commander Earl Haig as an incompetent butcher of men who had to be exposed. 'If only the generals had not been content', Churchill exclaimed, 'to fight machine-gun bullets with the breasts of gallant men, and think that that was waging war.' The possibility of personal enrichment encouraged frankness and revelation: Lloyd George had an offer of £90,000 for his memoirs. On the side of dissuasion, Hankey, the Lords of the Admiralty, and others issued warnings backed by the Official Secrets Act. Partly because of this and partly because he reached an accord with Haig who cleverly decided to help him with his research, Churchill was more lenient in his later writings on the field marshal.[26]

There was a special effort to hush up the secrets of Room 40 and especially the Zimmermann Telegram. A problem arose in 1921. In June of that year, the American journalist Burton J. Hendrick wrote to Ned Bell saying he was just back from London where he had spoken with Admiral Hall. Sir Reginald had briefed him on the Zimmermann affair and given him around twelve telegrams as evidence.

This could have been sensational. Hendrick was a Yale graduate who became one of the original generation of Progressive era 'Muckrakers', investigative journalists who after 1900 set out to lift the veil of secrecy that covered malpractices in business and government—Hendrick's own contribution had been an exposure of insurance industry scams. Now, he wanted to write the biography of Walter Hines Page. He planned to include the revelation about Room 40 codebreaking and how it affected America's entry into the war. He seemed to have accepted at face value the story that Bell had helped to decode the Zimmermann Telegram, and wanted Bell to tell him the details so that he could 'make the account as graphic & dramatic as possible'.

Bell replied agreeing to help with the biography, but issued a warning about the confidential nature of the Hall materials: 'It is unnecessary for me to point out that the one Government would be equally interested with the other.' He insisted that Page would never have released such material without obtaining official permission. Page's son Arthur, who worked with Hendrick at the magazine *World's Work*, now approached the State Department for permission, claiming he was doing so at the suggestion of the British government, which had already given its consent. He had also consulted Irwin Laughlin, who had been counsellor at the American embassy in the war, and although surprised, Laughlin had failed to disabuse him about what was likely to be the real British attitude. Hearing about this, Bell rebuked Laughlin, 'I only wish to Heaven that when this man approached you you had hit him with a sand-bag.'

The dispute dragged on and in 1923 Leland Harrison, by now assistant secretary of state, wrote to Secretary of State Charles Evans Hughes backing Bell. It was 'not seemly' that the information should appear in an unofficial biography. He recommended the prohibition of publication on the ground that it would be 'against the public interest'. The pressure appears to have worked. When Hendrick's biography appeared, he communicated Page's view that the Zimmermann Telegram brought America into the war, but his reference to Hall was muted. If he did understand the full story, he did not tell it.[27]

This was far from the end of the matter. In 1923, a US embassy official notified the State Department's code specialist Bill Hurley that 'one of the most important of our friends' ('friends' meaning, then as thereafter, British intelligence) had raised a concern. One of Hall's code clerks, Cleland Hoy, had fallen on hard times and wanted to sell his Room 40 memoir to an American publisher. Harrison intervened, every obstacle was thrown in Hoy's way on both sides of the Atlantic, excisions were thrust on the author, and his book did not come out until 1932.

Hall, too, fell under the censor's axe. He filed an affidavit in December 1926 with the German-American Mixed Claims Commission. The commission's purpose was to determine financial liability for German sabotage operations in the USA. Hall supplied the commission with hundreds of decrypted German messages. But when he started to write his memoir based on such materials, the Admiralty told him it was 'undesirable on naval grounds' for any reference to be made to 'intercepts'. Succumbing to this pressure, Hall returned his publisher's advance and sacrificed the payment he had made to a shadow writer.[28]

Then in 1927 Sir Alfred Ewing gave his lecture. At its conclusion he returned to the theme that his story was not 'a revelation of secrets'. Its details had been concealed for a few years, but then 'had been publicly referred to by Mr Churchill [in his war history *World Crisis*] under whom, as First Lord, the work of Room 40 was begun, and by Lord Balfour, under whom it was continued'. Clearly he had a premonition that the Admiralty would be unhappy with his lecture—at the time of delivery it was, in fact, the fullest account so far of the Zimmermann affair.

Still, Ewing escaped prosecution. Perhaps a lecture was deemed less harmful than a publication. His account was less authoritative than he claimed, and possibly considered less harmful for that reason. But he also escaped because of a powerful intervention on his behalf by Lord Balfour. The former foreign secretary knew Ewing not just from the war, but because he was a native of East Lothian and was chancellor of Edinburgh University. The Admiralty listened to Balfour when he pleaded that prosecution of his friend would be a 'purely retrograde step'.[29]

The reasons for the British authorities' stern approach do not entirely lend themselves to logic. Officials in the Wilhelmstrasse and Kremlin knew that the British secret service was in the business of codebreaking, so there was no reason to conceal that. More sensitive was the issue of whether Britain (or at least Hall) had tricked America into entering the First World War prematurely by manipulating the release of news about the Telegram in January–February 1917. Sensitive, too, would have been any hint that the

Anglophile American upper-class had conspired with its British friends to secure US entry. Given certain Anglophobic currents in American society, that story might have been political dynamite. It must remain speculative, as the joint suppression of that angle of the story was successful.

The secrecy impulse was still not played out. In 1932, Compton Mackenzie published the third volume in his wartime reminiscences. It was called *Greek Memories*, discussed his counter-espionage activities in Athens, and presented a biting portrait of the original 'C', Sir Mansfield Cumming, MI6 chief 1909–23. The Director of Public Prosecutions forced Mackenzie's publisher to withdraw the book, and Mackenzie faced charges under the Official Secrets Act. To ease his life, Mackenzie pleaded guilty and paid a fine. The whole episode was regarded as a farce. Even the Special Branch officer who served the summons on the author sympathized with Mackenzie and bought him several pink gins as consolation.

Mackenzie took his revenge on the intelligence establishment by publishing a satirical novel, *Water on the Brain* (1933). Perhaps because (like some in MI6) he suspected his prosecution had been an MI5 plot, his new novel lampooned the entire intelligence service. Its parade of characters included an 'American SS man' called Katzenschlosser who was 'the most important foreign agent on either side of the Atlantic'. Rather prophetically for real life, the British had to handle Katzenschlosser with kid gloves to avoid 'trouble with the American Embassy'. According to Mackenzie's biographer, in 1942 *Water on the Brain* was required reading for recruits at the fledgling Office of Strategic Services (OSS). But Mackenzie also contributed to the idea that it was right to lift the veil of secrecy when it hid so much that was foolish and unsavoury.

What puzzled people at the time was, why bother to prosecute Mackenzie? What he disclosed was hardly comparable to the Zimmermann secrets and was far removed from high policy. His lawyers and others at the time speculated that he was being used as an example to others—not just veterans of the intelligence community, but also former politicians like Lloyd George who might embarrass current governments with too-frank revelations. This may have been the case. At the same time, it seems clear from the cumulative evidence that Britain's culture of secrecy was solidifying.[30]

In America, Yardley found himself running into that same culture. In 1931, he published his book *The American Black Chamber*. It revealed how his unit had decoded Japanese diplomatic messages giving the Americans a bargaining advantage at the 1921–2 Washington naval conference when the

Pacific powers were negotiating naval tonnage reductions. The book caused a sensation in Japan. According to a neoconservative interpretation of Japanese history its publication contributed to distrust of America, and helped to set Japan on a military course. Following the success of that book, Yardley now planned another, 'Japanese Diplomatic Secrets', which would discuss Yap as well as Washington decodes in some detail and print the texts of many intercepted telegrams. Stanley K. Hornbeck, a Far Eastern specialist in the State Department, warned the book might have an unfortunate impact on US–Japanese relations. Japan had already occupied Manchuria, and Japanese anti-American feeling was running high.

On the authority of the Espionage Act of 1917, federal officers entered the New York premises of Macmillan publishers and seized the manuscript. In spite of its preoccupation with emergency legislation to fight the Depression, the Franklin D. Roosevelt administration reacted in a further way. It drafted a bill and steered it through an already desperately busy Congress. Signed by the president on 10 June 1933, the measure prohibited anyone with access to government code work from divulging any diplomatic transmissions, upon pain of up to ten years in prison. The law became known as the Yardley Act.[31]

In some ways, the Yardley case differed from the Mackenzie prosecution. Mackenzie was a satirist who attacked the intelligence establishment and excessive secrecy. In the 1930s, with Senator LaFollette presiding over his inquiry into labour espionage, Yardley might have made a similarly principled contribution to open government. However, his initial aim had been to promote not denigrate his profession, and there are still those who admire him for having done that. Later, embittered by the loss of the American Black Chamber and by his own dismissal, he revealed pecuniary motives when he tried to sell his wares first to the Japanese and then to the Canadians.

In spite of this, Yardley might be seen as a precursor of the intelligence apostates who opened up discussion in later decades. And his story is still similar to Mackenzie's in that it illustrates the culture of secrecy that was, even if perhaps with some justification in Yardley's case, taking a grip in Anglo-American intelligence circles.

The affair of the Zimmermann Telegram had wide-ranging consequences. Ned Bell died of a heart attack in 1924 and did not see it through, but the cryptographic cooperation epitomized by the affair inspired emulation of British intelligence practices in the USA. It announced also the beginnings of an Anglo-American intelligence imperium.

There were, however, limits to the affair's significance. First, SIGINT was not the only game in town. Other types of intelligence liaison were taking place. There was the military intelligence cooperation on the battle-front in the First World War, and human intelligence liaison over the issues of the Bolshevik Revolution and the shaping of post-war Europe.

In the 1930s, MI5 and the FBI operated in harmony in the counter-intelligence sphere. Notably, in 1938 the British authorities arrested the Glasgow-born German spy Jessie Jordan. A working-class woman who declared that 'nationality means nothing to her', she had acted as a courier between the German secret service and its major spy ring in the USA. The Scottish legal authorities refused to hand her over to American interrogators, but MI6 ensured that the FBI was sufficiently briefed to launch a successful prosecution in New York.[32]

Intelligence and with it intelligence liaison nevertheless fell into disrepute and disrepair in the 1920s and 1930s. There was an incipient challenge to gratuitous secrecy from the supporters of a more open society. There was a hint, here, of two nations beginning to march in tandem, but on issues of civil liberty and free speech rather than the practices associated with Zimmermann-era cooperation.

A final limitation was that the affair did not signify absolute trust and cooperation. Hall and his successors withheld the inner secrets of cryptography. Here, we can see a preview of Churchill's observation in July 1940: 'Are we going to throw all our secrets into the American lap? If so, I am against it. It would be much better to go slow, as we have far more to give than they.'

If a special intelligence relationship had germinated in the First World War, in the period of American neutrality at the start of the Second World War it had still to bloom. Information was too valuable a commodity to be squandered for no return. There was also the matter of security. With German-Americans serving in the US armed forces, Churchill feared that British secrets shared with the Americans would go 'pretty quickly to Berlin'.

Already, however, the prime minister was anticipating a change. 'Once it is war, very much better controls are operative.'[33]

4

The Special Intelligence Relationship in the Second World War

The first Sunday in December 1941 found Winston Churchill at Chequers, the Buckinghamshire mansion that is the prime minister's official country residence. German aggression culminating in the invasion of Poland in September 1939 had vindicated his views, previously considered sanguinary. The materialization of the Nazi menace had propelled him into his nation's highest political office with the mission of saving his country. As America was still neutral and much of Europe under Adolf Hitler's control, his chances of success were slim.

On that Sunday in the English countryside, Churchill knew that something was astir. The previous day he had received a decoded intercept from Bletchley Park, the new headquarters of the Government Code and Cipher School (GC&CS). The purloined message was from the foreign ministry in Tokyo, instructing the Japanese ambassador in London to destroy all codes and secret documents. War was imminent. But where and whom would Japan strike first? If the attack were on the British Empire alone, it would be a disaster, as the UK would still be alone, and with a new enemy.

Churchill at last entered the dining room in company with his two American guests, Ambassador John Winant and President Franklin D. Roosevelt's special envoy, Averell Harriman. Clementine was indisposed, and Harriman's daughter had escaped the scene. The prime minister summoned his butler, Sawyer, to place on the dining table a fifteen-dollar portable radio gifted to him by President Roosevelt's adviser, Harry Hopkins. They would catch the BBC's 9 o'clock news. Churchill switched on the radio. Winant remembered the occasion. 'For a moment there was a jangle of music, and then, suddenly, from the little black box, a voice announced that Japan had attacked our fleet at Pearl Harbor.'

Winant now telephoned Washington, and Churchill chimed in for a matter-of-fact conversation with the president. Over there in the White House, the domestic staff had Sunday night off. By the time Eleanor Roosevelt had served up a supper of scrambled eggs to twenty-four guests, the die was cast. As in April 1917, America would be coming to Britain's assistance.[1]

And as in relation to the preceding conflict, there have been suspicions that Britain manipulated America into entering the war. That Churchill seemed, on one reading of Winant's account, unsurprised at the BBC news item has been interpreted as meaning he knew all along the Japanese were going to attack America, and when. According to one theory, British codebreakers were on top of Japanese codes and ciphers, but Churchill did not want to forewarn Roosevelt as he could have, in case the president took pre-emptive action. For from the British point of view American public opinion, to arouse it from its neutralist torpor, needed a proper shock—such as that duly administered by Japan's slaughter of 2,000 men at Pearl Harbor. Later, according to the conspiracy theory, when given US decrypts of Japanese messages they could already read, the British pretended to be grateful—just to cover up what they had been doing and why. The suppression of all relevant documentation further fanned suspicions.[2]

Though Churchill, like Hall before him, would have been pleased to have contrived US entry into the war, the sensible verdict on the conspiracy theory is 'not even remotely proven'. The suppression of evidence is not in itself proof of the existence of a plot. As for Churchill's sang-froid, it is a characteristic of powerful leaders. They school themselves to appear to be in control, and never surprised. Indeed, President Roosevelt's bearing as he discussed the Japanese attack over scrambled eggs was just as unruffled as the British prime minister's—even if his supporters later insisted he *had* been surprised, in order to scotch further conspiracy fears about a president tricking his own nation into going to war.[3]

Similarities nevertheless exist between the First World War and Second World War scenarios, and they extend further than the retrospective disposition to generate conspiracy theories. On both occasions, there was extensive Anglo-American intelligence liaison. Britain having built up expertise because of prior entry to both conflicts, Americans twice went through a period of intelligence apprenticeship. Intelligence cooperation contributed to Allied victory on both occasions, and helped to shorten the war. The experience of what came to be a special intelligence relationship in the early 1940s laid the foundations for its post-war continuation. As in the First World War, there were tensions over such issues as autonomy, information control, and decolonization. Yet, and to a greater extent than in 1917–18, intelligence liaison in the Second World War contributed to the shape of the post-war world. The ill-fated dream of an 'American Century' was a joint enterprise.

In another similarity with the earlier war, American neutrality in the period 1939–41 developed into an intelligence sham. As in the 1914–18 conflict, the British sought partisan collaboration. The process was already under way when Churchill became prime minister in May 1940. Stewart Menzies, who took over at MI6 a few weeks after the outbreak of the war, had in the previous month sent William Stephenson on a mission to the USA.

From Winnipeg, Manitoba, and the son of a servant of the Empire who had been killed in the Boer War, Stephenson would play a special intelligence role. According to his deputy, the MI6 officer H. Montgomery Hyde, this was 'the same job' as that performed by Wiseman in the earlier war. In common with Wiseman, he had a slight physique and had been an accomplished boxer, in fact, world amateur lightweight champion. Like the Englishman, he had been gassed in combat in the First World War—before converting to the air service and winning recognition for outstanding gallantry. Stephenson in peacetime became a self-made millionaire specializing in pressed steel production. He was conversant with German industrial conditions and was one of those who warned Churchill, then in the political wilderness, about the danger posed by German rearmament. Known from 1940 by the code name 'Intrepid', he more tellingly bore the nickname 'The Quiet Canadian'. For like Wiseman, he conducted his business discreetly and stayed out of the limelight. As for his Canadian identity, it pointed to future trends in global intelligence liaison. More immediately, it gave him a double entry, making him welcome in both Britain and America.

Stephenson made headway where others had failed. The situation was at first difficult and, for the British, confusing. The British had not studied the pluralistic American scene with anything approaching the thoroughness with which the Americans periodically investigated UK intelligence. Hampered by this ignorance, they looked for a single source of authority with whom they could communicate. However, war not yet having concentrated minds in Washington, there was a marked diffusion of power there, with inter-service rivalries contributing to the lack of a unifying voice.

Given a bureaucratic twist or two, Assistant Secretary Adolf Berle was the successor to the undersecretary of state who had presided over U-1 until its dissolution in 1927. He was head of the Interdepartmental Intelligence Conference and there was an expectation that he would revive the coordinating role. Indeed one biographer offers the reflection that 'during World War II, Berle ran the State Department's worldwide intelligence network'. But in reality Berle was unenthusiastic, and even less keen on liaison with the British at the time when, as he reasoned, his country was neutral. He had minimal dealings with James Paget, the passport control officer who had served as the UK intelligence representative in the United States since 1937. He stymied the efforts of Hamish Mitchell, of the British Purchasing Commission, to establish relations with the FBI.

Berle also continued to distrust Wiseman. In one sense, he was here in touch with the times, for Wiseman had lost the confidence of officials in the Foreign Office and MI6. They could not both have been true, but charges that Wiseman was pro-Jewish and pro-Nazi were an indication of how the baronet-turned Wall Street magnate had dropped his magic wand. He no longer had his former capacity to generate confidence on all sides. At first he aspired to his old role, but by June 1940 was reconciled to Stephenson's ascendancy, while continuing to help from the wings.[4]

In a comment that sums up the problems for the British in the spring of 1940, the historian Douglas Charles observed that 'Berle opposed liaison with British intelligence while Hoover sought to monopolize it'. J. Edgar Hoover's prickly rivalry with other agency heads, and indeed with the British when he was so minded, would be a problem. Yet he did play a pivotal role in generating the special intelligence relationship. He explained to Winston Churchill how the State Department was sticking to neutrality in a way that made it difficult for the FBI to help the British. Churchill sent Stephenson to explain the problem to Roosevelt. The president was already using the FBI to harass and spy on politicians who campaigned against US intervention in the war. He now used his executive authority to put liaison into effect. 'There should be the closest possible marriage between the FBI and British intelligence,' he told Lord Lothian. It was just what the British ambassador wanted to hear.[5]

Berle continued to obstruct, and continued to be sidelined. On 31 May, he attended a meeting in Hoover's office attended by Van Deman and other representatives of the military. Though he had a 'pleasant time, coordinating', he objected to the centralization of foreign and domestic intelligence, and failed to see 'what the State Department has got to do with it'. But in the following month Stephenson returned to New York to replace Paget at Passport Control. He set up a worldwide intelligence organization called British Security Coordination (BSC), and started to campaign for greater US intelligence coordination. He found he was pushing on a door that was at least half-open.[6]

Hoover wanted his FBI to be at the fulcrum, with himself as the American central intelligence tsar. His bureau already had the foreign intelligence remit in Latin America. He had furthermore established an FBI codebreaking unit. Its cryptanalysts worked on Japanese, German, and Vichy French traffic, confirmation that the FBI was looking beyond the Americas. They shared information with BSC and its mother agency. MI6 in turn alerted Guy Liddell at MI5 and Alastair Denniston at Bletchley Park to the extent of the Hoover's activities.

Following a Lord Lothian initiative, the British and American military began to exchange information and to work towards technical compatibility. On the last day of August 1940 at a meeting with the British chiefs of staff, General George V. Strong of the US Army's G-2 revealed that Friedman and others in the US Army's Secret Intelligence Service were making progress with Japanese and Italian ciphers. He proposed a 'free exchange of intelligence'.

Apparently using an FBI channel, though the military had no intention of accepting Hoover's authority, Strong pressed his case requesting an 'interchange of cryptographic material'. Permanent Undersecretary Sir Alexander Cadogan intimated to his Foreign Office colleagues 'that we cannot possibly divulge our innermost secrets at this stage', and the Americans received a non-committal reply saying they were welcome to send over one of their experts for instruction. It was the old British brush-off. Yet it was also an indication of where senior American intelligence officials saw their future. It was not with their German counterparts.[7]

Berle did approve one FBI–UK venture. It must have seemed harmless enough, as it was a learning exercise. At the urging of Stephenson, the bureau sent two special agents to London to study British intelligence. Hugh Clegg and Lawrence Hince arrived in London on 1 December

1940, stayed for two months, and supplied Hoover with the data that formed the basis of two reports to the White House in March 1941. The first report addressed overall British strategy especially economic warfare, noting that London wanted to 'organize the [post-war] world' but assuring the president that this was with a view to 'profit' and curbing the spread of communism. The second report dealt, quite critically, with Britain's security arrangements. The work of its codebreakers, and of MI5 and MI6, came under scrutiny.[8]

On the suggestion of his new secretary of the navy, Frank Knox, President Roosevelt now sent William 'Wild Bill' J. Donovan on a further fact-finding mission to Britain. This was a significant move because Donovan would be one of the architects of the special intelligence relationship. He was of Irish extraction with a dash of Fenianism in his family. Yet he acquired an acceptable pedigree for membership in the Anglo-American intelligence elite: Ivy League, married into Protestant money, Wall Street law firm partner. He would bring new-boy enthusiasm to his role as Anglophile intelligence leader.

Donovan had charismatic leadership qualities. According to the British intelligence-liaison officer Bickham Sweet-Escott, he was 'a man of inimitable Irish charm'. Another British officer 'thought he was another Custer—an unintelligent, bombastic American', but he too noted that Donovan's colleagues 'loved him'. Donovan could bulldoze people, and was physically brave. He had played quarterback for Columbia University. In 1918, he served in the Meuse-Argonne offensive. He soldiered with, and then commanded, the New York 69th Infantry. The 'Fighting 69th' lost one-fifth of its men. Donovan escaped with non-disabling wounds, heavily decorated for bravery. Even his enemies, of whom there were a few, had to concede that Bill Donovan was a hero and a leader of men.

Knox wanted Donovan to study the Fifth Column menace in Britain with a view to counterintelligence measures that might be put in place in the USA. Donovan duly produced a volume on the subject. But Knox was not the only person to task the special emissary. The president took a hand, and for a pressing reason. In May 1940, the British Expeditionary Force retreated from the continental war, escaping to England by the skin of its teeth via the French port of Dunkirk. So in the summer of 1940, Britain was desperate. Hitler's forces having occupied much of the continent, the nation stood alone in Europe—and had already emptied its coffers into the war effort. President Roosevelt wanted to help financially, but had to be able to convince Congress and the nation at large that he was not wasting money on a lost cause. He asked Donovan to assess the resistance power of Britain. His obedient emissary returned to give Roosevelt the answer he wanted to hear: Churchill's compatriots would fight on.

Donovan's additional task, approved by Roosevelt and encouraged by Stephenson, was to study British intelligence as a whole with a view to US improvement in that field. For this reason as well as because the UK wanted a favourable report on its combative qualities, the British assiduously courted Donovan. Stephenson had a suite at Fifth Avenue's St Regis Hotel, and met Donovan there prior to his departure. Then on 14 July, who should be sitting beside Donovan not so accidentally on the London-bound Pan American flying boat, but Sir William Wiseman. Lord Lothian had meantime urged the Foreign Office to roll out the red carpet. George VI gave Wild Bill an audience, Prime Minister Churchill received him, and 'C' cultivated and briefed him. In December, Donovan again flew to England on a three-month fact-finding mission that would take him around the Mediterranean war theatre. In another message to the Foreign Office sent just a week before he died from uraemia, the diligent Lord Lothian asked for renewed special treatment. He assured his diplomatic superiors that the American had 'done splendid work for us' since his July visit and was 'a valuable champion of our cause and is on the inside of all pro-British activities'.[9]

Once back in the States, Donovan drove through his own vision of central intelligence at Hoover's expense. By July 1941, he had persuaded Roosevelt to set up the Office of the Coordinator of Information (COI), with himself in charge. There have been various claimants to the honour of being chief assistant persuader. Wiseman having arranged an introduction, Admiral John Godfrey of British naval intelligence pressed for reform in a meeting with Roosevelt, and his aide Ian Fleming (later known for his James Bond novels) drafted a proposal for the creation of such an agency. However, Stephenson partisans, including the 'Quiet Canadian' himself, have asserted *his* claim to paternity. Sceptics have portrayed Stephenson as a self-promoter. The diplomatic historian Warren Kimball has pointed out that there is no mention of Stephenson in any of the 2,000 telegrams exchanged between Roosevelt and Churchill. The controversy is testimony to the weight placed upon the founding of COI by those, chiefly defenders of the CIA, who believe in the mantra of centralization, and in its British inspiration. The idea of British origins became an essential element in the credo of the special intelligence relationship.[10]

In June 1942 with America now in the war, Roosevelt replaced COI with the multi-functional Office of Strategic Services (OSS). Donovan was the first and only director of OSS. The following year, Donovan, by some considered the father of the CIA, proposed 'the need for a continuing independent intelligence organization functioning in peacetime as well as wartime'. He offered in support of this idea an innocent version of history, maintaining that while other nations had always had their MI6 or Gestapo, America was at a disadvantage in having no such tradition.[11]

It seemed that the British had had their way. A single man, Donovan, now had the brief to run American intelligence. Not only this, but he was, in Stephenson's words, 'our man'. It was a curious situation. In spite of claims, then and since, that this idea of central command was British in origin, the British in fact had no such person themselves. In 1936, the Committee of Imperial Defence created a new Joint Intelligence Committee that had the job of coordinating British intelligence but it was, as is evident from its title, a group of people and not an individual.

Sweet-Escott in fact complained about chronic divisions and 'war' within British intelligence, and envied the fact (as he saw it) that 'the corresponding organizations in the States were all responsible to one man'. He was deluded. In practice, the Americans never achieved one-man-rule. It was just as well. Centralization is no panacea and the effort to create it can be counter-productive. The COI, once created, failed to anticipate Pearl Harbor. The OSS did not have a global remit—Hoover's FBI, for example, retained Latin America—and because of turf wars back home was always, in the words of British official historian William Mackenzie, 'looking over its shoulder'. OSS had a mixed record and generally underachieved. Fortunately for the war effort, it did not come close to coordinating the efforts of the armed forces and the FBI.[12]

None of this affected the pace of Anglo-American intelligence collaboration. As in the case of the First World War, this collaboration started long before the USA abandoned its theoretical neutrality. In fact, because of Nazi atrocities, the American government's departure from neutrality and acceptance of British intelligence guidance was more of a foregone conclusion in 1939–41 than in 1914–17.

According to Fisher Howe, sent by Donovan to London to help set up a COI outpost there, the Americans secretly began to invest money in British intelligence in advance of US entry into the war. American funds, apparently unvouchered, dribbled into the coffers of BSC. One of Howe's first actions following his recruitment in September 1941 was—again according to his own account—to insert $100,000 in small denominations into the accounts of the Special Operations Executive (SOE).

Established in 1940, SOE operated from a mundane office block in Baker Street, London. In 1942, Churchill would read John Steinbeck's new novel *The Moon is Down*, a tale of resistance to German occupation in a fictional European nation assumed to be Norway. In the American writer's account, the British made small arms and explosives drops to help the locals create mayhem. Inspired by the story, Churchill thought up a distinctly unprosaic mission for SOE. Its objective would be to arm, train, and generally encourage resistance groups operating in the German-occupied nations of Europe. In the prime minister's phrase, it would 'set Europe ablaze'.[13]

On the evening of 6 September 1941, Stephenson had some friends round to dinner at the St Regis. It was a Saturday, and they partook of cocktails before moving to the rooftop restaurant. But when the orchestra made low-decibel communication impossible, the group descended to the Quiet Canadian's suite, and conversation began in earnest. Tommy Davies was over from Baker Street, and wanted to know if an SOE training school could be established in North America. By the next day, Stephenson had set the plan in motion with the assistance of another of his guests. Alfred Taylor was a self-made millionaire from Vancouver. Tight-lipped like his old friend, he liked to move discreetly, and did. Taylor established a top-secret complex in Canada.

The BSC-SOE training facility known as Camp X received official authorization on 21 October. Located on the shore of Lake Ontario between the communities of Whitby and Oshawa it was (when not snowing) within sight of the halo created by the city lights of Rochester, New York. Once America had joined the war, it educated US students in the arts of clandestine warfare. Relations in the camp were not uniformly smooth. Carl Eifler, a hard-drinking, 250-pound former Los Angeles cop, was not inclined to accept British tuition unquestioningly. In the course of a training exercise, he once made his point by ambushing his unsuspecting instructors just as they were laying a didactic ambush for his own unit. But harmony generally prevailed, and some of Camp X's US graduates went on to achieve prominence. John Bross would take charge of the joint

Anglo-French-American Jedburgh missions into French occupied territory. The 'mastodon incarnate' Eifler would run an OSS operation in Burma.[14]

At SOE's insistence, UK tuition of American behind-the-lines operatives continued in the British Isles. There, the British were already coordinating an international force. From 1942, special services training took place in Wales, where in the words of one intelligence officer the 'coastline and mountains were ideal for commando training'. Recently invented, commando units specialized in such arts as silent killing. They existed primarily to create havoc on the super-dangerous peripheries of battlefields, but infiltration agents also received commando tuition, in addition to their intelligence training. In the interest of security, agents of different nationalities learned their dark arts in separate communities and in ignorance of each other. French resisters went through their paces in Criccieth, Dutch in Porthmadog, Belgians in Abersoch, Norwegians in Nefyn, Poles in Barmouth, and Italian-speaking Slovenians at an undisclosed location.

And then there was Aberdyfi. The SOE intelligence instructor John Coates recalled in a private letter that the unit training there was 'British/ Ha, ha!' They were Jews who had escaped to Britain. Some were from the Viennese haute bourgeoisie, others socialist volunteers from the Sudetanland who had fought against Franco. All wanted to 'strike back' at Hitler. Under Bryan Hilton-Jones ('Skipper'), they trained as 3 Troop, 10 Commando. Nobody had English as a first language (a Cambridge languages graduate, the Skipper's original medium was Welsh). For fear of reprisals against their families, all had to invent new identities and pass themselves off as British. Thus a certain Herr Freytag became Tommy Farr, naming himself after the Welsh heavyweight boxer who, in 1937, had taken Joe Louis to fifteen rounds in the Yankee Stadium, New York City. But the Jews did not forget how to speak good German, an advantage in light of their imminent destinations. Along with the other ethnic groups, the Jews of Aberdyfi were heavily deployed behind enemy lines, and suffered high mortality rates.[15]

Cooperation was already under way in a variety of shapes and forms by the time the Americans began to arrive. With the new arrivals, facilities multiplied. The locations were sometimes in requisitioned mansions surrendered by their owners—there was a national shortage of servants because of conscription, and running a mansion without underpaid help had become tedious. So 'Stately 'Omes of England' became a gibe at the SOE acronym, while OSS became 'Oh, So Social'. However, Scottish locations were also prominent and presented physical challenges. Like those in Wales, some of the Scottish training facilities were near rough terrain. For example, the former SOE–OSS training headquarters at Arisaig House on Scotland's west coast is a comfortable hotel, but its hinterland is as rugged today as it was then. As well as in Aberdyfi, Hilton-Jones trained men in Achnacarry, not far from Scotland's highest peak, Ben Nevis. US personnel trained with 'Jedburgh' units, named after the Scottish borders town where there was a training camp.

The SOE officer class enjoyed a sense of social superiority. M. R. D. Foot, who wrote the official history of the SOE in France, related how its officers were drawn from English private schools—in British parlance, the 'public schools' represented in the 'headmasters' conference'. Foot was taken aback when 'a few young reviewers [of his book] protested that this was a needless fragment of old-world snobbery'.

There were those in OSS who admired the British style. We can turn to the recollections of the English journalist Malcolm Muggeridge, who represented MI6 in Lourenço Marques, Mozambique, then part of the Portuguese empire:

They came among us, these aspiring American spymasters, like innocent girls from a finishing-school anxious to learn the seasoned demi-monde ways of old practitioners—in this case, the legendary British Secret Service. Most of the early arrivals were Yale or Harvard dons, who imagined themselves writing Ashenden-type stories when the war was over.

But was there resentment in the ranks? And did this have repercussions for Anglo-American relations? Most British people would have admired Paul Robeson, the left-wing African American voted their nation's most popular radio singer, rather than the officially fêted Bill Donovan. It might be added that the British people voted overwhelmingly against Churchill in 1945, helping to put in power the Labour government of Clement Attlee, and that soldiers old enough to vote in that election may well have contributed to Labour's 393 to 213 seat majority in the House of Commons. The balance of evidence suggests they did so because they remembered the depressed 1930s, not the war. Nevertheless, did ordinary British soldiers somehow resent the wartime experience with Americans?

There is a scarcity of evidence on what the lower orders thought. Certainly, there was some resentment. An SOE Jedburgh wireless operative—a sergeant—resented the Americans' conspicuous affluence: 'We could just not believe that such people existed.' Indications of friction do not, however, appear to be related to rank.

Power tussles between British and American officers mirrored the rivalries of their respective nations. When the 'Sussex' project was launched to infiltrate military intelligence agents behind German lines, SOE and OSS operated separate units. Jedburgh groups destined for France were supposed to be integrated. An American would serve alongside a Briton and a Frenchman. This did not always happen, and when it did could cause resentment.

At ground level, it was a mixed picture. A training officer in Milton Hall, Peterborough, complained the Americans were 'bloody undisciplined soldiers'. However, another Peterborough instructor recalled the wonderful 'bits and pieces' the OSS men supplied for breakfast, while at the end of the day the French contributed Algerian wine. Captain Tom Carew may have spoken for all ranks when he remarked of the Americans: 'We had a lot of rapport. There was no bullshit with them.'[16]

Local centres of intrigue developed as the war progressed. Cairo was one such place, Istanbul another. Of special importance to Anglo-American intrigue was London. The British capital was, of course, closer to the seat of war than Stephenson's New York. COI had a London post, and this became the London station of the OSS, which had responsibility for clandestine intelligence collection as well as operations.

Two sides of OSS London can be illustrated biographically. At the end of 1942, David Bruce became the station chief. As one historian of OSS London put it, Bruce's 'patrician background was obviously suited to easing relations with the British intelligence establishment'. Bruce came from an upper crust Virginian family and in a nod to the Yankee North had married Ailsa Mellon, daughter of the leading American financier. By the time Bruce reached London, Andrew Mellon was dead. His marriage to Ailsa was crumbling, and it ended in divorce in 1945. Three days later, Bruce married a colleague who had been working with him at OSS London. She had studied in Europe and spoke twelve languages. Like Ailsa, Evangeline had lost her father—Edward Bell. It may be surmised that First World War intelligence arrangements, their social dimensions included, were well remembered in the years when David and Evangeline were romancing.[17]

Whitney Sheppardson was a different kind of political animal. In June 1941 he became the first chief of SI (Secret Intelligence) at the London station. There was no surprise about his background—Rhodes scholar,

Harvard Law School, successful businessman—but he exemplified the critical twist in the OSS's outlook. Back in 1930, he had been disdainful of Philip Kerr's approach to imperial reform, perceiving that the future Lord Lothian had no intention of empowering non-white people in South Africa. His view was that one should take all national aspirations seriously, not just those of 'Anglo-Saxon' descent. In the European context, he thought the assertively nationalist Charles de Gaulle should be backed as the spokesman for France, and insisted on an independent collection facility for OSS. Nor was he out on a limb. Ambassador Winant was far more supportive of the British cause than his doubting predecessor Joe Kennedy. But he could see there was another side to British society. He had helped draft the New Deal's social security legislation, served as director of the International Labor Organization, took an interest in workers' education, and donated his personal American Studies library to an adult education college in Wales—among his books were Alain Locke's *The New Negro* and other works that would have gone down badly with defenders of the British Raj.[18]

So much for training and administration. How did SOE–OSS liaison work out in practice? The story is a stirring one, and at the same time a tale of turbulent relations. Operation Torch and more especially Operation Massingham that followed illustrate the point. They stemmed from an Anglo-American accord, an agreement that both reflected and contributed to an attempt by Washington and London to stitch up world politics for years to come.

In June 1942, Donovan and Bruce struck a deal with Oliver Stanley, secretary of state for the colonies, and SOE chief Charles Hambro. They divided the world into operational spheres. SOE would be in charge in India, East and West Africa, the Balkans, the Middle East, and western Europe. OSS would have swathes of territory that included China, Australia, and North Africa. Burma, Indochina, Germany, and Italy were amongst the joint responsibilities, and there was no agreement on the USSR, Spain, and Portugal. The plan included provisions for OSS to operate out of SOE territory, and vice versa.[19]

Agreement having been reached, Operation Torch, launched on 8 November 1942, was an American-dominated invasion of a region designated an OSS sphere of influence. French North Africa was an area that in principle owed allegiance to the Vichy regime in southern France that had settled for a truce with Germany. Torch would, if successful, reinforce British efforts against General Erwin Rommel, whose forces they had recently defeated in Egypt at the Battle of El Alamein. For President Roosevelt, it was crucially a way of demonstrating to the American public that America was at last launching an initiative, for, in the eleven months after Pearl Harbor, the USA had seemed to be on the defensive.

Donovan welcomed the attack as a means of demonstrating the OSS's usefulness. He participated in the strategic assessment of the operation's potential. He promised that the OSS would, through clandestine man-oeuvres, persuade the majority of the Vichy French not to resist the American landings. He predicted that OSS guerrilla and sabotage teams would smooth the way for the advancing regular soldiers, minimizing casualties and helping the Allies to establish a North African foothold with relative ease. This did not work out as planned. Within three days of the start of the operation 1,400 Americans lay dead. But it did result in Allied control of Algeria, creating the possibility for parachuting special forces into southern France.[20]

Massingham was the assigned name for a base, formerly a French 'adult play area', 12 miles west of Algiers. Secret agents trained there, and flew out of the base into fascist-controlled areas of Europe—Spain, France, Italy, Yugoslavia, and Czechoslovakia. Assigned the lead role in the Massingham operation, Donovan's OSS hoped to prove its worth at a time when people back home were wondering why the organization existed. After the Chinese nationalists proved to be uncooperative partners, it was the only significant proving ground assigned to the Americans.

There were all kinds of tensions at Massingham. Working-class lower ranks stole plastic explosives and used them for fishing. Spanish-based communist agents refused to give proper military salutes. English officers were condescending towards their American counterparts, and the Americans complained that the British had too little respect for their democratic values.

Yet, after a fashion, they all pulled together. Into France alone, Massingham dropped 400 agents—and, according to one estimate, about 40 per cent of the weapons and other supplies that the French Resistance received from abroad. Eleven purely OSS units, based in Massingham and at the Villa Magnol in Algiers, parachuted into France in July–August 1944, mostly into the Ardèche, where they inhibited German troop movements by attacking the railway lines of the Rhone valley. From the same North African base, 25 Jedburgh units flew into action out of a total of 93 sent to France altogether.

By the end of 1944, Massingham could claim to have contributed to the surrender of Italy (September 1943), facilitated the liberation of Corsica— and helped with the invasion of France.[21]

The story of the French Resistance and of the aid sent to it is one of many variations. By way of illustration, we can look at one particular community. Vabre, in the Tarn region, is about a hundred miles to the south-west of the Ardèche. It is one of those Resistance areas failing to make it into mainline narratives because historians simplify in the interest of clarity. But it was typical both in not being exceptional, and also in being different, for every Maquis (Resistance) unit had its own character.

Colonel Guy de Rouville narrated the history of the Vabre Resistance to a group of Scottish visitors to Vabre in June 2004. He did not speak in the proudly guarded Languedoc language. From a local family of industrialists, he spoke Parisian French having trained at the École Centrale des Arts et Manufactures in the capital. It was in Paris that he began his contribution to resistance in 1940 by issuing false identity papers to some of his firm's Jewish clients. Later he became a main leader of the Maquis in Vabre, where there were three companies, one of them consisting of Jewish fighters.

Rouville's wife Odile in a later letter reflected a widely held view in stressing the importance of the region's religious history. The city of Albi lay to the north, and Vabre had partaken in the Albigensian or Catharist 'heresy' in the twelfth century. Five centuries later, the area had been a stronghold of the Huguenots. These Protestants had been largely expelled from France by Louis XIV's revocation of the Edict of Nantes in 1685, but in Vabre they stubbornly held out, and a Protestant place of worship to this day dominates the square off which is found the Maquis Museum (curator, Colonel Rouville). In sum, resistance was historically ingrained into the Vabrian mentality.

Rouville regaled his Scottish audience with anecdotes. The Germans controlled the Vabre to Castres railway and the parallel telegraph line. But the railway workers placed every obstacle in the way of their efforts to deport Jews to the concentration camps. Meanwhile, the Maquis tapped the telegraph line to learn of German troop movements—and used it for their own communications. Then there was the occasion when the local German commander received a tip-off that Rouville was the Maquis boss. He visited the Rouville mansion, finding there the colonel's parents, his wife Odile, and their children living in bourgeois comfort. Believing the Nazi propaganda line that the Maquis were lowlife communists, the German cast aside his suspicions and exclaimed to the local mayor 'Ah, nicht terrorists [*sic*] nicht communist'.

Rouville's portrait of the local Maquis was of an organization that struck heavy blows and was lucky to escape with so few mortalities. Odile observed that maybe this was because the Germans had only lightly garrisoned this area of Vichy France. Whatever the reason may have been, the Resistance was already strong in Vabre by the time help arrived.[22]

At half-past nine p.m. on 6 August 1944, a specially modified RAF 624 Squadron Halifax bomber took off from Blida, Algeria. Its crew were part of a special duties unit that flew many missions into occupied France, flying in often at less than 500 feet to drop undercover specialists and supplies. On this occasion, it carried fifteen OSS men. So it was a British plane carrying American and Canadian fighters, but with no UK special forces and no French contingent. However, the team called 'PAT' had a French-speaking commander. Captain Conrad LaGueux had been born in Rhode Island of French-Canadian parents.

'PAT' were aiming for the drop zone known as Virgule, but a wind blew the parachutists off course and they landed in an area of thorny trees. Jacques Noyez was a member of the Maquis reception committee. He remembered a parachutist suddenly emerging from the bushes, menacing him with a Colt revolver. With a certain presence of mind, Noyez demonstrated his competence in English: 'I am French, welcome.' The reply came in French: 'Sergent chef Gautier, canadien du Quebec'.

Another member of the OSS unit, the Cuban-American Robert Esquenazi, was injured as he hit the trees. He spent the next few weeks recuperating in a hidden loft on the Rouvilles' property, tended to by Jérémie, the Rouvilles' gardener. Odile visited him there every day 'to give him news of the war'.

Her husband took against the Americans. The US-Quebecan contingent in turn aligned themselves with a rival Resistance group (there was a Catholic v. Protestant divide in the local movement, and the priest and the pastor sometimes had to be called in to impose peace). Guy de Rouville preferred the English 'even if they were obliged to bomb us'.

But OSS PAT overcame local rivalries. In spite of losing Esquenazi and then a Canadian and an American shot dead in an ambush a couple of days later, its men wrought havoc on the German occupiers. On 20 August 1944, LaGueux's special forces and their Maquis allies derailed a troop train, taking prisoner 60 officers and 5,800 men. They slowed down German troop movements, and contributed to the liberation of the city of Castres.[23]

On the night following the arrival of PAT, another Halifax approached the same drop site. It carried guns, ammunition, and chocolate for the natives. It carried a French army officer, a radio operator, and his equipment. Also on board was an Englishman.

(Acting) Major Hector Davies and his French co-parachutists had earlier that evening dined, along with two other units bound for France, at a restaurant in Blida. As their plane finally rose above the North African coast, Davies had watched the beach below, bathed in the light of a full moon. He had swum there earlier in the day, and recalled thinking that perhaps it was for the final time.

Davies does not feature in the records or history of SOE. Born in 1913 the son of a civil servant who was secretary to the Liberal peer Lord Grey (British foreign secretary, 1905–16), he had attended Rugby School. The former public school boy then worked for the Bank of England. Along the way, he acquired near-perfect French. Early in the war following the fall of France, he was aide de camp to the legendary Philippe Leclerc. He was with the aristocratic Free French leader when Major Leclerc led an attack on the Axis's African forces from a base in Chad.

Davies dropped into Virgule from 1,000 feet at 2 a.m. on 8 August with the moon still shining. A young man wearing a black beret extricated him from the customary bramble bush. As the Halifax bomber continued to circle and to drop supplies, a German force suddenly attacked. There was a firefight. The Germans secured all the precious guns and ammunition. Davies later expressed his fury in terms that hinted at his identity: 'The security of this operation was appalling.' In spite of requests to change, London had issued instructions using a 'burnt' code the Germans could easily have read. One could have done without the crowd of spectators that greeted one's arrival, and the reception committee should have been able to mount a counter-attack on the German troops to save at least some of the containers that the Halifax had dropped. Still, if only minutes before the German attack, Guy de Rouville had at least whisked Davies and his companions away to safety.[24]

Although technically subordinate to the French officer who accompanied him, Davies assumed inter-services command in the Tarn region. He organized the delivery of weapons, and decided which Resistance groups should get what. He ordered uniforms for four battalions of Resistance fighters saying the kit had to be American or British, but not mixed. He participated in military activities and for his gallantry was mentioned in dispatches.

However, Davies's speciality was intelligence assessment. For example, he tracked the retreat to Castres of a Panzer division driven out of Albi by the ferocity of Allied bombing attacks, and compiled candid estimates of the fighting capacity and battlefield retreats of the Maquis. In addition to being in touch with Massingham about more machine guns and ammunition, he communicated directly with 'C' in London. His reports to Menzies help to explain his absence from the historical record, as MI6, unlike SOE, remained forever reluctant to release information. The destination of his reports also reflected the power struggles back home, where Stewart Menzies and the old hands at 'six' resented the SOE parvenus and tried to keep their own tabs on affairs.

Davies was interested in politics (he later ran for office as a Liberal), and his assessments of the French Resistance show that. He was critical of the Maquis—that was his job—but also appreciative. He noted that while he was received by the well to do, the bulk of Resistance support came from the left. He observed that the Americans and the British were warmly welcomed in France, but 'the British in general can not... fully realize the contributions made by the French people after D-Day to help get rid of the enemy'. He would have deprecated attempts by later historians who claimed that the French made relatively little contribution to the success of the Allied landings, and he might have questioned the assumption that it was SOE/OSS who shortened the war by six months. When it came to nation building, he valued actual indigeneity rather than externally managed national aspirations, thus evincing a quality absent from many a future MI6 and CIA operation.[25]

Looking back at the fissures and events of 1940–4, Odile de Rouville many years later wrote, 'Sometimes it looked like a muddle but—at the end—it was victory for us all.' Yet Anglo-American rivalry was undoubtedly a problem that characterized, and in some cases blighted, joint operations. The power struggle between a declining and a rising empire played out in different parts of the world. There was, for example, K Project, named after the initial of Bulgarian businessman Angel Nissimov Kouyoumdjisky. Operating out of Istanbul, Kouyoumdjisky plotted with OSS from the summer of 1943 to the early months of the following year. They planned to detach three countries from Germany's grasp—Romania,

Bulgaria, and Hungary. A timely OSS-inspired intervention in Bulgaria would weaken Germany's military position, pre-empt a Soviet invasion, and preserve Kouyoumdjisky's business interests.

But this was an initiative too far. The Balkans were in the British sphere of influence. John E. Toulmin, director of OSS-Middle East, worried, 'I think that our cousins [British intelligence] are watching the "K" Mission very carefully and might possibly stoop to attempt a sabotage operation on it.' London dragged its feet. The moment passed. Germany sent five divisions into Hungary in March 1944, and by November the Red Army had rolled into both Bulgaria and Hungary. Looking back at the episode, Sweet-Escott feared the British attitude had been a 'mistake'.[26]

In Burma, the British faced not so much American rivalry, as American anti-imperialism. In 1942 OSS sent to the Far East a unit originally called Detachment 1 but in a display of chutzpah aimed at the British renamed Detachment 101. There was in fact only one unit. Under the command of Camp X-trained Carl Eifler, Detachment 101 had distinctly anti-Raj opinions. 101 came under the authority of the South East Asia Command (SEAC), the creation of Roosevelt and Churchill at the Quebec conference of August 1943. Alert to the opportunity to deconstruct an acronym, the wags of 101 made it 'Save England's Asiatic Colonies'.

Nevertheless, OSS and SOE worked together to further flights over 'The Hump', the southern spur of the Himalayas on the other side of which the Chinese were trying to repel the forces of Japan. OSS and SOE also worked together to reopen the Burma Road so that supplies could be sent overland. The intensity of operations redoubled when V-E Day, victory in Europe, made it possible to transfer Allied resources from one war theatre to the other.

Down on the ground where the fighting took place, Anglo-American harmony appears to have prevailed. Oswin Craster, with the SOE in Burma in 1945, submitted to an oral history interview four decades later. He could remember nothing about ambushes, and claimed to have forgotten about Japanese casualties and prisoners. His recall of other details was vivid—the use of Benzedrine to keep alert, the idiosyncrasies of porter elephants who could negotiate the narrowest of jungle paths but were fearful of open terrain. He especially remembered what a good job the Americans had done in keeping the Karen tribesmen friendly.

An English NCO who served with SOE in the Mawchi area of Burma in 1945 also had favourable memories. He unreservedly admired American

Lysander pilots who flew just ten feet above ground to make free-fall drops of essential supplies. Sergeant Patten could recall not a single instance when a bottle of whisky had been broken. He did not record any worries about the Yankee fliers' views on imperialism, and this whole issue became moot when Roosevelt forsook his earlier principles and decided that empire was a block against communism.[27]

The problem of communism was, however, a further irritant to the Anglo-American intelligence relationship. While the two countries shared a mutual antagonism towards totalitarian socialism, the British were more pragmatic—a generalization to which there were exceptions, but which nevertheless holds true.

Yugoslavia was a prime bone of contention. When the Germans overran Yugoslavia in April 1941, the army officer Draguljub Mihailoviç took to the hills with his Chetniks, a group with a history of resistance to Turkish rule in the Balkans. He was royalist and anti-communist, and at first seemed a good target for SOE–OSS help. The BBC dutifully built him up as a resistance hero and determined foe of the Nazis. But the Nazis were in fact even more anti-communist than the Allies, an attraction for Mihailoviç. By 1943, British intercepts of German signals traffic confirmed that Mihailoviç was siding with the Nazi enemy in their campaign against the communist-led partisans. Under the leadership of Josip Tito, these partisans were perhaps Europe's most effective anti-Nazi resistance movement. Churchill reluctantly ordered SOE to switch its support to Tito and his followers.

In a parallel decision, SOE began to help Enver Hoxha in Albania. They had found an effective leader to back. From the Muslim area in southern Albania, the tall and intelligent Hoxha had lived in France, was well educated, and if he was a dedicated communist that was something to overlook in the context of the times.

The result was an increasingly effective resistance movement up and down the Adriatic coast. It was at the cost, post-war, of communist dictatorships in both Yugoslavia and Albania. Foreseeing this, the Americans were uneasy. They had their representatives in Cairo, including an ex-FBI man who supervised pistol practice sessions and claimed to have shot John Dillinger. But, as the Balkans were a British sphere of influence during the war, the Americans had to yield to Churchill.

They were even more frustrated in later years when there were revelations about British intelligence headquarters in Cairo, which oversaw Balkan operations. Basil Davidson, who in 1942–3 headed the SOE

Yugoslav section in the Egyptian capital, had in the 1920s worked for the far-right Economic League. But he was an early advocate of the view that Tito should be supported, and in August 1943 parachuted into Bosnia to fight with the partisans. His unit included another of the same view, James Klugmann, a communist regarded by his Conservative-voting colleagues as hugely eccentric—according to Davidson, 'it was reported that he actually liked Egyptians'. Although Churchill made his decision strictly on pragmatic grounds, British intelligence's failure at the time to discover the political affiliations of Klugmann played badly when the truth emerged. The problem of communism would be a gritty impediment in the machinery of the Anglo-American intelligence relationship.[28]

Devoted though he may have been to the razzmatazz of special operations, Donovan was keen to develop also a more cerebral branch of the OSS. This was the Research and Analysis (R&A) division. R&A scoured America's campuses for talented scholars to inform the war effort on particular problems and on individual countries, and came to resemble a university faculty itself. As part of its activities, it sent people out into the field. With a dash of hubris, one historian of R&A observed that a 'full-scale Harvard invasion of North Africa' accompanied Operation Torch.[29]

By far the largest-scale outpost of R&A was within OSS London. Ambassador Winant with his New Deal background needed little persuasion to give embassy credentials to economists and other scholars. Historians Crane Brinton, Perry Miller, and A. M. Schlesinger Jr were there, as were the sociologist Edward Shils and the economist Walt W. Rostow. Two problems can be noted here. First, although the *raison d'être* of OSS was largely to do within liaison, this was achieved only imperfectly in the case of R&A. There was an administrative mismatch. According to Nelson Mac-Pherson in his history of the London station, 'R&A did not fit neatly into any single existing category of British intelligence work.' It appears that if the British had inspired the creation of OSS, they had neglected to form such an organization themselves. The second problem with R&A, back home as well as in London, is that policy-makers and military leaders largely ignored it. In the view of historian Barry Katz, this amounted to a 'tragic waste'.

In the longer term, though, R&A proved to have been a significant innovation. Seven of the forty historians who worked in R&A went on to be presidents of the American Historian Association, with obvious repercussions for the way in which the war came to be remembered, and its lessons applied. The 'country desk' approach within R&A, bringing diverse scholars together in an interdisciplinary fusion, helped to promote (though it did not originate) the 'area studies' approach so popular around the world in the Cold War years—and so heavily promoted by the CIA and Ford Foundation as a way of anti-communist 'nation building'. Finally, R&A was an antecedent of the CIA's Office of National Estimates (ONE), run by Harvard historian William Langer, who had directed R&A earlier. ONE, still taking some help from the British, was the Cold War's premier intelligence analysis unit outside the Soviet Union.[30]

In the realm of Allied codebreaking, the UK was off to a flying start. In part this was because of earlier entry into the war. In part, it was because Alastair Denniston had repeated a measure his fellow Scotsman, Alfred Ewing, had taken in the previous war. According to his son and biographer Robin, in the decade preceding the Second World War Alastair Denniston 'facilitated this sigint superiority over his American counterparts by touring British universities looking for mathematicians and linguists to work for him'. Finally, Britain's codebreakers received one of those intelligence gifts that make all the difference. The mathematician-cryptologist Marian Rejewski with two fellow Poles had managed to crack the Germans' five-wheel 'Enigma' encryption methodology. Via the French intelligence service, the Poles delivered intact an Enigma machine close in design to those used to set German military ciphers. By January 1940, the British were beginning to read Enigma traffic.[31]

According to Hugh Trevor-Roper who served in MI6 in 1941, GC&CS was now the main game in town. It outshone MI6. At 'six', Menzies 'drew his personal advisers from a painfully limited social circle', did not understand the war, and commanded little respect. But he managed to preserve his role as the person who delivered the fruits of GC&CS to the prime minister on a daily basis. By means of this feat, Trevor-Roper believed, he saved MI6 from extinction.

Certainly, GC&CS product was a precious asset. Yet in a departure from their First World War stance, the British ultimately shared their codebreaking methodology with the Americans. After US entry into the war, the cryptological effort in some essential areas became a joint Anglo-American effort. This made codebreaking an especially powerful tool, first during hostilities with the Germans and Japanese, and later in the Cold War.

At first, though, the British held out. Churchill remained reluctant 'to throw all our secrets into the American lap'. The British were concerned about power as well as security. By dispensing the fruits of Enigma without explaining how it worked, the hope was that the USA would make concessions to British war aims and strategy, as the price of staying within the informational loop. Morally, America was on weak ground so long as Tommies were dying in battle and the GI remained unscathed. By degrees, though, British resistance crumbled. There was a gentlemen's agreement that concessions would be made once the USA became actively engaged in the war. In addition to this, America developed its own cryptographic expertise, weakening UK bargaining power and suggesting there would be mutual advantage in sharing.

British–American codebreaking cooperation built up by fits and starts. In January 1941, a US Army team arrived at Bletchley Park. They appeared at midnight, and Denniston's personal assistant did not know what to do: 'I'd never met Americans before, except in the films. I just plied them with sherry.' The Americans had the advantage of having worked on Japanese codes, and the British wanted to partake of their expertise as they had a shortage of experts in the Japanese language. Not only this, but the Americans brought with them a prototype of the PURPLE machine being designed to break Japanese messages, and, as a goodwill gesture, gave it to Denniston's colleagues.

But the US Army mission had weaknesses: the absence of Friedman, who was having a nervous breakdown from which he later recovered, the junior status of the team, and the simultaneous presence in Britain of the Clegg and Hince team—though the FBI would not, in the event, develop as a serious codebreaking entity. The absence of a navy contingent was a further disadvantage—the US Army and Navy carried on their traditional rivalry in the Second World War. And, of course, Bletchley Park was guarding its secrets. In March, the British at last informed their American cousins how Bletchley Park was becoming literate in Enigma, but they still kept mum about their methods.[32]

Denniston did want to cooperate with his American counterparts, even if he could not yet do so fully. He assured them of this goal, and took reassuring steps. For example, leaving Scotland for the USA in August 1941, he telegrammed Washington, 'I should like to have full discussions with my opposite numbers and also visit OTTAWA if this can be arranged without any chance of meeting YARDLEY'. Profoundly distrusted by his former American employers for his book on the Black Chamber and subsequent advisory services he performed for the Japanese, Yardley was now helping the Canadians to set up their own cryptographic capability. Building trust with Washington, Denniston made clear he was having none of it. He followed up his communication with Washington by telling the Canadians they would have to choose between Yardley and intelligence help from Britain. The Canadians yielded the point and dismissed Yardley.[33]

Denniston continued his efforts to lay the dinner table even if he could not serve the full roast beef. He arranged a channel for the exchange of lesser information and for the means of transmission—microdot images of documents. In October 1941 he wrote to Captain Edward Hastings, GC&CS's representative in Washington. He would continue to use him as a 'postbox' for materials he was sending the US Army and Navy Departments; he hoped Hastings and Donovan were 'having success in coordination' but noted that when he was in the USA the army and navy 'were two shows each jealous of their own works'; the army's Friedman was the 'right man' but 'might wish to conceal his activities'; Ottawa would soon be rid of Yardley and 'the Admiralty are very pleased that you are managing to get the triangular cooperation going'. This last was American–British–Canadian cryptographic liaison, sometimes referred to as 'ABC'. It was another ingredient in the cooperative feast that was being prepared in contravention of the principle of neutrality; prepared, but not yet served.[34]

Some British gestures had a double-edged impact. A Churchillian admission prompted by Alastair is a case in point. Denniston reported in September 1941 the view 'in various quarters' that there should be no more interceptions of American diplomatic telegrams 'as the co-operation between the various departments of the two countries is now so intimate'. Although the Americans were not yet in the war, he anticipated that the British would no longer wish to spy on them. However, he cautioned that, 'in view of ultimate peace negotiations when we might wish to know American views fairly accurately', US diplomatic traffic should still be monitored.

Denniston additionally drew attention to the inherently dangerous fact that the State Department's encryption methods were insecure. A few weeks after Pearl Harbor, Churchill passed on this essential if unsavoury news to FDR. Making no mention of the fact that Britain had additionally been breaking US naval and military codes, he suggested that as the UK had found it easy to read US diplomatic traffic, 'our enemies' might do the same. His admission to spying on America confirmed, according to the historian

Stephen Budiansky, 'the US experts' worst fears about the British'. Britain would need to work harder to reassure America of its frankly good intentions.[35]

And the need for this display of goodwill had become more pressing. By the time Churchill sent his message, Bletchley Park was running into difficulties. Germany had developed a more sophisticated version of Enigma that made decryption a cripplingly slow process. In the meantime, the 'activities' that Friedman had sought to conceal were accelerating. The Americans were making cryptological progress. Unable to read Japanese fleet messages on the eve of Pearl Harbor, the US Navy now made such advances that, at the Battle of Midway in early June 1942, its battle group knew of a trap set by the Japanese admirals. The knowledge contributed to what turned out to be the decisive US naval victory of the war in the Pacific. With the advantage of more money, gifted personnel, and the assistance of high-technology businesses like IBM, the Americans were drawing level with the UK, and were in a position to pull ahead.

The time was ripe for more extensive cryptographic cooperation. First there was a more meaningful exchange of technology, and then came the Holden Agreement of September 1942. Sir Edward Travis led a Bletchley Park delegation that came to an understanding with the US Navy on exchanges of personnel and methodologies. This excluded the US Army, an omission that fuelled Yankee naval pride and nourished illusions of continuing independence in GC&CS. But the US Army continued to pepper Travis with precise requests for the minutiae of decryption; IBM punch-card technology was on offer in exchange. The BRUSA agreement of 17 May 1943 finally arranged for American participation in British Army and Air Force Enigma decryption. Twenty American experts, the first of many, arrived to learn and labour at Bletchley Park. As usual there were cultural problems, and as usual there were compensations. One of the cooks imported by the Americans had run a Philadelphia bakery, and his artfully distributed wares came to be mutually appreciated.[36]

Joint cryptography, a potent element in the special intelligence relationship that had never matured in the previous war, was up and running. Its impact must remain partly conjectural. There has been a disposition on the part of those involved to pluck figures out of thin air, and to claim that British intelligence alone shortened the war by several years. This is to forget not only other factors such as fighting men, but also the other side—Germany was reading Royal Navy signals in 1942–3. Still, in the absence of cryptography, especially joint cryptography, the Allied cause would have been weaker, and possibly less assured of victory.[37]

There had been a change in the balance of power in the special intelligence relationship. That the British had become more takers than givers is indicated in an exchange of November 1944. The US liaison officer at Bletchley Park complained that the British were holding back diplomatic intelligence on the Near East. He observed that Denniston, now demoted but still in charge of diplomatic codebreaking, occasionally overrode orders from on high to give the Americans what they needed. But he complained that on this occasion Denniston had been obliged to clam up. Called upon to explain, Denniston made another confession. The US Army's Signals Security Agency at Arlington Hall, Va., had his 'whole-hearted co-operation', but 'we have no more to give'.[38]

Another indicator of the change was the respective opinions of the two sides on the matter of permanence. Signs of relative US strength were evident at a meeting in Washington, DC, in October 1945 between American and British officials. With Germany and Japan defeated and OSS already dissolved, they discussed the future of communications intelligence. Travis, as head of GC&CS, made the case for a continuation of intelligence cooperation in peacetime. In the recorders' paraphrase, 'he stressed the fact that the field of communications intelligence is not readily adaptable to the separation of its several branches and that any cooperative effort will be severely weakened by any limitations to full collaboration'.

General Clayton Bissell responded for the Americans. Bissell represented US Army intelligence, and was about to take up the post of military attaché in London. He 'requested the views of Sir Edward Travis as to what conditions, if any, might control the termination of an Agreement such as he had proposed. Sir Edward Travis stated that such an Agreement could not be so concluded as to be permanently binding. He was in agreement with the idea of General Bissell that such an Agreement should be continued only so long as it is advantageous for both parties.' The British had come to perceive full collaboration as being to their advantage, but were obliged to concede the principle of possible termination.[39]

To the present day there is a tendency to assume that the British–American signals relationship holds together as if carved into some piece of Anglo-Saxon granite. According to one explanation, the two sides knew so much about each other that it was too dangerous to split apart. Another argument is that fascism drove British and American codebreakers to share their secrets, and that then communism and perhaps Al Qaeda stepped into the breach to perform the same function. However, the evidence from 1945 indicates that the communications crux of the special intelligence relationship was never written in stone, and that an American had been the first to point that out.[40]

This qualification is worth keeping in mind when summarizing the Anglo-American intelligence relationship in the Second World War. It was an alliance that contributed to victory and helped to shape the post-war world, and yet it is a mixed picture. The possibility that the Americans would withhold intelligence as the British had when they were in the ascendancy is part of that picture.

Looking beyond 1945, a significant feature of the alliance, the cultural bonding between Oxbridge educated public school boys and Ivy League humanities preppies, would come unstuck on the American side when intelligence performance dipped, technology became important, and the nation's ethnography changed. On the operational front, the SOE tie had put a spring in the step of the OSS which otherwise had an indifferent war record. There were reincarnations of the SOE–OSS act long after they were both dissolved. But there would also be recurrences of the tensions over how to handle communism and empire.

Turning to the realm of mutual learning, Denniston's comment that the UK had nothing more to give the Americans contained a kernel of truth, but British spies clung to their illusions. The British insistence that America was its apprentice and not vice versa would endure after the war. It was in itself a symptom of head-in-the-sand decline, and of a shifting intelligence relationship the nature of which was clearer to Washington than to London.

5

CIA: The New Model Agency

Stormie Seas was a sight to behold. A Greek fishing schooner modified to resemble a rich man's yacht, she weighed in at 43 tons. Four orange sails towered over her blue and gold hull as she scudded before an Adriatic wind.

On the evening of 3 November 1949, Sam Barclay supervised the activities of the *Seas'* Greek skipper. Representing himself as a painter, the 29-year-old Barclay had with him his younger friend John Leatham—writer. Contributing to an air of domesticity, the crew consisted also of Barclay's wife Eileen, together with the family dog, Lean-to.

As day gave way to darkness on a night chosen for its waning moon, the sparsely inhabited stretch of Albanian coast was barely visible. A new sound had taken over from the refrains of the rigging. It was the growl of the boat's engine, worryingly loud as the boat crept towards the Karaburun Peninsula.

The 90-horsepower thrust was needed to propel a heavy load. Below deck in dummy fuel compartments were German-made Schmeiser subma-chine-guns, ammunition, propaganda leaflets, and photographs of émigré leaders who had fled the communist dictatorship of Enver Hoxha. Add-itionally there were codebooks, and radio transmitters powered by a man-powered cycling mechanism designed to improve on the SOE prototypes that had depended on batteries.

Then there was the human cargo. Nine Albanians crouched in the hold. They awaited their opportunity to step ashore and start an insurgency against the Hoxha regime.

The vessel dropped anchor in the cove at 'Seaview', a point thus named six years earlier, when SOE's David Smiley had made a hasty departure from the same spot. It was by now past midnight. In the early hours of what would be a fatal day, the crew pulled in the dory, a small boat trailing in the schooner's wake. The tall English sailors bade farewell to their passengers, whom they had not too respectfully dubbed the 'pixies'. The dory ferried the Albanians ashore. Before the band of smaller men loomed a mountainous terrain, traversed only by goat tracks.[1]

It was the first Anglo-American covert operation of the Cold War. The below-deck contingent aboard *Stormie Seas* had trained under Smiley's supervision in Malta—as his American colleague Frank Wisner observed, 'Whenever we want to subvert any place, we find that the British own an island within easy reach.'

In Malta, the Albanians learned skills that SOE's veterans kept alive. MI6 took the lead role, but help came also from the Office of Policy Coordination (OPC). Established in September 1948 to conduct covert operations under Wisner's leadership, the OPC was a division of the Central Intelligence Agency (CIA), formed in the previous year. It operated semi-autonomously until the CIA ended its independence in 1950.

Over in Washington, an OPC–MI6 committee planned the operation. Wisner led the OPC team, and the British input came from MI6, with Kim Philby playing a role in the later stages—with the cover position of first secretary at the British embassy, Philby was responsible for MI6–CIA liaison. The committee agreed that the OPC would take care of northern, Catholic Albania, leaving the Muslim south to MI6.

Albania was a small country reduced further in functioning size by the mountains that covered two-thirds of its terrain. Small, but with big troubles. Internally, it was torn between competing tribes. Externally, it laid provocative claim on the neighbouring province of Kosovo, 90 per cent of whose inhabitants shared the Muslim faith of the majority of Albanians. It had two neighbours, Greece and Yugoslavia, which coveted parts of its own existing territory. A cross between a tinderbox and a quandary, Albania at first sight offered few rewards and many dangers.

Debate in the British Foreign Office nevertheless focused on the Albanian action as a means of asserting 'freedom' against 'communism', possibly producing, if successful, a knock-on effect in the rest of the communist world. There was also reference to the need to prop up the Greek government by eradicating communist exiles' raids on their mother country from bases inside Albania—Britain had recently helped crush the Greek communist movement in spite of the communists' wartime role in resisting German occupation. The British policy mandarins advanced two further arguments, both of them prophetic. The first was that the Americans were known to be planning a move, and it would be best to join with them in order to exert some influence over US policy. The second argument, discarded in the event, was that it was no good sending in a clandestine advance guard without a plan for proper military back up.

CIA analysts understood that the overthrow of the Stalinist Hoxha might be a match to the tinderbox, tempting Greece and Yugoslavia to move in and partition—a gift to Soviet propaganda. But they felt they could restrain those two countries, and still saw advantage in toppling a regime that so firmly aligned itself with the Soviet Union. Even if they did not get rid of communism in Albania, they might achieve, through the removal of Hoxha, a realignment of Albania towards Yugoslavia, where Tito was asserting the independence of his communist nation from Moscow's control. Even partial success in Albania, they reasoned, would be a psychological blow against Stalinism.[2]

The mini-invasion of the moonless night was a disaster. The Albanian army chief Beira Maluku had alerted the local population and deployed troops to surround the whole coastal area. Soon after disembarkation from the *Stormie Seas'* dory, the group of nine split into two smaller forces, one of which headed north. Within hours, three of this northern force had been killed; the fourth disappeared without trace. The other force of five men moved towards the south, the operational area of the Greek cross-border communist guerrillas. Tipped off by a farm girl that they were being hunted down and would be killed, they hid in caves, fought their way through two ambushes, and made it to safety across the Greek border with the loss of one man missing. They delivered an intelligence report: Albania might not be ready for an uprising.

Undeterred, the Anglo-American Allies continued with a policy that was kept secret from the voters back home, but otherwise was clandestine only in name. The *Stormie Seas* sailed again with MI6-sponsored contingents. The Americans poured good money after bad and continued to infiltrate would-be counter-revolutionaries until 1951. They had inherited from Ross's Research and Analysis division a 'Who's Who of Albanian Guerrillas'. They trained chosen candidates at a CIA facility in Heidelberg, Germany. Of the 250 graduates of the course, more than 60 parachuted into Albania. Only a handful got out alive.

Post-mortems on the Albania affair have identified tactical issues. Charges of incompetence included the observation that for reasons of plausible deniability the insurgents received not US/UK equipment, but inferior kit from other countries. With the same aim of disavowal, no UK or US

officers took part in the operation—this discouraged locals who remembered the Allies' more active role in the war. The *Stormie Seas* carried only
low-grade codebooks. The Allies used the same old landing bases—Seaview, Ibiza, and Degas were is use in the Second World War, and known to
communist security personnel who might well have used them themselves
when resisting fascist Italian and German occupation. Albanian émigrés
talked too much. So did Italian coastguard officers who trained their
telescopes on the *Stormie Seas* naively taking onboard Albanian 'pixies'
within plain sight of the Italian coast.

Then there was Kim Philby, who remained on the organizing committee—and was a double agent spying of behalf of the Soviet Union.
Depending on your point of view, he betrayed the operation or was a
convenient scapegoat for the failings of others. The authorized history of
MI6 rather eloquently fails to mention the part Philby played.[3]

All this has obscured the strategic shortcomings of the Albanian operation
and of its many sequels in the Cold War. In the rush to oppose communism,
the Americans jettisoned their republican principles and endorsed monarch-
ists, partisans of the former King Zog. Reversing their wartime judgement,
the Allies supported fascist elements—only to register horrified incredulity
when street demonstrators across the world assailed them with the word
'fascist'.

At the root of the strategy in the Balkans and elsewhere was destabilization through the encouragement of nationalism, with perhaps free enterprise and democracy as further goals although post-destabilization strategy
was not properly thought out. On the one hand, it was assumed that, given a
little help, patriotic Albanians and others would spontaneously rise up
against their oppressors. On the other hand, there was a patronizing disposition to guide—in the words of one anti-communist SOE/Albania officer,
'these people are like children and they need a firm hand'. The strategy of
synthetic spontaneity produced some apparent results, but contained the
seeds of its own destruction. As for the Albanian adventure, it ended in
a series of show trials of captured insurrectionists in the Albanian capital
in 1954.[4]

The Albanian operation proved to be not a cautionary lesson, but a
training exercise. It was the forerunner of further ventures that continued
long after the OPC had merged into the main body of the CIA. These
covert operations had mixed results, but persuaded some American policy-
makers that they could determine the shape of world politics by means of a

hidden hand. If often through their unintended consequences, US covert actions did and still do affect international security and insecurity.

The Albanian venture also signalled the beginning of ambitious plans by large-scale American secret agencies. Three of these came into existence in the early phase of the Cold War. The last of them was the Defence Intelligence Agency (DIA), established in 1961 to coordinate the work of the three separate armed forces. Before that came the National Security Agency (NSA), which combined the signals and communications efforts of those Second World War rivals, the army and navy.

But the CIA preceded both these agencies. Its impact may be likened to a development 300 years earlier, the formation of Oliver Cromwell's New Model Army. That force set new standards of professionalism. Raising the parliamentary banner, it defeated the royalist soldiers of Charles I in England's Civil War. In like fashion, the CIA set new standards following its inception on 1947. It fought for America's version of republican and democratic values. It became the totemic intelligence institution of the post-war era, the New Model Agency. It inflicted defeats on its opponents.

Was the CIA a British invention? Not really, but it is still a significant question, as we shall see after a review of the real causes of the agency's creation. Here, we can start with the long-term underlying cause of the rise of intelligence agencies in general—the aversion to war, the desire to seek out 'intelligent' and bloodless solutions to international problems. As it happens, there had been British articulation of this view. It will be recalled that the British journalist William Makin argued this case in asserting that espionage was divorced from ethics, yet made for peace. There was an economic as well as humane basis to this way of thinking. In 1945, the UK's Joint Intelligence Committee (JIC) explained, 'the less money we have to spend on preparations for war, the more important it is to have a first-class intelligence service in peacetime'. American presidents as diverse as Woodrow Wilson and Dwight D. Eisenhower held similar views.

Allied to this was a consciousness of American tradition. There were particular strands of memory: for example Evangeline Bell's recollections of U-1 may have affected the outlook at OSS London. But the consciousness was not limited to official circles. Interest in clandestine affairs was widespread in the 1940s, and a number of popular writers tried to meet and profit from the demand. Richard D. Rowan's potboiling *Story of Secret Service* appeared just before the war. George S. Bryan was another spinner of yarns, and his history *The Spy in America* appeared under the Lippincott trade imprint in 1943.

Where spy fiction is concerned, the public may at different times be in search of literal realism, deeper meaning, verisimilitude, or simply escape. At a particular moment, the genre can be a mirror of society. A new edition of James Fenimore Cooper's *The Spy* appeared at the height of the debate over post-war intelligence to remind Americans of their espionage trad-ition. First published in 1821, it was about General George Washington's intelligence service in the Revolutionary war. The only 'high literature' US spy novel to appear until the publication of Norman Mailer's *Harlot's Ghost* in 1991, it was both critical and deeply patriotic, and its republication signalled an American re-dedication to a profession that so often came in for abuse and contempt.[5]

More immediately, there was the memory of the intelligence failure at Pearl Harbor. In the absence of improved coordination, insisted Senator Millard E. Tydings (D-MD), 'we may have another Pearl Harbor'. This was by far the most prominent argument put forward in congressional hearings on the legislation that created the CIA. In its focus on surprise attack the argument was narrow in scope and possibly fallacious—the centralization mantra had already taken hold at the time of Pearl Harbor but failed to forestall the event, just as it would fail to counter future surprises ranging from the Yom Kippur War to 9/11. But the congressional debate in and of itself defined an essential feature—perhaps *the* essential feature—of the New Model Agency. Unlike its peers in the UK, the Soviet Union, and else-where, the CIA was democratically sanctioned. Once founded, the agency was subject to legislative scrutiny. President Dwight D. Eisenhower resisted such oversight and it fluctuated in intensity, but it would be permanent.

Just as urgently as the Pearl Harbor consideration, there was what Presi-dent Truman early identified as the Soviet threat to the security of America and its allies. The threat did not feature in congressional debate, but it did in the executive tasking of the CIA's immediate precursor, the Central Intelli-gence Group (CIG). The group's first directive identified a single target: 'There is an urgent need to develop the highest possible quality of intelli-gence on the USSR in the shortest possible time.' Clearly the Cold War was an important spur to the creation of the CIA.[6]

Under the acronym's broad umbrella, there was more than one CIA. There was the pure intelligence agency that spied out information and analysed it with a view to predicting both surprise attacks and longer-term threats. Then there were other branches and characteristics, each having its own causes and drawing on different traditions. The emphasis on training and professionalization drew on the entrepreneurial emphasis on efficiency and on the rise of business schools, as well as on 1920s campaigns to reform the foreign service, making it a meritocracy divorced from the patronage system.

The idea of problem-solution by means of a large centralized agency took shape in the Second World War but was also a continuation of the social reform impulses of the 1930s. The CIA was, amongst other things, the New Deal's last great agency. Its famous 'opening to the left' initiative whereby it reached out to social democrats in Europe and progressives elsewhere in the world to some extent reflects that provenance, as did the controversy that the opening to the left generated.

The clandestine action section of the CIA had roots of its own. The Second World War with its casualties had consolidated American anti-militarist attitudes, and in the Soviet Union, where the war-induced 'population deficit' had been 48–50 million, the feeling was the same. By mutual if unspoken consent, war was out. Instead, clandestine action was in.

CIA covert action also had a specific prehistory. As the Albanian case illustrates, there were repetitions of SOE–OSS practices, often carried out by the same people. The OPC/CIA's resort to covert actions furthermore stemmed from a pre-war development. It reflected the undertakings made at the Montevideo Pan American conference in 1933. On that occasion, realizing that US gunboat diplomacy on Latin America was losing hearts and minds and was counter-productive, President Roosevelt accepted a self-denying ordinance—no more military interventions in the internal affairs of other nations. When America did want to intervene in the Cold War era, clandestine action was the solution to the 'problem' Roosevelt had created.

So there is no shortage of credible explanations of the CIA's creation, and of the shape the agency assumed. This brings us at last to the British input, a contribution that was in some ways mythical, yet was still influential in its own special way.

The idea that the CIA was a British institution is partly an eddy in a broader stream of thought. Nineteenth-century Americans like Walt Whitman and Brooks Adams were keen on the idea of the migration of civilization. From China it passed to Egypt and Greece, thence to Britain, and now it was America's turn. In the eyes of its admirers, the British secret service was an inspiration for the new torchbearer of civilization. There was an outbreak of veneration for the British institution. The crack FBI agent Leon G. Turrou had remarked in 1939, 'the British have a real intelligence service; American has virtually none'.

So powerful was the reputation that US intelligence leaders had to offer reassurance that they intended to hold their own. Accused in 1944 of having allowed the British to run OSS, Donovan assured President Roosevelt that, on the contrary, OSS had penetrated MI6. CIG chief and future CIA director Hoyt Vandenberg told Congress in 1946: 'for months [in the war] we had to rely blindly and trustingly on the superior intelligence system of the British. . . . We should [now] be self-sufficient.'[7]

Steadily, the myth grew that British tuition at Bletchley Park and in the SOE training schools had been essential to the birth of the CIA via its OSS predecessor. The myth of British tuition was persuasive because it was grounded in some realities. In 1943 Prime Minister Churchill offered guidance when he sent across a description of how the British Cabinet Secretariat handled national security; there was the tuition offered at Camp X and by SOE on the British mainland; Bletchley Park had imparted know-how, even if it turned into a reciprocal arrangement. Arguing for the CIA in 1947, its future director Allen Dulles was nevertheless offering a hyped-up perspective when he spoke of the need to emulate MI6's 'long history of quiet effective performance'.

Along with the notions of British supremacy and rescue went the myth that there had been a pre-war lacuna in US intelligence arrangements. The American intelligence theorist George Pettee argued that the USA had been out of step with other nations before the Second World War: 'for thirty years this country has been surprised and dismayed by the development of world events.' Tom Troy, the official historian of the CIA's origins, acknowledged that there had been some activity before Stephenson and Donovan activated OSS, but advanced an amnesia hypothesis: 'U-1 was not just abolished; it passed into oblivion.' For Ray Cline, a Harvard history Ph.D. who had served in senior CIA positions before writing his memoir in 1977, it was 'almost a miracle' that the OSS and CIA emerged from the American intelligence wilderness, and the transformation owed much to Churchill's determination to make Americans 'face the strategic facts of life'.[8]

There were reasons for this deracination of United States history, and they were reasons that performed a significant function. To acknowledge the American roots of the CIA would be to imply that the lower level of intelligence preparedness that existed between the two world wars might have been sufficient. Maybe America would have had the resources to pick itself up without British assistance, and maybe the vast, permanent, and inflexible intelligence bureaucracy that developed after 1947 was inappropriate to peacetime needs.

The British were keen to support the myth. They were disposed to do so partly out of ignorance of American history, especially the history of US intelligence, which they had never systematically studied. Then there was the vanity factor, indirectly evidenced in British spy fiction. Not only did the fictional James Bond treat his American colleague Felix Leiter as a sidekick, but also his creator Ian Fleming claimed in 1957 and again in 1962 to have drafted, when a wartime naval officer, the charter for OSS. The 007 construct was an attempt to display British superiority at a time when Britain was in decline.

Finally, the misinterpretation of history was an exercise in persuasion—you needed us then, you still need us today, and (ever so politely) we look forward to receiving the secrets you owe us. This is still an article of faith—and policy—with senior British intelligence officials.[9]

The New Model Agency did not carry all before it. President Truman at first gave the CIA a low priority. In his retirement, he looked back and claimed he had had reservations about its covert operations. What he prioritized above all in 1945 was signals intelligence, SIGINT, and from the beginning he authorized collaboration with the British.

The UK was ready for that collaboration. In 1946 the nation's code-breaking unit acquired its present-day name, the Government Communications Headquarters (GCHQ). It moved from Bletchley Park to a London suburb, then in 1951 decamped to a new site on the outskirts of Cheltenham. The Gloucestershire spa town was known for its private 'Ladies' College' but the wags suggested the real reason for the move was the local horseracing track. Frivolities aside, it was notable that GCHQ remained a centralized outfit. America introduced cryptographic integration only with the formation of the NSA in 1952, when the informational demands of the Korean War made it seem urgent.

Until then, GCHQ continued to cooperate with individual branches of the US armed forces. Intelligence cooperation was, as usual, a bartering process. The degree of success you achieved depended on what bargaining chips you could bring to the table. America with its wealth, computer technology, and reservoir of university-trained experts was in a strong position. But the British, too, had assets. In addition to the residual expertise from Bletchley Park days, there was access to a global network of listening posts. These were located in the distant reaches of what had once been an extensive empire, the whiter parts of which were still considered to be trustworthy and sympathetic to the needs of western intelligence.

A second factor making for cooperation was the American desire, especially evident in the Republican-controlled Congress, to save taxpayers' money. The UK operated with even greater financial constrictions, and a codification of amendments agreed in July 1948 confirmed that burden-sharing would take place: 'the two parties will continue to effect elimination of unnecessary duplication in order to ensure the maximum exploitation of foreign communications.'

The result was, by 1948, a complex series of SIGINT undertakings involving the USA as 'the First Party', and Australia, Britain, Canada, and New Zealand as 'Second Parties'. The agreement embraced went beyond SIGINT, and contemporary documents used the acronym COMINT, standing for Communications Intelligence. This included not just codebreaking but also the interception of traffic (telegraph, radio, telephone, and later email and its derivatives), direction finding, translation, equipment exchanges, standardization of codewords, oceanic surveillance to detect Soviet surface and submarine vessels, and the purloining of documents and technical specifications. In a burden-sharing exercise, collection responsibilities were shared out, and each signatory also had specified regional duties. The collective name for the accords covering these broad activities was the UKUSA agreement.[10]

The UKUSA agreement helped to slow the decline of British power and to hasten the rise of America's. To the degree that it enhanced understanding of the Soviet Union it helped to keep the peace. For ignorance breeds fear, and fear lies at the root of aggression. Here, one's hostility to Stalinist communism should not be allowed to get in the way of an important qualification—the KGB and Soviet military intelligence, too, played a role in keeping the peace.

UKUSA experienced difficulties and tensions. Each party to the agreement was capable of denying the other party intelligence. As the senior partner, the USA had more to withhold, but the British could be reticent, too. For example, when London and Washington disagreed over the establishment of the state of Israel in 1948, JIC feared Zionist influence on US policy-making and withheld sensitive information it possessed on the

Palestinians. A better understanding on the part of JIC would have revealed a distinctly pro-Arab, anti-Israeli sentiment within the CIA; the failure to realize this is further evidence of a gap between the US and UK intelligence communities that did not amount to a yawning chasm, but existed nevertheless.

Venona was a further source of tension. This was the codeword for the US cryptographic offensive against Soviet codes. It was top secret, and the origin of the term 'Venona' remains obscure. The programme had started during the war, and the Americans told the British about it in 1945. On the UK side, GC&CS's Alastair Denniston had made some preliminary moves in the same direction in 1943, and, as Venona developed, the listening posts in Britain's overseas dominions proved to be an asset. Known to GCHQ by a different code name, Bride, the programme ceased to be effective in 1948—a communist mole in the Army Security Agency alerted Moscow, and the Soviet Union changed its encryption methods.

By this time, Venona had yielded a poisonous prize. It alerted Washington to the extent and effectiveness of Soviet atomic espionage, but in doing so generated suspicions about the existence of moles in MI6. These suspicions developed over the years and led to the exposure of Kim Philby and other spies embedded in the British secret service. The Americans came to entertain forebodings about the trustworthiness of their British allies and about the viability of the special intelligence relationship.[11]

This was a two-way process. The British also had reservations about the Americans. There was, for example, frustration over the McMahon Act of 1946. The act created the US Atomic Energy Commission (AEC), gave the AEC intelligence responsibilities, and ended the exchange of nuclear-related information with Britain.

Then there was the question of whom to talk to. The US Director of Central Intelligence (DCI) wore a second hat. As well as running the CIG/CIA, he was supposed to control the entire intelligence community. This gave him the unenviable challenge of overseeing the turf-jealous military intelligence establishments, the resentful FBI, and the rarefied world of atomic intelligence at the AEC. In 1949, the CIA established an Office of National Estimates (ONE) to try to pull things together. But centralized government remained uncongenial to many influential Americans, some of whom considered the Big Government initiatives of the 1930s and 1940s to be akin to crypto-communism. When he tried to coordinate the effort of the intelligence community as a whole, the DCI ran into difficulties. At least part of the reason why British intelligence found its American equivalent to be confusing was that the Americans were, in fact, in a muddle.

There were witnesses to this. It must be said that the Englishman Bertie Blount was not the best-organized person in the world. After his death, his family went through the homemade chemistry laboratory he had constructed above the garage attached to his house. They found he had neglected to dispose of several jars of anthrax left over from his SOE days, when he had planned to assassinate Hitler. But in his days as chairman of the inter-services science committee, even the shambolic Blount found the American intelligence scene to be disorderly. Visiting Washington in 1950, he discovered that the AEC and CIA retained separate scientific intelligence units that barely spoke to each other. He reported that 'American intelligence is inexperienced, overstaffed, wastefully run and rent by internal dissentions'.

Blount's observation reflected a wider British attitude to America's new intelligence system. There was no full UK investigation into that system, but in 1947 Air Chief Marshal Sir Douglas Evill had commented on it in the course of a review he conducted of the JIC. He doubted whether the National Security Act of that year, which unified the armed forces and created the CIA, would work either for US intelligence or for Anglo-American intelligence liaison. The Soviet explosion of an atomic device in 1949, two or three years earlier than intelligence officials had predicted, confirmed the jitters of those Jeremiahs who thought US espionage was inadequate.[12]

While the New Model Agency did not carry all before it, the CIA nevertheless became the prime intelligence agency of the modern era. It stood out partly because of the relative inadequacies of its friends. The shortcomings of MI6 confirmed the CIA in pole position. Assessments of MI6's deficiencies vary. According to one school of thought, its performance had been mediocre in the inter-war years. Hugh Trevor-Roper, the historian who had served in MI6 in the Second World War, was scathing about 'six' in the 1930s: 'Novels of clubland heroes might have given it fictitious lustre, but essentially it remained an amateur organisation with a slender budget . . . recruited by patronage, it acquired some of the character of a coterie.'

An extension of this critical view was the belief that MI6 mediocrity had continued in the war itself. Consistent with this was the perception that 'C' had ridden on the coat tails of GC&CS. Only by making himself the conduit between Churchill and Bletchley Park, to recall Trevor-Roper's verdict, did Menzies give himself the air of a man who mattered.

These views were, of course, anathema to the post-1945 school of CIA boosters who argued that British intelligence had been wonderful and had ridden to America's rescue in the Second World War. Yet it was true that MI6 had, like its counterparts across the Atlantic, suffered post-First World War funding retrenchment. After the second war, MI6 once again experienced cuts. It did absorb the remnants of the now-defunct SOE and thus acquired that additional dimension, covert operations, that the OSS and CIA embraced. Nevertheless, budgetary constraints made MI6 but a shadow of what it might have been, thus adding by default to the standing of the more generously funded CIA.[13]

The decisive element in the CIA's worldwide intelligence ascendancy was its democratic provenance and oversight. It would be years before the British government admitted the existence of MI5, MI6, and GCHQ. The names of their directors were also an official secret, and such secrecy, while pronounced in the British case, was not unusual in the many nations that practised espionage. In contrast, the CIA was very soon a household name. Its director was a public figure and sometimes a master of publicity. All this could be a double-edged sword. The public relations imperative could distort goals and run counter to the need for security. Democratic zeal could become missionary in character leading to loss of perspective and to atrocities that, in extreme cases like the 1960s Phoenix assassination programme against Vietnamese communist cadres, matched the ultimate depredations of Cromwell's New Model Army, which upheld Cromwellian dictatorship and committed atrocities in Ireland. In due course the CIA also ran into heavy criticism, such as accusations of crusaderism. Nevertheless, democracy was the lesson that the world new superpower wanted to teach, and the legislatively underpinned character of the CIA was appropriate to the task in hand.

Worldwide, the CIA became a model for national intelligence agencies, especially those newly formed. Gradually—and it was neither a sudden nor a complete process—it came to supplant MI6 as an enabling agency. Its relationship with other secret intelligence entities varied in both nature and outcome. Sometimes they were its clients, at other times modelled on its practices and beneficiaries of CIA training.

President Roosevelt had ordered FBI director J. Edgar Hoover to marshal the efforts of all intelligence agencies in Latin American nations in the undercover war against Nazi agents, and the CIA reaped some of the benefits of the resultant liaison and tuition in spite of J. Edgar Hoover's petulant lack of cooperation when told to give up his empire to the south of the Rio Grande.

West Germany's Bundesnachrichtendienst was a US-inspired new organization born of the Cold War partition of a nation. Garrisoned West Germany was a key area for Anglo-American scientific espionage, a potential window into Soviet atomic research. MI6 had jurisdiction in the UK zone of occupation and played a supporting role that preserved a glow in the dying embers of British intelligence prestige. But from 1949 the Bundesnachrichtendienst had a contractual relationship with the CIA. It continued to operate the old Nazi spy rings against the Red East. This appeared to be an asset until it transpired that communist moles had comprehensively penetrated West Germany's equivalent of the CIA.

Similarly the CIA's James Angleton took an active hand in the creation of the post-war Italian intelligence community, though it is unclear how much control the Americans exerted over it. The CIA in 1958 paid the salaries of 51 out of 691 employees of the Dutch security agency BVD. It supplied them with bugging equipment and arranged for three of them to study Chinese at Yale University. So concerned were some Europeans about all this control that the French, West German, and Dutch together with other European partners set up an independent anti-communist undercover unit. The ultra-conservative Interdoc came into existence in 1963. The Americans ended up influencing that, too.

Looking beyond the western hemisphere and Europe at another divided country, South Korea's intelligence organization was named after its US prototype. The KCIA, however, launched into extreme practices such as interference in domestic high politics in a way that was difficult for the CIA to control.

In Egypt, CIA officers enjoyed a special relationship with Gamal Nasser, after the 1952 revolution the most prominent leader of the newly independent nation. They imported FBI specialists to establish a new national police school. They nurtured Egypt's General Investigations Directorate (GID). It is a matter of debate whether the GID was a clone of the CIA—it also drew on German assistance and displayed indigenous traits. But the USA trained its senior officers and analysts and supplied them with surveillance and counter-surveillance equipment.

The CIA's epitomization of democracy had its limits. After all, its legislative underpinning was a domestic arrangement, and America's principles, like those of other democracies, all too often stopped at the waterline. In Iran, Guatemala, and Chile, the agency would be associated with the overthrow of democracies, ostensibly to save them from communism. When the CIA helped and trained its clones and clients, it did not insist on oversight mechanisms, indeed some of its imitators would have had much to fear from such scrutiny.

Yet it is difficult to resist the argument that the ultimate widespread adoption of more open practices sprang from the CIA model. The North Atlantic Treaty Organization (NATO), the defensive alliance of democratic countries established in 1949 under US leadership, underwent expansion when communism finally collapsed, and it would be an expected condition of membership that former communist dictatorships joining NATO would have to have their intelligence organizations democratically overseen. When the European Union imposed a similar requirement on new applicants for member state status, it repeated what was, thanks to the CIA model, an established requirement.[14]

The CIA played a prominent role in the implementation of the key postwar objective of Anglo-American foreign policy, the stabilization of Europe. The Marshall Plan of 1948 channelled what would become $14 billion in economic aid to democratic European countries that were prepared to join the Organization for European Economic Cooperation, a precursor of the present-day European Union. On the communist side of the Iron Curtain, the goal remained regime change using Albanian-style tactics. But for democratic western Europe, America adopted a policy whose goals included the elimination of nationalistic tariff barriers in the interest of peace and prosperity, the prevention of future wars, and the creation of a market for US exports. Talk in the United States of America of the creation of a 'United States of Europe' hinted at a nationalistic US narcissism. More importantly, however, the rejuvenated and united nations of western Europe were to form a bulwark against communist expansion. Although the United Nations had been formed in the United States in 1945 and remained based there, the more pressing American concern in the immediate post-war years was western European unity and economic viability.

European unity was neither an American invention nor a CIA plot. The concept was rooted in European history, and its post-war pioneers were a gifted generation of European leaders who were determined to avoid a repetition of the twentieth century's wars. France and West Germany, enemies in three successive conflicts, were pioneer signatories. While the British with their straitened circumstances and overstretched global commitments were heel-draggers, there was at least some British support for the idea of European federalism. The British ambassador Lord Lothian had thought that American-style federalism provided a solution for Europe's problems. Some European federalists consider him to have been a prophet without honour in his own country. Winston Churchill gave at least lip service to European unity, and the Conservative politician Duncan Sandys was a supporter.[15]

Yet it remains true that it was America's CIA that took the lead in conducting an undercover campaign for the Marshall Plan's successful implementation. The United States gave open assistance to the economies of approved European nations. On a much smaller but still substantial scale, the CIA invested secret funds to encourage the political success of the programmes. In post-war elections in France and Italy, the agency secretly subsidized non-communist campaigns and resorted to direct measures such as buying up newsprint supplies to prevent the appearance of communist publications. In 1947, the fledgling CIA allegedly hired Corsican gangsters to intimidate and murder communist strikers in Marseilles.

Channelling funds through front organizations, the CIA waged a cultural campaign, making sure that anti-communist artists received financial rewards and opportunities to succeed. In the field of education, the agency promoted programmes and conferences that challenged the communist worldview—one of its vehicles was America's own National Students Association. Frank Wisner, William J. Donovan, and Allen Dulles promoted European unity. Though officially retired from intelligence activities, Donovan chaired the CIA-funded American Committee on United Europe (ACUE).

Donovan encouraged the establishment, in 1950, of the College of Europe. The Bruges-based educational establishment would train the future leaders of Europe-wide institutions in a fraternal, counter-nationalist atmosphere. Valerie Plame was not the first American to study at the college. The young Princeton alumnus Peter Dodd attended its first session thanks to an ACUE fellowship. He reported that in class discussions 'national biases and prejudices were quickly exposed'. Jean Monnet, chairman of the European Coal and Steel Community, expressed his general appreciation to Donovan in 1952: 'we are proceeding to build a United States of Europe... The aid and encouragement of Americans which is marshalled by the American Committee on United Europe has done much to strengthen this great undertaking.' Between 1948 and 1960 the CIA spent $4 million on the promotion of European unity.[16]

The CIA's 'opening to the left' policy applied in the first instance to democratic European countries (later examples occurred in Africa and the Middle East, but in Latin America there was more ideological rigidity perhaps because it was the USA's 'back yard'). The aim was a tactical one, to undercut potential support for communist political candidates by promoting the campaigns of those on the democratic left. The tactic was part of what expanded into a broader strategy—keep open your 'back channel' communications with any group that may one day find itself in power and in a position to help.

But if the policy was pragmatic, there was also a subjective element. Some of the agency's early leaders, appointees as they were of New Deal politicians and their successors, were 'liberal' or 'left' themselves. Sidney W. Souers, President Truman's leading security adviser who served as the first director of the CIG and then as the first secretary of the National Security Council to which the CIA reported, declared himself to be 'just left of center'. Covert operator David Phillips described his colleagues as 'Ivy League, OSS, liberal'. The CIA contained some outright conservatives like the counterintelligence specialist James Angleton, yet there was a perception that liberal sympathies held the ground. Cord Meyer who worked with private organizations including student groups was, according to future CIA director Bill Colby, a keen promoter of 'democratic socialism' in Europe.[17]

In the case of Britain, there was no significant communist presence, so the CIA supported the more conservative wing of the Labour Party against that party's left wing. The results were less than gratifying. In office between 1945 and 1951, Labour nationalized the steel and coal industries. Then in opposition to the Conservative government, 1951–64, it sang to its own tune and opposed European unification.

Furthermore, to the dismay of its left wing, Labour supported the Conservatives' policy of having an independent British nuclear deterrent. The successful British nuclear bomb test of 1952 destroyed the simple USA–USSR balance of nuclear power and removed all moral impediment to nations that wished to join the atomic arms prestige race. The Labour Party favoured by the CIA thus delivered bipartisan support to the nuclear proliferation that was to be the bane of international security and American foreign policy.

While more open to public scrutiny than its foreign counterparts, the CIA concealed from the American public its support for the European left. There were pressing political reasons for this. In the 1950 and 1952 elections, the Republicans made a major issue of the dangers inherent in British 'Fabianism', and in New Deal-style 'creeping socialism' at home. They insisted that America should avoid such policies at all costs. They won both elections on that platform. And as if that were not enough, the Republican Senator Joe McCarthy now started his crusade against 'communists in government', inveighing against the Department of State and fixing the CIA in his sights.

In an ironic outcome, the CIA survived that attack from the American right only to become the bête noire of the very European left whose bills it had once paid. In 1953 the British socialist Gordon Stewart wrote the first-ever history of the CIA. It was bitterly critical of the agency's support of resistance movements in eastern Europe. Cord Meyer ended up being a target of the Labour Party's left-wing MPs, who in 1974 tried to have him removed from his position as CIA station chief in London.[18]

Though a young organization, the CIA from the beginning had the means to overshadow its British counterpart. It developed on distinctive lines and sought to universalize a new model for intelligence in democratic societies. Like any new model, it had its flaws. The world it attempted to influence was, moreover, complex and beset by varying perceptions and degrees of hostility.

It was not an ideal setting for international trust. Yet leaders of the agency realized it would be unwise to go it alone. They chose the devil they knew. With mixed results as illustrated by the Albanian debacle, they persisted with the US–UK special intelligence relationship.

6

Surviving Mistrust

Cold War Intelligence Episodes

The son of a German Lutheran pastor, Klaus Fuchs opposed the rise of Hitler. In danger because of this, he fled Germany in 1933.

Supported by an English Quaker family, Fuchs now pursued what would blossom into a scientific career at the University of Edinburgh and in England. In 1941, he joined the British atomic research project. When America entered the war, the British invested their knowledge into the newly started US atomic bomb programme. Towards the end of 1943, Fuchs accompanied a British team sent to New York to work on the Manhattan Project. In August of the following year, he transferred to the Los Alamos facility in New Mexico, where he worked on theoretical aspects of nuclear weaponry until mid-1946.

One day in the course of his stay in Manhattan, Fuchs visited the Lower East Side clutching a tennis ball in his hand. There, he hoped to encounter a man holding a green book and a pair of gloves. It was a prearranged meeting with his latest contact from Soviet intelligence, a man from the NKVD (precursor of the KGB, established in 1954). Fuchs had volunteered his services as a spy soon after joining the British atomic project. The man he was about to meet was an American communist, Harry Gold.

A working relationship with Gold having been established, Fuchs proved to have a gift for the double life. He survived three separate security investigations by British counterintelligence. Soviet documentation reveals that on the occasion of his first meeting with Soviet military intelligence (GRU) in August 1941, he warned of Nazi nuclear research in Leipzig and mentioned only in passing the equivalent British effort. But between 1941 and 1943, he went on to betray substantial information about both the UK and the US programmes.

To put the matter into perspective, Fuchs was not the only spy, and the betrayal was not entirely the fault of the British. Information derived from the US decryption of Soviet coded messages—the Venona programme—identified 349 Americans secretly tied to the NKVD and other Soviet intelligence agencies. Fuchs's NKVD and GRU controllers complained that he furnished them with too much theory and not enough technical information. But it does seem likely that Fuchs with his privileged access to classified data helped the Soviets to make an atomic bomb based on plutonium, which was cheaper and faster to manufacture than enriched uranium. It is estimated that he hastened their bomb production by between one and two years, and contributed also to the knowledge base that permitted the subsequent Soviet development of the more powerful hydrogen bomb. The Fuchs operation was the Cold War's most serious case of atomic espionage.

By the late 1940s, intercepted messages and FBI detective work had convinced the American authorities that the Soviets had stolen their secrets. Captured Gestapo files indicated Fuchs's membership in the Communist Party as early as 1933. Enquiries by the FBI's Robert Lamphere showed how Fuchs had been in contact with Soviet spies well before his arrival in America. One of Lamphere's discoveries suggested a very early date. It arose from the defection in 1945 of Igor Gouzenko, a code clerk at the Soviet embassy in Ottawa. One of the agents uncovered by Gouzenko had an address book, and in the address book was listed Klaus Fuchs at an old address, 84 Grange 'Lane' (it should have been Loan), Edinburgh. This indicated a longstanding relationship between the atomic spy and his Moscow controllers.

The matter was by this time urgent, as the Soviet Union in 1949, sooner than expected, exploded its first atomic device. Naturally there was a suspicion that information purloined from the West had hastened that event. As if this were not enough, Fuchs was by now head of the theoretical physics division at the British Atomic Energy Research Establishment in Harwell, England, and in a prime position to pass on more atomic secrets. He was arrested on 2 February 1950, and confessed.[1]

Ensuing events illustrate how FBI–MI5 relations were not in a state of prime health. The British tried to monopolize the interrogation of Fuchs partly out of a desire to cover up their lax security but mainly because of UK nuclear rivalry with the USA. The British were still developing their own nuclear bomb. They resented the fact that, through the McMahon Act of

1946, the Americans had unilaterally abrogated the sharing of nuclear research secrets with Britain and Canada. On the part of the United States, there may well have been a feeling that nuclear cooperation with Britain was not the only game in town. To look ahead, President Eisenhower's 'Atoms for Peace' speech to the United Nations in 1953 would contemplate the universalization of technology, and in 1956 Eisenhower looked for a way of explaining to Prime Minister Sir Anthony Eden that a declaration of joint Anglo-American nuclear collaboration would offend 'our other allies'.[2]

Alert to incipient unilateralist tendencies across the Atlantic, the British did not want Fuchs to impart any of their own secrets under FBI interrogation. To keep Fuchs sweet, they encouraged him to believe that they might treat him favourably. It was in the British interest to keep the impatient American interrogators at bay. FBI Director J. Edgar Hoover fumed at 'the sly British' for denying the FBI access to the scientist's interrogation process. He told London he was 'outraged at the lack of cooperation by the British Government and MI5 on the Fuchs case'.[3]

Eventually, the British allowed the Americans to interrogate Fuchs. He supplied the FBI with leads that helped in the apprehension of an extended ring of atomic spies orchestrated from Moscow with the assistance of leading officials from the Communist Party of the United States. Convicted on the evidence of Harry Gold, Julius and Ethel Rosenberg went to the chair in 1953. Even if they were minor characters compared with Fuchs, their trial was of iconic significance in the history of America's Cold War.[4]

It is tempting to see the Fuchs episode as signalling a fall from the high pinnacle of what Winston Churchill had only recently defined as the Anglo-American 'special relationship'. The former prime minister had dramatized the idea in his Fulton, Missouri speech of 1946 in which he defined the coming Cold War, famously warning that the Soviet Union had imposed an 'iron curtain' on Europe. For security reasons, he glossed over the intelligence issue in official pronouncements. With the passage of years, however, historians have come to view Churchill's words, backed up by his actions as war leader, as the defining moment and acme of the 'special intelligence relationship' between Britain and America.[5]

The Fuchs spat proved to be one in a series of potentially destabilizing episodes in the special intelligence relationship. Yet until the 1960s, at least, there was no precipitous decline in that relationship. In the 1950s when the Cold War was at its height, certain factors cemented the two countries together. To mutual fear, mutual social structures, and mutual culture was added mutual benefit.

Fears about Soviet arms escalation and intentions dominated security thinking in the West. Arriving at a sensible Soviet estimate was no simple matter. Because of the closed nature of Soviet society it was hard to find out what the Red Army was up to, and even harder to estimate the intentions of the Kremlin. Blind in this way, western estimators risked slipping into the error of mirror imaging, assuming that given the same circumstances Russians would behave in the same way as Americans. And there was a problem with the US military. Army, navy, and air force promoters respectively exaggerated the number of tanks, ships, and planes in the Soviet armed forces in order to win appropriations for their own service, and to win the competition with rival services at home.

The CIA, created by the National Security Act of 1947, counteracted the last tendency in being a civilian agency. By various means, for example by studying the Soviet economy's ability to sustain an arms race, CIA leaders like Allen Dulles and Richard Bissell arrived at more realistic estimates. They scotched the myths of the 'bomber gap' and the 'missile gap'. Their essential reasonableness was complemented on the other side of the Iron Curtain where, in spite of ideological rhetoric and bombastic speeches by the Soviet leader Nikita Khrushchev, an intelligent rationality underpinned policy-making.

Close as they were to the Americans, the British had an input. At the start of the 1950s, Britain still offered superior expertise in some areas, for example on the Soviets' development of guided missile systems.

Signals intelligence and codebreaking remained a cornerstone of UK–USA clandestine cooperation. From its formation in 1952, NSA indirectly bankrolled GCHQ. But this relationship was not one-way. There was continuing UK expertise, and there were also the British-enabled listening posts ranging from those in Fylingdales, Yorkshire, and Edzell, Scotland, to Pine Gap in Australia. Thus, one can speak of a jointly contrived UKUSA input into what came to be known as the US national intelligence estimates.

At least partly because they operated successfully in tandem, the intelligence communities of America and Britain refined security strategy and spending, on balance defused nuclear tensions, and promoted the economic interests of both countries. These were amongst the main reasons why the special intelligence relationship survived a series of episodes that fomented suspicion and mistrust.

Their mutual taste for social and even ethnic elitism also bound the countries together. In the period prior to the 1960s, the Anglo–American intelligence relationship retained its air of exclusivity. The French foreign intelligence station chief in Washington, Thyraud de Vosgoli, thought the 1950s CIA was in cahoots with the British and distrustful of foreign intelligence agencies and of the French in particular. General Charles de Gaulle claimed that 'the countries of continental Europe stood in danger of the development at their expense of an Anglo-Saxon world hegemony'. The French opinion was not groundless. Sir Eric Jones, who served as GCHQ director in the early 1950s and had shaken hands on the original SIGINT deal with the United States, is said to have 'hated to spend a night on the continent'.[6]

Sherman Kent commented on the Cold War Anglo-American intelligence relationship in his unpublished memoir. A Yale graduate and OSS Research and Analysis veteran, Kent was a history Ph.D. and a theoretician of intelligence. It was he who established America's national intelligence estimate (NIE) system in 1950, and he remained in charge of the Board of National Estimates for eighteen years. He recalled that Walter Bedell Smith, CIA director 1950–3 (and not an Ivy Leaguer), opposed 'junket' visits by US officials to the UK. But Smith still endorsed cooperation with Britain's Joint Intelligence Committee (JIC) on a 'when, as, and if basis'. Smith's successor Dulles (Princeton) encouraged cooperation, and Kent, with the CIA's Anglophile liaison man Ray Cline (Harvard history Ph.D.), cultivated their JIC colleagues: 'we were privileged to read most of the British JIC papers and the British . . . most of our NIEs . . . I do put a great importance in this exchange of information with our cousins.'

Though Kent was 'an old French Historian', he subscribed to Anglo-Saxon prejudice. He recalled with relish an occasion when Churchill refused to speak French to a Frenchman, calling him a 'wretched Froggy' for making the request. Also in his memoir, Kent ridiculed General Paul Grossin, head of the French intelligence service, whom he met in 1960. He depicted Grossin as a man with 'a peculiar idiosyncrasy of smoking cigars in a short holder which, from time to time he would remove from his lips and shove up one of his nostrils and breathe the cigar smoke through the nasal passages'. Kent recorded that the USA exchanged amenities with the French but nothing of substance to do with the NIEs: 'The U.S., of course, did not have the special intelligence relationship with the French, which obtained with our British cousins.'[7]

Partly because of the Fuchs case and Venona evidence, some Americans nevertheless had reservations about British intelligence. The bell began to toll for old school elitism when suspicion fell on the Cambridge spy ring. Members of the privately educated Anglo-Scottish elite who had come together as undergraduates at Cambridge University, these young men had rebelled against the political and sexual mores of their own social class. In the bitter years of the Great Depression when capitalism was discredited, they had developed communist sympathies. These sympathies endured. Unlike so many comrades who became quite rapidly disillusioned with Stalin's brand of dictatorship, the Cambridge group retained their external fealty and continued to serve the Soviet Union by becoming spies. The historian Victor Kiernan, who knew them at Cambridge and shared their views, described their outlook as one that made it impossible to be 'a "traitor" to the Washington plotters and their European jackals'.

Donald Maclean (bisexual) went to be first secretary at the British embassy in Washington in 1944, and by 1951 was head of the American department at the Foreign Office. He had access to the US Atomic Energy Commission. He passed on to his Soviet controllers information about the development and potential deployment of nuclear weapons, and possibly about Truman's war plans in Korea. Guy Burgess (gay) was not such a high flier, but was assigned to the Far Eastern Affairs section of the Washington embassy where he was in post at the outbreak of the Korean War in 1950.

Burgess was indiscreet and in any case US codebreakers had worked on intercepted messages that gave rise to suspicion regarding both him and Maclean. The Foreign Office sheltered them because chaps like us can't be traitors. But by 1951 the net was closing. Kim Philby (committed philanderer) now intervened. Harold Philby, nicknamed Kim from the boy in Rudyard Kipling's stories of empire, had joined MI6. He picked up an Order of the British Empire (OBE) award for his wartime service, served as head of MI6's Russian desk sabotaging British and American counterintelligence operations, and then went to Washington to be the liaison man with the CIA. He was thus sufficiently well informed to tip off his fellow Cambridge graduates Burgess and Maclean, who both fled to Russia in 1951.

By this time, the CIA's counterintelligence chief James Jesus Angleton was suspicious of Philby himself. He reasoned that the MI6 man must have betrayed the details of the Albanian operation to the communists. Recent scholarship suggests that Philby did not send detailed information and was not the key factor behind the mission's failure. The Englishman arrived in Washington too late for the key Albanian briefings, it is questionable whether the KGB would have risked such a prize asset by using him to defend Albania, and in any case the whole operation leaked like a sieve. Mike Burke, the US operative in charge of the Italian end of the operation, thought that, regardless of Philby, the operation could never have succeeded. In his book questioning the effectiveness of espionage, Sir John Keegan concedes that Maclean betrayed significant secrets, but sees Philby as 'a classic example of a spy spying on spies', rather than on a strategically important target.

In the long term nobody, least of all Philby, denied that the British double agent betrayed the general Albanian plan to Moscow and thus to Tirana. At the time, though, Philby's British colleagues could not find or would not believe the evidence against Philby. Following detective work by the CIA's Bill Harvey, DCI Walter Bedell Smith told MI6 that Philby was no longer welcome in Washington. The British authorities dismissed American suspicions, but did release Philby from MI6 in 1955. Even then, he received a golden handshake, and the future prime minister Harold Macmillan rose in the Commons to defend him. Ultimately the mandarins of British intelligence took the easy course and transferred Philby to the relative obscurity of Beirut. While they were angry with him, he was also a convenient scapegoat—when things went wrong for MI6, for example when the KGB outwitted them in the Baltic region, it was all too easy to blame Philby's betrayals. In 1963, Philby absconded from Beirut to Moscow, losing his OBE in the process but picking up Soviet awards instead.

It may be true, as Keegan suggested, that Philby was merely a spy's spy, but he did poison operational relations between MI6 and the CIA. John Bruce Lockhart, who oversaw MI6 work in Germany, recalled that in the years before 1963 'liaison with the CIA was nearly paralysed by the unresolved suspicions'.

The year following Philby's defection, still another member of the Cambridge 'Apostles' confessed—John Cairncross (polygamy enthusiast) had worked in the Treasury and given his Soviet controllers confidential economic information, for example about weapon systems.[8]

A further member of the 'Magnificent Five', Anthony Blunt, had been Cairncross's recruiter in Cambridge. Sir Anthony (as he was until stripped of his knighthood in 1979) survived even longer as a pillar of the British establishment. He had worked for MI5 in the war, conveying to his

Moscow masters the names of Allied agents—whose lives were thus imperilled once the Cold War started. Later, he was an art historian and Keeper of the Royal Pictures until, in 1979, Prime Minister Margaret Thatcher publicly named him as a spy. Like Burgess, and like Maclean, when he chose to swing in that direction, Blunt was gay, but in all five cases ideology appears to have been a more powerful motivating factor than sexuality or the threat of blackmail.[9]

Confirmed and unconfirmed stories about Moscow Centre's penetration of British intelligence were galling to the Americans. Knowledge of the penetration gave rise to further suspicions. Espousing 'rollback', the Americans were keen to extend covert anti-communist activities beyond Albania and into several other nations behind the Iron Curtain, but although the UK also ran such operations, they favoured a more cautious approach. Especially after Stalin's death in 1953, the British showed signs of accepting Churchill's 1944 'spheres of influence' accommodation with Moscow, with the Soviets and the West agreeing, in the interests of peace, which areas of Europe each would dominate. Given the known presence of double agents at the heart of the British intelligence establishment, such caution—though in due course justified by the collapse of rebellions in East Berlin and Hungary—could be misinterpreted.

Expressions of alarm were acute. At the end of 1951, the US Joint Chiefs of Staff received a report indicating that MI6 and the CIA had begun to 'foul each other up in some of their covert operations'. Ten years later, J. Edgar Hoover was still fuming over the Burgess and Maclean episode. One British intelligence officer remembered him 'sounding each syllable of their names with almost prurient venom'. The damage imposed by the betrayals was far reaching. Hoover saw a communist plot behind every domestic protest movement; Angleton developed acute worries about the possibility that the CIA might be penetrated; until the 1990s, homosexuals were barred from serving in America's intelligence agencies.[10]

Though sceptical about the amount of damage caused by Philby, Keegan estimates that the Cambridge spies collectively 'caused great harm . . . to Anglo-American trust' that lasted until the discovery of America's own spies later in the century. In a similar vein John Dumbrell, in a work on the overall Anglo-American relationship, notes how President Eisenhower and his secretary of state John Foster Dulles wanted to cultivate closer relationships with several countries, rather than pursue a special bond with the UK. However, too much was at stake and the benefits of cooperation were too large for either side to call for closure. Joint operations in Iran and in Berlin demonstrate, on the contrary, a determination to continue.[11]

Iran had become a democratic country with Mohammed Mosaddeq as its prime minister. The new leader wanted his country to benefit from its oil wealth, previously siphoned off into corporation profits by multinationals backed by western imperialist powers. After unproductive negotiations with the British, Mosaddeq decided with the support of parliament to nationalize the Anglo-Iranian Oil Company (AIOC). The British disapproved and wanted to retain control of their strategic asset; the Americans aimed at control for themselves and feared that Mosaddeq might turn to Moscow for support. Both countries were prepared to forget the setback in Albania and take another risk. The result was a significant Anglo-American operation conducted in secret—it was hidden, at least, from the voters back home. The Iranians, like the Albanians, were from the outset aware of the western powers' machinations.[12]

MI6 initiated the plan and mobilized the contacts and agents it had lined up in a country that fell within the British sphere of imperial influence. Through the medium of its own intelligence agency, the AIOC ran a propaganda campaign against Mosaddeq. Some of Iran's mullahs considered Mosaddeq to be too liberal, and played along with the campaign. The CIA stepped in with dollars, for example paying the inhabitants of Teheran's southern slums to demonstrate and riot against the Mosaddeq government. The result was the coup of 1953 that removed Mosaddeq from power. It placed the democratically elected leader under permanent house arrest and restored the royalist powers of Mohammed Raza Pahlavi, the Shah of Iran.[13]

The shah had sought refuge abroad and was in Rome when he heard the news. 'I knew it!' he exclaimed, 'They love me!' His reaction was at least partly delusional, though there were doubtless influential elements in Iran who wanted rid of the Mosaddeq government.

At the time, the whole affair seemed to be an Anglo-American intelligence triumph. Private firms continued to supply Iranian oil to the West, with the difference that Texaco and other US corporations supplanted AIOC and now controlled 40 per cent of the rights. Intelligence leaders revelled in the success. The CIA's Middle Eastern chief, Kermit Roosevelt, visited Sir Winston Churchill at 10 Downing Street to explain how it had been done. The ailing premier was in bed and scarcely able to hear or speak. He professed never to have heard of the CIA but said that MI6 was 'close to his heart' and sent Roosevelt away with the impression that he thoroughly approved of his actions. Reportedly MI6 was miffed by Roosevelt's taking of so much of the credit, but according to the CIA's internal history of the event the new 'C', Alexander Sinclair, was actually very happy 'not only because of the success of the operation per se, but because of the effect its success had already had and would continue to have upon SIS's reputation and relations with its superiors'.[14]

The Iranian coup was, however, a disaster in three respects. First, it condemned Iranians to live under successive tyrannies, the shah's until the disillusioned mullahs' revolution of 1979, and then the mullahs' own despotism. Second, anti-British sentiments in Persia that had existed prior to the coup now developed, in a portion of Iranian society, into a permanent alienation from the West with repercussions that are keenly felt today. Third, it emboldened a generation of covert adventurers to undertake even more irresponsible actions that resulted in the downfall of other democracies, and injured the long-term reputation and credibility of the United States and its allies, especially its closest ally.

In the United States Congress, there was concern about both the effectiveness and the appropriateness of the activities of the CIA. A number of subcommittees kept an eye on the agency, but there was a feeling that a more powerful mechanism should be established. President Eisenhower opposed the idea. CIA director Allen Dulles said it was 'primarily for Congress to decide', but campaigned against the proposal in private.

One reason for Dulles's and Eisenhower's reluctance was that the CIA had been a prime target of Joe McCarthy. Sniffing a wider conspiracy behind the CIA's opening to the left, the histrionic senator had scented a communist plot.

Another worry stemmed from the need to guard secrets. Congress was gossipy. Giving legislators access to prime secrets was asking for trouble. Senator Mike Mansfield (D-MT) therefore came up with the idea of a joint oversight committee. Drawn from both houses of Congress, this committee would consist of a limited and carefully selected group of individuals. The idea was that they would have access to all the secrets, and would keep them. By January 1955, Senator Mansfield had thirty-five co-sponsors of this proposal in the Senate.[15]

President Eisenhower was aware of the need to supervise the nation's spies. He had previously established an inquiry under James Doolittle that offered stringent critiques, for example of the quality of CIA personnel. However, Eisenhower had reservations about congressional oversight.

At the height of Mansfield's renewed campaign in January 1956, he proposed an alternative to the joint committee: a President's Board of Consultants on Foreign Intelligence Activities.

The Mansfield and Eisenhower initiatives sparked a report from the British embassy in Washington on the 'US Intelligence System'. Unlike American inquiries into British practices, this did not look for lessons that might be applied at home. The report was functional in a different way— how would the proposed changes affect Anglo-American intelligence cooperation? The report and the Foreign Office officials who studied it were very much against the idea of congressional oversight.

The embassy report was marked 'guard', meaning it had to be kept from American eyes. In the event of congressional oversight it anticipated what 'would be a grave loss', 'the termination or curtailment of the present intimate cooperation with the CIA'.

However, there were better tidings from 'our friends'. The feeling over in the CIA was that Eisenhower would opt for a board of consultants. Even this could be bad news. The former ambassador Joseph Kennedy might be on the board and he was unfriendly to the UK. But at least, in the report's paraphrase of the CIA viewpoint, the board might 'be of assistance as a defence against unwarranted criticism'.

In sum, the masters of MI6 equated even a modest initiative in open government with a loss of bilateral trust. They need not have worried in the short term, as behind the scenes lobbyists picked off Mansfield's supporters one by one, and he lost the Senate vote by the decisive margin of 59 votes to 27. But the potential for friction over oversight arrangements was evident, and would arise more urgently in the future.[16]

At this point, the Berlin tunnel operation was about to become another flashpoint in Anglo-American intelligence disquietude, though it should really be regarded as evidence of successful cooperation. The scheme originated in the mid-1950s. The West needed to know about Soviet military capabilities and intentions. However, as the totalitarian grip tightened in the strategic area of East Germany, MI6's assets there began to fade, and West Germany's spies in the same region were unreliable. The UK and USA decided on a joint venture. As with the Iranian operation, this indicated a return of Anglo-American trust in the aftermath of the Burgess and Maclean revelations.

MI6 and CIA dug a 1,000-yard tunnel from the American sector of West Berlin under the boundary with communist East Berlin. It terminated

under its target, a Soviet military communications post. The idea was to bug
this post. The tunnel was ready by February 1955. It was deep down to
avoid vibration detection, and air-conditioned to stop the snow melting
above it in a manner that would betray its presence. Six hundred tape
recorders using 800 reels a day now tapped 295 Soviet communication lines.

Teams of analysts and translators in London and Washington struggled to
keep up with the output. They passed to their political masters information
about the Red Army's capabilities. It emerged, for example, that the rail
system in communist East Germany was too inefficient to sustain a full-scale
military invasion of the West. Another crucial message derived from what
did not emerge: there was no evidence of a Soviet intention to commence
hostilities with the West. Put together with information from other sources
such as overhead flights by America's U-2 spyplanes that monitored missile-
testing sites, such data calmed US and British leaders, made them sceptical of
inflated threat estimates by their own military, and dissuaded them from
overreacting to the Moscow challenge. The Foreign Office was delighted
with the results, and Allen Dulles, CIA director at the time, remembered
the Berlin tunnel episode as 'one of the most valuable and daring [intelli-
gence] projects ever undertaken'.[17]

It is important to note that the project had a double denouement. First, it
turned out that the Soviet intelligence agency, the KGB, had yet another
agent within MI6. A gifted linguist of Egyptian-Jewish ancestry, George
Blake had fallen into the hands of the North Korean communists during the
Korean War. It was when a prisoner of the communists that he decided to
become a double agent. Because of Blake, the KGB knew about the tunnel
before it was even started.

In April 1956 the communist authorities announced the tunnel to the
world. They excavated the bugging terminus and turned it into a tourist
attraction. There was an even more embarrassing sequel. The British
rumbled Blake and he received a 42-year prison sentence after a secret
trial in 1961—but five years later he escaped from London's Wormwood
Scrubs prison and turned up in Russia.

In the West, a wail of despair issued from those commenting on the affair.
The assumption now was that the KGB had regulated the flow of tapped
messages, mixing trivia with disinformation. Perhaps all that reassurance was
make-believe, and Soviet intentions were menacing after all.[18]

But in the 1990s the arrival of détente heralded Stage 2 of the double
denouement. A puzzling aspect of the case had always been that the

communist authorities had waited until April 1956 before revealing the tunnel plot. Looking back at the episode and freed of the obligations of secrecy, KGB veterans now reminisced that even with the assistance of Blake's sketch it had taken some time to find the tunnel. However, there was a more important reason for the delay in disclosure. KGB did not want to sabotage the MI6–CIA operation. They may well have refrained from issuing disinformation. For they realized that western analysts might spot disinformation and look for a reason for it, leading them to suspect the KGB's asset, Blake. Additionally, they were pleased that the West would learn from an impeccable source that the Soviets had neither the where-withal nor the will to launch an attack through Germany. The KGB wanted to keep the peace, and may well have refrained from tipping off the Red Army about the tunnel's existence until they had to, for fear that the military might insist on conveying disinformation that would not only expose Blake, but also provoke the West.[19]

The Suez crisis followed on the heels of the tunnel exposure, and was a low point, perhaps the nadir, in the post-war diplomatic relationship be-tween the United States and Britain. The Egyptian leader Gamal Nasser wanted to rejuvenate his nation by constructing an additional dam across the river Nile, near Aswan. Once constructed in the 1960s, it would create a 200-mile long lake, improve flood control and irrigation, supply hydroelec-tricity, and contribute to the development of the Egyptian economy—rather like the Tennessee Valley Authority in 1930s America. In the 1950s Britain and America at first promised to finance the project. But Nasser flirted with the communist world. US cotton growers lobbied against a project that would result in competition from the newly irrigated plains of the Nile valley. Secretary of State John Foster Dulles withdrew his country's offer.

Nasser's response on 26 July 1956 was to nationalize the Suez Canal Company. Tolls paid by ships passing from the Red Sea to the Mediterra-nean had hitherto enriched British and French stockholders. Now, they would pay for the Aswan Dam. The scene was set for one of the great follies of British political leadership, and for an Anglo-American falling out with potential intelligence repercussions.

In spite of their miscalculation over the Aswan Dam, the Americans by and large recognized that Nasser was a symbol of the wave of post-colonial nationalism sweeping through the Arab world. Like the British they would have preferred to get rid of him, but there was at least some appreciation of the fact that he was not really a communist, but rather was playing the West against the East in order to get the best deal for his country. Kermit Roosevelt understood that, and when Nasser purchased Soviet weapons in 1955, it was Roosevelt who in a meeting at Nasser's home suggested the face-saving subterfuge of saying the arms came from Czechoslovakia.

According to one version of this event, the British ambassador Humphrey Trevelyan arrived in the middle of the conversation, and Roosevelt and his companion Miles Copeland hid upstairs while Trevelyan delivered London's unbending message—do not buy from Moscow. For the British view had atrophied. Compared with the CIA, MI6 was behind the game, relying for information on sources linked to the old royalist regime who portrayed Nasser in totalitarian hues. Prime Minister Anthony Eden needed little prompting. He equated Nasser with Mussolini, and in the wake of the nationalization of the Suez Canal saw Egypt as a country that should not be appeased. He had favoured the option of assassinating Nasser, but now determined on an alternative course. He authorized a military seizure of the Suez Canal zone to be undertaken jointly with France and Israel. Until it was actually under way, this operation was to be kept secret from the Americans.

Israeli tanks rolled on 29 October. In a flourish of waning imperial power, British paratroops followed. Conscripts whose motives went no further than loyalty to Queen and Country found themselves walking through unknown wadis and shot at by the locals—why did the Egyptians hate them?[20]

President Eisenhower and his colleagues expressed their outrage both privately and in public. They regarded the attack as a public relations disaster for the West. It was an event that had occurred at the wrong moment. For in Hungary, an uprising against Soviet control had begun on 23 October. It was a moment of hope for those who championed self-determination and democracy. But when Soviet forces invaded in strength on 4 November and crushed the Hungarian uprising using tanks, what could the United States and its allies now say? Of course, there were words of condemnation, but they sounded hollow against the background of Anglo-French violations of Egyptian territorial integrity.

Eisenhower was furious for a second reason, too. The Anglo-French-Israeli invasion had been planned and executed in secret, a betrayal of trust between Washington and its allies. The president had cause to be angry with his own intelligence services. Why had they not warned him of what

London and Paris were up to? Surely the USA should be spying on its allies in a more effective manner? More importantly and of special import for public consumption at a time when a presidential election was under way (Americans went to the polls on 6 November), Eisenhower was angry with the British for keeping him in the dark. In a display of power that exposed the toothless condition of the British imperial lion, he threatened to pull the economic rug from under London. In a humiliating climb down, the British, French, and Israelis had to withdraw their forces.

America had squashed its disappointing ally. There was a determination in Washington that Britain would from now on have to toe the line. When John Foster Dulles lay incapacitated by cancer in the Walter Reid Hospital in April 1959, he had a meeting with a small group that included his brother, CIA director Allen Dulles, and Christian Herter who had just taken over from him as secretary of state. The dying man warned that Harold Macmillan, Eden's successor as prime minister, would try to seize the initiative. He insisted, 'our allies must in the end realize that, if we give firm leadership, they will have to accept our positions'.[21]

But the special relationship was not dead. Macmillan, like Churchill half-American by birth, strove to mend fences. With the passing of Dulles and especially with the advent of John F. Kennedy to the White House, he would make better progress. On the intelligence front, in spite of friction and signs that America was the senior partner, the will to cooperate persisted. As events in the 1960s were to show, the Americans even felt they could continue to learn by studying UK intelligence practices.

7

Vietnam, Guyana, *Ramparts*
Trust in Decline

The United States and Great Britain remained tied together in 1960. Each of the powers had something to offer the other, even if the balance was changing. And as ever there was the common language and culture, not to mention the linguistic and cultural laziness that prevented the two English-speaking nations from looking too hard for alternative partners.

At the same time, though, Anglo-American rivalry persisted. It was as evident in the world of spies as in that of diplomats. There was even an American challenge to Britain's dominion in the sphere of spy fiction. CIA director Allen Dulles admired the novels of Ian Fleming and was aware that President Kennedy likewise professed admiration. However, there was a problem. In Fleming's novels the CIA was no more than a stalwart source of support for James Bond. Fleming put MI6 and 007 in the driving seat, with their American counterparts playing bit parts.

The CIA took remedial action. According to E. Howard Hunt, Dulles asked him to be a kind of press officer, responding to a rising tide of enquiries about the CIA's activities that occurred in the Kennedy years. From this, according to Hunt, there arose the effort to challenge the ascendancy of UK spy-fiction writers. He recalled that the CIA's Richard Helms encouraged the idea that 'I write an American counterpart to the popular James Bond series'.

Though an indifferent secret agent who botched more than one operation including the notorious Watergate break-in of 1972, Hunt was a gifted writer, and under the pseudonym David St John he duly wrote a series of novels featuring Peter Ward, America's answer to Bond. Unlike 007 they did not take Hollywood by storm, and in quality they did not match Hunt's own earlier work of fiction, *Bimini Run*. But the circumstances behind their publication are of interest as they indicate, in a trivial yet revealing way, a grievance-driven sense of rivalry.

There were other indications of strain in the special intelligence relationship. The Anglo-American relationship had been based on practical considerations of mutual benefit. Global decline made the UK a less valuable ally and intelligence partner. That decline was undeniable. Demonstrators against western imperialism increasingly focused their ire on Uncle Sam, and sometimes forgot to burn the Union Jack. However, the special relationship had also been evangelical in character. With their empire crumbling in the 1960s, the British built on this rhetorical tradition attempting to give new force to an old myth. They tried to construct a relationship with America that would preserve the illusion of British imperial power.[1]

The intelligence relationship between the UK and the USA persisted, but it was appreciably less special than it had been in the past. Steadily disappearing was the idea that Britain could pass on lessons in imperial governance to its precocious child, America. Going if not yet gone was the idea that there could be some kind of western hegemony jointly and equally administered by the USA and UK. However, if the 1960s were in some ways a turning point, the game was not yet over. The fortunes of bilateral liaison would still fluctuate both ways, up as well as down, and advocates of the very special relationship stuck doggedly to their guns.

In the 1960s, America was visibly undergoing changes that contributed to the widening of the US–UK gulf. The Ivy Leaguers, those self-appointed natural partners of the British elite, began to lose their grip. Eisenhower's Doolittle investigation had revealed mediocrity in the ranks of the CIA. It was an invitation to widen the basis of recruitment. Then came the Bay of Pigs disaster of 1961. The brainchild of Dulles (Princeton) and Richard Bissell (Yale), this was the attempt to get rid of the popular communist dictator Fidel Castro (Havana) by landing a force of CIA-trained 'patriots' on the shores of Cuba. The plan behind the ignominiously defeated adventure reflected a deep flaw in America's covert nation building philosophy. This was the idea that one could impose one's own brand of capitalistic nationalism regardless of the wishes of the local people, and get away with not revealing one's hidden hand. Neither the administration nor its critics learned that particular lesson, but there was plenty of emphasis on tactical failures such as the inability to keep Castro in the dark about the CIA's plot. Dulles and Bissell had enjoyed success in other spheres of intelligence analysis and President Kennedy (Harvard) was as responsible as they were for the Cuban folly, but the two CIA officials had to resign.

It had been part of the folklore of the Anglo-American intelligence world that recruitment took place informally, with reliable faculty chaps connected to the services approaching reliable student chaps in the colleges of Cambridge or Yale Universities or similar in a way that ran counter to public advertising and the problem of assessing the suitability of persons with whose background one was mercifully unfamiliar. The proverbial tap on the shoulder in the senior common room did not cease in the 1960s. In fact, it may have increased, because student protesters angry with the CIA's transgressions prevented the organization from recruiting openly on campus (the practice resumed in the 1980s). Nevertheless, new attitudes were developing about recruitment criteria.

Already by the time of President Johnson's election in 1964 CIA leaders were less likely to be Ivy Leaguers, and were increasingly technocrats rather than HUMINT enthusiasts. In that election year, the sociologist Digby Baltzell famously announced the demise of what he termed the White Anglo-Saxon Protestant (WASP) establishment. The change reflected a broader demographic and geographic drift in American society, away from the 'Anglo-Saxon' dominated north-east towards the south-west and 'sunshine belt' with their Hispanic and Asian immigrants. British intelligence leaders continued to insist they had rapport with their American counterparts, but their school ties were beginning to look threadbare and their complexions were doomed, in the coming years, to look out of place.

The world was still in the midst of an Anglo-American imperium. But it was a bit like the England test cricket team. Officially, it was the team of the England and Wales Cricket Board and players from the Welsh county, Glamorgan, sometimes made it into the team. In the eyes of the world, though, it was an England team. Just so, the Anglo-American intelligence consortium was really the CIA with occasional helpers. Nevertheless, as we shall see, British intelligence continued to make notable contributions, both to the joint successes and to the joint failures. Britain was in decline but not absolutely; the special intelligence relationship was in decline but far from extinct; both declines descended in a fluctuating curve, not in a sudden and terminal drop.

In the case of Vietnam, at least some influential Americans were still prepared to learn intelligence lessons from the British. The context was controversial. George McGee, newly promoted to the third most senior post in the Department of State in 1961, opposed direct US military intervention to prop up the anti-communist government in Saigon. At the request of National Security Affairs Adviser McGeorge Bundy and with the help of America's leading counterinsurgency expert Edward G. Lansdale, he prepared a memorandum drawing largely on British experience, a memorandum that challenged direct intervention, and pointed to a different way.

McGee noted the success of certain previous British and American campaigns. He pointed to the UK–US counterinsurgency efforts in Greece, the clandestine anti-communist assistance given effectively by Americans in the Philippines, and the British triumph in halting the march of communism in Malaya. He did warn that South Vietnam, with its long boundaries with communist North Vietnam, Laos, and Cambodia, was a different proposition:

> ...no one of these campaigns is directly comparable to the situation in Vietnam. In Malaya and the Philippines, there was no active contiguous sanctuary from which manpower and supplies could be furnished. The gradual closing off of the Yugoslav sanctuary from late 1947 [had a similar effect in Greece]...Malaya was unique in that a colonial power (the UK) was involved; the campaign was against an ethnic minority (the Chinese); and the tactics of the Chinese guerrillas were more terrorist than guerrilla.[2]

The Americans nevertheless enlisted British advice based on the recent Malayan 'Emergency'. To the dismay of Labour Members of Parliament who felt there should have been democratic consultation, the Conservative administration of Harold Macmillan had in July 1961 established the British Advisory Mission in Saigon. It was a bilateral initiative of the South Vietnamese and British governments, and this did not universally enhance its appeal in American circles. Nevertheless, its purpose, to draw on the Malayan experience to advise the regime of President Ngo Dinh Diem on how to crush the communist insurgency, seemed promising.

The mission's senior member was Robert G. K. Thompson. Thompson had attended a public school, Marlborough College, and was a 1930s history graduate of Cambridge University. As a senior colonial administrator and ultimately secretary of defence in Malaya, he had been associated with the strategic hamlets strategy—basically, the British put non-communist loyalists into fortified villages, looked after them well, and aimed to kill everyone else.[3]

After an initial chat with Diem and a trip to England to buy some acres on Exmoor, Thompson embarked for Vietnam. He travelled via Washington. At the White House, he parleyed with General Maxwell D. Taylor and National Security Adviser Walt Rostow. He had drinks with MI6's liaison man in Washington Maurice Oldfield, and with the CIA's Far Eastern chief, Desmond Fitzgerald: 'We devised names for each other so that we could talk more freely on the phone. Desmond was Sanders, I was Carruthers.'[4]

Thompson's contribution was a cautionary tale, however. 'Fritz' Nolting, the US ambassador in Saigon, was a Diem devotee, but took umbrage at the Vietnamese president's bypassing of the US diplomatic channels to deal directly with Thompson. He reported, 'Thompson mission is badly off rails from standpoint US'. Thompson had outlined a draft plan for Diem without consulting the Americans. He also advised Diem on military matters in spite of a promise, as Nolting understood it, to 'limit himself to intelligence and civil aspects of counterinsurgency effort'.[5]

Thompson overcame this distrust, and would be an adviser to Presidents Kennedy, Johnson, and Nixon. He was second only to Lansdale as an advocate of the 'hearts and minds' approach to counterinsurgency. However, his plans would suffer the same fate as those of his American counterpart—they could not hope to succeed, once the United States embarked on full-scale military actions causing widespread civilian casualties and discontent.

Thompson's star was at its brightest in the period before the United States resorted to shelling and bombing. He explained his approach to the sympathetic General Taylor. Author of the 'flexible response' doctrine that had so impressed President Kennedy, Taylor, while not shy of taking conventional military action, appreciated that Thompson was offering America another option. Thompson met the general in October 1961 and later impressed on him the 'striking' similarities between Vietnam and Malaya. The Mekong Delta, he thought, was an area where intelligence could be used to separate loyalists from insurgents. Having disposed of the latter, 'social and economic improvements which make an impact at the village level' would cement loyalty, and then the offensive could be broadened into other parts of South Vietnam. In March 1962, Thompson's plan for the Mekong Delta won approval. In July, the CIA reported the establishment of 2,000 strategic hamlets not just there but in other areas of South Vietnam, and announced plans for 7,000 more.[6]

No doubt because of Thompson's presence and advice, Malaya became a fixture in policy-makers' minds. US Secretary of Defense Robert S. McNamara was one person thus affected. In August 1962, he wrote to President Kennedy recommending a policy of food-denial to impair the activities of communist insurgents in the eastern province of Phu Yen. The number-crunching defence tsar reckoned a 'single helicopter can spray one acre [of crops] in about five seconds with very effective defoliant chemicals'. There might potentially be 'psychological' repercussions with the Viet Cong making a propaganda issue of starvation, but it was not really a problem because the local population, the montagnards, had already been resettled into secured areas. The region could be saved for freedom by making sure nobody else lived there. 'This would be the first trial of both the strategic hamlet concept and the complemental food-denial operations since the successful campaign in Malaya.'[7]

With the passage of time, it must have seemed increasingly unlikely that the counterinsurgency programme would work. Nevertheless, Thompson reported in March 1963 that 5,000 strategic hamlets had been established, that progress had been 'impressive', and that government forces were gaining the upper hand. He agreed with what President Diem had told him, that 'we are on the right track' and that 'the end might come quicker than many people forecast'.[8]

Less than six months later, Diem was dead, assassinated by South Vietnamese officers who acted in the knowledge that the new US ambassador, Henry Cabot Lodge Jr, considered him ineffective and wanted him removed. In reality the South Vietnamese president was perhaps more of a realist than some of his American advisers. He had incurred the ambassador's disapproval by making peace overtures to the communists. In reaction to the removal of his original sponsor, Thompson bent with the wind, or at least pretended to. On the day following Diem's death, Lodge cabled Washington: 'Thompson, British advisory mission, told me this morning that "If the generals stay together, the coup should help very much to win the war".'[9]

Thompson was straining to appear supportive of American policy. He acted against the background of Prime Minister Harold Macmillan's cultivation of a strong UK–US relationship, a relationship enhanced by the personal friendship between David Ormsby-Gore, the British ambassador from 1961 to 1965, and President Kennedy. But unsettling events were to happen in quick succession. Shortly before Diem's death, Macmillan resigned for reasons of ill health. Less than three weeks after the murder of the South Vietnamese leader, President Kennedy fell victim to an assassin's bullet. These happenings contributed to a progressive destabilization of the UK–US intelligence relationship.

British tuition failed to produce a successful outcome in Vietnam. This was at least partly because British lessons were improperly applied—bombing alienated the very people America was trying to win over. But the poor outcome did nothing to reinforce faith in the British. The apparent British fallibility preyed on the minds of those in Washington who were already having doubts about the US–UK relationship.

The Vietnam War would in fact become an increasing source of awkwardness in Anglo-American diplomacy. At a time when the United States needed foreign friends, the government of Harold Wilson, Labour prime minister from 1964 to 1970, remained annoyingly neutral regarding the conflict. As Wilson was asking the USA to make available some of its war-drained resources to prop up the weak pound, the UK's neutrality obliged it to make humiliating concessions elsewhere.

This happened in British Guiana. That nation (known as Guyana after independence in 1966) had a population of only 600,000. This is one reason why the story of the South American colony's transition to statehood has until recently not featured prominently in accounts of US diplomatic history—indeed the Guyana entry in one respected foreign policy encyclopaedia of 1997 reads '*See* Appendix 2', and there the tabular entry consists of just one line.

A more significant reason for British Guiana's erstwhile obscurity was the CIA's success in concealing what happened. The historian Stephen Rabe notes that the CIA systematically destroyed the documentation on what went on in Guyana, an indication in itself of the weight the Kennedy and Johnson administrations attached to that small nation. A recent study of the emergence of independent Guyana tells the story without even mentioning the CIA.[10]

The history of a country is always more than the story of a particular personality. But politicians in both London and Washington were so obsessed with Cheddi Jagan that it is helpful to explain Guyana's destiny with reference to that one man's career. The son of an overseer on a sugar plantation and the eldest of eleven children, Jagan became a promising student, debater, and cricketer. He moved to the United States to study at Howard University then at Northwestern, where he qualified as a dentist.

In Chicago, he met Janet Rosenberg, whose father threatened to shoot Cheddi Jagan on sight on the mistaken assumption that he was leading his daughter astray—Janet was already a left-wing political activist in her own right. Back home with his new wife, Cheddi Jagan founded the colony's first democratic political movement, the People's Progressive Party. When the British introduced home rule in 1953, the 35-year-old won election to the post of first minister. Like his wife, Jagan was a declared socialist. Prime Minister Churchill was sceptical of the Colonial Office's view that Jagan was a communist, but nevertheless sent in troops to depose him.

This did not have the desired effect. With the approach of independence, Cheddi Jagan continued to enjoy popularity with the Guyanan people, especially the majority who were descendants of indentured labourers imported from India—the 'East Indians'. In 1961, he was once again elected chief minister, a post he would hold for three years in the run-up to the pre-independence elections of 1964. His victories in one election after another rang alarm bells for the Kennedy administration, which had just suffered the humiliation of Fidel Castro's defeat of the CIA-led invasion of Cuba. Anti-British protests, including some serious unrest in February 1962 that caught the Americans by surprise, seemed to augur dangerous possibilities.

With the advantage of hindsight, it is plain that British Guiana was an unlikely Trojan horse for communism in Latin America. It was not only a small country, but also isolated within Hispanic South America in being an English-speaking one. However, Jagan openly admired the leadership of Fidel Castro, and like so many emergent nationalists talked of doing deals with the Soviet Union. President Kennedy and his advisers had nightmares about a second Cuba. The situation in British Guiana made them fear, in Attorney General Robert Kennedy's words, for the 'future of South America'.[11]

The Kennedy administration backed a rival political candidate. Forbes Burnham became America's man. He was a member of the smaller but still sizeable group of Guyanians who were of African descent, and enjoyed the support of African Americans in the United States. Burnham, too, was a socialist. Also, he was much less of a democrat and more of a racist than Jagan. But the Kennedys calculated that he was ambitious, and willing to comply with American wishes in order to gain power.

The Kennedy administration tasked the CIA to destabilize the premiership of Jagan in order to improve Burnham's prospects for success in the pre-independence election of 1964. At the agency's instigation, the

American Federation of Labor paid for a succession of strikes that undermined Guyana's economy. There was a campaign of disinformation about Mr and Mrs Jagan and about their marital relations, the drift of which was that Janet was a brainy libertine who controlled her emasculated husband. Opposition parties received covertly channelled CIA funds. The CIA poisoned Indian–African relations, and race riots followed with between 100 and 200 killed. All this gave the impression that the Jagan government was weak. America furthermore insisted on a system of proportional representation (PR). This was an arrangement eschewed at home by both the UK and USA, but it would enhance Burnham's prospects in the 1964 election.[12]

With the decolonization of the British Empire proceeding apace in the mid-1960s, one colonial governor after another was packing his bags to go home. Soon, Georgetown would be the capital of a fully independent Guyana. Against this background, the Johnson administration formed in the wake of Kennedy's death lost little time in seeking British support to prevent communists from exploiting the post-imperial scene. In December 1963 Secretary of State Dean Rusk travelled to Europe to press the American viewpoint on Colonial Secretary Duncan Sandys.

The colonial secretary had taken on board Macmillan's dictum that the Anglo-American alliance was more important than the fate of British Guiana, and gave Rusk an encouraging audience. The US secretary of state also met with the rather more recalcitrant defence secretary, R. A. ('Rab') Butler, and with Macmillan's successor as prime minister, Sir Alec Douglas-Home. Rusk's briefing paper indicated that the Macmillan–Kennedy accord would continue, and stated that President Johnson felt as strongly as Kennedy 'that we cannot have another communist state in the Western Hemisphere'.[13]

Rusk's position paper for Johnson when the president received Prime Minister Douglas-Home in Washington was even firmer. Passages in the paper that might have referred to the covert actions under way or being contemplated are still redacted. However, the rump of the document shows how LBJ would continue JFK's policy, insisting that there was 'a grave risk of Jagan's establishing a Castro-type regime should he attain independence'. Contrary to its publicly professed faith in self-determination, the US president would urge Britain to retain control over the colony, especially in regard to security matters. Rusk anticipated that Douglas-Home would want to continue the 'Macmillan/Kennedy understanding'. But he hinted at a rift. He feared that the prime minister would 'question the feasibility of a resumption of direct UK rule unless the grounds can be publicly shown to be fully justified'.[14]

The British did not want to cross a certain line. They were prepared to manipulate the democratic process to prevent Jagan from becoming the first premier of independent Guyana, and MI6 worked towards that end. But they resisted American pressure in that they refused to re-impose direct rule, took a minimalist approach to troop levels, and refrained from postponing the 1964 elections in Guyana. All this meant that the economic chaos and racial violence stirred up by the CIA produced, not just the intended block to class solidarity and socialism, but also a potentially counter-productive impediment to political stability.

A US intelligence memorandum of June 1964 throws further light on the foot-dragging approach of the British to American-style anti-communism. It recorded the success of the governor of British Guiana, Sir Ralph Grey, in persuading Jagan to share power with Burnham as an interim measure in the period leading up to elections. Jagan had been reluctant. He told Grey he would not trust Burnham with any further power: 'You don't know Burnham. He'll cut my throat.'

However, while Grey said he was opposed to 'communist control' in Guyana, he saw coalition as the most that could be achieved. Given the scale of discontent he conceded he might need to ask for more soldiers, but he 'wondered how many troops it would take' to calm the situation, and questioned the wisdom of an open-ended commitment when there was 'no real end in sight'. He was acutely worried about the racial violence. From this report it would appear that Grey either did not know the CIA was helping to foment the disorders or, more likely, was playing the innocent. For he concluded the interview by asking his interlocutor, 'incidentally, who is this Dr Singer of yours? I understand he is someone I should keep an eye on.' He received an evasive reply that promised Singer would exit the country by 16 August.[15]

The Americans remained convinced that an outright victory for Burnham could be achieved. To that end, they attempted to create religious fissures amongst the 'East Indian' ethnic group, playing off Muslims against Hindus. In this particular ploy they failed, for the effect of the prevailing racial violence was to cement the solidarity of Jagan's supporters.

The danger was that disorder, far from discrediting Jagan or causing an advantageous postponement in the election, might run out of control.

American officials tried to pin the violence on 'terrorists'. But it was becoming clear that what they had started might be difficult to stop. For Burnham was potentially unrestrainable. The outcome of a consideration of these issues at a secret Anglo-American meeting in London was to agree on PR with the aim of a coalition between Burnham and a third candidate, Peter D'Aguinar, whose support was small yet might produce an aggregate majority. The United States offered financial sweeteners in the event of a Burnham victory, and Sandys confirmed his approval of the plan at the end of July.[16]

In September 1964, a seven-person group convened in the White House to discuss British Guiana. It included National Security Adviser McGeorge Bundy, and a person whose name is redacted from the record. The meeting heard from Delmar Carlson. He was the US consul general in Georgetown, by now as influential a figure in the colony as its British governor. Carlson was worried that chaotic local conditions might force Burnham to accept a coalition government that included Jagan. Another problem was that Burnham was becoming less attractive by the day. He played the tactic of twisting the lion's tail, and the governor hated him—not a promising circumstance given US hopes for British backing for Burnham. He was a 'racist and probably anti-white' (not, after all, a charge that could be levelled against Jagan, who was married—happily, as it turned out—to a white woman from Chicago). Carlson damned Burnham with faint praise: the aspiring leader promised not to recognize the Soviet Union and to 'have nothing to do with Cuba' but only 'so long as he can find other people to buy British Guiana's rice'.[17]

A complication now occurred on the other side of the Atlantic. Douglas-Home's Conservative government was faltering, and it looked as if there might be a Labour administration headed by Harold Wilson. The US ambassador to the UK, David Bruce (the OSS London veteran), reported on the possible new scenario. Wilson, he thought, would toe the line. On 16 October 1964, the hypothetical became real. Wilson won a slender majority in the House of Commons and became prime minister—a result that would have been distinctly less probable under PR. Richard Helms, a senior CIA officer who had a watching brief on British Guiana and who had overseen liaison with MI6 in that country, now reported polls indicating that Burnham was likely to win under the PR system imposed on the colony. He was nervous about how Guyanians would react to that event, but noted with satisfaction that the new Labour government had moved two additional battalions into the Caribbean 'ostensibly on manoeuvres'. These soldiers could be deployed to Georgetown at short notice. Against this background, Burnham succeeded in the elections, and became Guyana's prime minister in waiting.[18]

America continued to back Burnham after the election, seeking to ensure that he remained in charge of a stable country in the period running through independence. The British tagged along. Pride-swallowing in silence was the order of the day.

Silence was not absolutely achieved, though. The CIA destroyed its records and Washington could usually be trusted to keep intelligence operations under wraps especially if they involved liaison. However, at the height of the 1970s investigations into the CIA, the State Department declassified one of its own memoranda indicating what the UK government had concealed from its own people and those of Guyana. It revealed the hand of Sir Patrick Dean, who had succeeded Ormsby Gore as British ambassador in Washington. Dean expressed the wish that 'the close cooperation now existing between our intelligence services will be continued'. He let it be known that the British agreed 'to authorize continued covert assistance to the anti-Jagan parties in British Guiana'. This revelation about British compliance and MI6 complicity occurred at a time when the world outside Guyana had developed other preoccupations, and the news caused not a ripple in the West.[19]

In the 1960s, Washington had been in a state of acute worry. Its officials feared that the contraction of the British Empire would mean an expansion of communism. A State Department briefing paper sent to Far Eastern embassies noted the problems of the UK economy, and the desire of the Wilson government to reduce defence spending at a faster rate than that previously contemplated by the Tories. Far from being in a position to help the USA in Vietnam, the Labour government wanted to withdraw militarily from east of Suez. Washington sent London a blunt message: it would support the pound sterling only if London promised not to reduce 'defense commitments without full consultation'. A surviving CIA report on British Guiana similarly put British policy into a wider context: the colony had been a drain on UK resources and London would not agree to postpone independence; to prevent a dangerous collapse of authority there and throughout the British West Indies, London might provide military cover on a temporary basis, but not much more could be hoped for.[20]

In the event, with Anglo-American help and because of his own ruthless tactics, Burnham remained in office. He consolidated his grip on power by fixing elections, trampling on civil liberties, manipulating, and in the process ruining, the economy, and excluding from representation the 65 per cent of the population not of African descent. He ran Guyana until 1980, and free elections did not take place there until 1992. His success reflected the operational effectiveness of US–UK intelligence cooperation in the 1960s even against the background of differing diplomatic priorities in Washington and London. At the same time, the wisdom of the operations was questionable. The US journalist Thomas B. Morgan estimated in his 1967 book *The Anti-Americans* that, even when the USA was suffering propaganda reverses over Vietnam, the CIA was the single greatest cause of America's worldwide unpopularity. Short-term UK–US covert operational triumphs did not augur well for a long-term successful relationship.[21]

US fears of Jeddi Jagan had been groundless. In the 1990s, Jagan would serve as president of Guyana and enjoy cordial relations with the administrations of George Bush senior and Bill Clinton. Soon afterwards, Janet Jagan served as prime minister then president—the first US woman to be in charge of any country. No doubt they had both mellowed by then. Yet they were never in the first place the ogres that the Americans made them out to be. The British had come to realize this by the 1960s but had been held over a barrel—not the best posture from which to conduct a trusting special relationship.

And there were other strains in the relationship. The renegade MI5 officer Peter Wright wrote in his memoir *Spycatcher* (1987) that the American intelligence services did not like Wilson's government because it was of the left and wanted defence cuts. According to Wright's personal recollection, CIA counterintelligence chief Angleton was one of those who thought British counterintelligence in general and MI5 in particular were shambolic and insecure.[22]

One reason why the US intelligence community took a critical look at its British cousin was that it was itself under the microscope. It therefore had to ask, anew, if there was something it could learn from the UK—or whether, on the contrary, the UK was below par and not to be wholly trusted.

It was not his forte, but President Johnson could see that there were shortcomings in the foreign intelligence he was receiving. This is evident from his retrospective interest in the immediate cause of direct US involvement in Vietnam, the Tonkin Gulf incidents. An impossible-to-verify story about communist torpedo-boat attacks on US spy ships cruising off the coast of North Vietnam had led Congress to adopt the Gulf of Tonkin resolution of 7 August 1964. On the face if it, this resolution was convenient for Johnson, as it gave him a mandate to use as much force in Vietnam as he wanted to.

In reality, it is questionable whether Johnson wanted a war that would drain America's economy and ruin his plans for social-reform expenditure, his 'Great Society'. A further episode in the Gulf suggests that, far from welcoming an excuse for war, he entertained doubts about Tonkin. On 18 September 1964 US surveillance ships once again reported they had come under fire, with the true sequence of events again obscure. This time Clark Clifford, the chairman of the President's Foreign Intelligence Advisory Board (PFIAB), led an inquiry into why the American intelligence apparatus seemed unable to explain—even at the second time of asking—what was going on in an area of vital importance to national security. Clifford's report for the president was a devastating indictment of intelligence inadequacies. The PFIAB's J. Patrick Coyne sent a copy of the report to Bundy, with a handwritten note saying, 'Because of the President's interest in the subject, you may wish to mention the highlights of the enclosed report to him'.[23]

This background suggests American questions regarding British intelligence were part of a broader concern. According to Wright, the president asked for a PFIAB 'review of British security'. He recalled that the task fell to Gordon Gray, formerly President Eisenhower's national security adviser, and his PFIAB colleague 'Gerald' Coyne (presumably Wright meant *Patrick* Coyne). Wright's MI5 duties meant he learned at first hand of a visit made to the UK in 1965 by Gray and Coyne, who were able to exploit the access to personnel and resources due to them on account of special relationship privileges. They turned in a 'devastating critique' of MI5 and of its leadership, and reported that British counterintelligence was under funded and badly organized.

For reasons that are easy to guess at, archivists and officials on both sides of the Atlantic remain reticent about the Gray–Coyne investigation. In the absence of corroborative evidence, Wright's account needs to be treated with caution. Because of his estrangement from MI5 and because he wanted to promote his book, he engaged in hyperbole. His assertion that Angleton was 'thrilled by the report' and saw an opportunity for 'the CIA to swallow MI5 up whole' can be taken with a dose of salt.[24]

Once having made these qualifications, though, one must allow that the Americans were unhappy about the low level of British security competence. Peter Jessup, a veteran CIA analyst now working as a staffer for the National Security Council, reflected US concerns in a memorandum for Walt Rostow. The memo was about George Blake's escape from prison in 1966. The escape 'raises some serious questions about the [word(s) redacted] security fabric of the UK today and points up the disastrously porous nature of their overall security'.

The British were too complacent about their own people, were wrong not to have actively vetted Blake on his return from North Korea, and needed to realize you have to 'sacrifice' some 'personal freedoms' if 'you are going to determinedly protect a security service in a free society'. The Wilson government appointed a commission under Earl Mountbatten (uncle-in-law to the queen) to look into prison security, and Jessup thought that might help 'the Wilson regime to weather this flap'. His idea that the British government might fall because of laxity in the security services was far fetched, but it did indicate the weight certain Americans placed on the issue.[25]

Presidential expressions of concern about the quality of US intelligence continued independently of these British worries—the PFIAB's Coyne in January 1967 reiterated the perennial anxiety about poor integration. Reciprocally and simultaneously, the British were critical of both their own set-up and the Americans'. Britain had been caught unawares by recent events in Rhodesia, and would again be surprised by the 1968 Soviet invasion of Czechoslovakia and later by a string of further crises—the Douglas Nicoll JIC-commissioned report of 1982 listed them. No intelligence organization can foretell all events and there were successes one tended not to hear about, but there was sufficient concern to prompt demands for reform.

In March 1967, British Cabinet Secretary Burke Trend produced the first of three reports on British intelligence organization. He noted that the CIA thought the British were superficial in their approach to analysis: 'This is what the Americans really mean when they accuse us—as they always do—of not being sufficiently "professional" in our attitude to intelligence.' Though CIA boosters had so admired British intelligence coordination, Trend thought it was deficient. His reports persuaded the Wilson government to create a new intelligence coordination post within the Cabinet Office.

Trend offered the reflection that Americans, obsessed with professional-izing intelligence estimates to keep them free of political influence, had got it wrong. He rejected the idea that in imitation of the USA the Foreign Office's (political) role in the JIC should be reduced. It was precisely the Americans' divorce of intelligence from politics that had brought about the Bay of Pigs mistake (he must have had in mind the failure to consider Cuban politics and the popularity of Castro before embarking on the venture; deeper reflection might have prompted Trend to consider Presi-dent Kennedy's political motive in authorizing the mission).[26]

It would be an overstatement to say that by early 1967 there was no love lost between the British and American intelligence communities. It was just that they were not lost in mutual admiration. Yet at this point, the CIA suffered another great embarrassment that caused American officials once again to turn to the British system for possible guidance.

In February 1967, the *New York Times* and *Washington Post* ran a full-page advertisement for the next issue of the West Coast quarterly magazine *Ramparts*. This was a publication that enjoyed quite a short life (1962–75), yet in its heyday performed a significant muckraking function. The adver-tised issue exposed the CIA's illegal financing of the National Students Association (NSA).

Over the years, the agency had secretly paid US student leaders to attend international conferences putting the anti-communist point of view, and had used them also to spy on their fellows. As the scandal developed, it became clear that the NSA was not the only American voluntary organiza-tion that had received covert funds in this way. In what the *Washington Post* called an act of 'moral imbecility', the American Newspaper Guild had accepted secret funding. The National Education Foundation, to which 983,000 American teachers belonged, had also received funds through a charitable foundation that was a CIA front. There were hundreds of other examples of private organizations that had, knowingly or otherwise, been conduits for clandestine dollars and purveyors of laundered information. In these ways, the CIA had contravened the congressional intention, based on civil liberties fears, that it should not operate at home.[27]

The *Ramparts* exposé revealed the scale of the CIA's covert activities, and showed that they had taken place in friendly, democratic nations as well as in communist or otherwise hostile countries. Britain was no exception. There, the agency had funded *Encounter*, a leading literary journal of the non-communist left. Subsequent research by Hugh Wilford has shown that the CIA also intervened quite substantially, though with indifferent success, to try to shape thinking in the Labour Party.[28]

At home in the United States, the CIA's actions provoked what Wilford terms 'universal political condemnation'. By suborning students, teachers, and the press, and by being caught in the act, the CIA had inadvertently signalled that America could not be trusted to uphold truth and free speech.[29]

There was a reaction abroad. Chester Bowles complained that the revelations 'hurt us throughout the world', especially in the nation where he was currently the US ambassador, India. In some places, the exposé merely confirmed previous expectations—a Cairo radio journalist remarked that the story added 'nothing to what we already know', and all it showed was that small countries had to be 'vigilant and keep watch on imperialist machinations'. In Europe, there was condemnation leavened by cynicism. The *Manchester Guardian* saw secrecy as the problem and wondered why students could not have been openly financed through an institution like the British Council (founded in 1934 and operating in eighty countries, the British Council dispensed around $30 million annually in cultural funds).

The English journalist Malcolm Muggeridge thought that subsidizing *Encounter* was a waste of money. He claimed that nobody was surprised at what the CIA was doing, whether they lived in France, Italy, or West Germany.

So the reactions were mixed. But it had now become evident to all that American emissaries could not be trusted to be what they said they were. As for the denizens of the espionage world, there was another take on trust. The CIA may not have been 'porous' in the sense of being penetrated, but neither could it be trusted to keep its secrets out of the press.[30]

The *Ramparts* affair was significant in still further ways. First, it was a preliminary step in the direction of greater openness in society. America would take the lead here in the 1970s, and Britain followed suit. Second, it gave rise to a specific US rejection of the British way of managing overseas propaganda.

Renewed American interest in British methods arose from the Johnson administration's need to assuage public outrage over the *Ramparts* disclosures. Here, a succession of stratagems yielded indifferent results. The CIA looked for dirt on *Ramparts* personnel, but the editors were liberal Catholics who reflected nothing more toxic than the culture of the San Francisco Bay area. CIA plans to organize an advertisers' boycott and to plant disinformation about *Ramparts* in the American press came to nothing. The White House tried the 'flashback' technique, pointing out that Johnson's three predecessors in the White House had all authorized secret subsidies. Helms later recalled that this plan did inhibit congressional probes, yet it was not enough. The administration felt obliged to set up two formal inquiries into the affair, the first chaired by Undersecretary of State Nicholas de B. Katzenbach, and the second by Secretary of State Dean Rusk. It was in the course of these investigations that American officials reviewed British practices.[31]

The Foreign Office's Information Research Department (IRD) carried out work that was quite close to some of the CIA's activities and had already attracted American attention. Established in January 1948 a full six months before the CIA's 'psychological operations' got under way, the IRD was at first intended to spearhead a British-led 'Third Way', an alternative to the Soviet and US duopoly. It was ultra secret, and destroyed its own records. It soon became clear that Britain did not have the means to pursue such an independent course, and the IRD then followed Anglo-American aims. It used 'grey' (misleading) and later 'black' (mendacious) 'publicity' (propaganda) against international communism. An early relatively benign example would be the translation into several languages of the anti-totalitarian works of George Orwell. There were, for example, high expectations for the efficacy of the Arabic translation of *Animal Farm*, as Muslims consider pigs to be unclean. Orwell was one of a number of democratic socialists who discreetly supported the programme as a means of opposing communism— it was Britain's own 'opening to the left'.[32]

The Americans knew about IRD and were aware it was something that could not be mentioned in public without breaching the secrecy protocols of Anglo-American intelligence liaison. In a move that foreshadowed the PFIAB's look at MI5, the CIA had in 1965 commissioned an inquiry into IRD's activities and structure. C. F. R. 'Kit' Barclay, the head of IRD, welcomed delegations from both the agency and INR, the State Department's intelligence unit. The CIA's Murray G. Lawson compiled the report on IRD and other British propaganda efforts and his colleague Oren Stephens distributed it to officials in the National Security Council, FBI, INR, and CIA.

The Lawson report reviewed British covert propagandists' use of the BBC, movies, television, the UK and worldwide press, the British Council, and 'covertly-owned' publishers like Ampersand and The Bodley Head.

Lawson noted that W. M. Barker, the head of IRD, had just completed a year's study at Harvard University's Institute for International Affairs, and that IRD might superficially resemble INR or his own propaganda unit in the CIA. But it was in reality a more hard-nosed anti-communist outfit. It enjoyed greater independence from the Foreign Office than INR did from the State Department, had more extensive publishing programmes, and ran 'International Front Organizations'.[33]

The IRD model would have been political dynamite in 1967 in being too close in its methods to the practices *Ramparts* exposed. Rather than dwell on IRD, the Department of State looked at other alternatives. Charles Frankel prepared a report outlining some options. A philosopher, Frankel was serving as assistant secretary of state in charge of education and culture. Though he was an authority on the advantages of democracy over totalitarianism he was no dogmatic Cold Warrior, and later in the year would resign in protest at US involvement in the Vietnam War.

Frankel tried, within the limited arena of educational affairs, to provide his government with democratic alternatives to the CIA's system of secret subsidies. His first suggested alternative was for State to take over the subsidization of students. It would be costly, as the current help totalled almost nine million dollars. It had the further disadvantage that people might think Foggy Bottom was getting involved with dirty tricks. Frankel's second alternative was the creation of 'an American version of the British Council'. This would have the advantage of 'open control', but might be 'too limited in scope'. His final idea was for 'a semi-autonomous Foundation for International Educational and Cultural Exchange'. Frankel was right to think that the State Department would shrink from immersion in a murky pond, and his third idea was too heavily marked with the fingerprints of his own fiefdom, so by default the British Council proposal was the one that attracted attention.[34]

Helms was a member of Katzenbach's committee, opposed a 'flat ban' on CIA secret subsidies, and demanded 'leeway'. However, the Katzenbach report recommended:

No federal agency shall provide any covert financial assistance or support, direct or indirect, to any of the nation's educational or private voluntary organizations... Where such support has been given, it will be terminated as quickly as possible...

The report envisaged the creation of a new institution to take up the funding slack, giving the British Council as its prime example. But although

1. **Winston Churchill**.
As First Lord of the Admiralty
1911–15, he promoted the
Room 40 codebreaking unit.
He later coined the phrase
'special relationship'.

2. **William Wiseman**.
An MI6 agent, he tied
the Americans into
British secret operations
at a time when the
USA was supposed to
be neutral.

The American Section.

Since my return from Washington the question of continuing to decypher diplomatic telegrams has been raised in various quarters, and I am asked if it is worth the effort, as the co-operation between the various departments of the two countries is now so intimate.

If you and the Foreign Office should decide that such work is unnecessary, I feel that perhaps in view of ultimate peace negotiations when we might wish to know American views fairly accurately, it might well be advisable to keep Miss Curtis as observer of the traffic passing so as to watch all cryptographic developments and where necessary ask the Research Section to investigate new systems which might occur.

When in Washington, I was told that the State Department had had little advice from the War and Navy Departments on the subject of their cyphers, which the two latter departments knew to be insecure but that early in this year the State Department had formed a committee including Friedman, chief adviser in the War Department and Safford of the Navy Department to advise on their cyphers and I therefore anticipate changes before so very long.

I should be grateful for an early ruling on this problem as among other questions, the censors abroad from time to time ask if it is necessary to receive American Government messages and I am inclined to answer in the negative.

A. G. D.

29th September, 1941.

3. Secret diplomacy on Racquet Club stationary. Ned Bell, the author of this letter, exemplified the elitism in Anglo-American intelligence relations.

4. An admission of past practice. Alastair Denniston, head of the Government Code and Cypher School, suggests in September 1941 that there should be a moratorium in British spying on U.S. diplomatic correspondence.

5. **Hector Davies.** Dropped into German-occupied France in 1944, Davies was supposedly part of an SOE-OSS-French team but actually an MI6 officer. He expressed the heretical view that the French were pulling their weight in the war.

6. **Allen Dulles.**
One of the founders of the CIA and its director, 1953–61. He oversaw the sober intelligence estimates of Soviet military capability that contributed to international security in the tense 1950s.

7. **America denies its secrets to the U.K.** This David Low cartoon indicated the fear that Britain would be marginalized now that the USA held the secret of the atom. *London Evening Standard* 29 July 1949.

8. **LBJ leans on PM Wilson.** The body language hints at the nature of the US-UK relationship.

9. **It's Christmas.** The Wilsons and the Johnsons celebrate in 1965. America was bailing out the pound, but demanded a price.

10. **LBJ and Forbes Burnham.** The president used the CIA as well as the almighty dollar to brush aside UK objections to Burnham's installation as the first leader of the former British colony of Guyana.

11. **Philip Agee**. Principled critic and advocate of open government or KGB agent of influence?

12. (*opposite*) **Agee–Hosenball Defence Committee poster**. The campaign prepared the ground for the ABC defence.

13. **ABC Defence poster**. The campaign in support of Crispin Aubrey, John Berry, and Duncan Campbell, 1977–8, helped to check abuses of the Official Secrets Act.

14. **Fingerprint expert**. Europol runs a photo competition for the best crime-fighting image and this French submission was one of the 2011 prizewinners.

15. Wall of shame. In the shabby dwelling beyond, a gang of international sex traffickers imprisoned and abused teenage girls. Europol intelligence operations led to their arrest and prosecution in 2010.

Helms signed the report, he wrote to the president indicating his dissent from it. He told President Johnson that an absolute ban of the type proposed would end the activities of the CIA's propaganda assets Radio Free Europe and Radio Liberty. It would also 'curtail the options available to the Government and its ability to react swiftly in situations which may develop abroad, comparable to the 1962 political crisis [following the February riots] in British Guiana'.[35]

Johnson now established his second inquiry, under Rusk. This time it had the specific duty of recommending alternative funding arrangements. The inquiries had already performed one function, providing the appearance of action being taken while time passed, time in which new issues captured the attention of voters, and in which moral indignation over the CIA's nefarious activities lost its heat. The Rusk committee, made up of heavy-weights from Congress as well as government figures and representatives from corporate America, proceeded in an unhurried manner and did not report until the summer of 1968.

The Rusk inquiry first considered the British Council model. It decided against it. The council seemed uniquely British, and had 'freedom from accountability'. What did that mean? Frankel had referred to the council's 'open control', meaning it was visibly subject to parliamentary and press scrutiny. Instead, the Rusk committee wanted accountability to govern-ment. It favoured a system of 'voluntary organizations' that would receive public subsidies and would have 'obvious governmental responsibilities'.[36]

In the event, America did tread, or rather re-tread, the road of guided voluntarism. The Ford Foundation had already worked hand in hand with the CIA's Paris-based Congress for Cultural Freedom. The foundation and other private agencies now received enhanced federal funds and instructions on what to do with them. Thus, for example, the Salzburg American Studies seminar continued to receive its one million dollar annual subven-tion. It was an arrangement that lasted for a while and then sank into desuetude as the CIA resumed business as usual—a Senate committee in 1976 found that the agency still deployed 'several hundred American academics'. Once again, the US government had considered the example of the mother country. Once again, the United States decided to follow its own path. Guiding the ways of the world was becoming more of an American mission, less Anglo-American.[37]

If the 1960s was framed on one side by the 1950s, a decade when the special relationship survived all mishaps, it was framed on the other side by the 1970s, a period when in some ways intelligence liaison recovered. At the start of the Richard Nixon administration (1969–74), the US government worked towards a strategic arms limitation treaty with the Soviet Union—talks came to fruition in the 'SALT' agreements of 1971 and 1972. Naturally, US intelligence specialists were on high strategic alert to ensure that Soviet negotiators did not pull the wool over the eyes of American negotiators. They passed on certain of their findings to the British, for example information on Soviet anti-submarine capabilities and data that helped improve the accuracy of UK Polaris missiles.

Lord Cromer, newly arrived in 1971 as the UK ambassador in Washington, visited the CIA and NSA and got the charm treatment. He impressed on the Foreign Office his view that 'We are in practice receiving a great deal more valuable knowledge and information than the formal agreements could be interpreted as entitling us to.' In seeming confirmation of this, one British intelligence official looked back at the 1970s and remembered a 'surge' in cooperation. He received the impression that the US intelligence community shared its 'crown jewels' with its cousin across the Atlantic.[38]

Yet in 1973 disaster struck. A premonition came in April 1972, when Secretary of State for Defence Lord Carrington sent a warning to Edward Heath, British prime minister from 1970 to 1974. He noted that the UK's economic straits were limiting military expenditure, and that negotiations were in progress with the French with a view to sharing the burden of developing nuclear defence. However, he now warned that the 'present arrangements . . . aimed at minimum expenditure, have made us dependent on the US' for vital facilities and intelligence, and that they 'effectively inhibit us from collaborating with third parties without permission'.

The background was that although Ted Heath was a visionary prime minister, he lacked the political empathy to keep UK–US liaison on an even keel. The United States had originally been a keen supporter of European integration, but Heath managed to court the European Economic Community with a degree of ardour that suggested to National Security Adviser Henry Kissinger a cooling in Anglo-American relations. Heath especially annoyed Kissinger by dealing with the EC without keeping him fully informed.

In 1973, at a time when Heath was pressing ahead with his European project and when the Nixon administration was jumpy because of the Watergate affair, Burke Trend, still in his Cabinet Office post if about to retire to head an Oxford college, flew out to meet Kissinger and try to calm the storm. He had a torrid time of it. Within days of Trend's last attempt to mend the breach, Kissinger telephoned the president to say, 'I am cutting [the UK] off from intelligence special information they are getting here.' As Heath was withholding bilateral candour on Europe, 'we can't trust Britain for special relationship'.[39]

Assessments of Kissinger's action vary. According to one British official, intelligence officers on each side of the Atlantic ignored Kissinger's instruction. There is some evidence that this happened. On the other hand, there is evidence that at least some materials were withheld, for example from the UK's Royal Air Force. There is also a suggestion that Heath's pique over his treatment was the reason why Britain remained neutral at the time of the Arab–Israeli war that suddenly—and to the surprise of both American and British intelligence—now broke out.

Resentful though the British may have been about American 'blackmail', Heath climbed down by the end of the year and began giving US officials the bilateral briefings on his European plans that they wanted. But the episode left its mark. Louis Heren, deputy editor of *The Times* and formerly its Washington correspondent, proclaimed in 1974 that the '"special relationship" is dead'. John Major's government (1990–7) worried that there might be another American intelligence cut off, and the anxiety persists to the present day.[40]

The Kissinger–Heath spat was high level. At other levels, British–American harmony often prevailed regardless of London–Washington happenings. Down in the parish, the Yankee vicar was working on ecumenical relations. Take the following example. A US Naval Security Group report on 'Anglo-American community relations activities for calendar year 1974' referred to Edzell in Scotland, where the USA had a listening facility. The naval group had a programme 'to intensify the superb relations already existing between the Scottish and American people'. The report noted that the Scots enjoyed 'dance, song, and fraternal conversation'. Americans had swung into action accordingly and had furthered the diplomatic goals of their nation by participating in traditional pastimes like 'First Footing' and 'Burns Suppers'.[41]

Further afield, there was a more contentious case. In 1975 in Australia, the Labour government of Gough Whitlam talked of curtailing US access to its eavesdropping facilities in Pine Gap. In a move that involved the queen's governor general in Australia as well as dark suspicions of CIA meddling, the democratically elected Whitlam was removed from office. Yet it was evident that Britain could no longer deliver unquestioning loyalty even in the white parts of what was now known as the Commonwealth. The fragments of empire that had gone into the UKUSA package seemed, all of a sudden, to be unreliable. The listening problem was, however, solved when Governor General Sir John Kerr sacked Whitlam. The move was profoundly undemocratic, but also an indication, especially with Harold Wilson back in office, that the British were keen on re-entry to the Anglo-American fold.[42]

In the later 1970s, concern arose over an issue supplying yet another contrast, Pakistan's apparent ambition to develop a nuclear bomb. Although America was the only country to have used such a bomb and Britain had contributed materially to proliferation beyond the Soviet–US balance of nuclear power, each country considered it had the authority to prevent further proliferation. They cooperated in the production of intelligence to this end.

The Americans at first concentrated on possible reprocessing facilities and gave Pakistan if not a clean bill of health, at least the benefit of the doubt. British intelligence focused on alternative fuel enrichment technology and suspected that Islamabad harboured real atomic ambitions. US officials questioned the 'quality and dependability' of the British finding. However, they came to realize that their intelligence partners were in this case correct (Pakistan finally tested two atomic devices in 1998). Sharp exchanges of difference over the matter served to emphasize that Britain could still offer informed dissent, and in that way be a useful intelligence partner.[43]

In the 1980s, President Ronald Reagan and Prime Minister Margaret Thatcher were political birds of a feather, and things looked promising for the special intelligence relationship. Although it had enjoyed a regional special relationship with Argentina, Reagan's America unofficially gave both military and intelligence assistance to Britain helping its old ally to win the 1982 Falklands/Malvinas War. In the view of one student of the Anglo-American special relationship, the help came 'unofficially on the Old Pals network between senior members of the Intelligence Service'. The European Community also helped Britain by placing an embargo on Argentina. But the Anglophonic/Europhobic British press channelled its gratitude bilaterally: 'Yanks a Million', said one tabloid.[44]

It nevertheless became apparent that the United States was looking away from the special intelligence relationship with Britain. It looked for relationships with other countries. It also displayed increasing symptoms of unilateralism. Then came the end of the Cold War in 1989 that not only removed the fear that bound old allies together, but also encouraged some Americans to believe that their nation, as the only superpower still standing, could rule alone.

The descent of the special relationship curve was a wobbly one, with regular upturns as well as rather larger dips. The decline had been especially evident in the 1960s. In the case of Guyana, President Johnson had used British economic dependency to ride rough shod over the policy prefer- ences of the Macmillan, Douglas-Home, and Wilson governments. On top of that, both America and its intelligence services visibly experienced social change that would weaken the old inter-elite ties.

Such changes imposed strain, as is evident in the story of the Heath government's attempt to reassert UK independence in the early 1970s and Kissinger's intelligence 'blackmail' response. American dominance could not on that occasion be withstood.

American dominance could also, however, take cultural forms, and with very different consequences. In the mid-1970s, a graphic illustration occurred, quite independently of top people's quarrels and reconciliations, of how American intelligence politics could reshape western democracy.

8

An American Gift

Government in the Sunshine

Duncan Wilson Archibald Campbell came from a respectable family. His father was a professor of economics at the University of Dundee. His mother received first class honours in mathematics at Glasgow University and had worked for the Government Code and Cipher School in the Second World War. Duncan followed in this tradition of excellence, gaining a first class honours degree in physics at Oxford University.

But the smooth path to bourgeois anointment did not appeal to Duncan Campbell. He abandoned science for radical journalism, and, on the evening of 18 February 1977, he ran into trouble. Not long afterwards, he would give an account of the event, in legal jargon a 'proof of evidence'. Setting forth his defence, the proof told what occurred on that February evening.

At 10.10 p.m. Campbell had just left the London flat inhabited by a former soldier, John Berry, and was trying to persuade *Time Out* staff writer Crispin Aubrey to drive him to Victoria Station. As they approached Aubrey's car, they realized they were not alone. Eight police officers materialized from the shadows. They separated the two journalists. A detective superintendent from Special Branch told Campbell he was being arrested under Section 2 of the Official Secrets Act. 'He then asked me who I was.'

This was encouraging. There must have been some kind of mistake. Campbell fumbled for his press card in an attempt to demonstrate his bona fides. But the officers now confiscated his briefcase, bundled him into a waiting vehicle, and told him he was being taken to Muswell Hill police station.

The Hillman Hunter police car drew parallel with the stated destination and drove straight past it. Campbell feared for a moment he was being abducted. But it was a mistake stemming from lack of street knowledge by officers whose duties were of an irregular nature. In a display of initiative, the officers now hailed a taxi, told the driver to go to Muswell Hill police station, and followed him there.

On arrival at the police station, Campbell was consigned to a small room with no bed or toilet, refused permission to see a solicitor on the Friday night of his arrest and for a further 48 hours, and not shown any of the specific charges against him. But he had an inkling, as the police had displayed such an interest in the contents of his briefcase. They included the transcript of his newly completed interview with John Berry.[1]

Campbell had been engaged in a campaign to demonstrate how the British state conducted an illicit programme of surveillance. In May 1976, assisted by the American journalist Mark Hosenball, he had published an article in *Time Out*. Though a cultural guide to London, the magazine doubled as an 'underground' publication, and Campbell's article outed the codebreaking institution GCHQ. It declared, 'Britain's largest spy network organisation is not MI5 or MI6 but an electronic network controlled from a country town in the Cotswolds.'

Campbell explained how, from its base in Cheltenham, GCHQ operated a worldwide network of signals intelligence, cooperating closely with America's NSA. Campbell and Hosenball supplied a map identifying 22 SIGINT sites in the UK. It pinpointed facilities such as the NSA's at Edzell in Scotland, various GCHQ-operated posts, and a collaborating BBC installation at Caversham Park. The Scottish-American pair portrayed an operation that involved spying on commercial rivals and on friendly nations, notably France. They raised issues of effectiveness as well as propriety— GCHQ operators listening in to the Soviet Air Force tended to get bored, and instead tuned in to concert broadcasts from Moscow.

Undoubtedly, GCHQ contributed to national—and international—security. Undoubtedly, too, it conducted or abetted illegal surveillance. For operational reasons and out of expediency, the very existence of GCHQ had been a state secret guarded with an emotional intensity. Campbell questioned a culture of secrecy that could mask incompetence and wrongdoing.[2]

For the three hours preceding the arrests of 18 February 1977, Campbell had been interviewing Berry over a bottle of Chianti. The ex-soldier had related his experiences at a GCHQ listening post in Cyprus. Aubrey had initiated the threesome, calling in Campbell because of his communications expertise, and he recorded the interview on his brand new tape recorder. All three, Aubrey, Berry, and Campbell, were now charged under Section 2 of the Official Secrets Act that had to do with the unauthorized release of official information. Later, the Crown preferred charges under Section 1 of the same law, which dealt with the more serious charge of espionage. Under the terms of the indictments Aubrey and Berry faced prison terms of fourteen years, and Campbell thirty.[3]

The Old Bailey trial of Aubrey, Berry, and Campbell came to be known as the 'ABC' affair. The authorities used tactics that, when disclosed, weakened their cause. Defying attempts at suppression, the radical press published the identity of the chief prosecution witness, 'Colonel B'. He turned out to be Hugh Johnstone, renowned for his participation in the British Army's efforts to subdue unrest in Cyprus. Given Cyprus veteran John Berry's whistle-blowing presence in the dock, Johnstone was not a brilliantly wise choice as a credible witness.

By September 1978 when the case came to court, the ABC defence was taking place outside as well as inside the legal precincts. Campaigners found support in the media. The television journalist Russell Harty ran an exposé suggesting there had been an official attempt at jury tampering, and for this reason the first trial had to be stopped. In the second trial with a new jury, Campbell was able to show that all the information he had collated had come from open sources. His 'Proof of Evidence' gave chapter and verse.

The proof also cited a November 1976 pronouncement by Home Secretary Merlyn Rees that seemed to undermine Section 2: Rees said it was government intention that the 'mere receipt of information should no longer be an offence'. When the trial judge described the use of Section 1 against Campbell as 'oppressive', the prosecution case was in shreds. In November 1978 all three defendants escaped with minor non-custodial sentences, and Section 2 of the Official Secrets Act was doomed.

The human rights lawyer Geoffrey Robertson saw the trial as the most important of the decade, and thought that by the case's end 'Britain was a less secret country'. The ABC affair was a landmark in the history of civil liberty and a turning point in the development of the British national security state. Painting a broad brush portrait, one could argue that hitherto there had been blind acceptance of government secrecy, trust in the authorities' management of national security issues, and even pride in Britain's ability to operate discreetly, projecting power by clandestine means without rushing to war. An irreversible change had now taken place.[4]

The argument in this chapter is that the impetus for greater openness in intelligence and national security affairs that affected Britain and other western countries in the last quarter of the twentieth century came in large measure from the United States. In the 1970s, American reconsidered some of the premises underlying its national security system, and with the collapse of the Cold War would resume its questioning in the 1990s. The American debate of the 1970s had a strong, if delayed, impact on other western countries.

It marked a turnaround in certain British attitudes. In the nineteenth century, it is true, Chartists and other reformers had admired American republicanism, democracy, and religious freedom. But in the twentieth century the British left was more critical. According to historian of the Labour Party Henry Pelling, the British left had become 'blind to the merits of American society'. In a reversal of attitudes, and in contrast to the staid and conservative leadership of the UK intelligence community who assiduously avoided the idea that anything might be learned from America, Campbell and others on the left now imported lessons from the USA.

Not that Britain lacked its own tradition of civil liberties. Without that tradition, the American seeds would not have germinated in British soil. Magna Carta had been a medieval stab at royal prerogative; assertions of parliamentary authority in the seventeenth century resulted in a civil war and then in the 1689 Bill of Rights; parliament abolished the slave trade in 1807. The Official Secrets Act of 1911, however, sent out a different message. The UK spied on other nations but was fierce in the defence of its own secrets. At home, the growing security services pried into the lives of individuals but refused to admit their own existence, let alone explain what they did and why they did it. In a century when people demanded personal privacy and public exposure to scrutiny, the British national security state delivered the opposite.

Compton Mackenzie's *Water on the Brain* (1933) had been a significant act of defiance directed at MI6. But of course it was fiction. Its author's prosecution under the Official Secrets Act had aimed to prevent him from revealing MI6 secrets, specifically the identities of 'C' and sixteen agents, and the fact that the Passport Control Office was one of MI6's covers. Thereafter, Mackenzie developed new interests such as Scottish independence—he had fallen in with the communist poet Hugh MacDiarmid and together they had been founder members of the National Party of Scotland.

Well before the 1970s, amnesia and the occurrence of competing events had blunted the impact of the Mackenzie case. He had become famous for something else. His work of comedic fiction *Whisky Galore*

(1947) portrayed a salvage effort by the islanders of Barra, off the coast of Scotland, following the wreck of a merchant ship. It was based on a real incident, the ransacking of the whisky-laden SS *Politician*, an act of plunder that goes some way to explaining today's high incidence of alcoholism on the isle of Barra. Ealing Studios made an evergreen movie of the book featuring Mackenzie himself as the ship's captain. Rarely are people remembered for more than one book, and Mackenzie's status as the man who tried to open up the affairs of MI6 sank with the *Politician*.[5]

By the 1960s, some underlying conditions preparing the way for greater openness had developed in Britain. A new group of radicals demanded greater transparency. The Labour Party's approval of an independent nuclear deterrent alienated an articulate minority that now came to be labelled the 'new' left. The new left espoused a range of causes including the ending of apartheid in South Africa. One of its most important causes was the exposure of nuclear weapons policy, and opposition to it.

The Campaign for Nuclear Disarmament (CND) was a prominent movement of the early 1960s. Some supporters of unilateral British nuclear disarmament formed a more radical group, the Committee of 100. Led by the philosopher Bertrand Russell, they broke away from CND with the aim of rendering 'government folly impossible'. In 1963, adherents of the Committee of 100 calling themselves 'Spies for Peace' broke into a military bunker in Reading. The bunker's purpose was to protect an elite in the event of a nuclear war. The committee sent out its message that the 'professors, top civil servants, air marshals and policemen' were 'quietly waiting for the day the bomb drops, for that will be the day they take over'. Duncan Campbell credited Spies for Peace as a significant British precedent for the drive for openness in the 1970s.[6]

Another British move in the direction of transparency was of a distinctly less radical character. Government officials started to release information in a controlled manner. They reasoned that publication of officially sanctioned histories might usefully correct misperceptions: the idea that British intelligence was crippled by moles, the notion that communists deserved most of the credit for European underground resistance to Hitler, the claims that America won the war and that the UK could not match the prowess of the CIA, and the proposition that espionage was a superfluous activity that burdened the British taxpayer. With an honest shilling to be made, there was no shortage of publishers ready to launch spy books based on the insider information that would now be available.

So the books began to appear. In 1962, the MI6 veteran H. Montgomery Hyde published his *Quiet Canadian*, a study of Sir William Stephenson, Britain's spy chief in the USA in the Second World War. Hyde had been one of Stephenson's agents. He was a controversial figure. For his advocacy of the decriminalization of homosexuality, the Conservative and Unionist Party in Northern Ireland had dropped him from its list of parliamentary candidates. However, his biography of Stephenson was acceptable to officialdom, for although it was a revelation, it was also a favourable account of British intelligence activities. The UK authorities decided to allow its publication and the *New York Times* greeted it as the greatest shock since *Lady Chatterley's Lover.*[7]

M. R. D. Foot's official history, *SOE in France*, appeared in 1966. There were several reasons for the authorization of this work. In the 1950s, the Conservative MP Dame Irene Ward had lobbied for an authoritative account that would confirm or dispel contemporary charges that incompetence at the helm of SOE had resulted in the deaths of a number of female agents who had fallen into the hands of the Gestapo. Another concern was that, as part of their 'we won the war' industry, the Americans were making claims for the prowess of OSS that seemed to diminish the role played by SOE, and by implication the need for British covert capabilities in the future. There was also resentment at the line being taken by French communist historians, who gave primacy to the role of communists in the French resistance (M. R. D. Foot's references to communists in his *SOE in France* were even-handed but sparse; the British like the Americans gave scant credit to the part played by the Red Army in the winning of the Second World War).

At the same time, the authorization of *SOE in France* was an attempt to guide the storm. If there was to be a flood of revelations about the intelligence services, the government wanted to be in a position to direct the flow, and thus to have the ability to switch it off at an advantageous juncture. Wherever one wishes to place the interpretative emphasis, *SOE in France* was a pioneering experiment in official intelligence history. The UK authorities having begun to ponder the virtues of publishing official histories, the work was an experimental start.

In the view of those who insisted that signals intelligence was the main course, Foot's narrative of special operations was just a taster. But some authors were already nibbling at the main feast, and in 1968 the UK opened up new possibilities by reducing the fifty-year-rule for the release of government documents to thirty years. This augmented the scope for authenticated histories of Second World War intelligence. To direct the flow, the government commissioned the intelligence veteran and Cambridge history professor Fred Hinsley to write an overall official history of intelligence in the Second World War. Official revelations about *wartime* SIGINT, at least, were now within sight though the first of Hinsley's volumes did not appear until 1979.[8]

America, too, had a tradition of civil rights. The Bill of Rights enshrined in the US Constitution listed press freedom and freedom from arbitrary arrest, and the states fought their own civil war resulting in the emancipation of slaves. Another strand in the tradition, a strand that was important to later open government initiatives, had to do with journalism. The golden age of investigative journalism—the 'muckraking era'—occurred in the period stretching from the late 1890s through the presidency of Theodore Roosevelt (1901–9). Writers like Upton Sinclair, Ida Tarbell, Ray Stannard Baker, and Lincoln Steffens targeted capitalist malpractices and political corruption. This was one reason why, when the Bureau of Investigation was formed in 1908–9, there was a vigorous public debate.

There were setbacks to the concepts of freedom from government intrusion and open democracy. Repression in the First World War and the Red Scare that followed were notable examples. So was the Yardley case. Like Mackenzie, H. O. Yardley found himself suppressed when he tried to reveal espionage secrets.

From an early stage in his administration, President Franklin D. Roosevelt authorized illegal wiretapping. Undertaken by the FBI, this practice at first targeted spies and others deemed to be a threat to national security. By the eve of the Second World War, it had assumed a political character. The Roosevelt government spied on its foreign policy critics. Because those anti-interventionists lost their campaign and were swamped by the patriotic fervour of war, the Rooseveltian misdeeds were forgotten—if only for the time being.[9]

In the 1950s, Joe McCarthy's anti-communist crusade promised to expose government secrets, but was a setback to the cause. The CIA with its supposed contingent of covertly liberal/left-leaning officers was one of the senator's prime targets. When McCarthy overplayed his hand and fell into disgrace, it gave secrecy a new if finite lease of life. For now, those who campaigned against secrecy could be, and regularly were, accused of being 'McCarthyist'. Furthermore, the 1950s and early 1960s were a period of

Cold War hypertension, and until the 1970s only a minority of Americans were sympathetic to attacks on the CIA or other icons of national security.

Yet the anti-secrecy bug was becoming virulent in America. *The Invisible Government* (1964) by journalists David Wise and Thomas B. Ross was the first in a stream of books that criticized secret intelligence, and it was well informed. In fact, Wise and Ross mentioned GCHQ as a 'British counter-part' of the NSA. Duncan Campbell made this a point in his defence as it showed he was not the first to reveal the existence of the Cheltenham unit. The *Ramparts* affair of 1967 was another notable event that helped set the agenda for the 1970s. And as the decade wore on, 'new left' opponents of the Vietnam War were building up a case against the excessive secrecy of the national security state. It was a campaign with international charisma.[10]

The 1960s yielded a piece of legislation aimed at the elimination of excessive secrecy. The Freedom of Information Act (FOIA) became law in 1966. It was not the first such legislation in the history of the West. Sweden had shown the way in its 'Era of Liberty' culminating in its Freedom of the Press Act of 1766 and there were more recent examples such as Finland's 1951 Act on the Openness of Public Documents and, in the following year, an initiative for the oversight of the Dutch intelligence services. Yet such developments had failed to register in the parochially monolingual Anglo world, and it was America's FOIA that would have an impact in Britain and beyond.

The US FOIA was the culmination of an eleven-year campaign by John Emerson Moss (D-CA), a Second World War navy veteran who had served in the House since 1953. Passed over the veto of President Johnson, it aimed at reversing the effects of the Administrative Procedure Act of 1946, which allowed officials to determine what was 'good cause' for the divulgence of information. The FOIA as enacted in 1966 was only partly successful. It applied just to documents, and left officialdom with tools, such as delay, prohibitively high charges, and concealment of filing methods, with which to keep secrets secret. So the consumer advocate Ralph Nader and Senator Edward Kennedy (D-MA) campaigned for an improved law. Enacted in spite of a further executive veto, the 1974 FOIA amendment made it an offence for federal employees to obstruct legitimate information requests. The FOIA, especially as amended, was a significant blow against unreason-able secrecy.[11]

A dramatic sequence of events in 1970s America now forced the open government issue onto the world stage. In 1971, the *New York Times* began to serialize the 'Pentagon Papers', leaked documents that painted the American decision to enter the Vietnam War as a mistake. President Nixon responded by authorizing a team of 'Plumbers' to stem future leaks. Exceeding their brief, the Plumbers broke into the Watergate complex in Washington, DC, to riffle through the records of the Democratic Party in the hope of finding dirt. They used tape to secure the bolt on a stairwell door, a blunder that led to their detection by a security guard, and to their arrest by the Washington police. This was in 1972, a presidential election year. In an action that would compound its future problems, the Nixon administration organized a cover-up.

The cover-up provoked American history's second muckraking era. The *Washington Post*'s investigative journalists Carl Bernstein and Bob Woodward hunted down the Nixon administration officials who had paid the Watergate burglars—it turned out that the burglars had FBI and CIA connections, and E. Howard Hunt was one of them. Press sleuths followed the smoke from the smoking gun until it led to the White House and forced President Nixon's resignation. An inside source referred to in their reports as 'Deep Throat' had assisted Woodward and Bernstein. Decades later, America learned that he was a senior, professionally frustrated FBI official, W. Mark Felt. Nixon's cover-up never stood a chance.

American withdrawal from the Vietnam War in 1973 followed by Nixon's resignation cooled two sources of controversy, but another rose in its place. This was the excesses of the CIA. In September 1974, the journalist Seymour Hersh revealed that the CIA had been implicated in the overthrow of the democratically elected government of Chile, installing instead the Pinochet dictatorship. Later that year, the same journalist showed that the CIA had conducted political espionage against opponents of the Vietnam War, a blatantly illegal operation. In February 1975, the award-winning television journalist Daniel Schorr exposed the fact that the United States had used assassination as an instrument of state policy. Notably, there had been a series of tragicomic attempts to kill the president of Cuba, Fidel Castro.

The CIA had become the prime focus of attention in the American press. A survey of 137 newspapers in the United States with an aggregate circulation of 28 million reveals that while in the calendar year 1970 there were no CIA-dominated editorials, in the calendar year 1975, the agency was the prime theme in no fewer than 227 editorials. Responding to public demand, Congress launched some of the largest investigations in its history. This attention did more than bring the CIA into disrepute. It encouraged a congressional challenge to the president's authority to conduct covert operations without legislative oversight, and to use the fig leaf of 'national security' to cover up significant truths.

Congress's assertion of constitutional privilege was a component in the American influence on British politics. When they supported the ABC accused, left-wing Labour politicians Peter Hain and Tony Benn attacked the growth of executive power in Britain. They were using unmistakably American political language.[12]

By this time, Watergate had shaped political consciousness on both sides of the Atlantic. Duncan Campbell thought that the whole ABC case was rooted 'in a counter-attack by the British intelligence and security services against the importation from the United States of post-Watergate investigative journalism, which had been adopted by radical and left journalists at a considerable speed during 1975'. According to Geoffrey Robertson who orchestrated the ABC defence, Campbell was 'one of a new breed of post-Watergate journalists'. Robertson noted that America had never had an Official Secrets Act and did not have an equivalent of the British 'D-Notice' system (since 1912, the UK government had used D[efence Advisory] Notices to prevent newspapers from publishing information it identified as national-security sensitive). Robertson greatly admired the First Amendment to the American Constitution that guaranteed a free press.

Attacking the Official Secrets Act, Campbell contrasted it to 'the United States tradition flowing from its plural democracy and federal government'. Others associated with the ABC trial wrote from a similar perspective. Aubrey chose 'Transatlantic Passage' as the title of a chapter he wrote on the case. He said he admired America's freedom of information legislation and contrasted it with the miseries of British official secrecy and D-notices. In supporting the ABC defendants, socialist historian E. P. Thompson praised America's 'very vigorous counter-attack' on the secret state, and demanded a US-style FOIA for Britain.[13]

American influence brought the British debate on secrecy to a tipping point. That debate was already finely balanced. *Time Out* journalist Tony Bunyan was writing a book on the history of political espionage. Seeing the cloud on the horizon, the political establishment intensified its effort at controlled disclosure. In 1971, Prime Minister Harold Wilson secured the agreement of leader of the Opposition Edward Heath to the launch of the series of official histories of Second World War intelligence.

Whitehall continued its policy of calculated tolerance. In 1972, it relaxed its opposition to the publication of a book on wartime deception operations by an insider—J. C. Masterman, the author of *The Doublecross System*, was an Oxford historian who had served in MI5. Then in 1974, Frederick Winterbottom published his memoir *The Ultra Secret*, about the codebreaking efforts at Bletchley Park.

One reason why Winterbottom's book saw the light of day was that Robin Denniston, the son of the GC&CS director Alastair Denniston, felt the authorities had treated his father shabbily by demoting him in the Second World War and paying him a meagre pension. Now an editor at Weidenfeld and Nicolson, Robin Denniston wanted to restore the codebreaker's reputation and pressed for the book's publication. Resigning himself to its appearance, Cabinet Secretary Burke Trend reasoned *The Ultra Secret* would show the positive side of British intelligence, and correct the damage inflicted by revelations about the Cambridge moles. Even if GCHQ's director was 'incoherent with rage' when Campbell jumped the gun in his 1976 *Time Out* article, *The Ultra Secret* had prepared the ground for the revelation that an entity in Cheltenham was eavesdropping on all and sundry.[14]

Against this background, the reporting of events in America had an impact. Additionally, individual US citizens had a direct influence. In his 'proof of evidence' for the ABC trial, Campbell explained the background to his 'Eavesdroppers' item. A 1974 article in the American magazine *Ramparts* had triggered his interest in signals intelligence. He then tried to identify a chain of British eavesdropping sites using his knowledge of microwave and other communications technology. He began to collaborate with the American journalist Mark Hosenball, and one of their most useful sources of information was another American, Perry Fellwock, better known by his alias, Winslow Peck.

Peck had worked at the NSA. In 1972, he had anonymously published a *Ramparts* article on the UKUSA network. He described it as a WASP arrangement that was not particularly effective at spying on the Soviet Union. He also supplied the *New York Times* reporter Tad Szulc with data for a 1975 *Penthouse* article on NSA that contained references to GCHQ. Only in the UK, it would appear, were the strange occurrences in Cheltenham still a secret.

Peck had developed a left-wing outlook. He supported the 'Winter Soldiers', veterans of the Vietnam conflict who had joined the anti-war movement. He cooperated with Norman Mailer's Organizing Committee for the Fifth Estate. He was so useful a source for Campbell's research that he inspired some Scottish scepticism: 'Mr Peck was fond of making as many sensational allegations as possible and was very happy to describe any aspect of his service experience with anyone'.[15]

Peck was one of a number of intelligence apostates who contributed in the first half of the 1970s to the demand within the USA for a more open climate. They included Patrick McGarvey, Victor Marchetti, and Sam Adams. Yet another of these American apostates would become a celebrity in the UK as well as the USA. His name was Philip Agee.[16]

Agee admitted to a 'privileged upbringing in a big white house bordering an exclusive golf club'. His parents told him not to kiss Anna Lily, his black nanny. He graduated from the Jesuit High School in Tampa, Florida, and then cum laude in philosophy from Notre Dame. He joined the CIA. Starting with six years in Ecuador and Uruguay, he ran agents and bugged his way around South America. He did so in the belief that he and others in the CIA were buying time for conservative reform by 'putting down the extreme left'. According to his account, he then realized the CIA was actually deferring reform. He underwent a socialist conversion. He left the agency, and by the autumn of 1972 had settled in England with the aim of completing a book exposing the Latin American activities of his former employer.

To avoid problems in the USA, *Inside the Company: CIA Diary* came out under the imprint of a London publisher. *The Economist* missed the point when it greeted its appearance as a 'godsend for the anti-American left'. The new British left was keen to back Agee and to gaze with restored faith at the way in which the American left conducted its affairs.[17]

Other whistleblowers had criticized the agency for its misdeeds or its inefficiency, but Agee went further. In an appendix, he named as many Latin American CIA officials, agents, and front organizations as he could. He maintained that this was the best way to neutralize their work.

Agee did not pioneer the naming of names. An East German publication had already outed a large number of alleged American spies and CIA front organizations, and the journalist John Marks had in 1974 explained how to spot CIA people by cross-referencing open sources like the Department of State's *Biographic Register* and *Foreign Service List*. Agee's contribution was to accelerate the trend. He and Marks were advisers to Fifth Estate's underground quarterly *Counterspy*, whose aim was to name spies in order to force them to go home, thus putting an end to US interventionist policies. The magazine named a further hundred agents.

Meantime in *Time Out*, the journalists Phil Kelly and Mark Hosenball, British and American respectively, published a 'Who's Who in the CIA'. It named scores of individuals amongst whom was the agency's London station chief, Cord Meyer. Concerned Americans Abroad (CAA), an organization originally founded to protest the Vietnam War, acted on cue. With help from a local theatre group and to the delight of the media on both sides of the Atlantic, it launched its 'Misguided Tours to the Stately Homes of Friendly CIA Operatives'. Participants were invited to 'see how the underhand live'. There was a vigil outside Meyer's Belgravia house, and there were calls in the House of Commons for the expulsion of CIA spies.[18]

The activities of Hosenball and Agee were unwelcome to the British government. Hosenball was applying the techniques of American investigative journalism to the British scene in a way that threatened the government's control over national security secrets—and in 1976 he would help Campbell 'expose' GCHQ. Agee's book had shocked the Washington establishment and his continuing dedication to intelligence exposures further alarmed senior Washington figures. It was not just the conservatives—Agee's critics ranged from former counterintelligence chief and right-winger James Angleton who criticized the UK for giving Agee a safe haven, to the liberal Frank Church whose Senate committee conducted a determined investigation of US intelligence, but who feared for the safety of named agents.

The British government did not want to hazard a special intelligence relationship that had been rocked by Henry Kissinger's blackmailing efforts, but otherwise seemed to be on the mend after the difficulties of the 1960s. The latest sterling crisis gave further reason not to alienate the USA. Ultimately, on 16 November 1976, British law officers served deportation orders on both Hosenball and Agee. Home Secretary Merlyn Rees told the House of Commons Agee had not only published information 'harmful to the security of the United Kingdom', but also 'maintained regular contacts harmful to the security of the United Kingdom with foreign intelligence officers'. Prime Minister Jim Callaghan told the House there had been no pressure from the Ford administration, and that he would not be consulting the incoming Carter administration.[19]

There followed a controversial deportation procedure. Denied a jury trial, Hosenball and Agee were allowed to appeal against their deportation orders only to a secretive panel of three titled and uncommunicative dignitaries the critics dubbed the 'silent knights'. The appeal was to no avail, and Agee was equally unsuccessful when he moved to Scotland to challenge the British deportation order in that country's courts.[20]

Prime Minister Jim Callaghan's Labour government received support from Shadow Home Secretary Willie Whitelaw, from Tory MPs like Winston Churchill (grandson of the wartime leader), and from much of the press. There was opposition from predictable quarters. *Time Out* attacked Rees's 'Star Chamber-style proceedings'. To mark the festive season, it offered a Deportation Game: 'any number of foreigners can play. Throw the dice, hang on to your political opinions and try to stay in Britain!' An Agee–Hosenball Defence Committee hastily formed at the headquarters of the National Council for Civil Liberties. It faced the task of whipping up instant support.[21]

That task was not quite as stiff as it might have been. CAA had over the years developed an agitation machine that involved not just Americans in exile but also a network of left-wing British citizens and organizations. It organized anti-deportation protest events. Attacking the Home Secretary's 'menacing phraseology that brings back to Americans memories of the McCarthy era accusations', a CAA circular appealed for campaign funds. On 13 December 1976, CAA dispatched a legation to the American embassy, where the counsellor, Loren E. Lawrence, assured them that the CIA was too 'chastened by the Watergate revelations' to risk being caught pressurizing the British government. Lawrence also had to respond to pressure from Democrats Abroad (UK), promising the embassy would follow the deportation case to ensure that Agee and Hosenball would not be deprived of 'due process'.[22]

The pro-Agee agitation was potentially potent because the American was already a well-known figure. He explained one reason for his popularity in a letter of 17 September 1975: UK 'interest remains high as one would suspect with topics like shellfish toxin and cobra venom popping up from day to day' back in America in congressional assassination hearings. He was in demand. 'Since publication of my book here in January I've really been busy and travelling a lot.' He wanted to promote *Inside the Company*, proselytize politically, and make a living. He was working on another book and on some movies. He was doing 'a speaking tour of factories and union halls in northern England and Scotland' and was lining up trips to Brussels, Zurich, Paris, and Toronto.

Agee's desk diaries reveal the extent of his contacts with leading British print journalists like Martin Walker, with the BBC, and with other western media such as Dutch and Swedish TV. He visited some establishment institutions like the aristocratic Magdalene College, Cambridge—he wrote it down phonetically as 'Maudling College'.

Mainly, though, Agee had sympathetic interaction with left wingers in and out of parliament. To give just a flavour of his many contacts in alphabetical order, he recorded appointments with Fenner Brockway, MP (CND), Tony Bunyan, Duncan Campbell, Robin Cook, MP (future foreign secretary), Michael Foot, MP (future leader of the Labour Party), Peter Hain (then under indictment in South Africa for 'terrorism' and prominent campaigner against apartheid, later minister of state for Wales), Eric Hobsbawm (Marxist historian), Bruce Kent (Catholic CND), Neil Kinnock, MP (future leader of the Labour Party), Joan Lester, MP (dissident member of the Labour cabinet and about to resign in protest against cuts), Ralph Milliband (New Left guru and father of Ed, future leader of the Labour Party), the Bertrand Russell Committee, and David Steel, MP (about to become leader of the Liberal Party and a future presiding officer of the Scottish parliament). It was a formidable, ready-made committee of defence not just for the Agee–Hosenball case, but also for the ABC trial that followed and for the principle of a more open democracy in the years to come.[23]

Other prominent public figures who lent their support to the Agee–Hosenball cause included Len Murray (leader of the Trades Union Congress), and 149 Labour MPs including cabinet ministers Barbara Castle, Judith Hart, and Tony Benn. The Liberals' David Steel asked a question in the Commons and Labour's Neil Kinnock spoke at a rally in Glasgow. However, not everyone on the left was enamoured. Agee's cultivation of Michael Foot flopped. The veteran campaigner said he favoured open government, but Agee should be expelled.

Benn accused Foot of being an 'extinct volcano'. Perhaps indeed Foot was mellowing with age. He was also a Callaghan loyalist. But there were other reasons why Agee was a less than ideal tribune for the export of open government.[24]

First, there was the charge by Merlyn Rees and others that Agee had cooperated with the KGB and its partners in Cuba. If proved correct, the allegation would have led to virtually universal condemnation of Agee in the western democracies. The idea that Agee may have been a double agent sowed doubt in the minds of his supporters on the left. How to react? Heinz Norden of the CAA in London read an August 1975 article from the US cultural magazine *New York* that suggested Agee might have worked for the other side. He chose just to clip out the article and file it.

Campbell did react. He put forward the idea that Hosenball, not Agee, was the real American promoter of reform in Britain. He noted that while

Agee may have been a 'figurehead' for the campaign, there were suspicions 'on the left about his book which was an admitted reconstruction', as distinct from a proper diary. Tony Benn stuck to his censure of Merlyn Rees. However, commenting in his diary on the charge that Agee had been 'in touch with foreign intelligence services', he worried, 'I don't know.'[25]

Agee denied having had contacts with the KGB and said that Rees should be dismissed as 'Uncle Sam's poodle'. Some evidence on the point turned up years later. Vasili Mitrokhin, a Soviet foreign intelligence officer who had enjoyed access to KGB archives before defecting to the UK in 1992, recalled that Agee approached the KGB in Mexico City in 1968. He further charged that Agee's campaign to out CIA officials was a KGB 'initiative'. A reviewer of Mitrokhin's book pointed out that, as independent historians had no access to the relevant KGB files in Yasenevo, there was no means of verifying or assessing the defector's account. One can speculate that Agee may have been an apostate as he claimed, or a double agent working for the KGB, or indeed a triple agent, pretending to defect as a cover for spying on the British left. Whatever the truth, the ambiguities undermined his appeal.[26]

A second circumstance that weakened Agee's impact was the political miscalculation behind the naming of CIA agents. There were serious political repercussions from an event that had occurred a year before the serving of the deportation order. On 23 December 1975 the Athens CIA station chief Richard S. Welch was returning with his wife from an embassy Christmas party. As they approached their house, three masked men stepped forward and shot the intelligence officer dead. The gunmen (it later emerged) were members of a terrorist group seeking to punish America for its support of the 1967–73 Greek junta.

The Republican administration of President Gerry Ford, for many months under the cosh from congressional intelligence investigators, seized the opportunity to make a martyr of Welch. It arranged for his burial to be at Arlington National Cemetery, normally reserved for military heroes. As the plane bearing his casket approached Andrews Air Force Base in readiness for the ceremonial interment, it circled for a full fifteen minutes to ensure breakfast TV could capture live images of the dead station chief's arrival.

CIA officials and their supporters alleged that the Athenian assassins had learned of Welch's identity from *Counterspy*, which had named him as an agency functionary. Agee's critics had always pointed out that the naming of names risked the lives of American operatives, and now they felt vindicated. Actually, when finally arrested in 2002, Welch's assassins claimed that they had never heard of *Counterspy*. The truth is that Welch had been outed previously as a CIA man. Earlier in his career he had been station chief in Guyana, winning the Intelligence Medal of Merit for his services to dictatorship in that country, and the Peruvian press had named him in 1974, earlier than *Counterspy*. The *Athens News* identified him just a month before he was killed, supplying his name, address, and telephone number. Or one could find out where he lived by boarding an Athens tourist bus, whose guide would point out the CIA residence as a point of local interest.

But the accusation against *Counterspy* was plausible at the time, and in any case Agee may well have endangered others' lives, if not Welch's. So strong was the political fallout from the story in the United States that it helped to inhibit the movement for open government and intelligence reform, and this had the secondary effect of weakening American reforms' impact in Britain.

The Agee affair did raise political consciousness in the UK. At the same time, it was a mixed blessing for Campbell and his co-defendants. It could not match the moral impact of their own 'ABC' campaign.[27]

Neither could it match the narrative strength of the main campaign over in America. The story of the American open government crusade was all the more significant because it achieved results. The list of American reforms in the years following the end of the Vietnam War is impressive. The joint Senate–House War Powers resolution of 1973 demanded consultation with Congress before any lengthy hostilities were launched, making it more difficult for the executive to wage surreptitious warfare. The Hughes–Ryan Act in the following year mandated the reporting of covert actions to no fewer than eight Senate and House committees—so open-ended was the requirement, that many of those concerned felt the need for voluntary restraint, and for a better arrangement that would stand the test of time. Accordingly, the Senate, in 1976, and the House in the following year established specialist intelligence oversight committees, and the Intelligence Oversight Act of 1980 restricted privileged knowledge of covert action to these committees alone. Meanwhile, the Government in the Sunshine Act of 1976 required that all meetings of all government agencies be open to public observation. There was an exemption in the Sunshine Act for national defence and thus intelligence, but the name of the law summed up the aspiration of a generation of Americans.

Government in the sunshine did not describe a smooth arc across a cloudless sky. The application of the principle in the realm of intelligence was vital in some respects, potentially fatal in others. President Carter soon began to emphasize how much he needed the CIA, and not just because of the Cold War. Reporting on a six-month investigation in May 1978, the Senate Governmental Affairs Committee concluded in light of 1,800 'major incidents' between 1970 and 1977 that international terrorism was 'a matter of the gravest concern'. Campaigning for the presidency in 1980, Ronald Reagan promised to 'unleash' the CIA. There were few critics of his administration when it promoted the Intelligence Identities Protection Act of 1982.

Nevertheless, things would not be the same again. With the end of the Cold War, there was even talk of abolishing the CIA. That came to nothing and the Bush Jr administration of 2001–9 not only boosted the size of the intelligence community in the aftermath of 9/11, but also slowed down information release. Yet that may well have been a blip. On the first day of his presidency Barack Obama issued a memorandum on 'Transparency and Open Government'. In March 2011, the Knight Open Government Survey found that the Obama administration had achieved a full half of its 'sunshine' goals.[28]

American debate and reform had a practical impact on nations in the democratic West. There are differing views on where the influence was most keenly felt. In his study of British intelligence accountability, Mark Phythian argues that while American reforms contributed to 'momentum' in the UK, British reform discourse 'lagged behind similar debates in the United States, Canada, and Australia'.

But did non-British countries surge ahead in terms of action? In Australia the response to intelligence controversy had to be rapid in the wake of the Crown's controversial removal, in 1975, of the democratically elected prime minister, Gough Whitlam. There was an early move towards openness. In 1977, Canberra for the first time officially acknowledged the existence of the Defence Signals Directorate, the Australian equivalent of GCHQ.

There, the process stopped. The Australians talked about parliamentary oversight and in 1994 a government investigation recommended it. Nothing happened. The Canadians managed to be just as sluggish. In 1984 they settled for a Security Intelligence Review Committee made up of appointees. The parliament in Ottawa sometimes flickered into life on the issue of civil liberties, otherwise the great and the good were allowed to get on with both running and overseeing secret intelligence.

Elsewhere, Scandinavia had a tradition of parliamentary oversight and also, since 1809 in the case of Sweden, the institution of a democratic ombudsman whose job was to look into abuses. In the 1990s Denmark had a revelatory impulse reminiscent of Duncan Campbell's exposures of US defence and intelligence installations in the UK. In 1995, Foreign Minister Niels Helveg finally acknowledged the fact that, contrary to assurances given by the Danish government, the United States had been allowed to build nuclear and intelligence facilities in Greenland and the Faroe Islands. This scandal and other lesser ones produced parliamentary inquiries in the Nordic countries. They were reminiscent of the 1970s US congressional investigations. Yet there was no emulation of the American arrangements for legislative oversight.[29]

The British response to the campaign for open government was not by these standards laggardly. It did happen slowly, though. The security crisis in Northern Ireland and a perceived need to cover up official miscarriages of justice in that province made politicians nervous about disclosure. Suspicions about Agee's motives in naming names and sympathy for the Reagan administration's promotion of the Intelligence Identities Protection Act dampened enthusiasm for reform.

In any case, new ideas take time to percolate through. After all, it took half a century for the Enlightenment to result in Russia's abolition of serfdom (1861) and America's ending of slavery (1865). In an age of instant mass communication, American ideas travelled rather more rapidly. Still, Callaghan was not disposed to rush things. His continuing instinct was to fudge the open government issue. Giving evidence to a parliamentary inquiry in 1986, he said he was 'not sure' what the accountability arrangements were for the intelligence services, adding, 'I am going to give you a very unsatisfactory answer. I do not know.'

In 1977, Foreign Secretary David Owen had nevertheless closed the secretive International Research Department, which had been directing a stream of black propaganda against critics of British policy. At first, this looked like a flash in the pan. Margaret Thatcher's Tory government (1979–90) was less keen on reform. Anticipating the informational reticence of her friend President Reagan, Thatcher blocked the appearance of further volumes in the official Second World War intelligence history series. In a further demonstration of her affinity with the Hollywood labour leader turned union buster who now ran America, she banned trade unions from GCHQ in 1984. When Foreign Secretary Robin Cook reversed the prohibition in 1997, a *Scotsman* journalist recalled the betrayals of the Cambridge spy ring and stated, 'there has never been a working class, ideological traitor'.

Reflexive secrecy seemed once again to be the order of the day. Following allegations that intelligence incompetence had been behind the UK's failure to anticipate Argentina's seizure of the Falklands/Malvinas islands in 1982, the Franks commission of inquiry heard from MI5 chief Sir Martin Furnival-Jones. He announced that any document was 'an official secret if it was in an official file'.[30]

As the decade wore on, however, the British rediscovered their liberal ways. The Labour MPs who had been sympathetic to the Agee–Hosenball and ABC defendants had their way when, in its 1983 election manifesto, the Labour Party committed to the principle of intelligence oversight by a select committee. The Conservative government felt it had to respond. The 1989 Security Service Act for the first time acknowledged the existence of MI5. It put that agency on a legal footing, and also created the possibility for legislative regulation. Like alcohol and drugs, espionage can be regulated once it's made legal. Six years later, a further law brought MI6 and GCHQ within the legislative fold.

At the time of the passage of the 1989 Act, Michael Mates addressed the issue of oversight. Mates was a Tory MP and chair of the Commons Select Committee on Defence. He made a special plea against parliamentary oversight of the intelligence services, arguing that it would make them the object of party political debate. His preference was for a British equivalent of the President's Foreign Intelligence Advisory Board—the secretive executive body set up by President Eisenhower to head off Senator Mike Mansfield's demand for congressional oversight in 1956.

The 1994 Intelligence Services Act regulating MI6 and GCHQ established an Intelligence and Security Committee (ISC). It was a compromise. The prime minister appointed the nine members of the ISC, drawing from both houses of parliament. Potentially, in being a committee of trusted parliamentarians rather than a parliamentary committee subject to the vagaries of politics, it could be trusted with a greater range of sensitive data. However, it did not oversee the deliberations of the Joint Intelligence Committee (JIC) or its military equivalents, and was open to the suspicion that it might be too loyal to its patron, the prime minister.[31]

To complete the legislative cycle, Britain passed two further laws in 2000. The Freedom of Information Act, like its American predecessor, exempted the intelligence services. But the Regulation of Investigatory Powers Act created a body to oversee surveillance activities and appointed judicial commissioners with that responsibility. The British secret services now had legislative, judicial, and executive oversight. The thinking was that this would create what David Omand, intelligence and security coordinator in the Cabinet Office, regarded as a just balance between open government and discretion. The hope was that the new balance would generate public trust in the security agencies. There was some evidence of that trust, with little public disquietude when MI5 expanded to take on new responsibilities in crime fighting and anti-terrorist activity in Northern Ireland.[32]

The flurry of British legislation did not come about entirely because of events in America. There were other reasons, too. In the 1980s, spy stories in the press indicated a need for confidence building. Notably, the disenchanted MI5 veteran Peter Wright published his book *Spycatcher*, in which he alleged (falsely, as it turned out) that his agency had tried to destabilize the supposedly left-leaning Labour government of Harold Wilson—a British version of Australian history.

Another factor was cases brought against the UK government in the 1980s under the terms of Article 8 of the European Convention on Human Rights (1950). The article protected the privacy of individuals against unwarranted surveillance. Essentially, it was a violation of a person's rights to bug his phone without legal backing. So for MI5 to eavesdrop in the interest of national security, it was necessary for it to become a legal entity governed by legislation.[33]

Still another circumstance was the end of the Cold War, with additional pressure arising from the fact that Senator Moynihan and others in the United States were asking new questions of the CIA and even proposing its abolition.

While there were various factors in play, there can, however, be no doubt that the American campaigns of the 1970s and their aftermath had an impact on Britain. British intelligence became more open in its practices. Whether that made it more humane or more effective is open to question. The ISC had a frustrating time trying to dissuade Prime Minister Blair from rushing into the Iraq War. But for better or not, the system had become more democratic.

For Campbell and his American colleague Hosenball, the 1970s campaign was the defining moment of their lives, something to look back on with 'immense pride'. It had been the time of a special gift from America—greater transparency in one of the murkier corners of human endeavour.[34]

9

The Distant Cousin

America Goes its Own Way

President Clinton gilded the lily when he said that Daniel P. Moynihan (D-NY) was a product of that desperate New York district Hell's Kitchen. The senator had grown up at least partly in the Midwest. Yet it was true that he had experienced the downside of life. The grandson of a County Kerry horse breeder, his more immediate memories were of a father who gambled, drank, womanized, and left his mother in 1937. The young Moynihan had accumulated dollars as a shiner of shoes and as a longshoreman. He attended high school on the unprivileged fringes of Harlem.

Early in his political career, Moynihan championed the cause of the poor and the rights of African Americans. In spite of this radical background, he must have seemed an unlikely person to lead the renewed attack on the CIA that took place in the 1990s. In some ways, he had become distinctly unradical. As with other self-made men, he felt he could be frank about the shortcomings of those who remained in poverty. He offended the left through his criticism of the morals of the black family, and was sufficiently conservative to serve in the administration of Richard Nixon. In fact, Moynihan resembled that well-known brand of neoconservative who started on the political left and ended on the right. That should have meant support for the CIA, as, by the 1990s, the agency had become a firm favourite of conservatives. Moynihan instead lent his prestige to a notable assault.

In the wake of the collapse of the Soviet Union in 1989, the time was ripe for renewed questioning of the CIA and of intelligence agencies generally. The removal of the Soviet threat meant one could criticize the CIA—or MI6/MI5—without feeling unpatriotic. With talk of peace dividends in the air, the intelligence agencies were in line for cuts. This was a threat to intelligence liaison, even if in principle liaison was a means to economy through burden sharing. Criticism also eroded confidence, an essential ingredient in the trust that enables liaison. If western intelligence agencies had played their part in hastening the fall of communism, they had become victims of their own success.

Moynihan attacked the CIA on two fronts. The first had to do with incompetence and mendacity. The nomination of Robert Gates to be director of the CIA gave the senator a chance to air his concerns. Gates was a career CIA officer—a Russian specialist—who believed that the United States and the CIA in particular had been instrumental in bringing about the fall of communism, which for him was the 'greatest of American triumphs'. Under the leadership of William Casey (its director, 1981–7) and with the backing of President Reagan, the CIA had conducted a campaign of economic sabotage against the Soviet Union, for example, attempting to drive down oil prices in 1985 to impoverish the oil-exporting communist bloc.

Again, in the early 1980s Gates and others induced Congress to allocate funds to the 'Star Wars' space war programme—in the belief that this would induce emulative and ruinously expensive military escalation in the Soviet Union. They were open to the charge that in order to cajole Congress into allocating funds to Star Wars, they inflated the CIA's estimate of the Soviet threat. True or false, their rearmament campaign contrasted with that pursued by the CIA in the 1950s, when DCI Allen Dulles, with the backing of President Eisenhower, had tempered the alarmist claims of America's 'military-industrial complex'.

Moynihan begged to differ from the 1980s CIA. He thought it was deplorable that the agency had 'lied repeatedly, and egregiously'. Indicating one reason for his animosity, he recalled how the CIA had deceived the Senate Intelligence Committee in 1984 by failing to apprise it of the covert operation to overthrow the government of Nicaragua (in protest, Moynihan had resigned as the committee's vice chairman). In an allegation that was potentially damaging to Gates, Moynihan further maintained that the CIA had for forty years 'hugely overestimated both the size of the Soviet economy and the rate of its growth' inducing *American* emulative spending that was corrosive of *American* prosperity. The CIA then failed to predict the economic collapse in the USSR and the resultant collapse of European communism. Moynihan could not have disagreed more strongly with Gates's triumphalism.[1]

The second ground on which Moynihan attacked was that of excessive secrecy. In 1981, he had gone along with a partial exemption of the CIA from the provisions of the Freedom of Information Act, arguing it was necessary to protect not only 'sources and methods' but also 'properly classified and other sensitive information'. But by the 1990s, influenced by the illegal behaviour of the agency in the previous decade and by the end of the Cold War, he took a different stance. He argued that, ever since its secret slogan of 1947—'Bigger than State by '48'—the CIA had engaged in expansionism. Its budget had grown at a rate of 17 per cent each year in the 1980s. Now that the Cold War was over, the nation should discard the CIA's illiberal and over-secretive tactics. The aggregated size of the intelligence budget (estimated unofficially at $30 billion) should be admitted and revealed. Harkening back to the days of U-1 and citing Truman's secretary of state Dean Acheson in his support, Moynihan proposed in his 'End of the Cold War Act of 1991' that the residual intelligence function of the CIA should return to the Department of State. He mounted a campaign in which he asserted that the term 'intelligence community' had become 'oxymoronic'.[2]

Moynihan went on to chair a federal commission on government secrecy, and to write a book on that subject. In the mid-1990s he was still advocating the abolition of the CIA. He shared these views with a senior Labour Party defence specialist, John Gilbert, who would serve in the Tony Blair government. He welcomed the advent of greater openness in Russia, and the long-delayed publication within the United States of information derived from the so-long-kept-secret Venona programme. Publications about Venona aired the evidence, kept out of the courts in the 1940s and 1950s for reasons of national security, that had occasioned the prosecution of the Rosenbergs as well as the arrest and trial of Alger Hiss on espionage-related charges. The libertarian left now had to confront realities conveyed by the long-buried evidence, and in this context the senator from New York was a distinctly conservative gadfly.

There were setbacks for Moynihan. Gates was duly nominated in spite of the senator's reservations, and headed the CIA, 1991–3. At first, this seemed to promise less secrecy. Gates convened a task force on greater CIA openness, and there was an acceleration in the declassification of records on past covert operations. The agency stepped up its production of official histories.

Yet although Moynihan's own commission called for less secrecy in 1993, within three years the number of classified documents had increased by 62 per cent, standing at 5,789,675. 'Madness', cried the disappointed Moynihan. When President Clinton commissioned a major inquiry into US intelligence, Moynihan's pleas fell on deaf ears. Next to the Church investigation of the 1970s, the Aspin-Brown investigation was the largest of the forty post-1946 government inquiries into intelligence. But it failed to endorse Moynihan's abolitionist demand, calling instead for a further effort at centralization. Aspin-Brown agreed with Moynihan that there should be budget disclosure, but failed to achieve it. The senator had reason to feel frustrated.[3]

In the event, though, his campaign against the CIA proved to have been a paragraph in a whole chapter of agency woes. Looking backwards from the perspective of 2008, the agency veteran Melvin Goodman would publish a book whose title conveyed its thesis: *Failure of Intelligence: The Decline and Fall of the CIA*. Goodman's was a widely held view.

Clearly, the decline and fall hypothesis needs to be qualified. The agency did not 'fall' in the sense of disappearing. It continued to perform some tasks effectively. It is an accepted if too often stated maxim that for fear of betraying its methods, an intelligence agency can rarely publicize its successes, so to dwell on failings can be a distortion of the true record. It might be added that charges of failure were nothing new in the agency's history, and stretched back to the 1940s underestimate of the speed at which the Soviet Union would develop its first atomic weapon. Moreover, some improvements were clearly visible—in the Bush Sr and Clinton administrations the agency broadened its talent pool by recruiting women and gays in a significant policy departure. There were improvements in other sections of the intelligence community, too. For example, with Louis J. Freeh as its director (1993–2001), the FBI began to haul in one Mafia boss after another, achieving successes against organized crime that had eluded the legendary bureau boss J. Edgar Hoover.

Yet it remains true that the failings of the CIA and broader US intelligence community were major, visible, and debilitating for the agency. In 1994, the FBI arrested Aldrich Ames, a senior CIA officer who turned out to have been spying for the KGB and its successor the Russian Intelligence Service. His treason had inflicted extensive damage on the US intelligence effort. If FBI partisans felt smug about this, their feeling was misplaced. For in February 2001 came the arrest of Robert Hanssen, an FBI agent who had performed similar services for the Russians. These were the two most prominent cases amongst a rash of betrayals. Now at last, the British could lay to rest their feeling of shame about the Cambridge spy ring—but at the same time, there was a case for pondering the security rating of their main ally.

The Al Qaeda terrorist assault on New York's Twin Towers in September 2011 (the '9/11' attack) resulted in roughly the same number of casualties as Pearl Harbor, and there were recriminations of a similar or even greater intensity. The FBI came in for criticism, but so did the rest of the intelligence community. After decades of heavy expenditure and false assurances, America was still vulnerable to surprise attack. Then came the Weapons of Mass Destruction (WMD) scandal. Iraq's secret development of chemical and nuclear weapons was the pretext for an Anglo-American military assault on that country in 2003 that actually had more to do with the protection of oil supplies and corporation profits. Both the CIA and MI6 succumbed to political pressure to back the WMD argument; no senior official in either agency subordinated his career to the national interest by telling the truth and/or resigning; there were comprehensive cover-ups, with Valerie Plame one of the victims. The resultant occupation of Iraq was a disaster for that country and exacted a cost that contributed to the economic decline of the USA and UK. Little wonder that the reputation of Anglo-American intelligence plummeted.

The Intelligence Reform Act of 2004 testified to the perception that there was a need for change. It created the Office of the Director of National Intelligence (ODNI), the latest attempt to have one person exert authority over the recalcitrant and feuding sections of the intelligence community. The CIA, though sometimes headed by a military person, had been essentially a civilian agency and a check on the military outlook. The DNI usurped the CIA director's role as head of the intelligence community. He talked the military talk of a man who was supposed to wage what President Bush called the 'war against terror', but was still, critics complained, a relatively feeble figure incapable of restraining the even more belligerent military-intelligence baronies. The new arrangement sidelined the CIA as a producer of intelligence estimates, consigning it instead to the practice of kidnap and murder or, to use the official language, 'rendition' (the capture of terrorist suspects and their transport to Guantanamo Bay and other locations under US control) and 'drone strikes' (the use of pilotless aircraft to kill suspected terrorists in foreign countries).

In terms of its proclaimed aims, the counter-terrorism programme was effective. The campaign of assassination by machine disrupted Osama bin Laden's network. The 2011 navy–CIA special forces operation against bin Laden's compound in Abbottabad, Pakistan, resulted in the terrorist leader's death.

However, there were questions to be asked about the health of the US intelligence community. Its conduct weakened the moral appeal of American democracy. The community's survival after the end of the Cold War had come to depend on the endless inflation of *Endless Enemies* (the title of one FBI agent's memoir). Each time the intelligence community failed, it was rewarded with more money—a politician's way of deflecting attention from his incompetence by suggesting failure was the result of intelligence under-expenditure—and a way, too, of buying the silence of intelligence officers who might blow the whistle on scandals like WMD.

But in straitened times expenditure became a problem. An internal report in 2009 accused the ODNI of allowing budget bloat, of financial mismanagement, and of lack of control over the very turf wars it had been created to halt. Critics complained there was too little bang for the bucks expended. In 2010 the Senate Intelligence Committee blasted the intelligence community for failing to collect and analyse information on the terrorist threat. In the same year, the intelligence budget peaked at $80 billion, perhaps a more honest figure than the £1.38 billion admitted to by British intelligence, but clearly on an entirely different plane even allowing for the relative sizes of the two nations. Given that level of expenditure, it was a serious matter when a Congressional Research Service report concluded that there was weak intelligence oversight and a widespread negative perception of the ODNI.[4]

Never a perfect instrument in itself—what institution is?—the American intelligence system had in the heyday of its cooperation with the British contributed to the defeat of fascism and then European communism. But by the end of the twentieth century it had developed, in addition to its inherent faults, a special weakness. It stood alone. Yes, it had loyal allies, but too loyal. It lacked real competition. Before the end of the Cold War, the KGB and Soviet military intelligence had provided an alternative interpretation of world events—an interpretation that was ideological in theory, but pragmatic in practice. After the collapse of the Soviet Union there were some alternative voices—the Qatarian broadcaster Al Jazeera began its service in 1996—but American intelligence and opinion dominated the scene. At home in the United States, it meant the American people were kept in the dark. Internationally, US intelligence domination was a recipe for subjectivity and discord.

General international cooperation was one alternative to US dominance. Moynihan was aware of President Wilson's observation back in 1919—if the League of Nations became an effective instrument for international peace, spying would cease to be necessary. In the event, Wilson had resigned himself to the necessity for an American Black Chamber and to other means of US espionage without considering the possibility that the League of Nations might be strengthened by having an intelligence service of its own. A similar question could have been asked of the United Nations—if the UN had its own intelligence, might it not prove to be an alternative to national intelligence services, or at least provide a different and more neutral perspective than that supplied by the intelligence service of a single nation state?[5]

Conor Cruise O'Brien did not think so. The Irish journalist and politician formed his view against the background of the 1960s Congo crisis. In the Congo, the Belgian colonial rulers had been a byword for ruthless exploitation and had done little to prepare the huge nation for independence. Joseph Conrad had coined the phrase 'heart of darkness' to describe the scene around 1900, Mark Twain was not far behind in the eloquence of his condemnation, and Barbara Kingsolver's more recent novel illustrates how little had improved by the end of Belgian rule. Part of the problem was the Congo's potential wealth, especially the mineral resources of its Katanga region. When Brussels suddenly conceded independence in 1960, both Moscow and Washington wanted the copper and cobalt resources.

Because the newly independent nation's elected prime minister, Patrick Lumumba, was left leaning, President Eisenhower demanded 'very straightforward action'. Accordingly the CIA delivered rubber gloves, a syringe and a lethal biological substance to be injected into Lumumba's food or toothpaste. Meanwhile the Belgians were scheming, ambitious Congolese were playing mutiny games, and there was a secession attempt in Katanga. Lumumba lasted only eleven weeks in office, and in 1961 was executed/assassinated having been betrayed into the hands of the Katangese rebels. The CIA's own assassination plans were thus made redundant as someone else had done the job, but at a cost to Congolese democracy.

In mid-1960, the United Nations sent in an armed force to restore order and prevent the secession of Katanga. The soldiers achieved the latter goal, but failed to contain a war that cost 100,000 lives and ended with the imposition of a dictatorial pro-US regime. Just as the Congo was sliding into a full-blown crisis, O'Brien found himself in the country as the special representative of Dag Hammarskjöld, the Swedish diplomat who served as UN Secretary General—and who would die in a mysterious plane crash in September 1961. *To Katanga and Back*, O'Brien's account of the Congolese imbroglio, explains how it was difficult to find out what was going on. The UN had no equivalent of the CIA or the Soviet intelligence service.

The UN did have Colonel Jonas Waern, the Swedish officer in command in South Katanga, who ran a spy ring in the strategic town of Elisabethville. The Katangan rebels saw Waern as a UN spymaster. O'Brien harboured thoughts of his own about the Swede: 'When you meet someone who is much taller, handsomer, richer and more socially exalted than yourself, you are quite likely to assume, on insufficient evidence, that he is less intelligent.' He confirmed that Waern's efforts were amateurish and 'a little comic'.

O'Brien's book carried the title *A Case History*, and he elevated Waern's deficiencies into two generalizations that would have considerable purchase in intelligence debate. The first was about ethics. He noted that while Hammarskjöld saw the absence of a UN intelligence network as 'a serious handicap' (O'Brien's paraphrase), the secretary general insisted that the UN 'must have clean hands' (Hammarskjöld's own words). O'Brien's second generalization was to do with practicalities. The UN with its cosmopolitan makeup 'could not ensure anything like the degree of security needed in serious intelligence work, and would be peculiarly liable to infiltration by agents of national services'.[6]

For many years, the UN was a cross between a sleeping giant and an emperor with no clothes. Article 99 of the UN Charter of 1945 authorized the organization to report and thus potentially to collect intelligence: 'The Secretary-General may bring to the attention of the Security Council any matter which in his opinion may threaten the maintenance of international peace and security.' Some smaller nations with fewer intelligence resources of their own to guard were keen to see a UN intelligence capability and Hammarskjöld was not the only secretary general to note that ignorance was an impediment to UN effectiveness. Hammarskjöld's successor U Thant saw the 'lack of authoritative information' as one of two 'insuperable obstacles' confronting him (the other was the doctrine of national sover-eignty). Yet in spite of such support and perceptions, Article 99 was rarely invoked and UN intelligence teetered between slumber and illusion until the end of the Cold War.

Walter Dorn, the Canadian scientist and peacekeeping activist who is the leading historian of UN intelligence, sees the pre-1990s period as one of dormancy. There was nevertheless some UN intelligence gathering and analysis in these Cold War years. Although the Swedish UN force com-mander in the Congo suggested the term intelligence should be 'banned outright' from UN discourse, his efforts to prevent civil war resulted in the creation of the mission's Military Information Branch whose unit heads called themselves 'chief intelligence officers'.

With the end of the Cold War, there was change. The UN conducted significant peacekeeping missions in the Congo once again as well as in Namibia and Rwanda. With these in progress and with communist Yugoslavia in end-of-Cold War meltdown, Balkan nationalism on the boil, and genocide in the making, there was a pressing need for a UN intelligence capability. A response came from Secretary General Boutros Boutros-Ghali. In 1993 he established a Situation Centre (SitCen), and within that an Information and Research Unit consisting of six intelligence officers supplied gratis by France, the UK, Russia, and the United States.

In 1999, the arrangement fell victim to a rebellion by poorer nations who saw it as a means of perpetuating UN control by the richer members who supplied personnel free of charge but with controlling strings attached. Nevertheless, in the first decade of the twenty-first century the UN continued to develop its intelligence facilities, venturing beyond its traditional reliance on HUMINT to draw on IMINT and SIGINT as well. By the end of the decade, the UN had 115,000 peacekeepers in the field. Only the USA had a greater number of personnel deployed in comparable activities, and there was a clear need for the UN to have intelligence back up. In 2006, it became a requirement that every UN peacekeeping mission in the field should contain a joint mission analysis centre.

These were significant developments on the tactical level. But ever since an initiative of 1988 by Argentina, Greece, India, Mexico, Sweden, and Tanzania, there has also been a demand for UN intelligence involvement in treaty verification and arms control. UN inspectors were involved on the ground in Iraq in monitoring the development (or otherwise) of weapons of mass destruction. Hans Blix, the Swedish diplomat in charge of the UN Monitoring, Verification, and Inspection Commission in Iraq, kept national intelligence services at arm's length. He regarded their product as contaminated politically. But he was unable to persuade the US and UK governments to accept his own unit's more authoritative estimates. In this case UN intelligence was competitive, but wilfully ignored.[7]

The slow rate at which the United Nations has emerged as a force in global intelligence is partly a consequence of its officials' idealistic rejection of dirty play. In turn, that reflects a broad definition of intelligence. Widely deployed since the Second World War, that definition assumes that intelligence is not just about information and analysis, but also embraces covert action and dirty tricks.

A second reason for UN tardiness has been US obstruction. America saw UN intelligence in two ways—positively as a source of potentially useful liaison, and negatively as a source of competitive estimates. The former fell victim to fears of the latter. For as ever, information was power. Just as Admiral Hall had denied codebreaking methodology to the Americans in 1917–19, so the Americans opposed the UN development of intelligence assets that would have involved the sharing of expertise as distinct from unilaterally selected information, and might have undermined their own capacity to deliver a US spin on world events.

The United States was committed to aspects of global collective cooperation that it favoured. A 1977 Senate committee on government operations review of US international policy noted that America's annual contribution to international organizations including UN agencies had risen from $129 million to $1.02 billion between 1949 and 1975. It concluded that to avoid 'diplomatic defeats', the USA needed to expend 'more effort'. There were intelligence dimensions to this contribution. For example, there was an American commitment to international police cooperation. A French initiative had established Interpol in 1914; the FBI began to cooperate with it in 1938; America increased its financial contribution to Interpol in 1974 and redoubled its enthusiasm when it assumed control of the organization in the 1980s.

In 1992, President George Bush Sr promised the UN general assembly US intelligence support for peacekeeping operations. CIA director Gates set the policy in motion. Wearing his director of central intelligence hat, Gates assigned the responsibility for UN support to the Defense Intelligence Agency. With peacekeeping crises in full spate in war-torn Rwanda and Bosnia, President Clinton repeated his predecessor's undertaking, promising in 1994 that America would 'share information, as appropriate, while ensuring full protection of sources and methods'.[8]

But President Clinton did not carry the day for US–UN liaison. Under his aegis, American officials opposed the use of the word 'intelligence' to describe functions undertaken by the UN, encouraging instead the use of the word 'information'. For their own reasons, they thus encouraged attitudes that already existed in the UN. The Americans' reasons were only partly to do with the protection of power. The charge that UN officials could not be trusted with secrets was still a motivating factor, even if it sounded strange coming from a nation that had produced Aldrich Ames. Hostility to the United Nations as a whole was another factor. The UN had been to an appreciable degree a US creation, but when membership proliferated with decolonization and America could not longer outvote its opponents in the General Assembly, the institution lost its charm. The nation that had spawned Tammany Hall politics now complained that the UN was corrupt and inefficient, and deserving only of reserved support.

Underlying this attitude, there was also a philosophical change in American politics. Out went the old-style neoconservative, radical in his youth and reactionary in later years. In came a new brand of neoconservative, professing admiration for the unilateralism of President Theodore Roosevelt (1901–9), architect of US naval might and wielder of the 'big stick' in foreign policy. American respect for legality, remarked on by Crevecœur in the eighteenth century and much in evidence since, now fell short of respect for international law. Under President Reagan, the CIA had mined the harbours of Nicaragua. The international court at The Hague condemned the action, but the new breed of neoconservative did not care. America would go it alone.

In the spring of 1992 President Bush's defence secretary, Dick Cheney, issued a draft Pentagon plan for national security. Largely written by Undersecretary for Policy Paul D. Wolfowitz, a leading neoconservative, it came to be known as the 'America Only' plan. Now the sole superpower, America would under the plan look after its allies, but should not countenance any threat to its authority. In Europe, where there were stirrings of an independent collective defence policy, the American-dominated NATO must remain the sole arbiter of power. And as the journalist Patrick Tyler put it, the America Only plan was 'conspicuously devoid of references to collective action through the United Nations'. The White House and Department of State disavowed the plan and the Republicans would lose the election of 1992. But Wolfowitz had articulated a significant viewpoint. It would be problematic for the Clinton administration long before Dick Cheney returned to office as an influential vice president, 2001–9.[9]

Reacting to a story that UN officials had leaked American secrets to Somalian warlords in a way that led to the deaths of eighteen US Rangers, Republicans in Congress drew up a series of proposals curtailing US intelligence cooperation with the UN. President Clinton refused to implement them, but the pressure increased when the Republicans won the mid-term elections of 1994. Responding to this political problem, the administration set several ascending levels of secrecy, restricting aid to the UN to the lower levels. In mid-decade, the issue attracted the attention of the Aspin-Brown inquiry. Aspin-Brown was in favour of burden sharing. Loch Johnson, an experienced intelligence investigator and scholar, helped to draw up the Aspin-Brown findings in 1996. He and his colleagues noted how the USA 'could benefit from intelligence sharing with other nations and with international organizations'.

At the time, the Clinton administration resembled an internationalist butterfly trying to escape its cage. The president signed the War Crimes Act of 1996 making it illegal for US citizens to violate the Geneva Convention of 1949, and (in 2000) the Military Extraterritorial Jurisdiction Act, making it possible to prosecute members of the US armed services for crimes committed abroad. In 2000, Clinton also signed up to the International Criminal Court to be established at The Hague for the purpose of trying the perpetrators of war crimes, crimes against humanity, and genocide. Even so, intelligence cooperation with the UN remained perilous political terrain. Aspin-Brown kept its recommendations deliberately vague for fear that congressional unilateralists 'might recoil at the idea of sharing information with the United Nations'.

Soon after 9/11, the United States once again distanced itself from the frameworks of international law. The Bush Jr administration dissociated America from the International Criminal Court. It decided to detain Al Qaeda suspects wherever they were found, and to imprison them in Guantanamo Bay, Cuba, as well as in a variety of undisclosed locations without benefit of trial until such time as they could be subjected to military tribunals. The CIA and other US intelligence agencies would be involved in the resultant procedures of kidnap and interrogation under torture. This was in the name of a 'war' against terrorism, but it was a 'war' only in a selective sense. In January 2002 President Bush suspended American compliance with the Geneva Conventions on the treatment of prisoners of war, on the ground that Al Qaeda operatives wore no uniforms and were 'illegal enemy combatants' not soldiers.

By 2010, with President Obama now in office, the United Nations was seeking the role of overseer. A UN special rapporteur on extralegal, summary, or arbitrary executions, the Australian Philip Alston, reported on the CIA's use of drones for purposes of assassination. He suggested that there might be better accountability if the military took over responsibility for the strikes. Another UN special rapporteur, Martin Scheinin from Finland,

drew up a 'Compilation of good practices on legal and institutional frameworks and measures to ensure respect for human rights by intelligence
agencies while countering terrorism'. Practice 30 stipulated that 'Intelligence services are not permitted to operate their own detention facilities or
to make use of any unacknowledged detention facilities operated by third
parties'. These are just two examples and US–UN cooperation continued in
a variety of ways, but such spats with America made the UN seem a risky
intelligence partner for other nations.[10]

Bilateral intelligence liaison thus preserved its relative pre-eminence.
Here, however, the United States was looking beyond its traditional partner, the UK. One factor accounting for this was the variegated nature of
intelligence liaison. A nation may have different liaison needs in different
parts of the world. It may also have an inner and outer tier of intelligence
collaborators. Again, intelligence runs to several different types, such as
technical, human, signals, imaging, covert operational, counter-terror, and
negative (counter-espionage). A bilateral relationship might involve one of
these types but not another, and take place at a higher or a lower level
of confidentiality. No one bilateral relationship is likely to involve all types
of liaison in every quarter of the globe at the highest level. In the case of
the US–UK relationship, there has been, in the estimate of one senior
official, consistently good interchange between the NSA and GCHQ over
SIGINT matters, and the 'bumps' in the relationship have been to do with
HUMINT and counterintelligence. With other intelligence partners, the
United States encountered different strengths and different weaknesses,
suggesting the need for a web of bilateral relationships, not just one.[11]

As Britain's global power continued to decline, America's need to look
elsewhere increased. Additionally, demographic change was continuing
apace. Immigration, always one of America's great strengths, was continuing
with undiminished vigour, and with a new diversity that did not help the
cause of traditional Atlanticists.

'Hispanic' migrants (many of native American extraction) flowed through
the porous US–Mexican boundary in an ever-increasing flood. In the years
after 2000, a million immigrants a year arrived, most of them from Latin
America, with China and India in second and third place. Californians of
European descent were now a minority of the population of their state, the
largest in the Union. Detroit had the greatest concentration of Arab speakers
of any city outside the Middle East. Like the urbanization of America that
culminated in the late 1920s, it was a transforming and irreversible trend—by

2012, fewer than half the annual births in America were to non-Hispanic whites.

Because of this changing demography as well as because of global interests, American perceptions changed. According to *Transatlantic Trends*, whereas in 2004 a majority of Americans still thought their vital interests lay mainly with Europe, by September 2011 only 38 per cent took that view, with a majority looking to Asia. President Obama envisaged a US 'pivot to the Pacific', with the nation swinging to concentrate naval and other resources in the Far East.[12]

Demography's influence on politics, diplomacy, and the tasking of intelligence agencies takes place slowly. Even if an immigrant arrives legally, and many from Latin America and Asia did not, it takes time to register for the vote and to muster up an interest in American politics and global policies. Already by the 1990s, however, there was an observable Hispanic presence in the CIA.

There were also social and geographic changes. In the 1960s, the increasing need for technicians and the Bay of Pigs disgrace had been a blow to the hitherto privileged and humanities-educated WASP. In the following decades, demographic development hastened the decline of Ivy League influence not just because of ethnic and social change, but also because America's population and voting power were no longer concentrated in the north-east. The 'Sunbelt' states stretching from Florida to California now held the cards. The new American nation no longer identified foreign policy priorities while looking eastward across the Atlantic. It gazed at new vistas, south across the Rio Grande, and west across the Pacific.[13]

Presenting an overview of US external liaison arrangements in 2006, Loch Johnson was still able to observe that there were 'close' intelligence relationships between, on the one hand America, and on the other hand, Britain and its white Commonwealth partners, Canada, Australia, and New Zealand. The US–UK link was 'a special case' because of the 'intertwined history between two enduring democracies that share a common language and culture'. He reflected a view widely held in the countries concerned. For example, Paul Monk, formerly an analyst with the Australian Defence Intelligence Organization, stated in 2003 that his country had 'a very special intelligence relationship with the Americans'.

While these were accurate observations, they referred to a limited spectrum. A number of factors undermined the 'special intelligence relationship' of old. There was the issue of the passive appendage. As it gradually supplanted MI6, the CIA had created a number of clones and clients—there were complaints, for example, that the Australian Secret Intelligence Organization (ASIO) colluded with the CIA to overthrow Prime Minister Gough Whitlam in 1975. Was ASIO an independent collaborator, or simply an extension of the CIA? Similarly, there were doubts about the independence of British intelligence over the WMD issue. British decline, US intelligence weaknesses, US unilateralism, and US demographic change all eroded faith in the Anglo-American special intelligence relationship.

The United States turned to other partners, yet became increasingly alone. It had plenty of potential friends, but did not want to trust them. This lack of trust applied both to single countries and to collective entities—the European Union, as well as the UN. There were some good reasons for this, such as the impossibility of finding a partner that could match America's intelligence resources and thus be an equal informational trading partner. There were also less good reasons, such an unwillingness to listen to other points of view, a reluctance that defied common sense. One reason behind this was a weakness inherited from the British Empire and its predecessors, imperial hubris and racial prejudice.

Loch Johnson indicated that Germany was in the upper section of the lower tier of US foreign intelligence partners, and 'closer to the norm' than the UK. Historically, Germany, and especially West Germany in the Cold War, had been strategically positioned to spy on the communist East, and had been rich, if unreliable, in the field of HUMINT.

Germany was another white country. In spite of the cosmopolitan makeup of the United States, 'Anglo-Saxon' prejudices lingered and helped to explain the Washington–Berlin axis. In contrast, US suspicions of Arab-Americans had contributed to the paucity of Arabic speakers in the American intelligence community. The danger of this ethnic bias became evident in retrospect. Intercepted Arabic-language messages would have given warning of 9/11, but the backlog was too great and they remained untranslated.[14]

There was at least some realization that in the post-Cold War environment intelligence officials from white nations might not always be the most effective partners. In January 2009, in the wake of a terrorist attack on Mumbai that killed 164 people, the former State Department analyst Wilter Andersen pointed to an urgent need for improved intelligence liaison between the USA and India.

More problematic but recognized as a critical ingredient in combating the Taliban in Afghanistan, and in stabilizing politics in a nuclear-armed nation, was the issue of US–Pakistani intelligence liaison. America suspected the CIA's partner, the Directorate of Inter-Services Intelligence, of harbouring Taliban sympathizers and of being untrustworthy. Pakistan, for its part, was embarrassed by, if complicit in, the CIA's drone strikes on targets within its borders—and angered by Obama's lack of consultation with Islamabad before sending in the team that assassinated bin Laden. Whereas in 2010 the *New York Times* reported that the US and Pakistani agencies had 'built trust', in the aftermath of the bin Laden strike the same newspaper indicated that America's 'broad security partnership with Pakistan is over'.[15]

There was an advantage in cooperating in certain intelligence fields with agencies that were otherwise unattached to the CIA, and here some accommodations were struck. The Russian Intelligence Service could be of assistance over environmental issues. Its Chinese rival was, in spite of military and trade competition with the United States, glad of US help in supplying listening stations along its Russian border.

And then there was Mossad, the Israeli intelligence service. Just as MI6 had done in the past, Mossad sometimes acted like an enemy service, spying on US secrets (in 1987, Jonathan Pollard of US naval intelligence went to prison having been found guilty of spying for Mossad). There were also questions about its reliability and expertise. There was a feeling that Israel tended to cry wolf about the atomic threat coming from Iran and Syria. Israel had to contend with memories of the sham-WMD scare over Iraq. To some observers, Israel seemed a less reliable source of information on the Arab world than Britain with its longstanding interests in the Middle East. But in the 2000s just as in the 1950s, America considered Mossad to be an indispensable ear to the ground in a region that was difficult to understand, and vital economically. It was an intelligence partnership, if of the minnow-and-whale variety.[16]

Turning back to Europe, there is some evidence that America, which had after all sponsored European unity in the 1940s and 1950s, was taking more seriously the advantages of cooperating in intelligence matters with the European Union (EU). Just after 9/11, the Dutch intelligence expert Cees Wiebes noted that as much as 60 per cent of the CIA's 'product' had, in the period of the Cold War, come from 'cooperating services'. He saw 'US–European intelligence liaison' as a way of keeping costs under control in America at a time of escalating efforts against terrorism. Another

European commentator reflected that America might want to nurture European defence integration, as it would release the USA from the obligation to resource NATO and allow it to concentrate on other parts of the globe. Still another stated that European officials were offering intelligence cooperation to the United States even as their political leaders denounced US foreign policy.

When the EU's counter-terrorism coordinator Gilles de Kerchove visited Washington in September 2011, he observed that the Obama administration was grateful for European support in winding down Guantanamo Bay. He further noted a willingness on the part of President Obama to solicit EU support for his positions, support he could deploy in internal US debate—an indication that the EU carried at least some weight. On the other hand, Kerchove reported continuing US confusion about the role the EU played, as distinct from the contributions of its member states.[17]

True though it may be that the US intelligence community obtains significant knowledge through its liaison arrangements, no one such arrangement as yet replicates the traditional bilateral relationship between the USA and the UK. Nor can it be said that any collective organization—the UN, NATO, or the EU—has hitherto supplied viable overall competition to the United States in the field of secret intelligence. None has constituted an alternative to American hegemony.

Against that background, the UK intelligence community has remained convinced that its relationship with its US counterpart is wise, and still 'special' in the sense that Britain is a privileged partner. Senior British intelligence officials are sometimes critical of US intelligence performance, but continue to see the special relationship with America as the best available option. In fact, they see an increase in the level of Anglo-American cooperation post-9/11. With the Americans supplying expensive high-technology output based on satellite and other means of espionage, the British conceive of themselves as having reciprocated with wisdom stemming from experience, expertise in specialist areas, and 'trusted peer review and second opinions'.[18]

Faith and trust are necessary to the success of a special intelligence relationship, and at the higher levels it has continued to exist in the UK regarding the US partnership. On the American side, too, there is some evidence of that faith. In June 2011, a group of a dozen middle-ranking US intelligence officials met with the author, under the auspices of the 'Georgetown salon', to discuss the state of Anglo-American cooperation. After drinks and surf-and-turf refreshment, they expressed some reservations:

the Pacific arena was now important; perhaps the British might consider a new special relationship with the emerging economic giant, India; British intelligence officials could be irritatingly condescending. However, all those present placed a high value on intelligence liaison, and none of them felt that the Anglo-American intelligence relationship had weakened.

So it is still possible for the British to speak of the Americans, in spy parlance, as 'cousins'. Yet, caution is in order. After all, if a group of men and women meet to discuss their nation's friendship with the British, they are likely to be Anglophiles. In wider American discourse less and less is heard about the special relationship with Britain. Writing on the special relationship in the 1990s, the political journalist John Dickie wrote, 'the term is rarely heard in Washington—even in the British Embassy'. Americans can find it amusing that the British harp on about the special relationship while US officials only employ the phrase to placate the British. In the view of some critics, the whole idea is a 'one-way' concept with the British doing the Americans' bidding in exchange for erratic titbits of information. The Pulitzer Prize-winning American journalist Ron Suskind was an admirer of British intelligence, but saw no evidence that the Bush administration had heeded the cautions British analysts had offered. Writing about the problem in 2008, he headlined his article 'How America Squanders Britain's Gift'.[19]

Senator Moynihan had voiced concerns about the CIA and about excessive government secrecy, and subsequent attempts at reform did little to halt the decline of US intelligence performance. US insistence on unilateralism by definition meant no reliance on any ally, and no trust in the UN. The American public and Congress were starved of access to genuinely different analyses of matters of vital importance like the WMD threat.

From the British point of view, assertions to the contrary notwithstanding, the cousin was now a more distant cousin. If the close reliance on America remained sacrosanct, it was at least partly because of the presumed absence of an alternative.

10

Europol

It was on the chilly south Hungarian plain. The arrests took place outside an obscure village, at a dwelling place that would have been indistinguishable from others, but for the high fence surrounding it. She had arrived at 6 a.m. It was the time agreed with colleagues in Vienna where a simultaneous raid was taking place. She took approximately 1,000 photographs. Because of the need to protect victim identities, just two of the images made it into the public domain. At 11 p.m. she quit the place, leaving behind a team of forensic specialists.

Angelika Molnar was born about 60 miles from Budapest in the village of Sarbogard. By the time she graduated in history from the Sorbonne, she was fluent in Hungarian, English, Spanish, and French. Slim, good looking, talented, the world was her oyster. She decided to work for the Hungarian National Police in Budapest. There, she specialized in intelligence and analysis. It was in Budapest that she began to partake in the effort to combat human trafficking. Her work against involuntary servitude included the detection of child labour and the exploitation of minors for sex and prostitution. She did not consider this to be stereotypically female work foisted on her by male colleagues; indeed much of her other work was to do with the importation of Chinese men who were being forced to toil in conditions of near-slavery.

By the time of the raid on 11 November 2010, she was working at the European Police Office in The Hague—Europol. A few days after the swoop, she agreed to narrate a discreet version of events. She spoke in English, with a restrained passion in her voice, but with an underlying matter-of-factness. The following account is closely based on her story.

The five victims found on site were Hungarian and Romanian. Under Hungarian law, the ethnic identity of victims and suspects cannot be revealed, nor their names except under special circumstances. However, at least two and possibly three of the three girls found on site were Roma, as was the chief suspect, a 54-year-old Hungarian man who ran the establishment with a 36-year-old female accomplice, his current wife. The Roma, sometimes mislabelled 'Gypsies' on the misunderstanding that they come from Egypt, are the result of an ancient diaspora from North India. Numbers of them escaped Hitler's attempts at extirpation in the Second World War. Around ten million Roma live mainly in eastern and east central Europe. They are still subject to persecution and discrimination and, like other oppressed people, have thrown up their own criminals.

The house in southern Hungary was a staging post for sex slaves. The ages of the girls who passed through the establishment ranged from 18 down to 13. They came from poverty-stricken backgrounds and would typically flee and seek independence because of family difficulties at home. The arrested suspect offered them an income earned through domestic service. After a while they were told they owed a large amount of money for board and lodging, which they could pay off with sex work. If they demurred they had to endure physical and psychological abuse. So barren was their emotional life that they would be influenced by false 'love promises'. It was a brain-washing process, and many of the girls involved came to believe that they had a good deal and would be worse off in any other situation. If under 18 they would be kept imprisoned and exploited within Hungary. Up to that age, police could lawfully intervene so they had to be kept hidden in one country. Once 18 and in possession of papers, the police would have to back off if they claimed they needed no help and were OK.

At 18, they would be ready for export to a more affluent country. Sent to Austria, the young women worked in 'studios', the euphemistic Austrian-German word for brothels. Denied any contact with their families, they were forced to entertain 15–20 clients a day, and to provide 'extreme sexual services'. They lived their lives behind boarded-up windows.

Once alerted to the problem, there were those who were willing to help. Newspapers were cooperative in supplying publicity. The English actress Emma Thompson campaigned against child exploitation. But, Molnar observed, passers-by in the street who might have been in a position to alert police were too often oblivious and indifferent to the crimes being committed under their noses.

What started as a bilateral Austro-Hungarian operation became a Europol concern when the international repercussions were evident. Realizing that the sex ring extended to Romania, the Hungarian police and the Austrian

Criminal Intelligence Service asked Europol for help. Specialists in Europol now tracked phone calls and banking records, supplied analytical and logistical help, and finally sent Molnar and other officers to the scenes of the arrests.

And so it came to pass that the Hungarian special forces struck in a 'rescue and free' operation in the early hours of that November day. Both Hungarian law and European Union Council of Ministers rules required a female presence in this kind of raid, and in addition to Molnar two Hungarian policewomen took part. The officials found their targets sleepy and unresisting. They led them away in handcuffs. In addition to the main suspect and his current wife, there were two male accomplices.

Molnar's busy camera recorded a luxurious dwelling place kept tidy by the enslaved labourers. It was crowded by crass displays of wealth and power ranging through jewellery, a leopard skin draped across one bed, the skins of rare (and illegally traded) snakes on the floor, ornate furniture, many motor scooters, six Harley Davidson motorbikes mostly gathering dust, 43,000 euros in cash, and a number of guns. Guns—under lock and key—were also found in a second house behind the first, a slum in which the girls were housed and abused.[1]

A few corridors and staircases away from the office of Angelika Molnar was that of Mauro Falesiedi, a senior specialist within the Criminal Finances and Technology Unit at Europol. He told another tale of detection, to do with his long-term work against money laundering. He recalled the raids of 25 May 2010 against the multinational criminal ring orchestrated by Christopher Kinahan and other members of the Kinahan clan in Ireland. The coordinated arrests of twenty-six people took place simultaneously at 4.30 a.m. in England, Spain, and Ireland. Seven hundred and fifty police officers searched premises and followed leads in Ireland, Belgium, Spain, and the UK, freezing bank accounts, restraining assets, and seizing cash, drugs, and guns.

Falesiedi described the sophistication of the Kinahan operation. Unlike the 'family' arrangements of the Mafia in his native Italy, the Kinahanites were highly professional in setting up a multi-disciplinary organized crime ring. They included specialized criminals, like the lawyers in Madrid who advised on money laundering. They filmed car movements near their places of operation to detect any unusual traffic, and traced the registration numbers. Pitted against them, however, were the intelligence resources of a number of national police forces. Europol helped with coordination and analysis. The agency deployed three mobile offices at the time of the raid. Europol officials were present at the Malaga, Dublin, and London venues, each carrying computers with direct access to Europol data. Falesiedi was present at the coordination centre set up by the UK's Serious Organized Crime Agency (SOCA) near London. Europol by 2010 had liaison officers from all European member states, natives of their respective countries who could help with urgent domestic requests for assistance, translation, and coordination issues.

Born in a medieval village in the Etruscan area of the Lazio region of Italy, Mauro Falesiedi was the son of a farmer who been the local mayor. His brothers were a doctor and a carpenter—he was the only police officer in his family. Though in possession of university qualifications including a master's in law from the Robert Schuman University in Strasbourg, he had worked his way up through the ranks, becoming a detective inspector and then deputy superintendent with the Italian state police. He worked against the Italian Mafia-type organizations before joining Europol in 2003.

His career and that of Angelika Molnar illustrate how Europol officers were mainly drawn from the ranks of existing national police forces. At first, there were whispers that only the less ambitious agreed to serve with Europol. It was a bit like a professor getting off the publication treadmill to serve for a spell with the CIA—when you returned to your post, others in your original place of employment had surged ahead in your absence. So if you were a go-getter, you clung to the treadmill in your own profession rather than stepping off to serve in a wider capacity. However, the hope was that those adventurous enough to accept a challenge with Europol were creating a new pan-European ethos, and a prestige of their own.[2]

The director of Europol exhibited a different career pattern from that of the detectives who arrived through the revolving door and expected eventually to return to their national police forces. Appointed in 2009, Rob Wainwright was already a career manager in the area of international policing. He became head of the UK Liaison Bureau at Europol in 2000 and then served as chief of the international department of SOCA, at the time of its inception in 2006 depicted as Britain's answer to the FBI.

With Hungary's Ferenc Banfi sponsored for the Europol job by a coalition of the EU's newer member states, supporters of Wainwright significantly had to fight to get their candidate appointed in succession to Max-Peter Ratzel. There had been a similar tussle over Ratzel's appointment in 2004. That the directorship of Europol had become a political prize was an indication that the young agency was beginning to carry some weight.[3]

In the year of Wainwright's appointment, Europol was just a decade old. It was the logical outcome of half a century of European integration, but also of a recent spurt of events. In 1991, Germany's Chancellor Helmut Kohl invigorated the debate over police cooperation when he called for a European FBI. In the following year, the Treaty of Maastricht accelerated integration by creating the European Union (EU). The treaty set up an operational and constitutional 'pillar' for Justice and Home Affairs, and gave it responsibility for fighting drugs, terrorism, and organized crime. Negotiations began on the creation of a European Police Office.

At this point, a reaction set in against anglophonic domination. When the EU's Council of Ministers debated the first Europol convention, the working papers and minutes were mainly in English. The French lodged several objections. It is easy to see how people might unconsciously recoil from a policing solution that was pre-packaged in the English tongue and seemed to be modelled on solutions in a far-off English-speaking country. Nevertheless, the founding member states of the European Union were united in their perception of the need for a common policing approach to combating the *threat du jour*, drugs cartels. The galloping processes of integration in themselves deepened that need. Notably the Schengen agreement of 1985, incorporated into EU law by the Treaty of Amsterdam in 1997, did away with border controls between participating nations. It was wonderful for business, trade, and leisure, but also an opportunity for international crime syndicates to go global. There was a need for countervailing police powers.[4]

In 1999, Europol began to function. Its headquarters were in The Hague. When the tourist alights from a train at the redbrick neo-renaissance Den Haag HS station, it is possible to purchase a humble raw herring sandwich before taking a clockwork-regular tram to view the modest royal palace. Redolent in these ways of Dutch tradition, the city nevertheless offers cosmopolitan advantages. It is close to Brussels, the administrative hub of the EU in neighbouring Belgium. It houses the UN International Court of Justice, located in the Peace Palace constructed in 1907–13 with money donated by the Scottish-American philanthropist Andrew Carnegie. The court has adjudicated in high-profile cases such as that arising from the CIA's mining of Nicaragua's harbours. The Hague was additionally the venue for the trial in 2000 (under Scots law) of the Libyans accused of the Lockerbie bombing of 1988. Following a decision made in 1999, the city would in 2002 become host to the EU's own anti-crime judicial cooperation unit, Eurojust. The Hague must have seemed an appropriate location when Jürgen Storbeck went to work as Europol's first director, appointed for a statutory four-year term and presiding over a staff of 144.

Europol developed new priorities in response to events. Indeed Claude Moraes, a member of the European Parliament's Committee on Civil Liberties, Justice, and Home Affairs, saw police politics as 'fashion driven'. A consortium of twelve European nations known as the Trevi group (they first met in Rome, site of the famous fountain) had called for a more coordinated approach to anti-terrorism in the wake of the 1972 anti-Israeli attack at the Munich Olympic Games. The 9/11 attacks in the USA gave a new urgency to the need to combat terrorism collectively. The European Council agreed on a 'Plan of Action' that envisaged a squeeze on terrorist finances, information sharing with the USA, the introduction of a European arrest warrant, the formation of Eurojust, and the expansion of Europol.

Even in the post-9/11 climate, Europol was expected to do more than fight terrorism. In the following year, 2002, a powerful core of EU member states adopted a common currency, the euro. Europol now had to focus on a new threat, that posed to the new currency by counterfeiters—in 2009, it would help Polish and Spanish detectives to arrest twenty-seven suspects and destroy an international ring.

Other main concerns of Europol arose from general criminal activity. Its activities against involuntary labour fell into this category. So did its operations against paedophile networks. One milestone in this never-ending task was reached in 2002, when Europol supplied intelligence analysis and image processing expertise to an operation codenamed TWINS that attacked an internet-based child pornography consortium that operated in Canada, the United States, and nine European nations. It resulted in fifty arrests.

Europol's development of a crime-scene website illustrated its intelligence-based approach. Launched in 2008 in conjunction with the European Network of Forensic Science Institutes, the research-based unit worked to introduce greater sophistication into investigations of DNA, crimes involving firearms, and the illegal trafficking of nuclear materials and technology. Investing further in computer technology, Europol sought to ensure that EU police forces could communicate quickly; it provided a specialist portal to assist collaboration between national anti-terrorism teams.

In a glossy publication issued to celebrate its tenth birthday, Europol confronted one of the reservations people entertained towards it, that it might prove a leaky vessel unsuited to intelligence activities. It asserted that internationally there was now 'growing trust' in its operations.

In one area, that may have been optimistic. In the aftermath of 9/11, Europol had, following European Council instructions, established a Counter Terrorism Task Force. But turf-protective national intelligence agencies proved to be less enthusiastic about the arrangement than their political masters. The operational argument they advanced was that it would be dangerous to trust Europol with information that might, if leaked, betray the identity of an informant or inflict some other damage.

Starved of the information essential to the performance of its job, the Task Force closed down. Information hoarding continued. Gilles de Kerchove (appointed EU Counter Terrorism Coordinator in 2007) complained, 'the intelligence community is not very eager to work with Europol'. Adrian Fortescue, a senior official at the European Commission, agreed: 'The one EU agency institutionally mandated to play an intelligence role, EUROPOL, has never [as of 2004] been provided with the material to conduct analyses which could add much substantive value to what the well-equipped Member States are willing to share on a bi- or tri-lateral basis with each other—and indeed with certain privileged third countries.'

Yet it began to become apparent that there were dangers in non-cooperation. As one of Kerchove's advisers put it in 2010, while it may have been hazardous to surrender information, it was even more dangerous *not* to divulge, for a terrorist incident might occur that intelligence distribution could have prevented. In the wake of lethal consequences, the mute had reason to fear retribution.[5]

In a decision made in 2008 and given force on 1 January 2010, Europol became a fully-fledged agency of the EU. Previously, individual contributions from member states had financed the agency, but in a new expression of trust it now had the power to submit an annual financial bid through the regular EU budgetary process. A simplified governance structure meant that, while the agency still reported to the EU Council of Ministers, a single member of the council would now chair a management committee overseeing the activities of Europol personnel, numbering 800 by 2012. A representative of the EU Commission, the civil service based in Brussels, would sit on the committee. Following ratification of the Treaty of Lisbon in 2009 with its enhanced powers for Brussels, there was furthermore an expectation that the European Parliament would have greater power of oversight over the agency. It was as if the FBI had broken free from control by a committee of state governors to become a federal agency at last. Europol was becoming a trusted instrument of EU government.[6]

Though it was a young institution, Europol inspired faith and expectations amongst its supporters. In 2004, Member of the European Parliament (MEP) Bill Newton Dunn issued a pamphlet, bearing the insignia of the UK Liberal Democrats but conveying his personal views, called *Europe Needs an FBI*. Like Chancellor Kohl, then, he thought the FBI was an admirable institution, and that Europe needed its own model.

Newton Dunn had watched the American scene. He conducted a dialogue with Bob Heibel, a former FBI deputy chief of counter-terrorism who, since his retirement, had taught at Mercyhurst University, Erie, Pennsylvania, an institution that offered remote and on-campus training for existing and intending intelligence personnel. Newton Dunn's pamphlet showed an awareness of the bureau's weaknesses, such as its fraught relations with the CIA. It also took note of the bureau's policy of leaving much of America's law enforcement to the local police. What this showed, Newton Dunn reassured his readers, was that a European FBI would not 'interfere in national policing'.

Newton Dunn wrote of a litany of problems that needed to be tackled urgently, including cyber crime, trafficking in heroin and people, gangs, money laundering, car theft, currency forgery, and identity theft. In all these areas as well as in the realm of terrorism, criminals posing a threat to EU citizens were organized internationally, both within and outside Europe. In his view, the European intelligence and policing response would only succeed if organized on the federal principle.[7]

Rob Wainwright spoke up for his agency for professional reasons. It is worth noting, though, that people—if lucky—do the jobs for which they are suited. Wainwright grew up Welsh-speaking in Pontyberem, Carmarthenshire, and attended Gwendraeth Grammar, the school that produced rugby legends Carwyn James, Barry John, and Jonathan Davies. His father, though, was English. The future Europol boss preferred Shakespeare to Dylan Thomas, took out a subscription to the *Economist* at the age of 13, and studied at the London School of Economics. His bicultural background gave him not so much a federalist inclination as an appreciation of cosmopolitanism. This was not to deny local and family influences. He was conscious of a family tradition of social radicalism—the tradition claimed as an ancestor Stephen Evans, a leader in the 1843 'nightly meetings' to destroy toll gates, in which men, to disguise themselves, dressed as 'Rebecca'. And he was fond of his maternal grandfather William David Griffith, chief librarian at the Carmarthen Public Library. Griffith had fought with the British expeditionary force in Norway in 1940, and Wain-wright appreciated the help the FBI had once given him as he searched for the locations of his grandfather's military encounters. Wainwright felt that his family background contributed to his strong desire to be of public service.

Like Newton Dunn and other Europol supporters, Wainwright saw the agency as a useful tool against terrorism. Looking to the future, he singled out another of Newton Dunn's concerns. Cyber security, he remarked in 2010, was emerging as a major threat. It was costing Europe €100 billion per annum in VAT avoidance alone. Europol offered the member states of the EU 'cradle to grave' support for operations against such threats. It was able to 'thread together' the disparate elements of complex cases. Given the international nature of modern crime, it was essential to have a 'European overview'.

As crime was not just Europe-wide but global, it was also vital to operate more widely, and Europol was working on such cooperation. Already there was outreach to about ten non-European countries such as Colombia and Israel, and in non-EU Europe he was forging links with Russia. Cooper-ation with the FBI was developing—here, Wainwright emphasized the traditional intelligence precept of the need for give as well as take on both sides.[8]

Some senior officials voiced concern about Europol's effectiveness. Analysis and intelligence (as opposed to on-the-ground police work) were the organization's main functions. According to CIA orthodoxy, the 'intel-ligence cycle' consists of the following activities: new requirements (tasking by political executives), planning and direction, collection, processing, analysis, and production, and dissemination. Europol's weakness, according to its critics, lay in its absence of any direct collection facility. The infor-mation it analysed came from the police forces of member states. Because it did not collect its own data, it could not offer choice morsels on an exclusive basis in exchange for offers of data from overseas agencies. Consequently Europol received, in the words of one senior EU official, only 'fag ends' of information from the CIA. A fellow EU official observed that the Americans made a major foreign intelligence-liaison effort in the aftermath of 9/11, but Europol was just one cog in the process. The same official noted that Europol was making no more than a modest contribution to anti-terrorism activities, though he conceded that the agency was effective in fighting globally organized crime syndicates.

Defenders of Europol pointed out that it was not meant to be a collection agency. The agency concentrated on analysing information that flowed in from police and other sources. It aimed to enlighten about general problems as well as about particular crimes and crises. For example, intelligence agencies in France and elsewhere took note of 'TE SAT', the Europol-produced EU Terrorism Situation and Trend reports. Publicly available annual TE SAT reports based on data from all EU member states assessed how the nature of threats was changing, and offered statistically based summaries of counter-terrorism efficacy on a Europe-wide basis and in individual countries.

This was not information that would be 'traded' with national intelligence agencies. Rather, it was the accessible result of a cooperative and centrally coordinated effort. A further step in the direction of cooperation had been the formation, in 2005, of the European Police College. Located in Hampshire, England, and described by the local Eurosceptic Conservative MEP as 'an appalling waste of money', the college aimed at harmonization of police practices across Europe, and ran courses in various EU countries on such topics as witness protection.[9]

Libertarian barbs directed at Europol have been more prominent than criticisms of its ineffectiveness. They reflected longstanding fears of the FBI-Gestapo bogeyman. There was an architectural dimension to this. In July 2011, Europol moved into a smart new building designed by the Dutch firm Quist Wintermans. As a visual statement it was reminiscent of the FBI's power-building erected in the 1970s, and it even stood on a street, Eisenhowerlan, named for the US Cold War president. Before that, Europol had occupied a building once requisitioned by the Gestapo.

But the libertarian critique of Europol stemmed also from that US gift, the campaign for government in the sunshine that had peaked in the 1970s, revived under the inspiration of Senator Moynihan and others, and had an impact on the rest of the world.

No doubt that helped to explain the caution in British political circles. In spite of strong support from the British police for the creation of Europol, the Home Office in 1995 shrank from the prospect of operational cooperation. In the words of its spokesman Peter Wrench, 'the original proposal for Europol envisages a sort of European FBI and that idea has not gone away on the part of some countries, but a clear majority are against going in that direction in the foreseeable future'. A House of Lords report warned of the need to be on guard against 'great dangers to individuals'.[10]

Prominent amongst the early critics was the UK civil liberties group Statewatch. One of its activists, Tony Bunyan, had been prominent in the US-inspired UK campaign for open government in the 1970s and 1980s. In 1995, Bunyan greeted the adoption of the Europol convention with a pamphlet arguing that the new organization was the result of a 1980s conspiracy by UK, German, and other police chiefs to promote 'the idea of a European-style FBI'. The convention had been 'drawn up in secret', the European Parliament had not been consulted, and there was no provision for parliamentary oversight. Statewatch's stance had not softened by the time Ben Hayes wrote on the issue in 2002. Hayes subtitled his tract 'towards an unaccountable "FBI" in Europe' while a section in the Statewatch website was titled 'EU-FBI surveillance plan'.[11]

According to Niels Bracke, a senior official at the General Secretariat of the EU Council charged with Europol and anti-terrorist liaison, Bunyan and his colleagues grossly overestimated the powers of Europol, and saw abuses where none existed. But Statewatch's critique won a sympathetic hearing in at least one conservative quarter, *The Daily Telegraph*. Commenting on a 45.9 per cent boost in Europol's budget post-9/11, a Brussels correspondent wrote in the *Telegraph* that Europol seemed to be developing into 'a sort of joint FBI/CIA wrapped together in The Hague'. It was further acquiring the kind of powers that had 'allowed the FBI in Washington to gain the whip-hand over the US state and city police forces'. Members of the British contingent in Brussels worried that any hint of an aggregation in Europol powers would provoke stories in the populist press about the return of 'jackboot' practices in Europe.[12]

The UK decided not to sign the additional Europol Protocol of 1996, whereby the European Court of Justice could rule on interpretations of the Europol Convention. The election of a new Labour government in 1997 seemed to promise a change in approach, with Foreign Secretary Robin Cook endorsing police cooperation at European level. But in 2003 the House of Lords (then still the forum for Britain's senior judges) issued a further report that was critical of a 2002 Europol/USA agreement facilitating the exchange of personal data. Perhaps perceiving a threat to the special Anglo-American relationship as well as to national sovereignty and personal liberty, it complained that 'the draft agreement was deposited very late, when it appeared that the text had already been agreed with the United States'.[13]

Critical voices came from other countries, too. The French security expert Jean-Claude Monet had been one of the first to complain about the lack of EU transparency in police matters. In the European Parliament, though, British dissent was prominent. MEP Sarah Ludford and her civil liberties allies spoke out in 2002 against the dangers of personal data sharing between the Schengen Information System (an internal EU crime data base) and Europol, and between Europol and non-EU countries like Russia and the USA. Ludford continued to voice her concerns, in 2005 warning about the dangers inherent in the retention of EU border-control personal details. Ludford's fellow parliamentarian Claude Moraes conceded that the small size of Europol, just 535 at the time of his remarks in 2005, made it too unthreatening to be regarded as Gestapo-like. But he, like his British compatriots, remained alert to the agency's shortcomings.[14]

There have been strenuous denials that Europol is a European FBI. In part, these denials were reactions to civil libertarian complaints such as those just described—how dare the critics suggest that Europol could be as bad as the FBI? In part, they were expressions of historical literacy—after all, Europe had its own police traditions and, in the case of Germany, an example of how police cooperation could succeed in a federal polity, so there was no need to borrow from an American example. In addition, FBI-denial was a symptom of the EU's determination to find a European way, and to be independent.

Chancellor Kohl in 1997 apologized for having used the phrase 'European FBI'. Within Europol itself, officials avoided the label. Willy Bruggeman, deputy director of Europol, stated in 2000, 'Europol is NOT an FBI and is not intended to become a comparable instrument of the EU.' Two years later, the sentiment found its way onto the FAQ section of the Europol website: 'Is Europol a European FBI? No.' Europol official Søren Kragh Pedersen noted in 2005 that there was no talk of the FBI at headquarters, even if he hinted at some ambivalence because the FBI was 'still a good brand name'. The Frenchman Yves Joannesse, Europol desk officer at the European Commission, observed in the same year that some commentators were ignorant of Europol. They designated the agency a European FBI only in a lazy act of 'copy and paste'.

It was not that EU officials were averse to learning lessons from abroad. In fact, in 2004 the EU's Directorate General of Justice, Freedom, and Security issued an edition of Adrian Fortescue's study, *A European View of the U.S. Department of Homeland Security*. Fortescue had conducted his research with the support of Harvard University after demitting office as director general for justice and home affairs at the European Commission. He noted that the FBI had not been incorporated into the Department of Homeland Security (DHS). Nevertheless, could the DHS offer lessons for Europe? But while Fortescue was receptive to American example, he also issued a counter-suggestion: 'EU might learn, but also perhaps teach.'[15]

It is controversial to say that Europol is a European FBI. In the aftermath of the Second World War America had been enthusiastic about the concept of a United States of Europe and about the development of federal European institutions. However, the FBI had no claim to paternity of Europol, nor was there a conscious EU effort to model Europol on the FBI. Nevertheless, federal entities may share some similar characteristics. FBI–Europol comparisons can usefully be made, and it is legitimate to ask whether the EU might learn from the FBI experience. It is instructive to approach these issues under three headings: powers, race, and oversight.

In the realm of powers, certain constitutional and legal facets of FBI history are of interest. In 2001 there were, according to one estimate, more than 3,300 federal crimes on the American statute books, with more in the offing as members of Congress saw political advantage in promoting 'get tough' legislation. Such a body of legislation gave the American agency the legal basis for its work. It was, however, a situation that had taken decades to develop. The corpus of laws for the FBI to enforce expanded only slowly. The 1911 Mann Act (also known as the White Slavery Act) empowered it to operate against those who operated the vice trade but only when that trade crossed state lines thus coming within the ambit of the interstate commerce clause of the US Constitution. In the First World War, the Espionage Act created further powers for the FBI, powers that were exercised again in the Second World War, the Cold War, and in the post-2001 recent 'war' against terror. The bureau's repertoire expanded in other respects, too, at least in the case of interstate crimes. By the 1920s, it was investigating automobile thefts. By the 1930s, it was hunting down kidnappers. The Civil Rights Act of 1964 and the Racketeer Influenced and Corrupt Organizations Act of 1970 added to its investigative duties.

There was still no federal crime of murder. It was a state crime. 'Jumping the fence' became a standard ruse for gangsters on the run—they would reach the state line where the city or state cops in hot pursuit would skid to a halt, with the FBI unauthorized to offer help except by circuitous means— Al Capone went to prison for tax evasion, not homicide. The National Association for the Advancement of Colored People's inter-war campaign for a federal anti-lynching law failed. Misuse of the US Forest Service's mascot 'Smokey Bear' risks a dawn raid by special agents of the FBI, but there is no federal crime of murder in the USA. In the case of many other serious crimes, too, FBI special agents simply advised on the basis of their specialist expertise, or assisted at the scene under local supervision.

In the twenty-first century wearers of cagoules marked 'Europol' began to appear at European crime scenes. But, whereas the FBI acquired the duty of enforcing a portfolio of federal laws, Europol has had not a single federal law to enforce, because there is no such thing as a European statutory crime. In the original debate over Europol's remit, the Greek presidency proposed that the new federal police agency would fight drugs trafficking and other serious international crime only where such activities occurred 'within the territories of at least two Member States', a provision that remains embedded in the Europol convention. There is a parallel with the US interstate commerce provision here, but the Greek presidency proposal went further. Europol would function only in cases where 'the form of crime is liable to prosecution in *all* Member States'. Its remit was to supply intelligence in the fight against organized crime, which, of course, applied by definition to crimes committed in more than one country. It could investigate murders, but only if the killing was conducted in an organized manner.[16]

As there was no constitutional provision for EU criminal law, the Council in 1997 adopted an action plan with the goal of 'harmonization of laws' in the member states. When a new European constitution was under discussion in 2005, it was envisaged that a European Public Prosecutor's Office would have powers to deal with 'serious crime having a cross-border dimension', but only after unanimous authorization by the EU Council of Ministers and after obtaining the consent of the European Parliament. The British opposed the measure, but the Treaty of Lisbon confirmed the principle of EU measures against cross-border crime, with some expectation that Eurojust should develop a facility for European public prosecution.[17]

Until the 1930s, FBI special agents rarely made arrests, and almost never carried guns—the FBI manual of 1927 expressly forbade the carrying of weapons except in extreme circumstances. All that changed in the 1930s, as the bureau's 'G-Men' waged war against the gangsters of the Al Capone era. One criticism later levelled at the FBI was that it developed an 'arrest culture' that undermined its detective and intelligence functions, rendering it ineffective as a counter-terrorism agency. According to Niels Bracke, in the EU there was no perception of any need for federal arrest-and-shoot practices, as the police forces of the EU member states were stronger and better organized than their equivalents in the states of the American Union.[18]

Some developments nevertheless occurred that helped both Europol and national police forces to facilitate the apprehension of suspected terrorists and other serious criminals. In 2002, in a further reaction to the 9/11 attacks, the European Council agreed on a formula for issuing European arrest warrants. In 2010, a new Council handbook on how to handle the legal side of making European arrests noted that the warrants were 'a radical change from the old extradition system'. In the first year of operation, 2004–5, EU warrants led to 836 arrests being made. By 2008–9, with EU membership having in the meantime expanded from 25 to 27 nations, the annual aggregate of EU-warrant arrests stood at 4,431.[19]

Eurojust was an addition to the EU's judicial machinery. It complemented the European Court of Justice in Luxembourg, the court of appeal since 1952 in matters of EU (non-criminal) law, and Strasbourg's European Court of Human Rights, the custodian of the European Convention on Human Rights established in 1959. Though it arose from earlier thinking, Eurojust took shape after 9/11. In 2003, it moved to its permanent head-quarters in The Hague. Each of the member states nominated national members who would be senior judges, magistrates, and police officers with appropriate experience. They and their stand-in assistants made up the College of Eurojust, around 50 in number by 2010, with a further 200 personnel in administrative support. In 2006, the US Department of Justice agreed to establish within Eurojust the position of US Liaison Prosecutor. But Eurojust's main business was the coordination of investigations and prosecutions across Europe. It cooperated with national police forces, for example the Belgian Federal Police in its 2008–10 operation against the computer pirating of movies and TV series. And it had the duty to assist and advise Europol.[20]

The Lisbon Treaty strengthened Eurojust and in February 2010 Aled Williams became president of the expanding institution. Of Welsh-speaking parentage, Williams grew up in England 'an Essex boy' and graduated in history from Cambridge University. Thereafter, he studied law, worked for the British Crown Prosecution Service as a Spanish liaison prosecutor, and married a Spanish woman. Well placed to take an objective view of British reservations about the EU and its growing powers, he thought the 'Eurosceptics vs. Europhiles' dogfight was just an invention of British journalists.

He preferred to see a discursive tension on the lines defined by Jean-Claude Piris, the long-serving legal counsel of the European Council. Piris framed the debate as one between 'integrationists' and 'cooperationists'.

Williams envisaged an increase in Eurojust work and responsibilities. For example, although Eurojust was casework driven, there was a need to implement Article 86 of the Lisbon Treaty, providing for a European Prosecutor 'from Eurojust'. Member states would need to entrust more information to Eurojust. Eurojust would facilitate the development of 'letters of request' as a means of putting information in the possession of one country into the hands of prosecutors in other countries.

It would, however, be a mistake to conclude that Eurojust, any more than Europol, was developing an arrest culture at the expense of informational and intelligence-based contributions to law enforcement and anti-terrorism. Williams saw no parallel between Eurojust and institutions in other federalized (meaning centralized) nations like the USA or Australia. It was a loose arrangement more akin to the work of IberRed, the Ibero-American Network for International Legal Cooperation, the prosecution exchange of expertise service for Latin America and the Iberian peninsula.[21]

Seen in these wider contexts, Europol was evidently increasing its powers, but the development of European arrest warrants and Eurojust prosecutorial activities did not mean it was adopting an arrest culture. Rather, they provided for Europe-wide arrest procedures that kept Europol relatively free from arrest responsibilities, giving it scope to concentrate on intelligence and analysis. If Europol was increasingly effective against organized crime, the reason was because of enhanced intelligence work.

The problem of racism is of critical importance in police and detective work. There is a need for the fair treatment of suspects, and for fair recruitment practices by police, detective, and intelligence authorities. For while fairness is desirable in all public and indeed private agencies, in the case of police and investigators it needs to be a goal that is especially and proactively pursued. To ignore a racial, ethnic, or religious minority in one's recruitment practices is often to deprive oneself of an intelligence asset. Then again, in most non-European countries as well as in the EU, the police come under the umbrella of an entity that calls itself 'Justice'. Should justice not be both done and seen to be done, a feeling of injustice ensues, with dire consequences for the victims of discrimination—and, potentially, for the rest of society, as the oppressed of our world have a long history of seeking retribution, whether through informal crime or through well-organized terrorism.

The history of the United States illustrates these points. There have been examples of judicial and police bias ranging from the poor treatment of slaves through the FBI's harassment of Martin Luther King to the non-recruitment of American Arabic speakers into the intelligence community in the 1990s. The Civil War, the race riots of the 1960s, and 9/11 are examples of the consequences. At the same time, America has adopted some fair practices, ranging from the creation of the Department of Justice in 1870 specifically to fight racism to policies of 'positive discrimination' to increase, for example, the numbers of African Americans in police forces, the FBI, and the CIA.

Europe, too, has a history of racial and religious discrimination with atrocities ranging from the Crusades to the Holocaust. Post-Second World War Europe contained survivors of previous persecution like the Roma, added to which there was the influx of Turkish workers to Germany, and post-colonial immigration from North Africa, Asia, the West Indies, and elsewhere. As of 2010, 31 million people who had been born outside Europe resided in EU countries, and many more were the descendants of immigrants. With the exception of the West Indians, the majority were Muslim or otherwise non-Christian. There was a need for equal treatment and equal hiring by police forces; equally there was an opportunity to employ minority members who might be useful for their language skills and other intelligence assets.

Europol did not fare well in this regard. Europol does retain the services of multi-cultural Dutch citizens, a reflection of Netherlands legal requirements—a visit to Europol headquarters will reveal the presence of non-white guards and secretaries. But as of 2005 the elite police-officer/ detective force was all white, with no Muslims. Following the EU's enlargement to the south and east, Europol set out to acquire a capability in the new European languages, but there was much less emphasis on Arabic and Farsi, in spite of the importance of those languages to anti-terrorist work.[22]

Europol and its supporters disputed the charge of prejudice on a number of grounds. While it could advertise lower-rank jobs in the local Dutch press, employees in the 'officer class' were either seconded by the police forces in their own member states, or successful applicants from police backgrounds in member states. Europol had no control over the hiring practices of those member state police forces. The suggestion was that, excepting the British police with its policy of proactive recruitment of minorities (a reaction to charges of 'institutional racism'), the police forces of Europe were largely prejudiced against minorities, a circumstance that affected Europol's recruitment pool. Another defence, one of the type that is heard in America, too, is that a minority-group applicant, for example, a Frenchman of Magreb ancestry, might have qualifications that were inferior to those of a white candidate, or he might be untrustworthy because he would sympathize with Muslim terrorists. Such persons should not be appointed merely to appease the advocates of political correctness.[23]

A further defence was that Europol is no worse than the EU's institutions as a whole, which are generally white and culturally Christian. This is true. In 2004, if Muslims had been elected to the European Parliament in proportion to the Muslim population in the EU, 24 of the 785 members would have been of that faith. The actual number was 8. If one attended a plenary meeting of the Committee on Civil Liberties, Justice, and Home Affairs in the European Parliament Building in 2005, one witnessed an imposing and crowded committee room that would dwarf the entire parliaments of some nations. Black-skinned tourist groups from former European colonies might occupy the back rows. For a few rows in front of them would sit privileged officials and observers, all white. The inner core consisted of committee members. Although the committee has contained MEPs of colour (Claude Moraes and Saj Karim, a British Muslim of Pakistani heritage), the inner core, too, would be almost uniformly white.[24]

Both because of his concern for racial justice and because he thought Jihadism was a real problem, Moraes had devoted thought to these problems, and in 2005 offered some additional reflections. Europol advertised posts, he thought, in places where ethnic minorities never looked. French post-colonial thinking prevailed—like Spain and Portugal in their New World colonies, France maintained the fiction (even through its race riots of 2005) that every inhabitant of metropolitan France had equal citizenship and opportunity, regardless of ethnic or religious background. According to this mode of thought, actively to seek non-white appointments would have been illogical and quite unnecessary. For Moraes, the problem was not just a French one. In eastern Europe with its newly acceded member states, the Roma were absent from the ranks of the local police and thus Europol.[25]

In the half-decade following Moraes's remarks, some developments took place. In Hungary, the police started to hire Roma officers. In Romania, the police reserved some places for Roma trainees in its Police Academy. The College of Eurojust could by 2010 boast of having two 'minority' members, both French and of North African heritage. At Europol in the same year, the director declared himself to be in favour of ethnic and religious balance in recruitment—though he conceded it was still more difficult to achieve than gender balance, where some progress had been made. The counter-terrorism unit at the council offices in Brussels talked of hiring an Arabic-speaker public relations officer. But as one observer who wished to remain anonymous noted, it was talk that had been going on for some time without action.

The European Union Ombudsman Jacob Söderman had noted in 2002 that there were plenty of EU rules and guidelines on the recruitment of ethnic minorities, but they did little good because of the 'passive attitude' of the European Commission. He recommended that statistics be collected to correlate the proportion of minorities in the population with the proportion in EU jobs. His advice apparently fell on deaf ears—eight years later Jonathan Faull, recently retired as director general of justice and home affairs, noted that neither the EU nor national census departments collected the data necessary to keep track on the progress or otherwise of ethnic and religious integration. It fell to Amnesty International to report that 70 per cent of Roma children in Slovakia were in institutional care, and that the unemployment rate for Roma living in Kosovo was 97 per cent. It was against this background that Europol and the EU justice system failed to ensure fairness in racial and religious matters. The failure was not to a demonstrably greater extent than in the rest of the EU's bureaucracies, but potentially it had more dire consequences.[26]

America had been a powerful intelligence partner for Britain and then for other countries, but also offered tuition. Here, the example the United States provided for legislative oversight was important. In a democracy, intelligence activities that are properly overseen command the confidence of the people. That increases the likelihood of budgetary support and operational cooperation within one's own nation, but also inspires confidence abroad. It is easier to place one's trust in an agency that is trusted at home and not likely to be minimalized or betrayed at source.

In the course of Europol's first decade, the EU Council provided the supervision. Through its members, it was indirectly responsible to the national legislators in member states, but there was a feeling that there should be more direct and transparent oversight from the European Parliament. Such an arrangement would make Europol more 'European', and less the creature of a committee of nations. Europol director Rob Wainwright was keen to build a firmer relationship with the European Parliament.

The European Parliament already had an interest in civil liberties. After a 2000 report to the European Parliament by the veteran campaigner Duncan Campbell, the legislature bickered with the UK and United States over the electronic surveillance programme, Echelon. The parliament continued to object to US activities, like the bank-account surveillance programme, Swift (aimed at terrorists), that potentially invaded the privacy of European citizens. In a similar mode, Sarah Ludford and others turned their vigilant eye on Europol.

The European Parliament continued to take an interest in civil liberty and privacy issues, whether external or internal in nature. The Lisbon Treaty struck a compromise, giving national parliaments more oversight responsibilities for Europol, but also giving the European Parliament budgetary oversight, access to Europol working documents, and the right to call the Europol director to give testimony.

Jonathan Faull noted that by 2010 the European Parliament had still not moved beyond its traditional concern of civil liberties—to look at, for example, the efficacy of Europol in the manner of congressional committees in the United States. That began to change on 14 March 2012, when the parliament created a special committee with a one-year mandate to investigate organized crime, corruption, and money laundering. They were all Europol concerns, and Europol supporter Newton Dunn was a member of the committee.[27]

As the work of Angelika Molnar and Mauro Falesiedi suggests, Europol, although a young organization, promised to be an effective tool in the fight against trans-national organized crime. At a time when the FBI was expanding its presence in most of the globe's major cities, Europol had become a viable alternative (in Europe, at least)—although if there was any competition with the Americans, the rivalry was friendly, and there was cooperation. Europol's contributions to counter-terrorism were more limited, and in comparison with its counterparts in the USA and perhaps the UK, too, it made little headway in the direction of racial fairness, and only partial progress towards effective oversight.

In Britain, it fell to the House of Lords to ponder Europol issues. On the eve of the implementation of the Lisbon Treaty, the House's European Union Committee welcomed, in this particular sphere, the idea of further cooperation and even integration. It noted the reluctance of member states to 'share sensitive information' with Europol, and censured what it saw as the communication shortcomings of police officers seconded to the agency:

'it is a matter of concern that four-fifths of the information exchanged by national liaison officers stationed at Europol is exchanged without actually going through Europol and is therefore not added to Europol's data base.'

There were plenty of British reservations about EU integration and about Europol deficiencies. Nevertheless, there was a perception in some quarters that the UK was giving Europol strong support. Hugo Brady, an Irish specialist with the London-based pro-integration think tank the Centre for European Reform, believed that Britain had 'invested heavily' in Europol, 'and now directs much of its international efforts against crime and terrorism through the organisation'.[28]

British cooperation with Europol, essentially a police intelligence organ-ization, provoked some debate but occurred without any great angst about the decline of the special Anglo-American intelligence relationship that had been so influential for so long. The idea of a European FBI was much less controversial than the idea of a European CIA.

11

The Quest for European Intelligence

Not every western nation marched in tandem with the dominant Anglo-American intelligence alliance. France was distinctly out of step. And in this French asynchronicity may be seen a significant contribution to the contemporary growth of European Union intelligence.

The cycle of recent French intelligence history invites attention. Like most countries with an established history of espionage, France has had a mixed experience with secret intelligence, and something of an anti-spy culture. French counterintelligence had disgraced itself in the 1890s by fabricating evidence purporting to show that a Jewish army officer, Alfred Dreyfus, had spied for German intelligence. It took an anti-racist campaign galvanized by the novelist Émile Zola to secure a reversal of Dreyfus's conviction.

In more recent years, the reputation of French espionage suffered a blow of comparable magnitude with the sinking of the *Rainbow Warrior* in Auckland, New Zealand. Responsible for this act of state terrorism was the Direction Générale de la Sécurité Extérieure (DGSE), the French foreign intelligence service nicknamed *La Piscine* after the swimming pool adjacent to its headquarters. The attack had aimed to stop the Greenpeace vessel's voyages of protest against French nuclear weapon testing in the Pacific. The two DGSE bombs timed to detonate within ten minutes of each other not only sank the ship, but also killed one of its crew who went to investigate the first bomb. Two DGSE agents fell into the hands of the New Zealand police and were convicted of the crime. French Defence Minister Charles Hernu had to resign, and the year of the event, 1985, was a low point in the history of French intelligence.

It was from this point that French intelligence began to march out of step with its American and British counterparts. Within a few years, it had recovered its poise and began an expansionist surge. According to Philippe Hayez, assistant director of the DGSE, 2003–6, one spur was the Gulf War of 1990, when the French military found itself engaged in action without adequate intelligence, reducing it to a state of dependency on others. For whatever reason, it came to pass that, at a time when other nations' intelligence policies were driven by considerations of 'peace dividend', France experienced instead a 'springtime of intelligence'. French expenditure on espionage escalated in the 1990s when other nations were paring back.[1]

One of France's aims was the provision of a satellite-based military surveillance capability. French Guiana, formerly a colony and now declared to be a part of metropolitan France, was a good launch site as it was near the equator where the earth's higher velocity meant it took less fuel and money to fire a rocket into space. From this base, French engineers could launch missiles designed to put satellites into orbit. France commenced a special programme in 1995. Splitting the costs with Belgium, Spain, Italy, Germany, and Greece, it used succeeding generations of Ariane rockets to place into orbit Helios satellites carrying high-resolution imaging equipment. With more information coming in, France reformed its analysis capability, in 2000 setting up a 'situation centre', charged with mounting a watch on crises that mattered to France in the Ivory Coast, Iraq, and elsewhere. The 39-year-old Hayez was first director.

Of course, France like other nations had a record not just of intelligence débacles, but also of intelligence achievement. For example, its intelligence people claimed to have issued an early warning of the Soviet Union's placement of missiles in Cuba in 1962. Similar prestige-boosting evidence emerged in 2007. In that year, the journalist Guillaume Dasquié published a story in Le Monde, based on 328 pages of purloined DGSE documents, claiming that French intelligence had communicated an advance intimation of the 9/11 attack.

It was a front-page splash. In a double-page spread in the paper's interior was a facsimile reproduction of a 5 January 2001 document warning Bill Murray, the CIA's station chief in Paris, that Al Qaeda planned to highjack aircraft in a plot to attack American targets. Other documents indicated that the DGSE had received reports from a mole in Osama bin Laden's organization since 1995. Later in 2007, Le Monde gently fumed at Dasquié's arrest and interrogation for refusing to identify the leaker within the DGSE. Yet it is reasonable to suppose that French intelligence took pride in the revelation—even if its warning had been one of many, most of them lacking in specificity and in DGSE's case pointing to US installations in Greece and Cyprus as the likely targets, not the Twin Towers in Manhattan.

Such stories can inflate the standing of an intelligence organization, and *La Piscine* was certainly enjoying a renaissance by the early years of the twenty-first century. The launch of a popular intelligence master's degree course at Sciences Po, the Paris Institute of Political Studies, was a symptom of the profession's rising reputation. The French began to refer to the 'singularity' of their achievement on the intelligence front. Hayez, though a scion of the professional classes with degrees from the Sorbonne, pointed to an egalitarian trend in his country. He told a meeting of the Oxford Intelligence Group that included senior British intelligence figures: 'In the French Civil Service system, there is no "Oxbridge" delivery mechanism... There has never been an "Old Boys network" in France', and the DGSE was particularly democratic.[2]

Developments in France were significant for their wider repercussions. They pointed to the benefits of cost sharing in expensive endeavours like spying from space. And they were evidence of intelligence life outside the Anglo-American fold. France having led by example, expectations about the EU's role began to rise.

The European Parliament in the 1990s considered the need for EU-wide intelligence, and the demands would intensify in the new century. Following the Madrid terrorist bombings of March 2004, Austria and Belgium called for a European CIA. John M. Nomikos of the Athens-based Research Institute for European and American Studies also called for a new EU agency based on the analytical model represented by the CIA, though rejecting that agency's covert operations. In France, one former intelligence official looked beyond his own country's initiatives. In the spring of 2006, Jean Heinrich, previously head of covert operations at DGSE, made the case for a 'European CIA'. These advocates had the CIA of yore in mind and did not take into account the demotion and changed nature of that agency in the wake of the US Intelligence Reform Act of 2004. 'European CIA' was less a precise term than aspirational shorthand. The use of the phrase did not imply a demand for imitation; rather it indicated a resolve in some quarters to achieve some form of EU foreign intelligence capability.[3]

The enthusiasm for such a capability was far from universal, and met with stiff opposition in some quarters. Britain's political leadership under Prime Ministers Tony Blair, Gordon Brown and David Cameron remained committed to their country's 'special' American alliance in intelligence matters.

European Commission President José Manuel Barroso said he was 'not happy' with Prime Minister Gordon Brown's tough talk of preserving British autonomy behind 'red lines' at the time of the 2007 Lisbon summit: 'Britain, which is always first to ask for global action against terrorism, appears not to be as committed as other members of the EU when it comes to Europe.'

However, in the first decade of the twentieth century the general drift was towards a desire for greater EU intelligence cooperation and autonomy. There were negative short-term reasons for this. These arose from the intelligence practices of the administration of President George Bush (2001–9). First, the 9/11 and Iraq WMD controversies pointed to a weak performance by US intelligence and its political overlords. There seemed to be a need for a better international arrangement than American-dominated intelligence, and perhaps the EU could help to remedy the deficiency.

Second, America's disregard for civil liberties at home and abroad seemed an overreaction to 9/11 and provoked European anger. There were ethical objections to the CIA's use of rendition (the kidnapping of terrorist suspects), surrogate torture, imprisonment without trial, and the use of drones to kill terrorist suspects in Pakistan, Yemen, and elsewhere. In 2005, representatives of the national parliaments of Europe called for the depoliticization of intelligence in EU member states and for a European code of intelligence ethics. This was not the same as an EU code of ethics, but it was still an expression of the collective European will and an implicit rebuke to America.

In the UK, there was resentment at the perceived threat by the USA to deny information to the UK intelligence services if London did not toe the Bush line. In the case of Binyan Mohamed, a tortured former Guantanamo detainee pressing a civil redress case in London, there were US requests to withhold from the plaintiff's counsel Anglo-American secret intelligence documents that might have assisted his defence. The British government found it difficult to discredit charges that it was covering up UK intelligence services' complicity in the torture used in Mohamed's interrogation, or succumbing to US threats to reduce intelligence cooperation, or both. The issue became so poisonous that in February 2010 the US embassy in London called off a commemorative event billed as 'A Special Relationship: 60 Years of Formal UK/US Defense Intelligence Co-operation'.

If the Bush administration recognized that information is power and acted accordingly, it was nothing new, and certainly not a novelty in the Anglo-American intelligence relationship. However, the controversy did fuel the perception that even the British might wish to reconsider their close alliance with Washington.[4]

While such negative factors played a role, there were also more positive considerations. Intelligence was becoming less toxic. It seemed to be moving beyond the secret pursuit of other people's secrets. In a digital age, the challenge was 'data mining', delving selectively and intelligently into what had now become available online—a mountain of evidence, much of it in the public domain. Intelligence analysis involved making sense of vast quantities of data collected from an expanding range of sources. For example, SOCMINT, or social media intelligence, tried to pluck out significant warning patterns from Facebook, Twitter, and so forth. The historian Richard Aldrich has suggested that one reason why the United Nations and the EU overcame their former distaste for intelligence was that espionage no longer had to rely on grubby operations. There was a potential trap here—data mining imperilled personal privacy. Campaigners in the European Parliament and elsewhere were keen to protect the rights of citizens. But there did seem to be a possibility for a newer, cleaner form of intelligence that would be acceptable in hitherto puritanical circles.[5]

In any case, Europe-wide intelligence was hardly a new idea. The prehistory of European intelligence integration goes back to the intelligence-gathering Proxenoi of classical Greece who were scattered over an area that embraces several present-day nations. Later international efforts were of a unilateral rather than cooperative nature, such as those associated with the Roman Empire, Charlemagne, and Napoleon. When collective efforts began in the modern era they were at first short-lived, a case in point being the 1898 meeting of police chiefs in Rome with a view to countering the terrorist threat posed by anarchists. But police cooperation over criminal matters did gradually develop in Europe, supplying a potentially supportive framework for intelligence integration.[6]

The continuous, institutional, collective background to European intelligence cooperation began with the establishment of western European cooperation in 1948, giving rise to the formation of the Western European Union (WEU) in 1954. The British refused to back the WEU, and the organization remained relatively dormant over the next four decades, the Cold War period when the Americans propped up western European defences, together with the intelligence capability that those defences required. Still, the WEU maintained its offices. Meantime, western Europe inched its way towards both single market arrangements and further political integration. In 1970, European Community member states launched the European Political Cooperation (EPC) programme. This was the year when Henry Kissinger ponderously quipped, 'When I want to speak to Europe, what number do I call', but it is possible that his scorn for disunity was already tempered by worry about EPC's potential success.

EPC aimed at a common foreign policy and flourished briefly at a time of European disagreement with America over Vietnam and trade policy. It lost momentum when the Middle Eastern oil crisis indicated there was still no substitute for American power. But from 1977, the Trevi group of European police chiefs cooperated on matters of mutual concern, and in 1985 the Schengen agreement between certain member nations of the European Community moved towards joint policing of migration, and a mutually maintained data bank on migrants. These were not in themselves substantial moves, but they were precedents, and indications of how intelligence cooperation might develop in the future.[7]

In the 1990s, the European Community beefed up its powers, and headed in new directions. Whereas it had hitherto concentrated on the creation of a single market, under the terms of the 1992 Maastricht Treaty it added two new 'pillars' to its responsibilities. One of these was Justice and Home Affairs, which opened the way to the creation of Europol. The other was the Common Foreign and Security Policy (CFSP), under the banner of which foreign intelligence fusionists thought they might achieve some advances. The European Community would henceforth be known as the European Union.

The reasons for this further integration will no doubt engage the attention of historians for years to come. From the intelligence point of view, the ending of the Cold War was an important factor. The removal of the Soviet threat meant that Europeans no longer needed America so urgently, yet they still depended on America for help in assessing a confusing new welter of dangers to peace and stability. Given the removal of the urgency, Europeans had the luxury of being able to wonder whether American intelligence could be relied on to serve their own particular interests in confronting these new dangers. Europe began to inch its way forward on the road to intelligence independence.

On the eve of Maastricht, there had been a perception arising from the Gulf War (1990–1) that Europe needed its own intelligence capability. The French, in addition to taking their own initiative, argued that their European colleagues needed a space-based surveillance capability.

The disintegration of Yugoslavia made the point even more emphatically. European cooperation after the Second World War had had as its objective not just the repulsion of Soviet advances, but also the prevention of future nationalist/ethnic conflicts. Yet the 1992–5 war in the formerly Yugoslav region of Bosnia-Herzgovina was a tragic ethnic conflagration at the very point where the First World War had begun. Europe struggled to meet its moral obligations in Bosnia and accepted US intelligence help. However, gratitude gave way to concern at the state of dependency that the European Union endured. That concern further stimulated an interest in European autonomy and self-reliance.

Negotiated by the EU member states in 1997, the Treaty of Amsterdam enhanced the effectiveness of the CFSP. It created the office of high representative for common foreign and security policy, filled in 1999 by former NATO Secretary General Javier Solana, who also took over as secretary general of the WEU with a view to integrating its functions into the CFSP's. This was a tentative step towards the establishment of an external relations capability for the EU, creating a potential need for a collective and autonomous intelligence capability. The treaty proclaimed that the 'Petersberg tasks' would be a CFSP responsibility. These stemmed from a 1992 meeting of the Council of the WEU in the Hotel Petersberg (just outside Bonn), which identified as tasks activities that included peace enforcement and crisis management. This would lead, after a further EU meeting at Helsinki in 1999, to plans for an EU rapid deployment force.

The Treaty of Amsterdam tentatively envisaged the incorporation of the WEU into the EU framework of governance. This would include the Intelligence Section that the WEU had established in 1995. With the election of a Labour government in the UK in 1997, the British seemed to be wavering in their opposition to European integration. Foreign Secretary Robin Cook endorsed European police cooperation, and at an EU summit in Austria in October 1998, the new British prime minister, Tony Blair, supported the incorporation of the WEU into the EU. The manner in which British and French leaders reached an agreement in Saint-Malo in December 1998 did not please those who preferred a more multinational approach, but it was significant that the British now signed up to the principle that the EU should have 'a capacity for analysis of situations, sources of intelligence, and a capability for relevant strategic planning'.[8]

In 1999, the Balkans once again sank into ethnic strife in a manner that reinforced demands for an EU intelligence capability. Ethnic 'cleansing' in

Kosovo led to a NATO bombing campaign there and in Yugoslavia, with the Americans once again taking the lead role and supplying the bulk of the intelligence. At the height of the bombing, EU leaders met in Cologne. They endorsed the Saint-Malo statement, and called for a reinforcement of EU intelligence capabilities.

One of the resources the EU leaders demanded in Cologne was a satellite centre. They had in mind an initiative already under way under the auspices of the WEU. Following a decision taken in 1991, the WEU had set up a satellite centre of sorts that was operational by 1997. Its duties included the verification of treaty implementation, assistance in arms control, and support of the Petersberg missions. It had the additional remit of environmental monitoring. However, it performed its task by ordering imagery from satellites sent into orbit by individual sovereign states, including non-EU states like India, Russia, Canada, and the United States.

Within the EU, a squabble broke out over where to situate the headquarters of what would be a more autonomous satellite-based system. Promoted by the French and known as Galileo, this system would rival American facilities as well as improved Chinese and Indian systems in the pipeline. French Guiana would be the EU's launch site, with Russian Soyuz rockets employed for the first launches in 2011.

This left open the issue of where the European Satellite Centre (SATCEN) would be based. SATCEN's role would be to coordinate space-based communications, and potentially to inform EU policy-makers and security officials. Newer member states like the Czech Republic objected to plans to establish the centre in Cardiff, and the older member states voiced security concerns about the formerly communist nations. In 2002, the contract went to Torrejón de Ardoz, just outside the Spanish capital, Madrid. Further operational centres for Galileo's Global Positioning System (GPS) facilities developed in Germany and Italy. On the one hand a sign of divisions within the EU, on the other hand the SATCEN scrap was an indication that independent intelligence EU facilities were now a prestigious asset.

The Galileo system would free EU member states from dependence on US, Russian, and Chinese satellites with their primarily military focus, and their susceptibility to shut out foreign clients at times of military crisis. The EU satellites would also shut down in military emergencies, but only in extreme circumstances, and they would supply more civilian intelligence and information.

SATCEN and the developing Galileo system were part of an expanding core of EU intelligence facilities. Informally, EU members together with Norway and Switzerland had cooperated since 1971 in an intelligence exchange forum called the Club de Berne. Now, however, there were more formal arrangements involving, in addition to SATCEN, Europol, an intelligence division of the EU military staff (EUMS INT) that supported Petersberg-task missions, and a civilian Joint Situation Centre. Elected EU legislators developed an incipient interest not just in political spoils— who would get such and such a facility—but also in the oversight of EU intelligence.

Compared with elected legislators in nation states, European parliamentarians' concern was at first more with civil liberties than with efficacy, and more with American than with European transgressions. In 1997, the European Parliament launched what would be a long-running investigation into Echelon, the US global signals surveillance network that aimed at greater security but intruded on the privacy of citizens. In 2005, there started a further round of investigations into prisons located in EU countries where the CIA had secretly incarcerated and abused terror suspects.

There was, however, a latent realization of a need to ensure the effectiveness and appropriateness of the actions of the burgeoning EU intelligence community. Between 2001 and 2003, the European Parliament and the European Council reached an agreement on legislative oversight. A select committee of five MEPs would be allowed access to sensitive information pertaining to matters that the parliament intended to debate. It included secret information that might have been supplied by non-EU agencies. However, this would be at the discretion of the Council, and items marked 'Top Secret' would be exempt from the arrangement.

It was a modest step forward, but one that flagged a vested democratic interest in EU intelligence developments. The signs were that the European Parliament would support those developments. For example, its president Hans-Gert Poettering in 2008 indicated his support for the gathering of satellite intelligence to guide EU peacekeeping missions in Georgia, Palestine, and ten other locations. Under the terms of an EU Galileo Implementation Regulation, the satellite budget now rose to €20 billion, with the expectation that it should be an independent and fully operational facility by 2013, with thirty satellites in orbit by 2019.

As for the Satellite Centre, Solana noted in 2008 that even without independent resources it was supplying valuable data for the fight against piracy, and in regard to crises in Chad and elsewhere. By 2010, it was delivering images to help with conflicts worldwide. It customers included the UN and EU member states, as well as the nascent Joint Situation Centre referred to above.[9]

SITCEN, as the Joint Situation Centre was known for the first decade of its existence, had its roots in the European Security and Defence Policy adopted in 1999. In that year, the newly appointed High Representative Solana put a group of analysts to work on open source intelligence. William Shapcott took charge, becoming SITCEN's first director in 2001. An Englishman who had served in the army but also studied politics and the social sciences, Shapcott argued that military intelligence cooperation was already under way and that there was scope, additionally, for civilian intelligence. Solana had to bide his time as the initiative for change had to come from member states of the EU, but in his lengthy tenure, Shapcott was able to shape SITCEN into an instrument that was helpful to the EU's diplomatic stances. The author of a paper prepared for the European Union Institute for Security Studies declared, at the start of 2004, 'although the fledgling Joint Situation Centre has only seven analysts, it deserves the label European intelligence agency since its function corresponds to that of an external intelligence agency'.[10]

In 2005, during the UK presidency of the EU, Home Secretary Charles Clarke stated in parliament that SITCEN 'monitors and assesses events and situations worldwide on a 24-hour basis with a focus on potential crisis regions, terrorism and WMD-proliferation'. By 2008, SITCEN had a staff of over 100 devoted to these tasks. Of these, 40 worked with open sources. However, 18 SITCEN personnel worked with more confidential intelligence materials. Thirteen of the latter were seconded from member states.[11]

SITCEN did not take part in any spectacular activities and for that reason was destined to have a lower profile than national agencies engaged in those 'covert action' activities now as a matter of course lumped in with the definition of intelligence—activities of the Castro assassination plot or *Rainbow Warrior* variety.

It operated in a quieter way. For example, intelligence assessments relating to piracy off the horn of Africa helped smaller EU nations that would have been unable to sustain watching briefs single-handedly. They may have been a factor in the North Indian Ocean deployment of the European Union Naval Force Somalia, which raided pirate logistic dumps in May 2012. It is of the nature of things that details of intelligence analysis do not come out at the time, and often the bad news precedes the good news because bad news makes for better stories. So far, the performance record of EU intelligence is a matter of surmise.

The Lisbon Treaty agreed in 2007 gave SITCEN a further responsibility. It arose from the work of the newly established European External Action Service (EEAS). The new service was intended to strengthen the EU's foreign policy coherence and profile. The slightly renamed high representative of the union for foreign affairs and security policy would direct the EEAS. The Englishwoman Catherine Ashton assumed that role on 1 December 2009 upon the retirement of Javier Solana. SITCEN would be incorporated into the EEAS and report to Ashton.

Further organizational changes took place between 2007 and 2012. In January 2007, there came into existence a Single Intelligence Analytical Capability (SIAC). This was a 'virtual analytical entity' leading to joint estimates by SIAC and its military equivalent, EUMS INT. All-source assessment could now be released to authorized consumers under the 'SIAC' imprint.

In December 2010, around forty members of SITCEN split off to form a dedicated 24/7 warning unit. The focus of this smaller group was less on intelligence work than on alerting EU leaders to events and problems around the world. High Representative Ashton appointed Agostino Miozzo to be in charge of the unit with the title of director for crisis response and operational coordination for the EEAS. Formerly an Italian government official charged with overseas emergency operations, Miozzo had experience of crises in locations ranging from Sri Lanka to New Orleans. To give an example of his EEAS activities, in April 2011 he would explain to a European Parliament committee how the EU might deliver humanitarian aid to strife-torn Libya in spite of an unpromising military background. As this testimony suggests, Miozzo's unit (known as SITROOM from March 2012) delivered unclassified information in real time—using, for example, text messages and emails.[12]

The majority rump of the old SITCEN now became the EU Intelligence Analysis Centre, with the acronym INTCEN. Shapcott having accepted a new post as personnel and administrative chief for the EU Council, there was hot competition to be the new director, with a French contender in the forefront for a while. Ultimately Ashton appointed Ilkka Salmi, the young director of Suojelupoliisin, the Finnish security service. His INTCEN still depended on member states' intelligence services for information as it had when an organ of the EU Council. But it now included commission staff, and indeed Ashton was first vice president of the European Commission. In this sense, INTCEN had become 'Europeanized' to a greater degree than its precursor.

Salmi's team of over 60 included 22 intelligence officers from member states. The unit produced security analyses, with between 5 and 12 reports per week going to Ashton and also to member states via the Political and Security Committee of EU ambassadors. The reports were classified on the EU hierarchical system ranging from 'restricted' through 'confidential' to 'secret'. To regulate all this, there was a 'Framework and Guidelines for Intelligence Support', and Ashton chaired an Intelligence Steering Board—not to task INTCEN, but to ensure that it functioned properly.

In the original SITCEN and its successor INTCEN, the EU had an intelligence agency that liaised with military counterparts, but was firmly civilian in character. It will be recalled that this had been one of the strengths of the 1950s CIA. But the young institution did have its critics. Although EU intelligence cooperation is in its infancy, it has already provoked discussion that illuminates what has happened, and perhaps gives an indication of historical trajectories. Contributions to the debate may be grouped into two broad categories, one that evinced a mixture of advocacy and hope, the other characterized by a greater degree of opposition and scepticism.

Advocacy and hope are evident in the literature that accompanied the initiatives of the late 1990s and early years of the twenty-first century. Not surprisingly, a study prepared under the editorship of Alessandro Politi and copyrighted by the Institute for Security Studies of the WEU evinced an upbeat tone. An independent Italian open source intelligence analyst, Politi tempered his views by observing that there should still be a mutually agreed division of labour between the EU/WEU and the United States, but he was optimistic about the development of a distinct European intelligence capability.

In 2000, Ole R. Villadsen conceded that the issue of national sovereignty was a prickly problem still to be overcome, but thought that 'European intelligence policy . . . is likely to improve in fundamental ways'. Villadsen was the recipient of the Walter L. Pforzheimer best-article award from the CIA's Center for the Study of Intelligence, not perhaps an indication of US approval of his views, but at least an endorsement of their coherence. A 2003 study by former German and NATO admiral Sigurd Hess sounded the customary notes of caution, but similarly predicted further developments, especially if Europe developed a multinational military force.

Hess quoted General Schuwirth of the EU Military Staff: 'The glass is half full and not half empty, or differently worded: Today the glass is half full, in 1998 it was empty.'

Although John Nomikos's 2005 article addressing the issue of EU intelligence focused on terrorism, in conceptual terms it ranged more widely, and began to ask questions about the CIA comparison. He observed that EU arrangements were still immature—they focused on imagery, or IMINT, and were weak on SIGINT and HUMINT. He noted that, while Belgium and Austria demanded a CIA-style EU agency, powerful member states including Britain, Germany, France, Spain, and Italy showed a reluctance to share intelligence. Just as Pearl Harbor had spurred the CIA, it was possible that events in the Balkans, 9/11, and the 2004 Madrid bombing might inspire EU intelligence cooperation, but, for the moment, EU intelligence might be best compared with the very early CIA, in the days before the American system matured. Nomikos nevertheless advocated an EU intelligence service.

Adrian Fortescue, the former director general for justice and home affairs at the European Commission who had accepted a position at Harvard University in order to study what lessons the EU might learn from the new US Department of Homeland Security (DHS), concluded in his report of 2004 that the DHS was weighed down by historical baggage such as turf wars. Europe, in contrast, was building its intelligence arrangements on a greenfield site. In concluding that there was 'no ipso facto reason why other countries or international organizations should seek to adopt the US model and subject themselves to all the accompanying disruption involved', he implied that Europe had cause to be upbeat about its indigenous security arrangements.[13]

Adverse comments on SITCEN did not—as in the case of Europol—concentrate on threats it might pose to civil liberties. There were some incipient concerns. Tony Bunyan, the director of Statewatch since 1990 and now active with the European Civil Liberties Network, voiced reservations on the ground that the EU Council directed its security activities in secret, and that this part of its work was therefore unaccountable. Reacting to the post-Lisbon scene, Bunyan went on to warn that EU policy-makers wanted a 'surveillance state' with 'unfettered powers' to gather data on private citizens in the name of protecting them against 'threats'.[14]

However, criticisms of SITCEN and EU intelligence arrangements mainly concentrated not on civil liberties, but on the issues of insignificance and ineffectiveness. Let us now turn to these critiques of SITCEN/INTCEN—and to a critique of the critics.

The Australian, a daily newspaper serving a successfully organized federal nation, took a keen interest in international intelligence affairs. It offered a devastating view of EU provision. In May 2005, its reporter Cameron Stewart noted that, after Madrid's 191 train-bombing mortalities, European leaders had offered 'strong words and lofty promises' of future cooperation to ensure pre-emptive intelligence. But this turned out to be 'lip-service'. The EU did not deliver a European intelligence agency. Cameron commented on the weakness of Gijs De Vries, the New York-born former Dutch deputy interior minister appointed in 2004 to the new post of EU counter-terrorism coordinator. He observed that De Vries had inadequate powers. Stewart concluded that the major member states were interested only in bilateral intelligence sharing.

Though its language was more sedate, a US Congressional Research Service (CRS) report reached a similar conclusion in the following year. Tellingly, the report dealt almost entirely with the efforts of individual countries. Its suggestion that Europe had been 'slow' to respond to the terrorist threat could be interpreted as offering encouragement to those who believed that closer cooperation was necessary. However, the report's single paragraph on the EU was dismissive in its brevity. The CRS made partial amends with a report on EU foreign and security policy in 2011, but still emphasized lack of coordination rather than progress, and made only fleeting reference to SITCEN.[15]

In interviews for this book, senior British intelligence and security officials offered stinging criticisms of SITCEN. One point made was that SITCEN contributed only a small part to the counter-terrorist intelligence effort, with member states individually doing a great deal more. Another criticism addressed the shortcomings of the satellite system on which SITCEN drew—its imagery and technologies were primitive compared with what the Americans could do.

A senior EU official offered the confidential rejoinder that the Americans were not sharing their imagery with the EU so it had to fall back on its own resources—and these resources were improving with the latest-generation 'Helios' satellite launches from French Guiana. He or she politely wondered whether the British critics had 'ever seen a Helios image'.

A further adverse comment, with some agreement from within SITCEN itself, was about the location of the politically fought-over satellite centre—in Spain instead of close to the analysts in Brussels. The lack of an EU SIGINT facility was a widely mentioned shortcoming, and SITCEN had no network of spies, thus no HUMINT of its own.

Here, the UK commentators offered the generalization, for them a criticism, that SITCEN was a receiver rather than an imparter of information. Lacking collection facilities, it could never match the performance of the bigger players in the intelligence game who did all the 'heavy lifting'. What SITCEN said in its reports might be news to security officials in smaller member states, but nations with significant intelligence services of their own would learn nothing that they had not already found out through bilateral exchanges, or simply by reading the newspapers.

Even within the EU community, there was a suggestion that Ashton's appointment of Salmi might have been a political sop to smaller EU nations and an indication that she placed a low value on intelligence. One British intelligence veteran came to her defence with the observation that Finland had spied effectively on the Soviet Union, and had an outstanding small-country intelligence service. Overall, though, British officials were keen to downplay EU intelligence prospects—as one of them put it, 'Don't expect a European CIA.'[16]

EU officials sympathetic to SITCEN criticized this British critique. To argue that INTCEN lacked a collection capability was to miss the point in two ways. First, EEAS had over 140 delegations and offices throughout the world supplying information on which INTCEN analysts could draw. The information thus relayed was less about the trivia of the closet than about political assessment, through both considered reports and real-time signalling of information. Second, INTCEN's function was to receive intelligence and to analyse it, and not to collect it through devious means.

Thus INTCEN was comparable not with, say, the CIA as a whole, but with its Directorate of Intelligence. To put it another way, SITCEN resembled Britain's JIC and the US Department of State's Bureau of Intelligence and Research (INR) more than, say, MI6 or DGSE. JIC and INR inspired confidence in spite of not running their own secret agents, and so should SITCEN.

Another criticism of EU intelligence focused on the issue of trust. Intelligence leaders in major countries sometimes say trust is easier to develop bilaterally than with a greater number of parties. British defenders of the Anglo-American intelligence relationship are fond of advancing that view.

Associated with this is the 'third party' problem—Country A will tell a secret to Country B but not if Country B is in danger of sharing the information with Country C whose level of discretion or indiscretion is beyond Country A's ken and ability to monitor. According to the 'institutions are not enough' view, the EU can develop intelligence mechanisms until it is blue in the face, but the whole exercise is irrelevant in the absence of trust.[17]

Three rebuttals of such doubts are, first, untrustworthiness has been a hallmark of intelligence history, affecting bilateral relationships and even single countries. Second, the monitoring of trustworthiness is not impossible where more than two countries are concerned—it is just harder work requiring an unblinkered cultural outlook. Third, in an era of open source data mining, secrets are to a certain degree becoming obsolete, as is the need for a trusty single partner.

In testimony to the House of Lords in December 2010, by now speaking as a former director of the centre, Shapcott justified SITCEN's mission. He argued that people 'subconsciously recognised' that security issues were now too challenging for individual member states to handle alone. While the EU did not seek to 'Europeanise national security', it could be of assistance. The creation of the External Action Service meant there was now 'a much closer joint interest . . . in sharing information'. In no case was this more vital than in matters of cybersecurity, a main threat on the horizon. The European Parliament would now have a role in contributing 'to the legitimacy of some of the actions taken at EU level', and Shapcott thought that, instead of being frightened by that, people should welcome the development.

Shapcott further observed that, while SITCEN 'has had no operational role', the EU was increasingly 'doing operational things' in countries like Iraq, and there was a pressing need for 'punctual operational information'. He noted that, in the main, the United States did 'not try to engage with the EU operationally'. But America needed to be alert to change. US officials were blind to the expertise SITCEN and its network already had in certain regions, for example Georgia's fought-over boundaries with the self-declared republics of South Ossetia and Abkhazia: 'I think that they miss a trick; the EU has 300 people on the ground in Georgia.'[18]

Shapcott's own country, the UK, continued to voice reservations about EU-wide security coordination. While intelligence people put forward doctrinal reasons for not sharing security assets, it might be tempting to espouse a less benign explanation. A person of critical disposition might argue the case as follows. Like many Americans, the majority of the British are monoglot and averse to the risk of conversing with a foreign culture, even if it is in the national interest to do so. Transfixed as they were by the history of the Anglo-American special intelligence relationship and cocooned by complacency-inducing privilege in the landscape of an increasingly inegalitarian society, it could be argued that the leaders of Britain's intelligence community were prejudiced against the EU, and unable to swim with the tide, let alone supply leadership.

Such generalizations are, of course, dangerous. British intelligence has always contained cosmopolitans, for example its Arabists. Recently, there has been a stated intent to recruit more broadly. Again, intelligence is not separate from the body of the church. Intelligence leaders may inform political leaders, but they are also obliged to take their cue from them, and British politicians have been noisily chary of the EU. For example, Foreign Secretary William Hague greeted the development of the EU's External Action Service with a display of reserve, and warned against its 'competence creep'.[19]

Yet, as in the case of other countries, one can distinguish between what UK politicians say for public consumption, and what they do. One thing London appears to have done is to work to secure British appointments of a certain kind. Since the 1990s, a remarkable number of British people have served in senior EU security and intelligence posts: Jonathan Faull as director general of justice and home affairs, Adrian Fortescue as his predecessor in the post, Shapcott at SITCEN, Rob Wainwright as director of Europol, Aled Williams as president of Eurojust, and more recently, at the political level, Ashton as high representative for foreign and security policy.

How has this come about, and what does it mean? While EU posts are expected to go to people on merit, there is also a process of international bartering to ensure that the top, influential posts are distributed equitably amongst member states, and according to their preferences and interests. Land-locked Austria, for example, would have little interest in pressing one of their citizens' claim to be European commissioner for fisheries and maritime affairs, while that would be a priority for countries which have large fishing fleets such as Portugal, Spain, or Greece (whose Maria Diminaki became commissioner in 2010). In surrendering your interest in some posts, you expect to make ground in those areas that for you have a high priority. It is hard to resist the conclusion that, for all their bluster, the British had a strong interest in EU security and intelligence, and fought to place their candidates in relevant posts. This may have been with sabotage or at least monitoring in mind, and the pro-EU enthusiasm of some of the appointees may be no more than an instance of administrative exiles 'going native'. Common sense suggests otherwise.

Brussels was gradually asserting Europe's independence from the United States. Yet it would be a serious overstatement to say that INTCEN and the rest of the EEAS apparatus by the second decade of the twenty-first century was a fully-fledged alternative to the intelligence activities of major European nations and the Anglo-American intelligence axis. The reasons were only partly to do with intelligence itself. They sprang from the constitutional, political, and economic state of the European Union.

Politically, a conservative brand of liberalism held sway in the EU. Business received a franchise to operate multinationally within a single market, but member states' leaders limited the growth of countervailing powers for the European Parliament. As Shapcott, Wainwright, and some European parliamentarians recognized, intelligence needed democratic governmental sanction in order to flourish.

The euro crisis of 2011–12 intruded against this background. The euro impasse both stemmed from weak government and, paradoxically, contributed to a decline in faith in strong government. It threatened to sap intelligence budgets and, as economic crises do, general confidence. SITCEN and its successor INTCEN had developed rapidly, but might have grown faster still but for inhibiting constitutional, political, and economic factors.

12

Beyond the Old West

Spies have always been detested, but in the twentieth century espionage gained a certain respectability. Against the background of horrific bloodlettings and atrocities, mostly planned in secret, clandestine intelligence acquired the reputation of being not just a means of winning wars, but a means also of preventing them.

Anglo-American intelligence cooperation proved to be an instance of two minds being better than one. The British intelligence veteran Michael Herman explained the dangers of a single nation's spies living in an 'insulated world', and suggested that 'external examiners' from 'invisible colleges' could play a role in 'keeping national systems intellectually honest'. In the twentieth century, the intelligence communities in the UK and USA kept a watchful eye on each other, and that helped them to be vigilant about actual and potential enemies. The merits of their undoubted impact on world history will forever be debated, but there can be little doubt that they contributed to the security of the West.[1]

Competitive estimating was one strength of the alliance. Sharing secret intelligence, Britain and America trained two pairs of eyes on the same data, and then compared their conclusions. The process was evident in the Second World War, then in the Cold War. When it came to non-Cold War problems like nuclear proliferation, the procedure was at first full of promise as, for example, one can see in the scrutiny of Pakistan's secret atomic research programme in the 1970s.

Another aspect of the alliance was mutual learning. From Ned Bell's report on British intelligence in 1919 to the post-9/11 congressional inquiry into whether the FBI should be reshaped to make it more like MI5, American intelligence experts regularly studied the practices of their Transatlantic cousins. British research into US practices occurred periodically but was less frequent, less thorough, and less open minded.

However, the United States did teach one lesson. When it came to the CIA and the promotion of democracy, that democracy for Americans started at home. There had been a congressional debate over the creation of the FBI, there was another over the creation of the CIA, and in the 1970s secret intelligence became for a while the main item on the American political agenda. In pursuit of the goals of 'government in the sunshine' and 'freedom of information', Congress passed new laws and strengthened its intelligence oversight mechanisms. This had an immediate impact on political debate in Britain.

Thereafter it took some time, but UK governmental and intelligence practices did follow American precedents and became more open. The American example inspired other nations, too, both in the West and beyond. It remains to be seen whether more open societies will in the long run produce more ethical and efficacious practices.

The Anglo-American special intelligence relationship went into decline. Specific rows had always occurred over issues such as British codebreaking trickery and Henry Kissinger's intelligence blackmail. They generally did not upset the whole applecart and would fade away after a while. But from the 1960s, a downward trajectory set in for more general reasons.

The relationship had been unequal before, when Britain was top dog, but now that America was the senior partner, it was difficult for London to swallow its pride and for Washington to treat the ageing canine patiently and with respect. The ham-fisted decolonization of Guyana was an object lesson in how American power could override what was, on that particular occasion, superior British wisdom.

As America became more racially diverse, other cracks began to appear. At the beginning of the twentieth century, the privileged classes in Britain and America had bonded, running espionage and secret diplomacy in a manner that held at bay not only competing nations, but also what they viewed as repugnant elements in their own societies. Fifty years later, the Ivy League, the East Coast Establishment, and Anglo-Saxon heritage still conferred great advantages in America, but they were no longer as important as they once were. The traditional US preoccupation with matters European was fading. All this affected intelligence, as it did the rest of the Anglo-American relationship.

With power and empire on the wane, the UK intelligence community tried to cling on to old ways. It annoyed the British scientific intelligence adviser R. V. Jones. Recalling the 1940s in a book he wrote in 1978, he poured scorn on certain of his compatriots who cultivated their US cousins 'and so [built] up their positions in Britain by achieving reputations for "getting on with" and "being trusted by" Americans'. Perhaps he underestimated the historical contribution made to Anglo-American relations by diplomatically skilled spies. However, he did identify the weakness in a one-sided relationship.

Over the years, the Americans when not pursuing a unilateralist course would adopt what one might call a 'terms of trade' approach to intelligence liaison—they defined advantage in relative terms, and conducted informational commerce with a number of partners. Jennifer Sims, deputy assistant secretary of state for intelligence coordination, 1994–8, saw this as a characteristic of the post-9/11 situation, when, she asserted, 'the role of intelligence liaison has taken center stage in the global war on terror'. She offered a justification for jumping ship rather than being stuck with a traditional bilateral relationship: 'If complacency sets in, formerly symmetric intelligence relationships can become asymmetric, costly enterprises for one party, sustained more by institutional inertia and professional courtesy than self-interest.'[2]

The British approach was less flexible than this. UK intelligence officials did appreciate the benefits of complex liaison, but the United States remained the star in their firmament long after it had faded in the eyes of others. Being entrusted with secrets by the Americans came to be a prestige fix for intelligence leaders as much as for their political masters, even when it was a goal with poor outcomes such as the protracted occupations of Iraq and Afghanistan.

The credibility of the Anglo-American espionage system as a means to western security may not have collapsed entirely, but the Weapons of Mass Destruction scandal and its sequels have been nails in the coffin of the nearly dead. Herman's general principle still held true, and there remained a case for cooperating with and attempting to steer America. But looking beyond the ways of the Old West, where could the British look for additional and alternative succour, and who could the Americans now find to look over their shoulders and *really* correct their mistakes?

The intelligence institutions of the European Union invite attention. Here, ignorance and lack of trust are obstacles. Not many Americans have trodden the trail blazed by Peter Dodd, the CIA-sponsored Princeton graduate who attended the first session of the College of Europe at Bruges. Valerie Plame was one successor. But American interest in the EU in the 2001–9 Bush administration turned out to be witheringly negative.

The United Kingdom, too, although a member of the EU, took a sceptical view of EU institutions as they began to take off in the new century. There were reasons to look away from America. The moral appeal of the US Secret Service's fight against Ku Klux Klan terrorism in the 1870s had degenerated into the moralism of the crusade against jihad. The upholding of democratic principles was still present in rhetoric, but frequently absent in practice when it came to countries like Guatemala and Palestine. Threats to security such as cyber warfare did not require responses identical to those prompted by Nazi Germany and the Soviet Union.

Yet suspicions remained that it was imprudent to confide in continental European countries. Like breeds like. A poll of five leading EU states in 2011 found that only a quarter of those polled thought the British were trustworthy. Europol and INTCEN emerged, then, against a background of mutual suspicion.[3]

Neither of them was the finished article, neither of them an organism for the British to turn to as a satisfying alternative partner, or for the Americans to view as a source of helpfully competitive intelligence analysis. Each of them had its weaknesses, Europol in being reflective of European racial prejudice, INTCEN in operating within a constitutionally weak political framework.

There was also the question of appearances. Like the United Nations intelligence units, the EU institutions operated on a cooperative model and, in an age of IT and data mining, were less obsessed with secrets. To their supporters, this was an attraction. To people set in the ways of the Old West, Europol and INTCEN did not look like the real thing.

Yet European Union intelligence was at least about intelligence, as distinct from foolish adventurism. It was on an upward trajectory and, unlike UN intelligence, could not be reined in at their convenience by the United States or any other external power.

Abbreviations Used in the Notes

LOCATIONS

CCC	Churchill College, Cambridge, England
CSR	Center for Southwest Research, General Library, University of New Mexico, Albuquerque
DNSA	Digital National Security Archive (Chadwyck/ProQuest)
EUCL	European Union Council Library, Brussels
FDR	Franklin D. Roosevelt Library, Hyde Park, New York
GUL	Georgetown University (Lauinger Memorial) Library, Washington, DC
HST	Harry S. Truman Library, Independence, Missouri
IWM	Imperial War Museum, London
JFK	John F. Kennedy Library, Boston, Massachusetts
LBJ	Lyndon B. Johnson Library, Austin, Texas
MLC	Manuscript Collections, Library of Congress
NA	National Archives, Washington, DC
NA2	National Archives of the United States, College Park, Maryland
SGM	Seeley G. Mudd Library, Princeton University, Princeton, New Jersey
SNA	Scottish National Archives, Edinburgh
TL	Tamiment Library, New York University
TNA	The National Archives, London
YUL	Yale University Library, New Haven, Connecticut

COLLECTIONS

ACUE	American Committee on United Europe Papers, GUL
AWD	Allen W. Dulles Papers, SGM
BC	Berlin Crisis collection, DNSA
CEU	Council of the European Union Records, EUCL
CJB	Charles Joseph Bonaparte Papers, MLC
DPM	Daniel P. Moynihan Papers, MLC
DS	David Stafford collection, Anglo-American intelligence liaison papers, gifted to the author
EI	US Espionage and Intelligence collection, DNSA

EMH	E. M. House Collection, YUL
FMS	Ferenc M. Szasz Papers, CSR
FO	Foreign Office papers, TNA
HN	Heinz Norden Papers, TL
JN	John Newman Papers, JFK
JSI	Jedburgh Sound Interviews, IWM
LH	Leland Harrison Papers, MLC
MD	Monro-Davies family papers, privately held in Edinburgh
NNP	Nuclear Non-Proliferation collection, DNSA
NSF	National Security File
PA	Philip Agee Papers, TL
PK	Papers of Philip Kerr, 11th Marquess of Lothian, SNA
SCMD	Small Collections, Miscellaneous Documents, FDR
SK	Papers of Sherman Kent, YUL
WHS	Papers of Whitney Hart Shepardson, FDR
WJD	William J. Donovan Papers (on microfilm), CCC
WRH	Papers of Admiral Sir (William) Reginald Hall, CCC
WW	Papers of Sir William Wiseman, YUL

Endnotes

CHAPTER I

1. Whitley report, 29 September 1871, 10, 17, 22, 30, RG60: General Records of the Department of Justice, Letters Received, Chronological Files, 1871–84, Treasury, NA2.
2. Knott, *Secret and Sanctioned*, 50; Whitley reports, 29 September 1871, 72–3, 15 September 1872, 67; 'Table 1: Enforcement Act and Internal Revenue Prosecutions in South Carolina, 1871–73', in Jeffreys-Jones, *FBI*, 29.
3. Mahan, *Influence of Sea Power*, 2.
4. Dorwart, *Office of Naval Intelligence*, 32; Perkins, *Hands Off*, 43.
5. Dorwart, *Office of Naval Intelligence*, 48, 60.
6. 'Appropriation for Secret Service, War Department', *House Document* 537, 55 Cong., 2 sess., 14 June 1898.
7. Carranza's letter to his cousin Admiral J. G. Ymay, 26 May 1898, fell into the disconsolate hands of the US Secret Service and was reproduced in Wilkie, 'Secret Service', 433–6. Other parts of Carranza's letter may have been (as its author claimed) a Secret Service forgery.
8. Wilkie, 'Catching Spain's Spies', *Boston Sunday Herald*, 2 October 1898.
9. Smith, 'American Road', 3; Campbell, *Great Britain and the United States*, 5; Chamberlain to Aberdeen, 6 June 1898, quoted in Jeffreys-Jones, *American Espionage*, 38.
10. Roosevelt quoted in Noakes, 'Enforcing Domestic Tranquillity', 80.
11. Press sentiment summarized in the Pittsburg *Leader*, n.d., in Scrapbooks, vol. 14 (1908), Box 261, CJB.
12. Roosevelt to (Speaker of the House) Joseph Cannon, 29 April 1908, *Letters*, VI, 1019; Gatewood, *Art of Controversy*, 250–5; Hiley, 'Re-entering the Lists: MI5', 425 n. 1.
13. Jeffery, *MI6*, 6.
14. Quotations from 'Note on the history of the secret service vote', n.d. but possibly 1921–2, cited in O'Halpin, 'Secret Service Vote', 348–9; Fergusson, *British Military Intelligence*, 10.
15. Alan Johnstone, 'Secret Memorandum', 17 October 1905, quoted in Davies, 'Organisational Development', 92; author's interview with a senior British intelligence veteran.

16. Boghardt, *Spies of the Kaiser*, 6. While the origins of British intelligence may not have been rooted in morality in the American sense, UK intelligence activities were not necessarily unethical. For a study of the philosophy of intelligence ethics, see Bellaby, 'What's the Harm?'

17. Moran and Johnson, 'Service of Empire', 2; Svendsen, 'Painting', 15; Shpayer-Makov, *Ascent of the Detective*, 6, 194–202; Jeffreys-Jones, 'Profit over Class', 235–6, 242–3.

18. Hiley, 'Decoding', 59; Oppenheim, *Mysterious Mr Sabin*, 339; Panek, *Special Branch*, 7, 18, 22, 32.

19. Moran and Johnson, 'Service of Empire', 12–13; William Le Queux, *The Great War in England in 1897* (London: Tower Publishing, 1894); Le Queux, *Invasion*, 4, 15; Stafford, *Silent Game*, 7; Melville quoted in Andrew, *Defence of the Realm*, 8.

20. Le Queux letter to the *Manchester Guardian*, 4 January 1910, quoted in Andrew, *Defence of the Realm*, 21.

21. Andrew, *Defence of the Realm*, 3.

22. Fergusson, *British Military Intelligence*, xvi.

23. Fergusson, *British Military Intelligence*, 8; Porter, *Plots and Paranoia*, 73–6; O'Halpin, 'Secret Service Vote', 349; Rowan, *Story of Secret Service*, 590; Wilkinson, *Secrecy and the Media*, 496; Boghart, *Spies of the Kaiser*, appendix 2, 149; Smith, *Six*, 3; Davies, 'Organisational Development', 86; West, *MI5*, 37; Jeffery, *MI6*, 9, 12; Hiley, 'Re-entering the Lists', 416–17, 449; Boghardt, *Spies of the Kaiser*, 143–5; Andrew, *Defence of the Realm*, 23, 28.

CHAPTER 2

1. Adolph Berle, Memorandum of Conversation, 'British Relations', 14 September 1939, File 740.00111A/47, Central Decimal File, General Records of the Department of State, Record Group 59, NA2; Berle and Jacobs, *Navigating*, frontispiece (a contemporary photograph from *Life* magazine) and 253–4; Jordan A. Schwartz, biography of Berle in the *American National Biography Online*; Adolf A. Berle Jr and Gardiner C. Means, *The Modern Corporation and Private Property* (1932), argument and impact summarized in Schwartz, *New Dealers*, 158–9.

2. Bell memorandum, 1 May 1919, enclosed with Bell to Leland Harrison, 2 May 1919, file 'British Intelligence', Box II 102, LH. For a similar academic verdict, see Hiley, 'Failure', 860.

3. Boghardt, *Spies of the Kaiser*, 143; Pöhlmann, 'German Intelligence', 2.

4. Robertson, *Public Secrets*, 58; Vincent, *Culture of Secrecy*, 91; chapter 1 in the forthcoming book *Classified: Secrecy and the State in Modern Britain* (Cambridge University Press), by Christopher R. Moran who showed a pre-publication draft to the author; Hofstadter, *Age of Reform*, 148–63. A notable

prosopographical tilt at Hofstadter was Thelen, 'Social Tensions', 331, table 1, and see Brinkley, 'Hofstadter Reconsideration', 471–4.

5. Ewing, 'Special War Work. I', 196, 199; Stafford, *Churchill and Secret Service*, 15–16; Beesly, *Room 40*, 16.

6. Gaunt, *Yield of the Years*, title page, and 11, 13, 172, 190; Kahn, 'Edward Bell', 144; Memo, Bell to Harrison, 1 May 1922, in folder 3, file 'Page-Hendricks', Box 7, General Correspondence 1915–1918, Records Kept by Leland Harrison, RG 59, NA2.

7. Bell to Harrison, 13 December 1917, folder 'Miscellaneous Corresp. 1917' and Bell to Harrison, 25 January 1918, folder 'Miscellaneous Corresp. January–August, 1918', both in Box II 115, LH; Diary of Frank Polk, 12 April 1920, EMH.

8. Roberts, 'Anglo-American Theme', 333–40, 343, 347–50, 355; Moser, *Twisting the Lion's Tail*, 3; Doerries, *Imperial Challenge*, 5, 6.

9. Manuscript and typescript genealogical fragments, n.d., folder 'Harrison Personal', Box II 18 and Harrison to House, 21 January 1916, folder 'H', General Correspondence, Box II 1, both in LH.

10. Roosevelt quoted in Kahn, 'Edward Bell', 144; Beesly, *Room 40*, 251.

11. Auchincloss diary, 30 March, 15 November 1917, EMH; Bell to Harrison, 30 December 1918, folder 'Misc. Corresp. September–December 1918', Box II 115, LH.

12. Memo, 'Friends of Irish Freedom', 23 May 1916, file 'German Espionage Activities', Box 3, General Correspondence 1915–1918, Records Kept by Leland Harrison, RG 59, NA2.

13. Bell to Harrison, 16 January 1918, folder 'Miscellaneous Corresp. 1917', Box II 115, LH; Arthur Murray (of British military intelligence) to Wiseman (forwarded to House), 22 June 1918, WW.

14. *The Re-Conquest of America* (The Statesman Press, July 1919); Spence, 'Englishmen', 531, 536 n. 113.

15. *The Re-Conquest of America*; Winslow to Hurley, 15, 17 September 1920, 7, 25, 31 January 1921, Hurley to Winslow, 22 December 1920, 12 January 1921, Bannerman to Hurley, 6 January 1921, all in file 'Sir Wm–Wiseman', Box 7, General Correspondence 1915–1918, Records Kept by Leland Harrison, RG 59, NA2.

16. Link, *Wilson the Diplomatist*, 26–7.

17. Spence, 'Englishmen', 522; *The* [London] *Sketch*, 15 October 1916; Tuchman, *Zimmermann Telegram*, 125–6.

18. Rintelen, *Dark Invader*, 129; Moynihan, *Secrecy*, 101–3.

19. Unpublished Reginald Hall autobiography, Draft D, Chapter 25, 6, folder 6, Box 3, WRH; telegram from German Admiralty to Rudolf Nadolny (handler of secret Irish operations), 25 January 1915, quoted in Doerries, *Imperial Challenge*, 180; Room 40 decodes of Bernstorff correspondence of 1915–16 relating to the sabotage of the Canadian Pacific Railway and other plans, in folder 'German messages intercepted by British and forwarded by Edward Bell

and Walter H. Page from London [in August 1918]', Box 3, General Correspondence 1915–1918, Records Kept by Leland Harrison, RG 59, NA2; Doerries, Introduction to Rintelen, *Dark Invader*, xxix.

20. Press release no. 31–83, 31 May 1942, general records of the Department of the Treasury, office of the secretary, general correspondence, NA; Paper quoted in Jones, *German Spy*, 55.

21. Jones, *German Spy*, 38, 88–91; Ward, *Ireland*, 108; Doerries, *Prelude to the Easter Rising*, 23; memoranda on various Irish American activities, 15, 22, 23 May 1916, W. J. Flynn to Secretary of State, 15 September 1916, all in file 'German Espionage Activities', Box 3, General Correspondence 1915–1918, Records Kept by Leland Harrison, RG 59, NA2. On 'Wilsonianism' and nationalism, see Rebecca E. Karl, review of Manela, *Wilsonian Moment*, *American Historical Review*, 113 (December 2008), 1474–6.

22. Kamath, *United States and India*, 104; *Gadar Memorial* (San Francisco, n.d.), pamphlet in folder 'Gadar Materials', Box 289, Part II, DPM; Wilhelm II quoted in Doerries, *Imperial Challenge*, 147.

23. Paraphrase of Hopkinson's claim in Popplewell, *Intelligence and Imperial Defence*, 156; Mathur, *Indian Movement*, 23, 28, 55; Doerries, *Imperial Challenge*, 148.

24. Popplewell, *Intelligence and Imperial Defence*, 160. On 2 April 2011, Richard Aldrich, Keith Jeffery, Michael Smith, and Peter Hennessy, authorities on British intelligence history, took part in an Oxford Literary Festival panel at Corpus Christi College on 'Intelligence Organisations and Secret Britain'. In response to a question by the author, they were hesitant on the subject of British peacetime assassination policy, but all agreed that in wartime British intelligence regarded assassination as a legitimate course of action.

25. Quotation from Popplewell, *Intelligence and Imperial Defence*, 250; Brown, 'Hindu Conspiracy', 54, 67; Jeffreys-Jones, *American Espionage*, 110–12.

26. Hess, *America Encounters*, 10–11; pamphlet on the Gadar Memorial in San Francisco and other materials enclosed with Avindash C. Pandey, Consulate General of India, San Francisco, to office of US Senator Daniel P. Moynihan, 18 June 1996, in folder 'Gadar Materials', Box 289, Part II, DPM.

27. Popplewell, *Intelligence and Imperial Defence*, 252; Gaunt, *Yield of the Years*, 149; Wiseman to Cumming, 7 October 1917, quoted in Spence, 'Englishmen', 530.

28. O'Halpin, 'British Intelligence in Ireland', 76; Bennett, *Morton*, 79, 83; Larsen, '1916 Mediation Mission', 683–7, 697, 702; Denniston's suggestion of discontinuation in memorandum, 29 September 1941, in 'UKUSA Sigint relations: cooperation with FBI', HW 14/45, TNA. On the history and conclusion in 1941 of British decryption of American messages, see further Christopher Andrew, 'The CIA and U.S. Intelligence: The View from Moscow and London', after dinner speech at the 'Landscapes of Secrecy' conference, University of Nottingham, 29 April 2011, audio version available at: <http://backdoorbroadcasting.net/2011/04/chris-andrew-the-cia-and-us-intelligence-the-view-from-moscow-and-london/>.

CHAPTER 3

1. Alfred W. Ewing (the principal's son) recalled his father's features, *Man of Room 40*, 178.
2. Ewing, 'Special War Work. I', 194–5, 'Special War Work. II', 36, 38; Denniston, *Thirty Secret Years*, 12; Admiralty circular of 16 December 1927 quoted in Freeman, 'Zimmermann Telegram Revisited', 110 n. 22.
3. Winkler, *Nexus*, 5–6, 208.
4. Unpublished Reginald Hall autobiography, Draft D, Chapter 25, 13, 15, 17, 22 (quoting Balfour memorandum of 20 February 1917), folder 6, Box 3, WRH; Freeman, 'Zimmermann Telegram Revisited', 124; Millis, *Road to War*, 404; Gathen, 'Zimmermann Telegram', 34.
5. 'Relations between the United States and Great Britain', memorandum of 8 March 1917 quoted in Jeffery, *MI6*, 116.
6. Unpublished Reginald Hall autobiography, Draft D, Chapter 25, 12, 13, 21, folder 6, Box 3, WRH; Eckhart, telegram to Imperial Chancellor, '2uth' March 1917, and Berlin to Mexico telegram, 4 April 1917, both in 'Zimmermann Telegram file', HW 7/8, TNA. On the delay, see Andrew, *Secret Service*, 111 and the 1945 account by the Room 40 codebreaker Nigel de Grey published in 1999 as appendix III in Kahn, 'Bell', 153–6 at 155. In her classic account of the affair published in 1958, Barbara Tuchman cited only the need to fool Germany: *Zimmermann Telegram*, 156.
7. Bell to Harrison, 29 October 1917, folder 'Miscellaneous Corresp. 1917', Box II 115, LH. For assumptions about British 'misinformation' directed at the Americans, see Freeman, 'Zimmermann Telegram Revisited', 99, 121, and cf. Jeffery, *MI6*, 115.
8. United States Army Intelligence Center, 'Evolution', 22; Tuchman, *Zimmermann Telegram*, 199.
9. United Stated Army Intelligence Center, 'Evolution', 23.
10. Menzies quoted in Brown, *C: Menzies*, 107.
11. Andrew, *Secret Service*, 167; Pershing's subordinate Arthur Conger quoted in Beach, 'Origins', 233.
12. Fredrick M. Glenwright, biography of Friedman in *American National Biography Online*; Clark, *Man Who Broke 'Purple'*, 4–5; Van Deman, telegram to military attaché London, 23 January 1918, folder 'Miscellaneous Corresp. January–August, 1918', Box II 115, and Bell memorandum, 1 May 1919, 21, enclosed with Bell to Leland Harrison, 2 May 1919, Box II 102, both LH; Jensen, *Price of Vigilance*, 123; Talbert, *Negative Intelligence*, 27; Ellis, *Race*, 53; Brown, *C: Menzies*, 120, 124.
13. Jeffery, *MI6*, 78–82; Smith, *Six*, 313; Popplewell, *Intelligence and Imperial Defence*, 258, 331.
14. Angleton quoted in Powers, *Man Who Kept the Secrets*, 283; author's interviews with two senior British intelligence officers.

15. Bell to Harrison, 21 January 1918, in folder 'Miscellaneous Corresp. January–August, 1918', Box II 115, LH; Polk Diary, 9 August 1918, EMH; Gardner, *Safe for Democracy*, 66–8.

16. Gray, *History of Jerusalem*, 287; notice issued by the Pasha of Jerusalem, n.d. (probably early December 1917) and Bell to Harrison, 28 February 1918, both in Box 2, Correspondence of Leland Harrison and Edward Bell, Records Kept by Leland Harrison, RG 59, NA2.

17. Maugham, *Short Stories*, III, 44.

18. Hyde, *Secret Intelligence*, 75; Andrew, *Secret Service*, 150; Hastings, *Secret Lives*, 222; Minute of conversation with the Bullitt Mission's Lincoln Steffens enclosed with J. Y. Simpson, Political Intelligence Department, Foreign Office, to Philip Kerr, 13 June 1919, GD40/17/847, PK; Jeffreys-Jones, 'Maugham', 91, 95, 98, 102.

19. Bell to Harrison, 21 January 1918, folder 'Miscellaneous Corresp. January–August, 1918', Box II 115, LH.

20. US Constitution, article 1, section 5; President Wilson quoted in Daniel P. Moynihan's Senate speech in favour of the End of the Cold War Act, *Congressional Record*, 102 Cong, 1 sess., 17 January 1991, 988; Yardley, memorandum to Van Deman, 12 December 1918 in folder 'Miscellaneous Corresp. January–August, 1918', Box II 115, and Yardley to Bell, 29 January 1919, folder 'Miscellaneous Corresp. January–February 1919', Box II 115, both LH; Yardley, *American Black Chamber*, 2; Kahn, *Yardley*, 46–7; Churchill, memorandum, 'Permanent Organization for Code and Cipher Investigation and Attack', 16 May 1919, reproduced in Kahn, *Yardley*, 54.

21. Bell memorandum, 1 May 1919, 19–21, enclosed with Bell to Leland Harrison, 2 May 1919, and Harrison's reply of 5 May 1919, both in file 'British Intelligence', Box II 102, LH. Harrison encouraged Bell to keep in touch with Basil Thomson, who as head of Special Branch investigated political crime.

22. W. W. Hicks, 'Memorandum on British Secret Service Activities in this Country' (stamped War Department, 9771-145, 2 November 1920), 2, 5, enclosed with and anticipated by Nolan, memo for the Chief, Negative Branch, 26 October 1920, and anon., 'British Espionage in the United States' (stamped War Department, 9944-A-178, 15 February 1921), 3, 5, 7, all in DS.

23. Winkler, *Nexus*, 213, 277; Denniston, 'Yardley's Diplomatic Secrets', 85–6, 106–8.

24. Denniston, 'Code and Cipher School', 47; Grew, *Turbulent Era*, I, 699, 705; C. Hartley Grattan, 'Walter Hines Page–Patriot or Traitor?' *Nation*, 25 November 1925, cited in Olmsted, *Real Enemies*, 27; Moser, *Twisting the Lion's Tail*, 76; Makin, *Brigade of Spies*, 17.

25. O'Reilly, *Racial Matters*, 13–14; Louis Bois, Governor of Bermuda, and C. W. Orr, Governor of the Bahamas, to Leo Amery, Secretary of State for the Colonies, respectively 20 and 25 November 1928, both in file 'Marcus Garvey activities', CO 318/391/12, and anonymous Foreign Office

memorandum detailing steps taken against Garvey in Nigeria, Jamaica, and Canada and titled, 'Marcus Garvey and the Universal Negro Improvement Association and African Communities League', c.1930, in file 'Movements of Marcus Garvey', CO 318/399/3, all in TNA.

26. Churchill, *World Crisis*, 1190; Prior, *Churchill's 'World Crisis'*, 220, 262; See also chapter 2 in the forthcoming book *Classified* by Christopher R. Moran.

27. Hendrick to Bell, 17 June 1921, Bell (from Tokyo) to Hendrick, 13 July 1921, Laughlin to Bell, 28 July 1921, Arthur Page to Undersecretary of State H. Prather Fletcher, 22 August 1921, Bell to Laughlin, 24 August 1921, Harrison to Hughes, 22 May 1922, all in file 'Page-Hendrick', Records Kept by Leland Harrison, General Correspondence, Mexican to Propaganda, Box 7, RG 59, NA2; Freeman, 'Zimmermann Telegram Revisited', 109; Hendrick, *Life and Letters of Page*, II, 214–15.

28. Boylston A. Beal to William L. Hurley, 26 March (with Hurley to Harrison cover note) and 15 May 1923 in file 'Admiralty Secrets', Records Kept by Leland Harrison, General Correspondence, Mexican to Propaganda, Box 7, RG 59, NA2; Hugh Cleland Hoy, *40 O.B.: Or, How the War Was Won* (London: Hutchinson, 1932); Freeman, 'Zimmermann Telegram Revisited', 109–10; Admiralty opinion quoted in Kahn, *Yardley*, 160.

29. Ewing, 'Special War Work. II', 39; Balfour quoted in chapter 2, Moran, *Classified*.

30. Wallace, 'Mackenzie'; Mackenzie, *Water on the Brain*, 276–8; Linklater, *Mackenzie*, 249–50, 256; Moran, *Classified*.

31. Kahn, *Yardley*, 161–70.

32. A. P. Duffes, KC, Jordan's lawyer quoted in the *Daily Herald*, 17 May 1938; P. J. Rose to (MI5 director) Vernon Kell, 26 July 1938, Criminal Case File, Jessie Wallace or Jordan, HH16/212, SNA.

33. Churchill, minute to Hastings Ismay, 17 July 1940, quoted in Gilbert, *Finest Hour*, 672.

CHAPTER 4

1. Stafford, *Roosevelt and Churchill*, 114–15; Winant, *Letter from Grosvenor Square*, 198–9.

2. Rusbridger and Nave, *Betrayal*, 28, 178–9. Rusbridger and Nave's source, Winant, refrained from saying that Churchill was surprised, but did not comment on his sang-froid as a special feature of the evening.

3. Stinnett, *Day of Deceit*, 2–3.

4. Hyde, *Secret Intelligence*, 75; Jordan A. Schwartz, biography of Berle in the *American National Biography Online*; Bennett, *Morton*, 369 nn. 45, 46.

5. Charles, 'Before the Colonel', 227; Charles, *Hoover and Anti-interventionists*; President Roosevelt quoted in Hill et al., *British Security Coordination*, xxv.

6. Berle and Jacobs, *Navigating*, 320.

7. Alvarez, *Secret Messages*, 73; unsigned letter to 'Robertson' copied to Liddell and Denniston, 17 July 1940 and draft reply to Strong, 22 November 1940 enclosed with F. G. Beaumont-Nesbitt letter, containing Strong and Cadogan paraphrases, sent on 22 November to undisclosed recipient and copied to Rear Admiral J. Godfrey and Air Commodore A. B. Boyle, all in 'UKUSA Sigint relations: cooperation with FBI', HW 14/45, TNA; Strong's request of 31 August 1940 quoted in Gladwin, 'Cautious Collaborators', 120.

8. Hoover reports of 3, 5 March 1941 quoted in Charles, 'Before the Colonel', 232.

9. Sweet-Escott, *Baker Street Irregular*, 127; Oliver H. Brown's impressions of Donovan, 10 February 1992, Reel 3, 12423, JSI; Donovan and Mowrer, *Fifth Column Lessons for America*; Jeffreys-Jones, *Cloak and Dollar*, 133–8; Lothian quoted in Jakub, *Spies and Saboteurs*, 11.

10. Brown, *Last Hero*, 163; Kimball cited in Troy, *Wild Bill*, 179; John Godfrey, 'Intelligence in the United States', 7 July 1941, in Bradley F. Smith, 'Admiral Godfrey's Mission to America, June/July 1941', *Intelligence and National Security*, 1 (September 1986), 445–50; Jakub, *Spies and Saboteurs*, 25, 27, 29–30; Jeffreys-Jones, 'British Intelligence Mythologies', 7.

11. 'Memorandum on the Need for a Permanent Independent Intelligence Organization for the United States', 10 September 1943, 2, Reel 117, Box 15, WJD.

12. Stephenson to 'C' 19 June 1941, quoted in Bennett, *Morton*, 257; Sweet-Escott, *Baker Street Irregular*, 130; Mackenzie, *Secret History of SOE*, 389; Jeffreys-Jones, *Cloak and Dollar*, 143–51.

13. Howe's recollections conveyed in Jakub, *Spies and Saboteurs*, 33, 247; Stafford, *Churchill and Secret Service*, 238–9; Churchill quoted in Foot, *SOE*, x.

14. Anonymous quotation in Stafford, *Camp X*, 76.

15. Quotations from handwritten five-page memoir and CV incorporated in a letter to Gillian Edwards (secretary of the Harlech History Society) by SOE veteran John Gordon Coates (1918–2006), dated 13 October 1998 and supplied to the author by Brian Willis-Jones, the owner of Llanllwyni, the house in Harlech where Coates gave intelligence tuition for Inter-Allied Commando (Coates was a Cambridge-educated linguist who went on to serve behind enemy lines in Hungary, winning the Distinguished Service Order); Masters, *Striking Back*, 53, 61, 74.

16. Creighton, 'Robeson's British Journey', 130; Foot, *SOE*, 66; Davidson, *Special Operations Europe*, 155–6; Muggeridge, *Infernal Grove*, 190–1; Crang, 'Politics on Parade', 215, 226; Addison, *Road to 1945*, 149; oral history contributions by Major Oliver Brown, Captain Tom Carew, Sergeant Norman Smith, and Captain Aubrey Trofimov, all in Bailey, *Forgotten Voices*, 212–13.

17. MacPherson, *London OSS*, 71; Bruce, *OSS against the Reich*, 207.

18. Shepardson to Kerr's assistant J. H. Oldham, 14 February 1930, in folder 'PHK', WHS; Jakub, *Spies and Saboteurs*, 61. Winant's donation was to the Elphin Lloyd Jones room of the library at Harlech (adult education) College, which commemorated the short life of the son of Tom Jones, Lloyd George's secretary. It is probably a coincidence that the intelligence training facility for SOE's Inter-Allied Commando Troup 10 was located in Harlech: Coates memoir.

19. Jakub, *Spies and Saboteurs*, 50–1.

20. Walker, 'Democracy Goes to War', 82–3, 90, 92.

21. Estimate of Colonel Douglas Dodds-Parker, senior SOE officer at Massingham, in Wales, 'Massingham', 45; Wales, 'Secret War in the South', 205.

22. German officer quoted in Rouville to author, n.d., received 14 December 2011; Rouville's remarks to a small group including the author in his office and then in the course of a tour of the Maquis Museum, 21 June 2004; Odile de Rouville to author, 3 December 2011. Some of the details in this and the following account come from the website 'Maquis de Vabre': <http://maquisdevabre.free.fr/mvintro.htm>.

23. Norma LaGueux-Hamilton email to author, 10 January 2012; Jacques Noyez and Odile de Rouville oral histories on the above website 'Maquis de Vabre'; Guy de Rouville to author, n.d., received 14 December 2011; 'LaGueux Memorial Dedicated in CIA Garden', *OSS Society Newsletter* (Fall 2002), 7 accessed 26 March 2012 at <http://www.osssociety.org/pdfs/oss_fall_02.pdf>. Author's translations.

24. Hector Davies, 'War in the Languedoc Rouge, "Aux armes, citoyens"' (five-page memoir, 1945, accessed 7 September 2012 on the 'Maquis de Vabre' website at <http://maquisdevabre.free.fr/mvdocs-rpdavies.htm>), 11 (veterans of the Maquis published this memoir on their website after the expiry of the fifty-year confidentiality rule imposed by the French government); author's collective interview with the Monro-Davies family, Edinburgh, 30 December 2011; M. R. D. Foot to Thérèse Duriez (née Monro-Davies), 5 June 1992, MD; Hector Davies, 'With the Maquis in France', undated notes in MD.

25. Hector Davies, 'With the Maquis in France', Le Colonel Commandant les F.F. I. du Tarn, Ordre de Mission, 1 September 1944, Davies's uniform requisition, 30 August 1944, Davies pre-enciphered notes to Menzies, n.d., Foot to Duriez letter above, all in MD; Davies, 'War in the Languedoc Rouge', 1–3, 5; Foot, *SOE in France*, xxx; SOE–Resistance controversies discussed in obituaries of M. R. D. Foot, *Guardian*, 22 February 2012, *Economist*, 3 March 2012, and chapter 8 in the forthcoming book *Classified* by Christopher R. Moran.

26. Odile de Rouville to author, 3 December 2011; Toulmin to Whitney Shepardson, 7 February 1944, Reel 123, Box 15, WJD; Sweet-Escott, *Baker Street Irregular*, 194. Shepardson was by now with OSS London; Sweet-Escott used the spelling 'Kouyoumdjeff'.

27. Smith, *OSS*, 286; Oswin Edmund Craster interview, 6 July 1992, Reel 3, 12612, and Ronald Eric Chatten interview, 22 April 1998, Reel 2, 17992, both in JSI.

28. Bennett, 'Mihailoviç and Tito', 527–8; Bailey, 'OSS–SOE Albania', 33; Bailey, *Wildest Province*, 55–6, 63; Smiley, *Albanian Assignment*, 8; Davidson, *Special Operations Europe*, 84, 103–5.

29. Katz, *Foreign Intelligence*, 181.

30. MacPherson, *American Intelligence in London*, 105; Katz, *Foreign Intelligence*, xii, 196; Morpurgo, 'American Studies in Britain', 19.

31. Denniston, *Thirty Secret Years*, 167; Milner-Barry, 'Hut 6', 92; Jones, *Reflections*, 214; Budiansky, 'Difficult Beginnings', 54.

32. Trevor-Roper, *Philby Affair*, 72 n. 1, 73–4; Barbara Abernathy quoted in McKay, *Secret Life of Bletchley Park*, 204; Smith, *Ultra-Magic Deals*, 54–5; Budiansky, 'Difficult Beginnings', 55.

33. Denniston telegram to Washington, 5 August 1941, in 'UKUSA Sigint relations: cooperation with FBI', HW 14/45, TNA; Kahn, *Yardley*, 210.

34. Denniston memo to Travis, 15 August 1941, in 'UKUSA Sigint relations: cooperation with FBI', HW 14/45, TNA.

35. Denniston memo to Director, American Section GC&CS, for the attention also of the Foreign Office, 29 September 1941, in 'UKUSA Sigint relations: cooperation with FBI', HW 14/45, TNA; Budiansky, 'Difficult Beginnings', 52, 70 n. 8.

36. Budiansky, 'Difficult Beginnings', 59, 61, 65; Bayly (of the US Army's code-breaking facility at Arlington Hall, Va.) memo to Travis, 30 April 1943 and Arlington telex offering IMB card technology to both the UK and Canada, 25 December 1943, both in 'GC&CS Misc.: papers USA Liaison (European) 1943–1945', HW 57/1, TNA; Aldrich, *GCHQ*, 43; Budiansky, *Battle of Wits*, 299.

37. Clark, *Man Who Broke 'Purple'*, 113. F. H. Hinsley thought it was a 'conservative estimate' to say that intelligence shortened the war by four years, and by that he meant British intelligence—no doubt because he was a veteran of Bletchley Park and wrote the official history of British intelligence, he paid scant heed to the American contribution: Hinsley, 'British Intelligence', 10.

38. Denniston to Walter Fried, 11 November 1944, quoted in Gladwin, 'Cautious Collaborators', 142.

39. Minute, prepared by John V. Connorton and Robert F. Packard, of the joint meeting of the [US] Army–Navy Communication Intelligence Board and the [UK] Army–Navy Communication Intelligence Coordinating Committee, 15 October 1945, available at <http://www.nsa.gov/public_info/declass/ukusa.shtml>.

40. Author's interviews with intelligence officers in the UK and USA; Smith, *Ultra-Magic Deals*, vii.

CHAPTER 5

1. Bethell, *Betrayal*, 1–2, 44, 77; Smiley, *Albanian Assignment*, 162.

2. Wisner quoted in Philby, *Silent War*, 160; Smiley, *Albanian Assignment*, 159; Jeffery, *MI6*, 715; Aldrich, *Hidden Hand*, 153; Callanan, *Covert Action*, 73.

3. Bethell, *Betrayal*, 78, 81, 83; Winks, *Cloak and Gown*, 394, 399; Bailey, *Wildest Province*, 328; Jeffery, *MI6*, 715–16.

4. Report by Wing Commander Tony Neel (SOE), 1944, quoted in Bailey, *Wildest Province*, 330.

5. Makin, *Brigade of Spies*, 17; JIC quoted in Huw Dylan, 'Good, but not good enough: The organization of British intelligence after the Second World War', paper delivered 2 May 2009 under the auspices of the International Politics Department, University of Aberystwyth, at the conference '100 Years of British Intelligence', Gregynog, Powys, and furnished by its author. Cooper's *The Spy* was republished in 1946. See, on the functions of spy fiction, Fletcher, 'Sense and Sensationalism', and Svendsen, 'Painting rather than Photography', and for evidence on US ambivalence towards espionage, Jeffreys-Jones, *American Espionage*, chapter 15, 'The Spy in the Mind', 200–17.

6. Tydings in Williams, 'Legislative History', 30; Barrett, *CIA and Congress*, 142; Sidney W. Souers memo, 'Development of Intelligence on the USSR', 29 April 1946, in Thorne and Patterson, *Emergence*, 344.

7. Valero, 'Coordination of American Intelligence', 57–65; Erickson, 'Soviet War Losses', 258; Turrou, *Nazi Spy Conspiracy*, 18; Donovan to Roosevelt, 7 November 1944, Reel 117, 15–23, WJD; 'Statement of General Hoyt S. Vandenberg, Director of Central Intelligence', in Williams, 'Legislative History', 36.

8. George Elsey's memorandum of 17 April 1951 acknowledging Churchill's input, quoted in Valero, 'Coordination of American Intelligence', 42; Dulles memorandum of 25 April 1947 quoted in Hugh Wilford, *The Game-Players: The Early Years of the CIA in the Middle East* (New York: Basic, forthcoming); Pettee, *Future of Intelligence*, 1; Troy, *Wild Bill*, 207; Cline, *CIA*, 21, 309.

9. Christopher Moran, 'Ian Fleming and the Early Public Profile of the Central Intelligence Agency' (forthcoming, *Journal of Cold War Studies*); Troy, *Wild Bill*, 127; author's interviews with senior British intelligence officials.

10. 'Outline of British–U.S. Communication Intelligence Agreement', 1 November 1945: <http://www.nsa.gov/public_info/_files/ukusa/draft_agrmt_1-nov45.pdf> and 'Appendices to U.S.–British Communication Intelligence Agreement', 15–16 July 1948: <http://www.nsa.gov/public_info/_files/ukusa/appendices_jul48.pdf> (both accessed from the NSA website on 15 October 2011); Richelson and Ball, *Ties that Bind*, 5–6; Aldrich, *GCHQ*, 103.

11. Hugh Wilford, *The Game-Players: The Early Years of the CIA in the Middle East* (New York: Basic, forthcoming); Aldrich, *GCHQ*, 79–80, 97.

12. Blount quoted in Goodman, *Nuclear Bear*, 133; 'Review of Intelligence Or-
    ganisations, 1947', Mis/P(47) 31, 6 November 1947, CAB 163/7, TNA
    (reference supplied by Philip H. J. Davies); Jones, *Reflections*, 8.

13. Trevor-Roper, *Philby Affair*, 69; Murphy, 'Keith Jeffery', 720–1. Wesley Wark
    argued that British intelligence was weak between the wars, but recovered in
    the nick of time: Wark, *Ultimate Enemy*, 233, 240.

14. Franklin D. Roosevelt confidential directive, 16 January 1942, SCMD and FBI
    Latin American summaries in Boxes 22, 23 OF 10b, FDR; Gehlen, *Memoirs*,
    164, 204; Mistry, 'Approaches to Italy', 255; Graaff and Wiebes, 'American and
    Dutch', 46–7; Scott-Smith, 'Interdoc', 356, 369; Maddrell, 'British–American
    Collaboration', 90; Bruneau and Matei, 'Intelligence in Developing Democ-
    racies', 761, 764; Hugh Wilford, *The Game-Players: The Early Years of the CIA
    in the Middle East* (New York: Basic, forthcoming).

15. Andrea Bosco, 'National Sovereignty and Peace: Lord Lothian's Federalist
    Thought', in John Turner, ed., *The Larger Idea: Lord Lothian and the Problem
    of National Sovereignty* (London: The Historians' Press, 1988), 108, 122, and, in
    the same collection, John Pinder, 'Prophet not Without Honour: Lothian and
    the Federal Idea', 145–7, 149–51. In forming his views on the American
    Constitution, Lothian had been influenced, at least in part, by his fellow
    Scotsman's study of one of its framers: Frederick S. Oliver, *Alexander Hamilton:
    An Essay on American Union* (London: Archibald Constable, 1906): Oscar Gass,
    memorandum to Harry Dexter White, 'The Newly-Appointed British
    Ambassador', 1 May 1939, Henry Morgenthau Diary, vol. 187, FDR, 93–6.

16. William J. Donovan, 'The Struggle to Create a United Europe', *San Francisco
    Chronicle*, 17 February 1952; Peter C. Dodd, 'Report on the College of Europe'
    (typescript, 1951) and Jean Monnet to Donovan, 2 October 1952, both in Box
    1, ACUE; Rebattet, 'European Movement', 294, 299 n. 2, 307 n. 1; Aldrich,
    Hidden Hand, 343.

17. Souers interview, 16 December 1954, PPF memoirs file (Associates), folder
    'Souers, Sidney, 15–16 December 1954', 5, HST; Phillips, *Night Watch*, 33;
    Colby, *Honorable Men*, 127–8.

18. Flynn, *Road Ahead*, 9, 75; Moser, *Right Turn*, 7, 59, 177–8; Pisani, *CIA and
    Marshall Plan*, 6; Wilford, *CIA, British Left*, 1, 2, 225; Stewart, *Cloak and Dollar
    War*; Richard Aldrich, 'The CIA and the British Left', forthcoming in Chris-
    topher R. Moran and Christopher J. Murphy, eds, *Intelligence Studies in Britain
    and America since 1945: Essays in Historiography* (forthcoming, Edinburgh
    University Press).

CHAPTER 6

1. Goodman and Holloway, 'Interrogation of Fuchs', 123, 133; Lamphere,
   FBI–KGB War, 10–12, 134–5, 144; Granatstein and Stafford, *Spy Wars*, 63–4;

Memo, Lamphere to Meredith Gardner (of the Venona project), 29 September 1949, National Security Agency Venona Collection, reproduced in Benson and Warner, *Venona*, 141–3; Haynes and Klehr, *Venona*, 12, 305.

2. Suggested reply, Eisenhower to Eden, 12 October 1956, NNP.
3. Hoover quoted in Sibley, *Red Spies*, 192; Andrew quoting Hoover from Security Service archives in *MI5*, 388.
4. 'Report [to FBI director] of Hugh H. Clegg and Robert J. Lamphere covering interviews with Klaus Fuchs in London, England', 4 June 1950, 4, 10, 43, 44, in FMS; Jeffreys-Jones, *FBI*, 151–4.
5. Foreign Secretary Lord Halifax referred to a 'special association' in 1940. Churchill used the phrase 'special relationship' in a private letter of 16 February 1944. A Google advanced books search yields no examples of the phrase 'special relationship' being deployed in the diplomatic sense prior to Churchill's speech of 5 March 1946. See Dickie, *'Special' No More*, x; Dumbrell, *Special Relationship*, 7.
6. Craddock, *Know your Enemy*, 277–9; Prados, *Soviet Estimate*, 56–7; Ernst, 'Economic Intelligence in CIA', 306; Zelikow, 'American Economic Intelligence', 167; Gaiduk, 'Soviet Policy'; Porch, *French Secret Services*, 291; De Gaulle paraphrased in Max Beloff, 'The Special Relationship', 151; Richard Aldrich, remark on Jones's attitude at a round table discussion on GCHQ, at Aberystwyth University's Centre for Intelligence and International Security Studies biennial conference in Gregynog, 13 May 2011. When France refused to follow the American security line at the time of the Anglo-US invasion of Iraq in 2003, 'French fries' became 'Freedom Fries' and French toast temporarily disappeared from restaurant menus.
7. Transcribed Kent memoirs, Series III, Tape No. 1, 8–12, Subject File, Group 834, Box 42, SK.
8. V. G. Kiernan, 'On Treason', *London Review of Books*, 25 June 1987; Knightley, *Philby*, 161; Keegan, *Intelligence in War*, 387; Bailey, *Wildest Province*, 253, 327–8; Corke, *Covert Operations*, 3; *Sunday Times*, 31 August 2008; Bower, *Red Web*, 191; Lockhart paraphrased in Bower, *Perfect Spy*, 132; Martin, *Wilderness of Mirrors*, 52–6; Andrew, *MI5*, 173.
9. The American Michael Straight was another 1930s Cambridge recruit for Soviet intelligence but appears to have been reluctant to spy once he returned to the United States. See Costello, *Mask of Treachery*, 381.
10. Heuser, 'Covert Action', 66, 78; report of Robert Joyce to the US Joint Chiefs of Staff recorded in minutes of a meeting held on 12 March 1952, quoted in Aldrich, *Hidden Hand*, 323; other quotation from Wright, *Spycatcher*, 128.
11. Keegan, *Intelligence in War*, 486; Dumbrell, *Special Relationship*, 53.
12. Donovan, 'U.S. Intelligence on Iran', 77.
13. Elwell-Sutton, *Persian Oil*, 151, 241–2; Bayandor, *Iran*, 146, 149.
14. Jeffreys-Jones, *CIA*, 90; Pahlavi quoted in Kinzer, *All the Shah's Men*, 184; Churchill quoted in Donald Wilber, 'Overthrow of Premier Mossadeq of Iran,

November 1952–August 1953' (CIA Clandestine Service History, March 1954, partially released in 2000), accessed on 28 January 2011 at <http://www.gwu.edu/~nsarchiv/NSAEBB/NSAEBB28/9-Orig.pdf>.

15. Bayandor, *Iran*, 149; Dulles to James E. Mooney, 14 November 1955, Box 68, AWD; Jeffreys-Jones, *CIA*, 79.

16. J. E. Coulson for the British ambassador to the Foreign Office, 13 February 1956, a report enclosed with a discussion sheet of the same date with comments by E. G. Andrews and other officials, FO 371/120373; Barrett, *CIA and Congress*, 142, 226, 233.

17. Dorril, *MI6*, 527; Dulles, *The Craft of Intelligence* (Guilford, Conn.: Lyons Press, 2006 [1963]), 206.

18. For a review of the literature of despair, see Stafford, *Spies beneath Berlin*, 177–8.

19. See Stafford, *Spies beneath Berlin*, 178–83.

20. Lucas and Morley, 'The Hidden "Alliance"', 95, 104; author's conversation with Henry Cowper, a Scottish conscript who took part in the invasion.

21. Joseph N. Greene Jr, memorandum of conversation, 23 April 1959, BC.

CHAPTER 7

1. Hunt, *Undercover*, 132–3; 'Everette Howard Hunt', in McCormick and Fletcher, comps., *Spy Fiction*, 143–4; E. Howard Hunt, *Bimini Run* (New York: Farrar, Straus, 1949); Danchev, 'On Specialness', 740.

2. Baltzell, *Protestant Establishment*, 9; Memo, McGhee to Bundy, 21 November 1961, enclosing the eight-page report, 'Decisive Factors of the Counter-Guerrilla Campaigns in Greece, Malaya and the Philippines', in folder 'Counterinsurgency, Special Group, 2/61–4/61 and undated', #12, Box 414, Robert Komer, NSF, JFK. On McGhee, see Newman, *JFK and Vietnam*, 140–1.

3. Ellis, *Britain, America*, 2; Clutterbuck, 'Sir Robert Thompson', 140.

4. Thompson, *Make for the Hills*, 125.

5. Telegram, Frederick E. Nolting to Secretary of State, 30 November 1961, folder 'November 1961: 28–30', Box 6, JN.

6. Thompson to Taylor, 5 January 1962, together with approving comments in General Lionel G. McGarr to McNamara and McGarr to Admiral Harry D. Felt (commanding, Pacific), both 6 January 1962, all in folder 'Vietnam, 1962, 092 January–June', Box 108, Office of the Assistant Secretary for Defense and International Security Affairs, Secret and below General Files, 1962, RG330, NA2; Smith, *International History*, II, 58–9.

7. Memo, McNamara for the president, 8 August 1962, folder 'Vietnam, general, 8/1/62–8/14/62', #10, Box 196A, NSF/Country, JFK.

8. Thompson paraphrasing Diem, Memo, 'The Situation in South Vietnam', 11 March 1963, folder Vietnam. RKG Thompson memoranda, 3/63, #1, Box 3, Roger Hilsman Papers, JFK.

9. Telegram, Lodge to Secretary of State, 3 November 1963, folder 'November 1963: 2–3', Box 17, JN.

10. Jentleson and Patterson, *Encyclopedia U.S. Foreign Relations*, II, 269 and IV, 407; Rabe, *Intervention*, 92–3; Palmer, *Jagan*. John Prados, like Rabe, has pieced together some of the evidence on the CIA: *Safe for Democracy*, 14–19.

11. Palmer, *Jagan*, 64, 178; Robert Kennedy quoted in Rabe, *Intervention*, 81.

12. Rabe, *Intervention*, 9, 11, 79, 126, 128; Prados, *Safe for Democracy*, 13, 18.

13. Rabe, *Intervention*, 102; memo on British Guiana by William R. Tyler, European Division, Department of State, for Secretary of State, 12 December 1963, folder 'British Guiana Special File', Box 5, Intelligence File, NSF, LBJ.

14. Rusk, Memorandum for the President, 6 February 1964, folder 'British Guiana Special File', Box 5, Intelligence File, NSF, LBJ.

15. Memo of 28 June 1964, names of sender and recipient redacted, folder 'British Guiana Special File', Box 5, Intelligence File, NSF, LBJ.

16. 'British Guiana, Anglo-U.S. Consultations, July, 1964', 'Top Secret' minute of meeting, dated 17 July 1964, and Sandys to Rusk, 30 July 1964, both in folder 'British Guiana Special File', Box 5, Intelligence File, NSF, LBJ.

17. Gordon Chase, memorandum for the record dated 14 September of meeting on 11 September 1964, in folder 'British Guiana Special File', Box 5, Intelligence File, NSF, LBJ.

18. Bruce to Tyler, 9 September 1964 and Helms, memo for Bundy, 18 November 1964, both in folder 'British Guiana Special File', Box 5, Intelligence File, NSF, LBJ.

19. Memo, Richard H. Davis, European Division, for Secretary of State, 9 July 1965, folder 'United Kingdom Memos, Vol. VII, 7/65–9/65 (1 of 2)', Box 208, Europe and USSR–UK, Country File, NSF, LBJ. The State Department declassification was on 3 November 1976.

20. Department of State briefing for embassies in Kuala Lumpur, Singapore, Canberra, etc., 4 September 1965, and quotation from telegram, Rusk to London embassy, 7 September 1965, both in folder 'United Kingdom Cables, Vol. VI, 7/65–9/65 (2 of 2)', together with CIA report on 'Britain and Its Dependencies in the Western Hemisphere', 29 October 1965 in folder 'United Kingdom Memos, Vol. VII, 10/65–1/66 (2 of 2)', all in Box 208, Europe and USSR–UK, Country File, NSF, JBJ.

21. Morgan, *Anti-Americans*, 9–10. Cf. Parmar, 'Anti-Americanism', 184.

22. Wright, *Spycatcher*, 273–5.

23. Coyne memo for Bundy, 19 October 1964, enclosing Clark M. Clifford, Memorandum for the President, 'Intelligence-Related Aspects of 18 September 1964 Gulf of Tonkin Incident', in folder 'Foreign Intelligence Advisory Board', Vol. 2 (3 of 4), Box 6, Intelligence File, NSF, LBJ.

24. Wright, *Spycatcher*, 273–5.

25. Memo, Jessup for Rostow, 1 November 1966, in folder 'Blake, George', Box 2, Intelligence File, NSF, LBJ. On the politics of the Mountbatten enquiry, see Terence Morris in *The Times*, 14 November 1980.

26. Memo, Coyne for Walt Rostow (McBundy's successor as national security affairs adviser), relaying PFIAB findings based on Helms's inquiry into counterintelligence, 31 January 1967, folder 'Foreign Intelligence Advisory Board', Vol. 2 (2 of 4), in Box 6, Intelligence File, NSF, LBJ; Michael S. Goodman, 'Avoiding Surprise: The Nicoll Report and Intelligence Analysis' (Nicoll listed the 1973 Yom Kippur attack on Israel, the 1978 Chinese attack on Vietnam, the 1979 Soviet attack on Afghanistan, the 1979 Iraqi attack on Iran, and the 1980 Soviet intervention in Poland), forthcoming in Richard J. Aldrich and others, eds, *Spying on the World: The Joint Intelligence Committee and Events that Shaped History* (Edinburgh University Press); 'Minute from the Secretary of the Cabinet, Burke Trend to the Prime Minister, Harold Wilson, with Section B of Attached Memorandum, 13 March 1967' reproduced in Young, 'Wilson Government's Reform', 137–42.

27. *Washington Post* quoted in Wilford, *Wurlitzer*, 242; Jeffreys-Jones, *CIA*, 157–8.

28. Wilford, *CIA, British Left*, 297–301.

29. Wilford, *Wurlitzer*, 241.

30. Bowles quoted in Jeffreys-Jones, *CIA*, 162; Cairo radio and *Manchester Guardian* source: USIA report, 'Use of CIA Funds', 21 February 1967, in file 'Packet #3', Box 193, Oversize Attachments, Confidential File, NSF, LBJ.

31. Wilford, *Wurlitzer*, 243; Jeffreys-Jones, *CIA*, 160.

32. Lucas and Morris, 'Very British Crusade', 86–7; Wilford, *CIA, British Left*, 58–63.

33. Memo, Lawson for Stephens, 'Some Observations About the British Information (& Related) Departments in London (June 28–July 9)', 23 August 1965, enclosed with memo, Stephens to FBI and others, 1 September 1965, in folder 'United Kingdom Memos', Vol. VI, 7/65–9/65 (1 of 2), in Box 208, Europe and USSR–UK, Country File, NSF, LBJ.

34. Memo, Frankel to Katzenbach, 'The Reorganization of International and Cultural Activities', 23 February 1967, in file 'Packet #3', Box 193, Oversize Attachments, Confidential File, NSF, LBJ.

35. Memo, Katzenbach for president, 17 March 1967, and Katzenbach report with covering note from President Johnson dated 29 March 1967, both in folder 'Ramparts–NSA–CIA', Box 44, Subject File, NSF, LBJ; Helms to president, 25 March 1967, in file 'Packet #3', Box 193, Oversize Attachments, Confidential File, NSF, LBJ.

36. 'Report to the President of the Committee on Overseas Voluntary Activities' (the Rusk committee), 4 June 1968, file 'Packet #1', Box 192, Oversize Attachments, Confidential File, NSF, LBJ.

37. Quotation from 'Foreign and Military Intelligence' (Final Report of the Select Committee to Study Governmental Operations with Respect to Intelligence

Activities, 5 Books, Book 1), *Senate Report*, 94 Cong., 2 sess, no. 94–755 (26 April 1976), 188–9.

38. Telegram, Cromer to Foreign Office, 17 April 1971, quoted in Kristan Stoddart, *The Sword and the Shield: Nuclear Weapons and International Security since 1945* (Palgrave Macmillan, forthcoming, excerpt supplied to author); recollections of an intelligence officer at a recent conference, anonymized under Chatham House rules.

39. Memorandum, Carrington for the Prime Minister, 11 April 1972, quoted in Stoddart, *Sword and Shield* (see previous note); transcript of recorded telephone conversation, Kissinger talking to Nixon, 9 August 1973, quoted in Robb, 'Kissinger', 308.

40. Author's interview with a senior member of the British intelligence community; Aldrich, *GCHQ*, 289–92; Robb, 'Kissinger', 308–9; Heren quoted in Rossbach, *Heath, Nixon*, 203; information on Major government conveyed to author by Richard Aldrich on 31 May 2011.

41. Report enclosed with 'U.S. Naval Security group Activity Edzell, Scotland, Command History for Calendar Year 1974' (1975), item EP00887, EI.

42. Jeffreys-Jones, *CIA*, 207; Cain, *Terrorism and Intelligence in Australia*, 184–5.

43. Paraphrase of US view in Foreign Office report, 'Export of Inverters to Pakistan', 18 April 1978, quoted in Malcolm Craig, 'Britain, America, and Non-proliferation: The Cases of India and Pakistan, 1974–1980' (Ph.D. in draft, Edinburgh University), used with Mr Craig's permission.

44. Dickie, *'Special' No More*, 5; *Daily Mail*, 21 December 2000; *Sun* headline quoted in Boyce, *Falklands War*, 92.

CHAPTER 8

1. 'Proof of Evidence', compiled by Campbell, he thinks before May, and certainly prior to September 1978, 117–19. Viewed in the course of the author's interview with Campbell, Edinburgh, 2 August 2010, from which supplementary information is also derived.

2. Campbell and Hosenball, 'The Eavesdroppers', *Time Out*, 21 May 1976, 8–9.

3. Aubrey, *Who's Watching*, 86; Robertson, *Justice Game*, 104.

4. Campbell, 'Proof of Evidence', 62ff.; Aubrey, *Who's Watching*, 193–5; Robertson, *Justice Game*, 104.

5. Pelling, *America and the British Left*, 4, 6; Linklater, *Mackenzie*, 249–50, 256.

6. Bertrand Russell, 'Civil Disobedience', *New Statesman*, 17 February 1961; Spies for Peace, *Danger*, 1, 8; Campbell, 'Official Secrecy', 75.

7. Aldrich, 'Policing the Past', 937–8; Stafford, *Roosevelt and Churchill*, 157.

8. Foot, *SOE in France*, 103, 124; Aldrich, 'Policing the Past', 923; Murphy, 'Origins', 939.

9. Charles, *Hoover and Anti-interventionists*, 3, 30–1.

10. Wise and Ross, *Invisible Government*, 198 in the 1968 Mayflower paperback edition (Campbell cited 209 in the 1965 Jonathan Cape edition).

11. Robertson, *Public Secrets*, 160; Aldrich, 'Intelligence and European Union', 635; Archibald, 'Early Years', 726, 728, 730.

12. Figures compiled from data in *Editorials on File*, 1970, 1975 (New York: Facts on File); Hain citing Benn in *Political Trials*, 14.

13. Robertson, *Justice Game*, 106–7, 111; Campbell, 'Official Secrecy', 75; Aubrey, *Who's Watching*, 93, 109; Thompson, *Writing by Candlelight*, 152, 176–7.

14. Porter, *Plots and Paranoia*; Bunyan, *History Political Police*; Aldrich, 'Policing the Past', 931, 949; Aldrich, *GCHQ*, 354–5; Denniston, *Thirty Secret Years*, 164; author's conversations with Robin Denniston who was in Edinburgh studying for a master's degree in US intelligence history, 1991–2; quotation from Duncan Campbell, interview with author, Edinburgh, 2 August 2010.

15. Campbell, 'Proof of Evidence', 18, 19, 33, 46, 52.

16. On the apostates, see Jeffreys-Jones, *CIA*, 172, 184, 187.

17. Agee, *On the Run*, 12; Agee, *Inside the Company*, 137, 562; 'Philip Agee–Biographic Data', in folder 'Concerned Americans Abroad–Agee, Philip and Hosenball, Mark–Correspondence 1975–77', Box 3, HN; *Economist*, 11 January 1975.

18. Agee, *Inside the Company*, 599–624; Mader, *Who's Who in the CIA* and *Yellow List*; Marks, 'How to Spot a Spook', *Washington Monthly*, 1974, reproduced in Agee and Wolf, eds, *Dirty Work*, 29–39; Olmsted, *Challenging*, 151; Steering Committee, CCA to Concerned American, 11 June 1975 in folder 'Concerned Americans Abroad–Correspondence, 1974 [*sic*]', Box 2, HN; *Washington Post*, 21 May 1975; *Time Out*, 9 May 1975.

19. *Guardian*, 19 November 1976; Theoharis, *Central Intelligence Agency*, 235; Rees quoted in *Times*, 19 November 1976.

20. Kelly, 'Deportations', 295.

21. BBC radio interviews cited in Castillo, 'British Left', 39; *Time Out*, 10–16 December 1976, 24 December 1976–6 January 1977.

22. 'Wanted: Money: For the Agee/Hosenball defense' (n.d.) in folder 'Concerned Americans Abroad–Correspondence, 1974 [*sic*]', Box 2, Heinz Norden, 'Report of a Deputation from Concerned Americans Abroad to the American Embassy' (n.d.), in folder 'Concerned Americans Abroad Minutes, Agenda', Box 3, and Lawrence to Rita Maran (cc: Anthony Hyde, Chairman, Executive Committee Democrats Abroad UK), 13 January 1977, in folder 'Concerned Americans Abroad–Agee, Philip and Hosenball, Mark–Correspondence 1975–77', Box 3, all in HN.

23. Agee to Thérèse, 17 September 1975 in folder 'Correspondence 1970–1980', Box 2, and Agee 'scribbling diaries' for 1975, 1976, and 1977, all in PA.

24. *Guardian*, 3 February 1977; Benn, *Conflicts of Interest*, 50; Morgan, *Foot*, 338.

25. Aaron Latham, 'A Defection in the Family', *New York*, 11 August 1975, clipping in folder 'Concerned Americans Abroad–Agee, Philip and Hosenball, Mark–Correspondence 1975–77', Box 3, HN; Campbell, 'Official Secrecy', 75; Benn, *Against the Tide*, 645.

26. Agee quoted in *The Scotsman*, 18 February 1977; Andrew and Mitrokhin, *Mitrokhin Archive*, 300, 303; J. Arch Getty (an authority on Soviet communism at UCLA), review of *Mitrokhin Archive* in *AHR*, 106 (April 2001), 685.

27. Olmsted, *Challenging*, 152–3.

28. Smist, *Congress Oversees*, 119–20; 'An Act to Combat International Terrorism', *Senate Report* No. 95–908, 95 Cong. 2, sess., 23 May 1978, 2; Morton H. Halperin, 'The CIA's Distemper', *New Republic* (9 February 1980), 21–2; National Security Archive report on the 2011 Knight survey at <http://www.gwu.edu/~nsarchiv/NSAEBB/NSAEBB338/index.htm> (accessed on 20 April 2011).

29. Phythian, 'British Experience', 67; Weller, 'Oversight', 486; Farson, 'Parliament and its Servants', 225, 232–3; Robertson, *Public Secrets*, 155; Weller, 'Political Scrutiny', 182, 184.

30. Callaghan quoted in Phythian, 'British Experience', 68; Wilford, *CIA, British Left*, 73; Aldrich, 'Policing the Past', 950; Alan Cochrane, 'Traitors in a Class of their Own', *The Scotsman*, 15 May 1997; Furnival-Jones quoted in Hain, *Political Trials*, 209.

31. Phythian, 'British Experience', 69, 76; Mates, *Secret Services*, 57–8; Leigh, 'Intelligence and the Law', 642, 646.

32. Omand, *Securing the State*, 253, 300.

33. See the references to *Malone* v. *U.K.* and *Hewitt, Harman* v. *U.K.* in Omand, *Securing the State*, 283.

34. Phythian, 'British Experience', 82; Author's interview with Campbell, Edinburgh, 2 August 2010.

CHAPTER 9

1. Hodgson, *Moynihan*, 11, 21, 25; Gates, *From the Shadows*, 552; Wills, *Reagan's America*, 462; Schweizer, *Victory*, xii, 242; Moynihan statement to the confirmation hearing by the Senate Intelligence Committee, 1991, 7, 10, in folder 11, 'Gates, Robert, nomination as director', Box II/268, DPM; Moynihan, 'The Soviet Economy: Boy, Were We Wrong!' *Washington Post*, 11 July 1990.

2. Moynihan statement, Senate Committee on Intelligence hearing, 21 July 1981, 97 Cong., 1 sess., *Intelligence Reform Act of 1981* (Washington, DC, GPO, 1981), 5–6; *Congressional Record*, 102 Cong., 1 sess., 17 January 1991, 988, 990; Acheson, *Present at the Creation*, 159; Moynihan, 'Do We Still Need the CIA? The State Department Can do the Job', *New York Times*, 19 May 1991.

3. Mistry, 'Approaches', 247–8; Moynihan to Gilbert, 23 April 1996 and Moynihan to Jonathan Brent (editorial director at Yale University Press, publisher of books on the Venona project and of Moynihan's book, *Secrecy*), 23 April 1996, both in folder 3, 'Commission on Secrecy: Central Intelligence Agency', Box II/279, DPM; Moynihan quoted in Hodgson, *Moynihan*, 386; Johnson, *Threat on the Horizon*, xv; Johnson, *National Security Intelligence*, 162.

4. Johnson, *Threat on the Horizon*, 387; Holcolm, *Endless Enemies*; *New York Times*, 2 April 2009; Federation of American Scientists, 'Intelligence Budget Data' at <http://www.fas.org/irp/budget/index.html> (accessed 5 January 2012); Best, *Intelligence Reform*, 6, 7. The British figure is from the government's 2004 spending review provision for the Single Intelligence Account that funds MI6, MI5, and GCHQ, and is reportedly an underestimate: Simon Usborne, 'Top Secret: A Century of British Espionage', in *The Independent*, 6 October 2009.

5. Moynihan quoting President Wilson in *Congressional Record*, 102 Cong., 1 sess., 17 January 1991, 988.

6. Joseph Conrad, *Heart of Darkness* (1903); Mark Twain, *King Leopold's Soliloquy* (1905); Barbara Kingsolver, *The Poisonwood Bible* (1998); 'Alleged Assassination Plots', 15, 19, 24; O'Brien, *To Katanga and Back*, 75–6.

7. U Thant to Ambassador Samar Sen (India), 30 March 1971, quoted in Dorn, 'Keeping Tabs', 263; Major General Carl van Horn (Sweden), quoted in Dorn, 'United Nations Peacekeeping Intelligence', 284; Wiebes, *Intelligence in Bosnia*, 36; Dorn, 'Intelligence-Led Peacekeeping', 805; Norheim-Martinsen and Ravndal, 'Intelligence-Driven Peace Operations', 460; Dorn, 'U.N. Should Verify Treaties', 13; Jones, *Failing Intelligence*, 40.

8. 'U.S. Participation in International Organizations', *Senate Document*, 95 Cong., 1 sess., no. 95–50 (February 1977), 9, 14; 'Increasing the Limit on Dues for United States membership in the International Criminal Police Organization. Report', *House Report*, 93 Cong., 2 sess., no. 93–1160 (27 June 1974), 1–2; Monet, *Polices et sociétés en Europe*, 27; Anderson, *French Police*, 3, 5, 28–9; Wiebes, *Intelligence in Bosnia*, 33; Clinton quoted in Jeffreys-Jones, *Cloak and Dollar*, 283.

9. Author's several conversations with Walter Dorn, senior common room, Trinity College, University of Toronto, autumn 1993, in the wake of Dorn's services for the UN in field missions and in New York; excerpts from the Pentagon's draft of 'Defense Planning Guidance for the Fiscal Years 1994–1999' and Tyler article, both in the *New York Times*, 8 March 1992; *New York Times*, 11 March 1992.

10. Wiebes, *Intelligence in Bosnia*, 34; Johnson, *Threat on the Horizon*, 350; Bellaby, 'What's the Harm?' 214; *New York Times*, 27 May 2010; UN General Assembly, Human Rights Council, 14th session, *Compilation of good practices on legal and institutional frameworks and measures to ensure respect for human rights by intelligence agencies while countering terrorism*, by Martin Scheinin (17 May 2010), 33.

11. Author's interview with a senior British intelligence officer.

12. Transatlantic Trends, 'Survey: Americans say Asia is more important than Europe' (14 September 2011): <http://trends.gmfus.org/?page_id=3226> (accessed 9 November 2011); *New York Times*, 10 May 2012; US Census Bureau figures reported in *New York Times*, 17 May 2012.

13. Heale, *Contemporary America*, 44–5, 173, 252–3; Baltzell, *Protestant Establishment*, 314; author's interview with another senior British intelligence officer (who noted the rise of Mormons as well as Latinos in both the CIA and FBI—another western phenomenon as the Mormons' strength lay in Utah).

14. Paul Monk quoted in the *Sydney Morning Herald*, 5 April 2003; Johnson, 'Liaison Arrangements of the CIA', 110.

15. *India Times*, 2 January 2009; *New York Times*, 24 February 2010, 25 December 2011.

16. Richelson, *U.S. Intelligence Community*, 299–300; *New York Times*, 21 April 2009; plaintiff's memorandum, *Rosen v. American Israel Public Affairs Committee et al.*, Superior Court for the District of Columbia, 14 December 2010. The critique of Israel's intelligence utility to the United States comes from a middle-ranking official in RELEX, the foreign relations division of the European Commission, speaking to the author in 2010 on condition of anonymity.

17. Cees Wiebes, 'Improve the International Intelligence Liaison', contribution to the *Intelligence and National Security* Intelligence Forum, 8 October 2001, at <http://lists101.his.com/pipermail/intelforum/2001-October/005646.html> (accessed 18 January 2012); Toje, *EU, NATO*, 14–15; Aldrich, 'US–European Intelligence', 123–4; private source of information.

18. The words of a senior British intelligence official interviewed in 2011. The paragraph expresses a consensus, a composite, and strongly expressed view conveyed in several such interviews.

19. Meeting at Georgetown University's Center for Peace and Security Studies, Mortara Center, Washington, DC, 20 June 2011; Dickie, *'Special' No More*, x; remarks of the QC Philippe Sands, 'Torture and International Law in the War on Terror', paper given at Aberystwyth University's Centre for Intelligence and International Security Studies biennial conference in Gregynog, 13 May 2011, available in audiovisual format at <http://www.aber.ac.uk/en/interpol/research/research-centres-and-institutes/ciiss/pastevents/2011conf/>; Suskind in the *Sunday Times*, 24 August 2008.

CHAPTER 10

1. Author's interview with Angelika Molnar at Europol headquarters, The Hague, 19 November 2010.

2. Author's interview with Mauro Falesiedi at Europol headquarters, The Hague, 19 November 2010.

3. *Independent*, 24 November 2004; *Guardian*, 14 November 2005; Judith Crosbie, 'Row Over Europol Top Job Intensifies', *European Voice*, 26 March 2009, at <http://www.europeanvoice.com/article/imported/row-over-europol-top-job-intensifies/64396.aspx> (accessed on 31 January 2012).

4. General Secretariat (Council of the European Union), 'Proceedings of the Europol Group on 29 and 30 March 1994', document 6018/94, Brussels, 7 April 1994 and General Secretariat (Council of the European Union), 'Outcome of proceedings of Europol Working Party', document 6200/94, Brussels, 12 April 1994, both in CEU. Unless otherwise stated, the historical background on Europol's creation and development given here is taken from Europol, *Ten Years*.

5. Author's interview with Claude Moraes, Brussels, 22 November 2005; Aldrich, 'Intelligence and European Union', 630; Europol, *Ten Years*, 45; Kerchove quoted in Fägersten, 'Resistance to Europol', 508; author's interview with Natalie Pensaert, a Belgian adviser to her compatriot Kerchove on the staff of the Council of the EU, Brussels, 8 March 2010; Fortescue, 'The Department of Homeland Security: A Partner but not Necessarily a Model for the European Union' (Paper given at the Weatherhead Center for International Affairs, Harvard University, 19 July 2004, accessed 2 February 2012 at <http://www.wcfia.harvard.edu/fellows/papers/2003-04/fortescue.pdf>), 26.

6. Author's telephone interview with Jonathan Faull, recently retired from his position, 2003–10, as director general of justice and home affairs (later, justice, freedom, and security), European Commission, 8 March 2010; Andrew Duff, MEP (Alliance of Liberals and Democrats for Europe spokesman on constitutional affairs), 'Europol Powers to be Reviewed after Enforcement of Lisbon Treaty', press release 17 January 2008, at <http://andrewduff.eu/en/article/2008/041956/europol-powers-to-be-reviewed-after-enforcement-of-lisbon-treaty> (accessed on 2 February 2012); Claude Moraes, MEP (Labour), letter to *The Guardian*, 13 August 2008.

7. Author's interview with Bill Newton Dunn, Brussels, 22 November 2005; Newton Dunn, *Europe Needs an FBI* (n.p.: Liberal Democrats, 2004. This pamphlet has no pagination, but is divided into enumerated sections and subsections), Sections 6.2, 8.3, 8.6, and *passim*.

8. Author's interview with Rob Wainwright, The Hague, 18 November 2010; David Williams, *The Rebecca Riots: A Study in Agrarian Discontent* (Cardiff: University of Wales Press, 1955), 246, 279.

9. 'Figure 2.1, The Intelligence Cycle', adapted from CIA sources, in Johnson, *National Security Intelligence*, 38; author's interviews with two senior and critical EU officials, with other officials who defended Europol, and with a senior official in French intelligence; *TE-SAT 2011* (The Hague: European Police Office, 2011), 9–14; Aldrich, 'Intelligence and European Union', 622; Daniel Hannan, MEP, quoted in the *Telegraph*, 17 February 2011.

10. House of Lords, Select Committee on the European Communities, session 1994–5, 10th report, *Europol* (25 April 1995), 11, 25.

11. Tony Bunyan, *The Europol Convention* (London: Statewatch, 1995), 1, 9; Ben Hayes, *The Activities and Development of Europol: Towards an Unaccountable 'FBI' in Europe* (London: Statewatch, 2002).

12. Author's interview with Niels Bracke, principal administrator, General Secretariat, EU Council of Ministers, Edinburgh, 28 November 2005; Ambrose Evans-Pritchard in *The Daily Telegraph*, 27 April 2002. On the 'jackboot' fears, author's interview with Charles Williams, administrator, DG Justice and Home Affairs, European Commission, Brussels, 21 November 2005, with a similar point being made by Bill Newton Dunn, Dunn interview.

13. *Europol and the EU's Fight against Serious and Organised Crime* (Foreign and Commonwealth Office background brief, May 1997), front cover and 2; House of Lords, Select Committee on the European Communities, session 2002–3, 5th report, *Europol's Role in Fighting Crime* (28 January 2003), 16.

14. Monet, *Polices et sociétés en Europe*, 303; Ludford quoted in *European Voice*, 31 October–6 November 2002; author's eyewitness notes on Ludford speech on the Visa Information System in plenary session of the European Parliament's Committee on Civil Liberties, Justice and Home Affairs, Brussels, 23 November 2005; Moraes interview.

15. Verbruggen, 'Euro-Cops', 152; Ellermann, 'Vom Sammler zum Jäger', 567; Willy Bruggeman, 'Europol: A European FBI in the Making?' (lecture under the auspices of the Cicero Foundation, Paris, April 2000, accessed 2 February 2012 on <http://www.cicerofoundation.org/lectures/p4bruggeman.html>),11; Europol FBI denial copyrighted in 2002 and still current in January 2006: <http://www.europol.eu.int/index.asp?page=faq>; author's interview with Søren Kragh Pedersen, Public Relations Unit, Europol, The Hague, 17 November 2005; author's interview with Yves Joannesse, Expert National Detaché, Lutte contre le terrorisme, le trafic et l'exploitation des êtres humains, et Coopération policière, DG Justice et Affaires intérieures, Commission européenne, Brussels, 22 November 2005; Adrian Fortescue, 'Department of Homeland Security', 11, 31. Sir Adrian died shortly after giving his paper, and in his honour the DG Justice, Freedom, and Security issued a new edition of it under the title *A European View of the U.S. Department of Homeland Security*.

16. *Christian Science Monitor*, 25 June 2001; Presidency (Council of the European Union) to Working Party on EUROPOL, 'Presidency proposal concerning Article 2', document 6016/94, Brussels, 28 March 1994 (emphasis added), CEU; De Moor and Vermeulen, 'Europol: FBI Perspective', 83; *Europol Convention* (Luxembourg: Office for Official Publications of the European Communities, 2004), Title I, Article 2, 8.

17. 'Action Plan to Combat Organized Crime', adopted on 28 April 1997 (97/C 251/01) in Council of the European Union, *Customs, Police and Judicial Cooperation in the European Union: Selected Instruments* (Brussels, 1998), Volume A, 5–6;

David Phinnemore, *The Treaty Establishing a Constitution for Europe: An Overview* (London: Royal Institute for International Affairs, 2004), 17; Valentina Pop, 'Europe Lacks Resources to Tackle Cross-border Crime, Says Eurojust', *EUObserver*, 17 March 2010, at <http://euobserver.com/22/29703> (accessed 6 February 2012).

18. Department of Justice, Bureau of Investigation, Manual of Instruction, 1927, *FBI Manuals, 1927–1978*, 16; author's telephone interview with Niels Bracke, 9 November 2005.

19. 'European Handbook on How to Issue a European Arrest Warrant', annexe to minutes of Council of the European Union meeting of 17 December 2010, 4, at <http://register.consilium.europa.eu/pdf/en/10/st17/st17195-re01.en10.pdf> (accessed 7 February 2012).

20. 'Brief notes', *American Journal of International Law*, 101 (January 2007), 226; Eurojust press release, 8 September 2010 at <http://www.eurojust.europa.eu/press_releases/2010/08-09-2010b.htm> (accessed 7 February 2012).

21. Author's interview with Aled Williams, The Hague, 19 November 2010; Piris, *Lisbon Treaty*, 46.

22. Katya Vasileva, 'Population and Social Conditions' (European Commission, Eurostat, 34/2011, accessed 8 February 2012 at <http://epp.eurostat.ec.europa.eu/cache/ITY_OFFPUB/KS-SF-11-034/EN/KS-SF-11-034-EN.PDF>); author's interview with Niels Bracke, Edinburgh, 28 November 2005. The Americans had by this time realized the importance of Farsi and other non-European languages—see 'Building Capabilities: The Intelligence Community's National Security Requirements for Diversity of Language, Skills, and Ethnic and Cultural Understanding', *Hearing of the Permanent Select Committee on Intelligence*, 108 Cong, 1 sess, 5 Nov 2003.

23. Interviewees who made these points to the author said that they did not personally hold these prejudices, and they wished to remain anonymous.

24. Author's interview with Claude Moraes, Brussels, 22 November 2005; Maruta Herding, 'Muslims in European Politics', *Euro-Islam.Info*, 2012, at <http://www.euro-islam.info/key-issues/political-representation/#foot note_7_8852> (accessed 8 February 2012); Dunn interview; author's visit to plenary session of the European Parliament's Committee on Civil Liberties, Justice, and Home Affairs, Brussels, 23 November 2005.

25. Moraes interview.

26. Molnar interview; 'Building Trust Between the Police and Roma and Shinti Communities', *OSCE Magazine*, 4 June 2010, accessed 8 February 2012 at <http://www.osce.org/odihr/69579>; author's interview with Merete Bilde, a Danish adviser to Gilles De Kerchove on the staff of the Council of the EU, Brussels, 8 March 2010; author's interview with anonymous EU Commission official; 'Ombudsman Criticizes Commission's Passive Attitude Towards Possible Racism in Recruitment', press release 4/2002, 20 February 2002 at <http://europa.eu/rapid/pressReleasesAction.do?reference=EO/02/4&for-

mat=HTML&aged=1&language=EN&guiLanguage=en>, and 'Decision of the European Ombudsman on Complaint 777/2001/1JH against the European Commission', 17 June 2002 at <http://www.ombudsman.europa. eu/en/cases/decision.faces/en/1573/html.bookmark> (both accessed on 9 February 2012); Faull interview; 'Discrimination against Roma in Europe' (Amnesty International Media Briefing, 4 April 2012), 8, 14.

27. Wainwright interview; *Mirror*, 30 May 2001; *Herald*, 6 July 2000; *Guardian*, 6 July 2000; *New York Times*, 15 June 2010; Ludford quoted in *European Voice*, 31 October–6 November 2002; author's eyewitness notes on Ludford speech on the Visa Information System in plenary session of the European Parliament's Committee on Civil Liberties, Justice, and Home Affairs, Brussels, 23 November 2005; UK House of Commons, European Scrutiny Committee, 9 February 2011, 'National Parliaments' Scrutiny of Europol' (EU Commission communication), clause 10.7 at <http://www.publications.parliament.uk/pa/ cm201011/cmselect/cmeuleg/428-xvi/42812.htm> (accessed on 10 February 2012); Faull interview; Dunn, email to author, 28 March 2012.

28. House of Lords, European Union Committee, *EUROPOL: Coordinating the Fight Against Serious and Organised Crime: Report with Evidence* (London: The Stationery Office, 2008), 8; Hugo Brady, 'Britain's Schengen Dilemma' (Centre for European Reform, 10 February 2009), <http://centreforeuropean-reform.blogspot.com/2009/02/britains-schengen-dilemma.html> (accessed on 10 February 2012).

CHAPTER 11

1. Phrases translated from Hayez, 'Le Renseignement: son importance', 2.
2. Jeffreys-Jones, *CIA*, 136; Hershberg, 'Men in Havana', 173 n. 127; *Le Monde*, 17 April 2007 and (editorial) 26 December 2007; Goodman, *Failure of Intelligence*, 219; quotations from Hayez, 'Le Renseignement: son importance', 1 and Hayez, 'Tribes in Need of a Flag: The New French Intelligence Community', an address at Nuffield College, Oxford, 21 May 2009, supplied by its author with permission to quote. Hayez's father was an archivist and his mother an engineer. He attended the University of Paris 1 Panthéon, a derivative of the Sorbonne: *Who's Who in France* (Paris: Lafitte, 2012), 1061. The French are not opposed to elitism. Their École Nationale d'Administration, based in Strasbourg, trains a high-flying cadre of future top civil servants and politicians (including the current French president, François Hollande), but it represents the apex of a meritocratic republic, not of a pyramid of privilege.
3. Keohane, *EU and Counter-terrorism*, 31; Nomikos, 'European Union Intelligence Service'; Heinrich, 'Case for European CIA', 138–9.
4. Barroso quoted in *Observer*, 14 October 2007; Parliamentary Assembly, Council of Europe, 'Democratic Oversight of the Security Sector in Member States',

23 June 2005 at <http://assembly.coe.int/main.asp?Link=/documents/adop-tedtext/ta05/erec1713.htm> (accessed on 23 February 2012); Ellen Naka-shima, 'Intelligence Chief [Director of National Intelligence Dennis C. Blair] Acknowledges U.S. May Target Americans Involved in Terrorism', *Washington Post*, 4 February 2010; *Times*, 26 July 2007; *Guardian*, 30 July 2009, 11 February and 11 March 2010; Andy Davies, 'Exclusive: UK/US Intelli-gence Event Called Off', Channel 4 News, 23 February 2010 at <http://old.cageprisoners.com/articles.php?id=31100> (accessed on 23 February 2012).

5. David Omand and others, *#Intelligence* (London: Demos, 2012), 10; Aldrich, 'Intelligence and European Union', 630.

6. 'Fig. 1: Distribution of Proxenoi Engaged in Intelligence Activities', in Ger-olymatos, *Study of the Proxenia*, 137; Occhipinti, *European FBI*, 239.

7. Young, *Unity of Europe*, 86; Lundestad, *'Empire' by Integration*, 30–1; on the contested historiography of European integration, Young, *Britain and European Unity*, 12–18, 43 and Foot, 'American Origins of NATO'; Kissinger quoted by Martin Walker, 'Future of Europe's Foreign Policy', 73.

8. Saint-Malo declaration quoted in Villadsen, 'Prospects', 82.

9. Honor Mahoney, 'Security Issues Cloud Galileo Seat Discussions', Euobser-ver.com, 13 September 2006; 'Galileo a step closer to Orbit', EurActiv.com, 8 April 2008; *Guardian*, 21 October 2011; Müller-Wille, 'Improving', 121; Agence France-Presse report on Poettering, 10 November 2008; Solana's statement to EU foreign and defence ministers, November 2008, quoted in Frank Ashbeck (director), 'EU Satellite Center—A bird's eye view in charge of ESDP operations', *ESDP [European Security and Defence Policy] Newsletter*, 8 (Summer 2009), 3; European Union Satellite Centre, 'The Centre's Users', at <?http://www.eusc.europa.eu/index2.php?option=com_content&task=view&id=7&itemid-15&pop=1&page=0> (accessed on 24 February 2012).

10. Björn Müller-Wille, *For Our Eyes Only? Shaping an Intelligence Community Within the EU* (Paris: EU Institute for Security Studies, 2004), 37.

11. Clarke in *Hansard*, 27 June 2005: <http://www.publications.parliament.uk/pa/cm200506/cmhansrd/cm050627/text/50627w19.htm> (accessed on 24 February 2012). Information here and in some places below comes from confidential sources.

12. EU Directorate for the Media press release, 15 April 2011.

13. Alessandro Politi, ed., 'Towards a European Intelligence Policy', Chaillot paper 34 (Paris: EU Institute for Security Studies, December 1998): <http://www.iss.europa.eu/publications/detail/article/towards-a-european-intelligence-policy/> (accessed on 28 February 2012); Villadsen, 'Prospects', 92; Hess, 'Intelligence Cooperation in Europe', 67–8; Nomikos, 'European Intelligence Service', 193–4; Adrian Fortescue, 'The Department of Homeland Security: A Partner but not Necessarily a Model for the European Union' (Paper given at the Weatherhead Center for International Affairs, Harvard University, 19

July 2004, accessed 2 February 2012 at <http://www.wcfia.harvard.edu/fellows/papers/2003-04/fortescue.pdf>), 33.

14. Bunyan quoted in *Sunday Telegraph*, 4 October 2004; Bunyan, *Shape of Things to Come*, 5, 37.

15. *The Australian*, 9 May 2005; Archick et al., *European Approaches to Security*, (i), 2; Mix, *European Union*, (i), 14.

16. Author's interviews with officials who were British citizens and who were working in or recently retired from senior positions in British intelligence and in the EU's Brussels bureaucracy. Andrew Rettman, 'Ashton Picks Finn to be EU "Spymaster"', *EU Observer*, 17 December 2010 at <http://euobserver.com/18/31541> (accessed on 4 May 2012).

17. Walsh, 'Intelligence-Sharing', 626, 630.

18. Oral evidence of William Shapcott, 6 December 2010, House of Lords Select Committee on the European Union, 'Inquiry into The EU Internal Security Strategy', at <http://www.parliament.uk/documents/lords-committees/eu-sub-com-f/ISS/issoralandassocev.pdf> (accessed on 28 February 2012).

19. Hague quoted in Edward Burke, 'What Europe's new diplomatic service can do for Britain', 10 January 2012, at <http://centreforeuropeanreform.blogspot.com/2012/01/britain-should-stop-undermining-eu.html> (accessed on 29 February 2012).

CHAPTER 12

1. Herman, *Intelligence Power*, 209.

2. Davies, *Intelligence and Government*, I, 2; Jones, *Most Secret War*, 603; Sims, 'Foreign Intelligence Liaison', 195, 197–8.

3. ICN poll of a sample of 5,000 in France, Germany, Poland, Spain, and Britain reported in the *Guardian*, 22 March 2011.

Bibliography

Acheson, Dean. *Present at the Creation: My Years in the State Department* (New York: Norton, 1969).

Addison, Paul. *The Road to 1945: British Politics and the Second World War* (London: Cape, 1975).

Agee, Philip. *Inside the Company* (Harmondsworth: Penguin, 1975).

——*On the Run* (Secaucus, NJ: L. Stuart, 1987).

——and Louis Wolf, eds, *Dirty Work: The CIA in Western Europe* (Secaucus, NJ: L. Stuart, 1978).

Aldrich, Richard J. *The Hidden Hand: Britain, America and Cold War Secret Intelligence* (London: John Murray, 2001).

——'Policing the Past: Official History, Secrecy and British Intelligence since 1945', *English Historical Review*, 119 (September 2004), 922–53.

——'US–European Intelligence Co-operation on Counter-Terrorism: Low Politics and Compulsion', *British Journal of Politics and International Relations*, 11 (January 2009), 122–39.

——*GCHQ: The Uncensored Story of Britain's Most Secret Intelligence Agency* (London: HarperPress, 2010).

——'Intelligence and the European Union', in Erik Jones et al., eds, *The Oxford Handbook of the European Union* (Oxford: Oxford University Press, 2012), 627–42.

'Alleged Assassination Plots Involving Foreign Leaders' (An Interim Report of the Select Committee to Study Government Operations with Respect to Intelligence Activities), *Senate Report*, 94 Cong., 1 sess., no. 94–465 (20 November 1975).

Allen, David. 'The Common Foreign Policy and Security Policy', in Erik Jones et al., eds, *The Oxford Handbook of the European Union* (Oxford: Oxford University Press, 2012), 643–58.

Alvarez, David. *Secret Messages: Codebreaking and American Diplomacy, 1930–1945* (Lawrence: University Press of Kansas, 2000).

American National Biography Online (New York: Oxford University Press, 2000–).

Anderson, Malcolm. *The French Police and European Co-operation* (University of Edinburgh: Project Group European Police Co-operation, *c.*1992).

Andrew, Christopher. *Secret Service: The Making of the British Intelligence Community* (London: Heinemann, 1985).

——*The Defence of the Realm: The Authorized History of MI5* (London: Allen Lane, 2009).

Andrew, Christopher and Vasili Mitrokhin. *The Mitrokhin Archive: The KGB in Europe and the West* (London: Penguin, 2000).

Archibald, Sam. 'The Early Years of the Freedom of Information Act. 1955 to 1974', *PS: Political Science and Politics*, 26 (December 1993), 726–31.

Archick, Kristin, et al. *European Approaches to Homeland Security and Terrorism* (Washington, DC: Congressional Research Service, 2006).

Aston, George. *Secret Service* (London: Faber and Faber, 1930).

Aubrey, Crispin. *Who's Watching You?* (Harmondsworth: Penguin, 1981).

Bailey, Roderick. 'OSS–SOE Relations, Albania', in David Stafford and Rhodri Jeffreys-Jones, eds, *American–British–Canadian Intelligence Relations 1939–2000* (London: Frank Cass, 2000), 20–35.

—— *The Wildest Province: SOE in the Land of the Eagle* (London; Jonathan Cape, 2008).

—— *Forgotten Voices of the Secret War: An Inside History of Special Operations during the Second World War* (London: Ebury, 2009).

Baltzell, E. Digby. *The Protestant Establishment: Aristocracy and Caste in America* (New York: Random House, 1964).

Barrett, David M. *The CIA and Congress: The Untold Story from Truman to Kennedy* (Lawrence: University Press of Kansas, 2005).

Bayandor, Darioush. *Iran and the CIA: The Fall of Mossadeq Revisited* (Basingstoke: Palgrave Macmillan, 2010).

Beach, Jim. 'Origins of the Special Intelligence Relationship? Anglo-American Intelligence Co-operation on the Western Front', *Intelligence and National Security*, 22 (April 2007), 229–49.

Beesly, Patrick. *Room 40: British Naval Intelligence 1914–18* (London: Hamish Hamilton, 1982).

Bellaby, Ross W. 'What's the Harm? The Ethics of Intelligence Collection', Ph.D. thesis, Aberystwyth University, 2011.

Beloff, Max. 'The Special Relationship: An Anglo-American Myth', in Martin Gilbert, ed., *A Century of Conflict, 1950–1950: Essays for A. J. P. Taylor* (London: Hamish Hamilton, 1966), 151–71.

Benn, Tony. *Against the Tide: Diaries 1973–1976* (London: Hutchinson, 1989).

—— *Conflicts of Interest: Diaries 1977–1980* (London: Hutchinson, 1990).

Bennett, Gill. *Churchill's Man of Mystery: Desmond Morton and the World of Intelligence* (London: Routledge, 2009).

Bennett, Ralph, et al. 'Mihailoviç and Tito', *Intelligence and National Security*, 10 (July 1995), 526–8.

Benson, Robert L., and Michael Warner, eds, *Venona: Soviet Espionage and the American Response, 1939–1957* (Washington, DC: NSA and CIA, 1996).

Berle, Beatrice, and Travis Jacobs, eds, *Navigating the Rapids: From the Papers of Adolf A. Berle* (New York: Harcourt Brace Jovanovich, 1973).

Best, Richard A., Jr. *Intelligence Reform after Five Years: The Role of the Director of National Intelligence (DNI)* (Washington, DC: Congressional Research Service, 2010).

Bethell, Nicholas W. *The Great Betrayal: The Untold Story of Kim Philby's Biggest Coup* (London: Hodder and Stoughton, 1984).

Boghardt, Thomas. *Spies of the Kaiser: German Covert Operations in Great Britain during the First World War Era* (Basingstoke: Palgrave Macmillan, 2004).

Bower, Tom. *The Red Web: MI6 and the KGB Master Coup* (London: Aurum, 1989).

—— *The Perfect English Spy: Sir Dick White and the Secret War 1935–90* (London: Heinemann, 1995).

Boyce, D. George. *The Falklands War* (Basingstoke: Palgrave Macmillan, 2005).

Brinkley, Alan. 'Richard Hofstadter's *The Age of Reform*: A Reconsideration', *Reviews in American History*, 13 (September 1985), 462–80.

Brown, Anthony C. *Wild Bill Donovan: The Last Hero* (New York: Times Books, 1982).

—— *'C': The Secret life of Sir Stewart Graham Menzies, Spymaster to Winston Churchill* (New York: Collier, 1987).

Brown, Giles T. 'The Hindu Conspiracy and the Neutrality of the United States, 1914–1917', Ph.D. thesis, University of California, Berkeley, 1941.

Bruce, David K. E. *OSS against the Reich: The World War II Diaries of David K. E. Bruce*, ed. Nelson D. Lankford (Kent, Oh.: Kent University Press, 1991).

Bruneau, Thomas C., and Florina C. Matei. 'Intelligence in the Developing Democracies: The Quest for Transparency and Effectiveness', in Loch K. Johnson, ed., *The Oxford Handbook of National Security Intelligence* (Oxford: Oxford University Press, 2010), 757–73.

Bryan, George S. *The Spy in America* (Philadelphia: Lippincott, 1943).

Budiansky, Stephen. *Battle of Wits: The Complete Story of Codebreaking in World War II* (London: Viking, 2000).

—— 'The Difficult Beginnings of US–British Codebreaking Cooperation', in David Stafford and Rhodri Jeffreys-Jones, eds, *American–British–Canadian Intelligence Relations 1939–2000* (London: Frank Cass, 2000), 49–73.

Bunyan, Tony. *The History and Practice of the Political Police in Britain* (London: Quartet, 1977).

—— *The Shape of Things to Come: The EU Future Group* (Nottingham: Spokesman Books, 2009).

Cain, Frank. *Terrorism and Intelligence in Australia: A History of ASIO and National Surveillance* (Melbourne: Australia Scholarly Publishing, 2008).

Callanan, James. *Covert Action in the Cold War: US Policy, Intelligence and Covert Operations* (London: I. B. Tauris, 2010).

Campbell, A. E. *Great Britain and the United States, 1895–1903* (London: Longmans, 1960).

Campbell, Duncan. 'Official Secrecy and British Libertarianism', in Ralph Miliband and John Saville, eds, *The Socialist Register 1979: A Survey of Movements and Ideas* (London: Merlin Press, 1979), 75–88.

Castillo, Mark. 'The British Left and America's Discontent with Intelligence' (University of Edinburgh M.Sc., 2010).

Charles, Douglas M. ' "Before the Colonel Arrived": Hoover, Donovan, Roosevelt, and the Origins of American Central Intelligence, 1940–41', *Intelligence and National Security*, 20 (June 2005), 225–37.

——*J. Edgar Hoover and the Anti-interventionists: FBI Political Surveillance and the Rise of the Domestic Security State, 1939–1945* (Columbus: Ohio State University Press, 2007).

Churchill, Winston S. *The World Crisis, 1911–1918* (London: Odham Press, 1950 [first published in 1923–31]).

Clark, Ronald W. *The Man Who Broke 'Purple': The Life of the World's Greatest Cryptologist, Colonel William F. Friedman* (London: Weidenfeld and Nicolson, 1977).

Cline, Ray S. *The CIA under Reagan, Bush and Casey: The Evolution of the Agency from Roosevelt to Reagan* (Washington, DC: Acropolis Books, 1981).

Clutterbuck, Richard. 'Sir Robert Thompson: A Lifetime of Counter-Insurgency', *Army & Defence Quarterly Journal*, 120 (April 1990), 140–5.

Colby, William. *Honorable Men: My Life in the CIA* (London: Hutchinson, 1978).

Cooper, James Fenimore. *The Spy; or, A Tale of the Neutral Ground* (New York: Dodd, Mead, 1946 [1821]).

Corke, Sarah-Jane. *US Covert Operations and Cold War Strategy* (Abingdon: Routledge, 2008).

Costello, John. *Mask of Treachery* (New York: William Morrow, 1988).

Craddock, Percy. *Know your Enemy: How the Joint Intelligence Committee Saw the World* (London: John Murray, 2002).

Crang, Jeremy. 'Politics on Parade', *History*, 81/262 (1996), 215–27.

Creighton, Sean. 'Paul Robeson's British Journey', in Neil A Wynn, ed., *Cross the Water Blues: African American Music in Europe* (Jackson: University Press of Mississippi, 2007), 125–44.

Danchev, Alex. 'On Specialness', *International Affairs*, 72 (1996), 737–50.

Davidson, Basil. *Special Operations Europe: Scenes from the Anti-Nazi War* (London: Gollancz, 1980).

Davies, Philip H. J. 'Organisational Development of Britain's Secret Intelligence Service 1909–1979', Ph.D. thesis, Reading University, 1997.

——*Intelligence and Government in Britain and the United States*, 2 vols, I: *Evolution of the U.S. Intelligence Community*, II: *Evolution of the U.K. Intelligence Community* (Santa Barbara, Calif.: ABC CLIO/Praeger, 2012).

De Moor, Alexandra, and Gert Vermeulen. 'Shaping the Competence of Europol: An FBI Perspective', in Marc Cools et al., eds, *EU and International Crime Control: Topical Issues* (Antwerp: Maklu, 2010), 63–94.

Denniston, Alastair. 'The Government Code and Cipher School between the Wars', *Intelligence and National Security*, 1 (January 1986), 48–70.

Denniston, Robin. 'Yardley's Diplomatic Secrets', *Cryptologia*, 18 (April 1994), 81–127.

——*Thirty Secret Years: A. G. Denniston's Work in Secret Intelligence 1914–1944* (Clifton-upon-Teme: Polpero Heritage Press, 2007).

Dickie, John. 'Special' No More: Anglo-American Relations: Rhetoric and Reality (London: Weidenfeld and Nicolson, 1994).

Doerries, Reinhard R. Imperial Challenge: Ambassador Count Bernstorff and German–American Relations, 1908–1917, trans. Christa D. Shannon (Chapel Hill: University of North Carolina Press, 1989).

——Prelude to the Easter Rising: Sir Roger Casement in Imperial Germany (London: Frank Cass, 2000).

Donovan. Michael P. 'U.S. Political Intelligence and American Policy on Iran, 1950–1979', Ph.D. thesis, University of Edinburgh, 1997.

Donovan, William, and Edgar Mowrer, Fifth Column Lessons for America (Washington, DC: American Council on Public Affairs, 1940).

Dorn, A. Walter. 'U.N. Should Verify Treaties', Bulletin of the Atomic Scientists, 46 (July/August 1990), 13–14.

——'Keeping Tabs on a Troubled World: UN Information-Gathering to Preserve Peace', Security Dialogue, 27 (September 1996), 262–76.

——'Intelligence-Led Peacekeeping: The United Nations Stabilization Mission in Haiti (MINUSTAH), 2006–07', Intelligence and National Security, 24 (December 2009), 805–35.

——'United Nations Peacekeeping Intelligence', in Loch K. Johnson, ed., The Oxford Handbook of National Security Intelligence (Oxford: Oxford University Press, 2010), 275–95.

Dorril, Stephen. MI6: Fifty Years of Special Operations (London: Fourth Estate, 2000).

Dorwart, Jeffery M. The Office of Naval Intelligence: The Birth of America's First Intelligence Agency, 1865–1918 (Annapolis, Md.: Naval Institute Press, 1979).

Dulles, Allen W. The Craft of Intelligence (London: Weidenfeld & Nicolson, 1963).

Dumbrell, John. A Special Relationship: Anglo-American Relations in the Cold War and After (Basingstoke: Macmillan, 2001).

Ellermann, Jan. 'Vom Sammler zum Jäger: Europol auf dem Weg zu einem "europäischen FBI"?' Zeitschrift für europarechtliche Studien, 5/4 (2002), 562–87.

Ellis, Mark. Race, War and Surveillance: African Americans and the United States Government during World War I. Bloomington: Indiana University Press, 2001.

Ellis, Sylvia. Britain, America, and the Vietnam War (Westport, Conn.: Praeger, 2004).

——Historical Dictionary of Anglo-American Relations (Lanham, Md.: Scarecrow Press, 2009).

Elwell-Sutton, Laurence P. Persian Oil: A Study in Power Politics (Westport, Conn.: Greenwood, 1975).

Erickson, John. 'Soviet War Losses: Calculations and Controversies', in John Erickson and David Dilks, eds, Barbarossa: The Axis and the Allies (Edinburgh: Edinburgh University Press, 1994), 255–77.

Ernst, Maurice C. 'Economic Intelligence in CIA', in H. Bradford Westerfield, ed., Inside CIA's Private World: Declassified Articles from the Agency's Internal Journal, 1955–1992 (New Haven: Yale University Press, 1995).

Europol. Ten Years of Europol, 1999–2009 (The Hague: European Police Office, 2009).

Ewing, Alfred W. *The Man of Room 40: The Life of Sir Alfred Ewing* (London: Hutchinson, 1936).

Ewing, J. Alfred. 'Some Special War Work: Part I' (comp. David Kahn), *Cryptologia*, 4 (October 1980), 193–203.

——'Some Special War Work: Part II' (comp. David Kahn), *Cryptologia*, 5 (January 1981), 33–9.

Fägersten, Björn. 'Bureaucratic Resistance to International Intelligence Cooperation: The Case of Europol', *Intelligence and National Security*, 25 (August 2010), 500–20.

Faligot, Roger. *Les Services secrets chinois de Mao aux J.O.* (Paris: Nouveau Monde éditions, 2008).

Farson, Stuart. 'Parliament and its Servants: Their Role in Scrutinizing Canadian Intelligence', in David Stafford and Rhodri Jeffreys-Jones, eds, *American–British–Canadian Intelligence Relations 1939–2000* (London: Frank Cass, 2000), 225–58.

Fergusson, Thomas G. *British Military Intelligence, 1870–1914* (London: Arms and Armour Press, 1984).

Fletcher, Katy. 'Sense and Sensationalism in American Spy Fiction', in Rhodri Jeffreys-Jones and Andrew Lownie, eds, *North American Spies: New Revisionist Essays* (Edinburgh: Edinburgh University Press, 1991), 218–40.

Flynn, John T. *The Road Ahead: America's Creeping Revolution* (New York: Devin-Adair, 1949).

Foot, Michael R. D. *SOE: An Outline History of the Special Operations Executive 1940–1946* (London: Pimlico, 1999 [BBC, 1984]).

——*SOE in France: An Account of the Work of the British Special Operations Executive in France, 1940–1944*, 3rd edn. (London: Frank Cass, 2004 [HMSO, 1966]).

Foot, Peter. 'The American Origins of NATO: A Study in Domestic Inhibitions and West European Constraints', Ph.D. thesis, University of Edinburgh, 1984.

Fowler, Wilton B. *British–American Relations 1917–1918: The Role of Sir William Wiseman* (Princeton: Princeton University Press, 1969).

Freeman, Peter. 'The Zimmerman Telegram Revisited: A Reconciliation of the Primary Sources', *Cryptologia*, 30 (2006), 98–150.

Gaiduk, Ilya V. 'Soviet Policy towards U.S. Participation in the Vietnam War', *History*, 81 (January 1996), 40–54.

Gardner, Lloyd C. *Safe for Democracy: The Anglo-American Response to Revolution, 1913–1923* (New York: Oxford University Press, 1984).

Gates, Robert M. *From the Shadows: The Ultimate Insider's Story of Five Presidents and How they Won the Cold War* (New York: Simon & Schuster, 1996).

Gatewood, Willard B., Jr. *Theodore Roosevelt and the Art of Controversy: Episodes of the White House Years*. Baton Rouge: Louisiana State University Press, 1970.

Gathen, Joachim. 'Zimmermann Telegram: The Original Draft', *Cryptologia*, 31 (2007), 2–37.

Gaunt, Guy R. A. *The Yield of the Years: A Story of Adventure Afloat and Ashore* (London: Hutchinson, 1940).

Gehlen, Reinhard. *The Gehlen Memoirs* (London: Collins, 1972).

Gerolymatos, André. *Espionage and Treason: A Study of the Proxenia in Political and Military Intelligence Gathering in Classical Greece* (Amsterdam: J. C. Gieben, 1986).

Gilbert, Martin. *Winston S. Churchill*, 6 vols, VI: *Finest Hour* (London: Heinemann, 1983).

Gladwin, Lee A. 'Cautious Collaborators: The Struggle for Anglo-American Cryptanalytic Co-operation 1940–43', in David Alvarez, ed., *Allied and Axis Signals Intelligence in World War II* (London: Frank Cass, 1999), 119–45.

Goodman, Melvin A. *Failure of Intelligence: The Decline and Fall of the CIA* (Lanham, Md.: Rowman & Littlefield, 2008).

Goodman, Michael S. *Spying on the Nuclear Bear: Anglo-American Intelligence and the Soviet Bomb* (Stanford, Calif.: Stanford University Press, 2007).

——and David Holloway. 'The Interrogation of Klaus Fuchs, 1950', in R. Gerald Hughes and Len Scott, eds, *Exploring Intelligence Archives: Enquiries into the Secret State* (London: Routledge, 2008), 123–39.

Graaff, Bob de, and Cees Wiebes. 'Intelligence and the Cold War behind the Dikes: The Relationship between the American and Dutch Intelligence Communities, 1946–1994', in Rhodri Jeffreys-Jones and Christopher Andrew, eds, *Eternal Vigilance? 50 Years of the CIA* (London: Frank Cass, 1997), 41–58.

Granatstein, Jack L., and David Stafford. *Spy Wars: Espionage and Canada from Gouzenko to Glasnost* (Toronto: McClelland and Stewart, 1992).

Gray, John. *A History of Jerusalem* (London: Robert Hale, 1969).

Grew, Joseph C. *Turbulent Era: A Diplomatic Record of Forty Years, 1904–1945*, 2 vols (London: Hammond, 1953).

Hain, Peter. *Political Trials in Britain* (Harmondsworth: Penguin, 1985).

Hastings, Selina. *The Secret Lives of Somerset Maugham* (London: John Murray, 2009).

Hayez, Philippe. '"*Renseignement*": The New French Intelligence Policy', *International Journal of Intelligence and Counterintelligence*, 23 (June 2010), 474–86.

——'Le Renseignement: son importance, ses transformations', *Cahiers français*, 360 (January–February 2011), 1–6.

Haynes, John E., and E. Harvey Klehr. *Venona: Decoding Soviet Espionage in America* (New Haven: Yale University Press, 1999).

Heale, Michael J. *Contemporary America: Power, Dependency, and Globalization since 1980* (Chichester: Wiley-Blackwell, 2011).

Heinrich, Jean. 'The Case for a European CIA', *Europe's World* (Spring 2006), 138–9.

Hendrick, Burton J. *The Life and Letters of Walter H. Page*, 3 vols (London: Heinemann, 1922–6).

Herman, Michael. *Intelligence Power in Peace and War* (Cambridge: Cambridge University Press, 1996).

Hershberg, James G. 'Their Men in Havana: Anglo-American Intelligence Exchanges and the Cuban Crises, 1961–62', in David Stafford and Rhodri Jeffreys-Jones, eds, *American–British–Canadian Intelligence Relations 1939–2000* (London: Frank Cass, 2000), 121–76.

Hess, Gary R. *America Encounters India, 1941–1947* (Baltimore: Johns Hopkins Press, 1971).

Hess, Sigurd. 'Intelligence Cooperation in Europe, 1990 to the Present', *Journal of Intelligence History*, 3 (Summer 2003), 61–8.

Heuser, Beatrice. 'Covert Action within British and American Concepts of Containment, 1948–51', in Richard J. Aldrich, ed., *British Intelligence, Strategy and the Cold War, 1945–51* (London: Routledge, 1992), 65–84.

Hiley, Nicholas. 'The Failure of British Counter-Espionage against Germany', *Historical Journal*, 28 (1985), 835–62.

——'Decoding German Spies: British Spy Fiction, 1908–18', in Wesley K. Wark, ed., *Spy Fiction, Spy Films and Real Intelligence* (London: Frank Cass, 1991), 55–79.

——'Re-entering the Lists: MI5's Authorized History and the August 1914 Arrests', *Intelligence and National Security*, 25 (August 2010), 415–52.

Hilfrich, Fabian. 'West Germany's Long Year of Europe: Bonn between Europe and the United States', in Matthias Schulz and Thomas A. Schwartz, *The Strained Alliance: U.S.–European Relations from Nixon to Carter* (Cambridge: Cambridge University Press, 2010), 237–56.

Hill, Tom and Gilbert Highet, Helen MacInnes, Roald Dahl, and Giles Playfair. *British Security Coordination: The Secret History of British Intelligence in the Americas, 1940–45* (London: St Ermin's Press, 1998 [1945]).

Hinsley, Fred H. 'British Intelligence in the Second World War: An Overview', *Cryptologia*, 14 (January 1990), 1–10.

Hodgson, Godfrey. *The Gentleman from New York: Daniel Patrick Moynihan: A Biography* (Boston: Houghton Mifflin, 2000).

Hofstadter, Richard. *The Age of Reform: From Bryan to FDR* (New York: Vintage, 1955).

Holcolm, Raymond W. *Endless Enemies: Inside FBI Counterterrorism* (Washington, DC: Potomac Books, 2011).

Hunt, E. Howard. *Undercover: Memoirs of an American Secret Agent* (New York: Berkeley/Putnam, 1974).

Hyde, H. Montgomery. *The Quiet Canadian: The Secret Service Story of Sir William Stephenson (Intrepid)* (London: Hamilton, 1962).

——*Secret Intelligence Agent: British Espionage in America and the Creation of the OSS* (New York: St Martin's Press, 1982).

Jakub, Jay. *Spies and Saboteurs: Anglo-American Collaboration and Rivalry in Human Intelligence Collection and Special Operations, 1940–45* (Basingstoke: Macmillan, 1999).

Jeffery, Keith. *MI6: The History of the Secret Intelligence Service, 1909–1949* (London: Bloomsbury, 2010).

Jeffreys-Jones, Rhodri. 'Profit over Class: A Study in American Industrial Espionage', *Journal of American Studies*, 6 (December 1972), 233–48.

——'W. Somerset Maugham: Anglo-American Agent in Revolutionary Russia', *American Quarterly*, 28 (Spring 1976), 90–106.

——*American Espionage: From Secret Service to CIA* (New York: The Free Press, 1977).

——'Lord Lothian and American Democracy: An Illusion in Pursuit of an Illusion', *Canadian Review of American Studies*, 17 (Winter 1986), 411–22.

——*The CIA and American Democracy* (New Haven: Yale University Press, 1989).

——'The Role of British Intelligence in the Mythologies Underpinning the OSS and Early CIA', in David Stafford and Rhodri Jeffreys-Jones, eds, *American–British–Canadian Intelligence Relations 1939–2000* (London: Frank Cass, 2000), 5–19.

——*Cloak and Dollar: A History of American Secret Intelligence* (New Haven: Yale University Press, 2002).

——'Wiseman, Sir William George Eden (1885–1962)', in Henry C. G. Matthew et al., eds, *Oxford Dictionary of National Biography*, 62 vols (Oxford: Oxford University Press, 2004), vol. LIX, 850–1.

——'The Idea of a European FBI', in Loch Johnson, ed., *Strategic Intelligence*, 5 vols, IV: *Counterintelligence and Terrorism* (New York: Praeger, 2007), 73–96.

——*The FBI: A History* (New Haven: Yale University Press, 2007).

——'Rise, Fall and Regeneration: From CIA to EU', *Intelligence and National Security*, 24 (February 2008), 103–18.

——'Angleton's Self-Invalidating Fallacy', *Diplomatic History*, 34 (September 2010), 761–4.

——'The End of an Exclusive Special Intelligence Relationship: British–American Intelligence Co-operation before, during and after the 1960s', *Intelligence and National Security*, 27/5 (October 2012), 707–21.

Jensen, Joan M. *The Price of Vigilance* (Chicago: Rand McNally, 1968).

Jentleson, Bruce W. and Thomas G. Paterson, eds, *Encyclopedia of U.S. Foreign Relations* (New York: Oxford University Press, 1997).

Johnson, Loch K. *The Threat on the Horizon: An Inside Account of America's Search for Security after the Cold War* (Oxford: Oxford University Press, 2011).

——*A Season of Inquiry: The Senate Intelligence Investigation* (Lexington: University Press of Kentucky, 1985).

——'The Liaison Arrangements of the Central Intelligence Agency', in Athan Theoharis et al., eds, *The Central Intelligence Agency: Security under Scrutiny* (Westport, Conn.: Greenwood, 2006), 85–120.

——ed. *The Oxford Handbook of National Security Intelligence* (Oxford: Oxford University Press, 2010).

——*National Security Intelligence* (Cambridge: Polity, 2012).

Jones, Brian. *Failing Intelligence: The True Story of How We Were Fooled into Going to War in Iraq* (London: Biteback, 2010).

Jones, John P. *The German Spy in America: The Secret Plotting of German Spies in the United States and the Inside Story of the Sinking of the Lusitania* (London: Hutchinson, 1917).

Jones, R. V. *Most Secret War* (Sevenoaks: Coronet, 1981 [1978]).

——*Reflections on Intelligence* (London: Heinemann, 1989).

Kahn, David. 'Edward Bell and his Zimmermann Telegram Memoranda', *Intelligence and National Security*, 14 (Autumn 1999), 143–59.

——*The Reader of Gentlemen's Mail: Herbert O. Yardley and the Birth of American Codebreaking* (New Haven: Yale University Press, 2004).

Kamath, M. V. *The United States and India, 1776–1976* (Washington, DC: The Embassy of India, 1976).

Katz, Barry M. *Foreign Intelligence: Research and Analysis in the Office of Strategic Services 1942–1945* (Cambridge, Mass.: Harvard University Press, 1989).

Keegan, John. *Intelligence in War: Knowledge of the Enemy from Napoleon to Al-Qaeda* (London: Hutchinson, 2003).

Kelly, Phil. 'The Deportations of Philip Agee', in Philip Agee and Louis Wolf, eds, *Dirty Work: The CIA in Western Europe* (Secaucus, NJ: L. Stuart, 1978), 286–300.

Keohane, Daniel. *The EU and Counter-terrorism* (London: Centre for European Reform, 2005).

Kinzer, Stephen. *All the Shah's Men: An American Coup and the Roots of Middle East Terror* (New York: Wiley, 2003).

Knightley, Phillip. *The Master Spy: The Story of Kim Philby* (New York: Vintage, 1990).

Knott, Stephen F. *Secret and Sanctioned: Covert Operations and the American Presidency* (New York: Oxford University Press, 1996).

Lamphere, Robert J. *The FBI–KGB War: A Special Agent's Story* (New York: Random House, 1986).

Larsen, Daniel. 'British Intelligence and the 1916 Mediation Mission of Colonel Edward M. House', *Intelligence and National Security*, 25 (October 2010), 682–704.

Lathrop, Charles E., comp. *The Literary Spy: The Ultimate Source for Quotations on Espionage and Intelligence* (New Haven: Yale University Press, 2004).

Leigh, Ian. 'Intelligence and the Law in the United Kingdom', in Loch K. Johnson, ed., *The Oxford Handbook of National Security Intelligence* (Oxford: Oxford University Press, 2010), 640–56.

Le Queux, William T. *The Invasion of 1910* (London: Eveleigh Nash, 1906).

Link, Arthur S. *Wilson the Diplomatist: A Look at his Major Foreign Policies* (Baltimore: Johns Hopkins Press, 1959).

Linklater, Andro. *Compton Mackenzie: A Life* (London: Hogarth Press, 1992).

Lucas, W. Scott, and Alistair Morey, 'The Hidden "Alliance": The CIA and MI6 before and after Suez', in David Stafford and Rhodri Jeffreys-Jones, eds, *American–British–Canadian Intelligence Relations 1939–2000* (London: Frank Cass, 2000), 95–120.

——and C. J. Morris. 'A Very British Crusade: The Information Research Department and the Cold War', in Richard J. Aldrich, ed., *British Intelligence, Strategy and the Cold War, 1945–51* (London: Routledge, 1992), 85–110.

Lundestad, Geir. *'Empire' by Integration: The United States and European Integration, 1945–1997* (Oxford: Oxford University Press, 1998).

McCormick, Donald, and Katy Fletcher. *Spy Fiction: A Connoisseur's Guide* (New York: Facts on File, 1990).

Macintyre, Ben. *For your Eyes Only: Ian Fleming and James Bond* (London: Bloomsbury, 2009).

McKay, Sinclair. *The Secret Life of Bletchley Park: The History of the Wartime Codebreaking Centre and the Men and Women Who Were There* (London: Aurum, 2010).

Mackenzie, Compton. *Water on the Brain* (London: Cassell, 1933).

——*Greek Memories*, with Postscript to 1932 Preface (London: Chatto & Windus, 1939 [1932]).

Mackenzie, William J. M. *The Secret History of SOE: The Special Operations Executive, 1940–1945* (London: St Ermin's, 2000).

MacPherson, Nelson. *American Intelligence in War-Time London: The Story of the OSS* (London: Frank Cass, 2003).

Maddrell, Paul. 'British–American Scientific Cooperation during the Occupation of Germany', in David Stafford and Rhodri Jeffreys-Jones, eds, *American–British–Canadian Intelligence Relations 1939–2000* (London: Frank Cass, 2000), 74–94.

Mader, Julius. *Who's Who in the CIA: A Biographical Reference Work on 3,000 Officers of the Civil and Military Branches of the Secret Services of the USA in 120 Countries* (East Berlin: Julius Mader, 1968).

——*Yellow List: Where is the CIA? A Documentary of Organizations and Institutions Set Up as Camouflages* (East Berlin: Julius Mader, 1970).

Mahan, Alfred T. *The Influence of Sea Power upon History, 1660–1783* (London: Methuen, 1965 [1890]).

Mailer, Norman. *Harlot's Ghost* (London: M. Joseph, 1991).

Makin, William J. *Brigade of Spies: An Account of Espionage Today* (London: Robert Hale, 1937).

Manela, Erez. *The Wilsonian Moment: Self-Determination and the International Origins of Anticolonial Nationalism* (Oxford: Oxford University Press, 2007).

Martin, David C. *Wilderness of Mirrors* (New York: Harper, 1980).

Masterman, John C. *The Double-Cross System in the War of 1939–1945* (London: Sphere, 1973 [1972]).

Masters, Peter. *Striking Back: A Jewish Commando's War against the Nazis* (Novato, Calif.: Presidio, 1997).

Mates, Michael. *The Secret Services: Is There a Case for Greater Openness?* (London: Institute for European Defence and Strategic Studies, 1989).

Mathur, L. P. *Indian Revolutionary Movement in the United States of America* (Delhi: S. Chand, 1970).

Maugham, W. Somerset. *Collected Short Stories*, 4 vols (Harmondsworth: Penguin, 1971), III (published as *Ashenden* in 1928).

Millis, Walter. *Road to War, America, 1914–1917* (Boston: Houghton Mifflin, 1935).

Milner-Barry, Stuart. 'Hut 6: Early Days', in Fred H. Hinsley and Alan Stripp, eds, *Codebreakers: The Inside Story of Bletchley Park* (Oxford: Oxford University Press, 1993), 100–12.

Mistry, Kaeten. 'Approaches to Understanding the Inaugural CIA Covert Operation in Italy: Exploding Useful Myths', *Intelligence and National Security*, 26 (April–June 2001), 246–68.

Mix, Derek E. *The European Union: Foreign and Security Policy* (Washington, DC: Congressional Research Service, 2011).

Monar, Jörg. 'Justice and Home Affairs', in Erik Jones et al., eds, *The Oxford Handbook of the European Union* (Oxford: Oxford University Press, 2012), 613–26.

Monet, Jean-Claude. *Polices et sociétés en Europe* (Paris: La Documentation française, 1993).

Moran, Christopher R. *Classified: Secrecy and the State in Modern Britain* (Cambridge: Cambridge University Press, 2012).

——and Robert Johnson. 'In the Service of Empire: Imperialism and the British Spy Thriller 1901–1914', *Studies in Intelligence*, 54 (June 2010), 1–18.

——and Christopher J. Murphy, eds. *Intelligence Studies Now and Then: Themes, Methods and Trajectories* (Edinburgh: Edinburgh University Press, 2012).

Morgan, Kenneth O. *Michael Foot: A Life* (London: HarperCollins, 2007).

Morgan, Thomas B. *The Anti-Americans* (London: Michael Joseph, 1967).

Morpurgo, Jack E. 'American Studies in Britain', in Robert E. Walker, ed., *American Studies Abroad* (Westport, Conn.: Greenwood Press, 1975), 53–7.

Moser, John E. *Twisting the Lion's Tail: Anglophobia in the United States, 1921–1948* (Basingstoke: Macmillan, 1999).

——*Right Turn: John T. Flynn and the Transformation of American Liberalism* (New York: New York University Press, 2005).

Moynihan, Daniel P. *Secrecy: The American Experience* (New Haven: Yale University Press, 1998).

Muggeridge, Malcolm. *Chronicles of Wasted Time*. Part 2: *The Infernal Grove* (London: Fontana: 1975).

Müller-Wille, Björn. 'Improving the Democratic Accountability of EU Intelligence', *Intelligence and National Security*, 21 (February 2006), 100–28.

Murphy, Christopher J. 'The Origins of SOE in France', *Historical Journal*, 46 (December 2003), 935–52.

Murphy, Philip. 'Keith Jeffery's *MI6*', *Intelligence and National Security*, 26 (October 2011), 720–3.

Newman, John M. *JFK and Vietnam: Deception, Intrigue, and the Struggle for Power* (New York: Warner, 1992).

Noakes, John Allen. 'Enforcing Domestic Tranquillity: State Building and the Origins of the (Federal) Bureau of Investigation, 1908–1920', Ph.D. thesis, University of Pennsylvania, 1993.

Nomikos, John. 'A European Union Intelligence Service for Confronting Terrorism', *International Journal of Intelligence and Counterintelligence*, 18 (Summer 2005), 191–203.

Norheim-Martinsen, Per Martin, and Jacob Aasland Ravndal. 'Towards Intelligence-Driven Peace Operations? The Evolution of UN and EU Intelligence Structures', *International Peacekeeping*, 18 (August 2011), 454–67.

O'Brien, Conor Cruise. *To Katanga and Back: A U.N. Case History* (London: Hutchinson, 1962).

Occhipinti, John D. *The Politics of European Police Cooperation: Toward a European FBI?* (Boulder, Colo.: Lynne Reiner, 2003).

Ochiai, Yukiko. 'Intelligence Assessment and U.S. Policy towards the Vietnam Conflict 1962–1965', Ph.D. thesis, University of Edinburgh, 2011.

O'Halpin, Eunan. 'The Secret Service Vote and Ireland, 1868–1922', *Irish Historical Studies*, 23 (November 1983), 348–53.

——'British Intelligence in Ireland, 1914–1921', in Christopher Andrew and David Dilks, eds, *The Missing Dimension: Governments and Intelligence Communities in the Twentieth Century* (Basingstoke: Macmillan, 1984), 54–77.

Olmsted, Kathryn S. *Challenging the Secret Government: The Post-Watergate Investigations of the CIA and FBI* (Chapel Hill: University of North Carolina Press, 1996).

——*Real Enemies: Conspiracy Theories and American Democracy, World War I to 9/11* (Oxford: Oxford University Press, 2009).

Omand, David. *Securing the State* (London: Hurst, 2010).

Oppenheim, E. Phillips. *Mysterious Mr Sabin* (London: Ward, Lock, 1898).

O'Reilly, Kenneth. *'Racial Matters': The FBI's File on Black America, 1960–1972* (New York: Free Press, 1989).

Palmer, Colin A. *Cheddi Jagan and the Politics of Power: British Guiana's Struggle for Independence* (Chapel Hill: University of North Carolina Press, 2010).

Panek, LeRoy L. *The Special Branch: The British Spy Novel, 1890–1980* (Bowling Green, Oh.: Bowling Green University Popular Press, 1981).

Parmar, Inderjeet. 'Anti-Americanism and the Major Foundations', in Brendon O'Connor and Martin Griffiths, eds, *The Rise of Anti-Americanism* (London: Routledge, 2006), 169–94.

Pelling, Henry M. *America and the British Left, from Bright to Bevan* (London: Adam & Charles Black, 1956).

Perkins, Dexter. *Hands Off! A History of the Monroe Doctrine* (Boston: Little, Brown, 1941).

Persico, Joseph E. *Roosevelt's Secret War: FDR and World War II Espionage* (New York: Random House, 2001).

Pettee, George S. *The Future of American Secret Intelligence* (Washington, DC: Infantry Journal Press, 1946).

Philby, Kim. *My Silent War* (New York: Ballantine, 1983 [1968]).

Phillips, David Atlee. *The Night Watch* (New York: Atheneum, 1977).

Phythian, Mark. 'The British Experience with Intelligence Accountability', in Loch Johnson, ed., *Strategic Intelligence*, 5 vols, V: *Intelligence and Accountability* (New York: Praeger, 2007), 67–88.

Piris, Jean-Claude. *The Lisbon Treaty: A Legal and Political Analysis* (Cambridge: Cambridge University Press, 2010).

Pisani, Sallie. *The CIA and the Marshall Plan* (Edinburgh: Edinburgh University Press, 1991).

Plame Wilson, Valerie. *Fair Game* (New York: Simon and Schuster, 2010 [2007]).

Pöhlmann, Markus. 'Towards a New History of German Military Intelligence in the Era of the Great War: Approaches and Sources', *Journal of Intelligence History*, 5 (Winter 2005). URL: <http://www.intelligence-history.org/jih/poehlmann _intro-5–2.html>.

Popplewell, Richard J. *Intelligence and Imperial Defence: British Intelligence and the Defence of the Indian Empire 1904–1924* (London: Frank Cass, 1995).

Porch, Douglas. *The French Secret Services: From the Dreyfus Affair to the Gulf War* (New York: Farrar, Straus and Giroux, 1995).

Porter, Bernard. *Plots and Paranoia: A History of Political Espionage in Britain, 1790–1988* (London: Routledge, 1992).

Powers, Thomas. *The Man Who Kept the Secrets: Richard Helms and the CIA* (New York: Knopf, 1979).

Prados, John. *The Soviet Estimate: U.S. Intelligence Analysis and Soviet Strategic Forces* (Princeton: Princeton University Press, 1986).

——*Safe for Democracy: The Secret Wars of the CIA* (Chicago: Ivan R. Dee, 2006).

Prior, Robin. *Churchill's 'World Crisis' as History* (London: Croom Helm, 1983).

Rabe, Stephen G. *U.S. Intervention in British Guiana: A Cold War Story* (Chapel Hill: University of North Carolina Press, 2005).

Radosh, Ronald. *American Labor and United States Foreign Policy: The Cold War in the Unions from Gompers to Lovestone* (New York: Vintage, 1969).

Rebattet, François X. 'The European Movement, 1945–1953: A Study in National and International Non-Governmental Organisations Working for European Unity', Ph.D. thesis, Oxford University, 1962.

Richelson, Jeffrey L. *The U.S. Intelligence Community*, 4th edn. (Boulder, Colo.: Westview Press, 1999).

——and Desmond Ball. *The Ties that Bind: Intelligence Cooperation between the UKUSA Countries, the United Kingdom, the United States of America, Canada, Australia and New Zealand* (Boston: Allen and Unwin, 1985).

Rintelen, Captain von [Franz Rintelen von Kleist]. *The Dark Invader: Wartime Reminiscences of a German Intelligence Officer* (London: Frank Cass, 1998 [1933]).

Robb, Thomas. 'Henry Kissinger, Great Britain and the "Year of Europe": The "Tangled Skein"', *Contemporary British History*, 24 (July 2010), 297–318.

Roberts, Priscilla. 'The Anglo-American Theme: American Visions of an Atlantic Alliance, 1914–1933', *Diplomatic History*, 21 (Summer 1997), 333–64.

Robertson, Geoffrey. *The Justice Game* (London: Vintage, 1999).

Robertson, Kenneth G. *Public Secrets: A Study in the Development of Government Secrecy* (London: Macmillan, 1982).

Roosevelt, Theodore. *The Letters of Theodore Roosevelt*, ed. Elting E. Morison, 8 vols (Cambridge, Mass.: Harvard University Press, 1951–4).

Rossbach, Niklas H. *Heath, Nixon and the Rebirth of the Special Relationship: Britain, the US and the EC* (Basingstoke: Palgrave Macmillan, 2009).

Rowan, Richard W. *The Story of Secret Service* (Garden City, NY: Doubleday, Doran, 1937).

Rusbridger, James, and Eric Nave. *Betrayal at Pearl Harbor: How Churchill Lured Roosevelt into World War II* (New York: Summit, 1991).

Schwartz, Jordan A. *The New Dealers: Power Politics in the Age of Roosevelt* (New York: Vintage, 1994).

Schweizer, Peter. *Victory: The Reagan Administration's Secret Strategy that Hastened the Collapse of the Soviet Union* (New York: Atlantic Monthly Press, 1994).

Scott-Smith, Giles. 'Interdoc and West European Psychological Warfare: The American Connection', *Intelligence and National Security*, 26 (April–June 2011), 355–76.

Shpayer-Makov, Haia. *The Ascent of the Detective: Police Sleuths in Victorian and Edwardian England* (Oxford: Oxford University Press, 2011).

Sibley, Katherine A. S. *Red Spies in America: Stolen Secrets and the Dawn of the Cold War* (Lawrence: University Press of Kansas, 2004).

Sims, Jennifer. 'Foreign Intelligence Liaison: Devils, Deals, and Details', *International Journal of Intelligence and Counterintelligence*, 19 (Summer 2006), 195–217.

Smiley, David. *Albanian Assignment* (London: Chatto & Windus, 1984).

Smist, Frank J., Jr. *Congress Oversees the United States Intelligence Community, 1947–1989* (Knoxville: University of Tennessee Press, 1990).

Smith, Bradley F. 'Admiral Godfrey's Mission to America, June/July 1941', *Intelligence and National Security*, 1 (September 1986), 441–50.

——*The Ultra-Magic Deals: And the Most Secret Special Relationship, 1940–46* (Shrewsbury: Airlife, 1993).

——'The American Road to Central Intelligence', in Rhodri Jeffreys-Jones and Christopher Andrew, eds, *Eternal Vigilance? 50 Years of the CIA* (London: Frank Cass, 1997), 1–20.

Smith, Michael. *Six: A History of Britain's Secret Intelligence Service*. Part 1: *Murder and Mayhem 1909–1939* (London: Dialogue, 2010).

Smith, R. Harris. *OSS: The Secret History of America's First Central Intelligence Agency* (New York: Delta, 1973).

Smith, Ralph B. *An International History of the Vietnam War*. 2 vols, II: *The Struggle for South-East Asia 1961–65* (London: Macmillan, 1985).

Spence, Richard B. 'Englishmen in New York: The SIS American Station, 1915–21', *Intelligence and National Security*, 19 (Autumn 2004), 511–37.

Spies for Peace. *Danger! Official Secret: RSG-6* (London: Committee of 100, 1963).

Stafford, David. *Britain and European Resistance, 1940–1945* (London: Macmillan, 1979).

——*Camp X: SOE and the American Connection* (Harmondsworth: Viking, 1987).

Stafford, David. *The Silent Game: The Real World of Imaginary Spies*, rev. edn. (Athens: University of Georgia Press, 1991).

—— *Churchill and Secret Service* (London: John Murray, 1997).

—— *Roosevelt and Churchill: Men of Secrets* (London: Little, Brown, 1999).

—— *Spies beneath Berlin* (London: John Murray, 2002).

Stewart, Gordon. *The Cloak and Dollar War* (London: Lawrence and Wishart, 1953).

Stinnett, Robert B. *Day of Deceit: The Truth about Pearl Harbor* (New York: The Free Press, 2000).

Svendsen, Adam D. M. 'Painting rather then Photography: Exploring Spy Fiction as a Legitimate Source Concerning UK–US Intelligence Co-operation', *Journal of Transatlantic Studies*, 7 (March 2009), 1–22.

—— *Intelligence Cooperation and the War on Terror: Anglo-American Security Relations after 9/11* (London: Routledge, 2010).

Sweet-Escott, Bickham. *Baker Street Irregular* (London: Methuen, 1965).

Talbert, Roy, Jr. *Negative Intelligence: The Army and the American Left, 1917–1941* (Jackson: University Press of Mississippi, 1991).

Thelen, David P. 'Social Tensions and the Origins of Progressivism', *Journal of American History*, 56 (September 1969), 323–41.

Theoharis, Athan, et al., eds, *The Central Intelligence Agency: Security under Scrutiny* (Westport, Conn.: Greenwood, 2006).

Thompson, Edward P. *Writing by Candlelight* (London: Merlin, 1980).

Thompson, Robert. *Make for the Hills: Memories of Far Eastern Wars* (London: Leo Cooper, 1989).

Thorne, Thomas C., and David S. Patterson, eds, *Foreign Relations of the United States: Emergence of the Intelligence Establishment* (Washington, DC: Government Printing Office, 1996).

Toje, Asle. *The EU, NATO and European Defence: A Slow Train Coming* (Paris: European Union Institute for Security Studies, 2008).

Trevor-Roper, Hugh. *The Philby Affair: Espionage, Treason, and Secret Services* (London: William Kimber, 1968).

Troy, Thomas F. *Wild Bill and Intrepid: Donovan, Stephenson, and the Origin of the CIA* (New Haven: Yale University Press, 1996).

Tuchman, Barbara W. *The Zimmermann Telegram* (New York: Macmillan, 1966 [1958]).

Turrou, Leon G. *The Nazi Spy Conspiracy in America* (London: Harrap, 1939).

United States Army Intelligence Center and School, *The Evolution of American Military Intelligence* (Fort Huachuca, Ariz., 1973).

Valero, Larry A. 'From World War to Cold War: Aspects of the Management and Coordination of American Intelligence, 1941–1953', Ph.D. thesis, University of Cambridge, 2001.

Verbruggen, Frank. 'Euro-Cops? Just say Maybe. European Lessons from the 1993 Reshuffle of U.S. Drug Enforcement', *European Journal of Crime, Criminal Law and Criminal Justice*, 13/2 (1995), 150–201.

Villadsen, Ole R. 'Prospects for a European Common Intelligence Policy', *Studies in Intelligence*, 9 (Summer 2000), 81–95.

Vincent, David. *The Culture of Secrecy: Britain, 1832–1998* (Oxford: Oxford University Press, 1998).

Wales, Thomas C. 'The "Massingham" Mission and the Secret "Special Relationship": Cooperation and Rivalry between the Anglo-American Clandestine Services in French North Africa, November 1942–May 1943', *Intelligence and National Security*, 20 (March 2005), 44–71.

——'The Secret War in the South: The Covert Center in Algiers and British and American Intelligence in the Western Mediterranean 1941–1944', Ph.D. thesis, University of Edinburgh, 2005.

Walker, David. 'Democracy Goes to War: Politics, Intelligence, and Decision-Making in the United States in 1942', in Rhodri Jeffreys-Jones and Andrew Lownie, eds, *North American Spies: New Revisionist Essays* (Edinburgh: Edinburgh University Press, 1991), 79–101.

Walker, Martin. 'The Future of Europe's Foreign Policy', in Robert J. Guttman, ed., *Europe in the New Century: Visions of an Emerging Superpower* (Boulder, Colo.: Lynne Reiner, 2003), 69–78.

Wallace, Gavin. 'Mackenzie, Sir (Edward Montague Anthony) Compton', *Oxford Dictionary of National Biography* (online, 2004–11).

Walsh, James J. 'Intelligence-Sharing in the European Union: Institutions are not Enough', *Journal of Common Market Studies*, 44 (September 2006), 625–43.

Ward, Alan J. *Ireland and Anglo-American Relations 1899–1921* (London: Weidenfeld & Nicolson, 1969).

Wark, Wesley K. *The Ultimate Enemy: British Intelligence and Nazi Germany, 1933–1939* (Oxford: Oxford University Press, 1986).

Watt, Donald C. 'The Historiography of Intelligence in International Review', in Lars C. Jenssen and Olav Riste, *Intelligence in the Cold War* (Oslo: Norwegian Institute for Defence Studies, 2001), 173–97.

Weller, Geoffrey R. 'Oversight of Australia's Intelligence Services', *International Journal of Intelligence and Counterintelligence*, 12 (Winter 1999), 484–503.

——'Political Scrutiny and Control of Scandinavia's Security and Intelligence Services', *International Journal of Intelligence and Counterintelligence*, 13 (Summer 2000), 171–92.

West, Nigel, pseud. Rupert Allason. 'Keegan's Disputable Thesis', *International Journal of Intelligence and Counterintelligence*, 18 (Summer 2005), 360–3.

——*MI5: British Security Service Operations 1909–1945* (London: Triad/Granada, 1983).

Wiebes, Cees. *Intelligence and the War in Bosnia, 1992–1995* (Münster: Lit Verlag, 2003).

Wilford, Hugh. *The CIA, the British Left and the Cold War: Calling the Tune?* (London: Frank Cass, 2003).

Wilford, Hugh. *The Mighty Wurlitzer: How the CIA Played America* (Cambridge, Mass.: Harvard University Press, 2008).

Wilkie, John E. 'The Secret Service in the War', in [Anon.], *The American–Spanish War: A History by the War Leaders* (Norwich, Conn.: Charles C. Haskell, 1899).

Wilkinson, Nicholas. *Secrecy and the Media: The Official History of the United Kingdom's D-Notice System* (London: Routledge, 2009).

Williams, Grover S., ed. *Legislative History of the Central Intelligence Agency as Documented in Published Congressional Sources* (Washington, DC: Congressional Research Service, 1975).

Wills, Gary. *Reagan's America* (New York: Penguin, 1988).

Winant, John G. *A Letter from Grosvenor Square: An Account of a Stewardship* (London: Hodder & Stoughton, 1947).

Winkler, Jonathan R. *Nexus: Strategic Communications and American Security in World War I* (Cambridge, Mass.: Harvard University Press, 2008).

Winks, Robin W. *Cloak and Gown: Scholars in the Secret War, 1939–1961* (New York: William Morrow, 1987).

Winterbottom, Frederick W. *The Ultra Secret* (London: Weidenfeld and Nicolson, 1974).

Wise, David, and Thomas B. Ross. *The Invisible Government* (London, Mayflower, 1968 [1964]).

Wright, Peter. *Spycatcher: The Candid Autobiography of a Senior Intelligence Officer* (New York: Viking, 1987).

Yardley, Herbert O. *The American Black Chamber* (London: Faber and Faber, 1931).

Young, John W. *Britain, France and the Unity of Europe, 1945–1951* (Bath: Leicester University Press, 1984).

——*Britain and European Unity, 1945–1992* (New York: St Martin's Press, 1993).

——'The Wilson Government's Reform of Intelligence Coordination, 1967–68', *Intelligence and National Security*, 16 (Summer 2001), 133–51.

Zelikow, Philip. 'American Economic Intelligence: Past Practice and Future Principles', in Rhodri Jeffreys-Jones and Christopher Andrew, eds, *Eternal Vigilance? 50 Years of the CIA* (London: Frank Cass, 1997), 164–77.

Illustrations Acknowledgements

Plate 1: U.S. National Archives photo no. 111-sc-89383; **Plate 2**: From W. B. Fowler, *British-American Relations, 1917–1918: The Role of Sir William Wiseman*, plate no. 1. Copyright 1969 by Princeton University Press; **Plate 3**: U.S. National Archives; **Plate 4**: The [U.K.] National Archives, ref. HW14/45; **Plate 5**: Courtesy of the Monro-Davies family; **Plate 6**: CIA/U.S. National Archives photo no. 306-PSA-59-17740; **Plate 7**: *London Evening Standard* 29 July 1949, British Cartoon Archive, University of Kent LSE7606, www.cartoons.ac.uk; **Plate 8**: LBJ Library photo no. A280-32; **Plate 9**: LBJ Library photo no. C1045-7; **Plate 10**: LBJ Library photo no. A2815-15A; **Plate 11**: Box 3, folder 5, Norden Papers TAM 122, New York University Library; **Plate 12**: Box 3, folder 5, Norden Papers TAM 122, New York University Library; **Plate 13**: Box 3, folder 5, Norden Papers TAM 122, New York University Library; **Plate 14**: Copyright Europol/Stéphanie Adzou Colongo; **Plate 15**: Courtesy of Angelika Molnar and Hungarian National Police.

Index